Species Conservation

Lessons from Islands

This book brings together leading conservation practitioners to reflect on their response to the current global biodiversity crisis through the lens of island species recovery and management. Initial chapters cover the biological understanding of small-population biology and the growing threat of invasive species, while subsequent chapters discuss the management of these threats and the complexity of leading projects within a dynamic and still relatively unknown system. Multiple case studies from islands worldwide illustrate key points, allowing readers to draw on the first-hand practical experience of respected professionals. This resource will be invaluable to both current and future conservation professionals, helping them to go beyond disciplinary 'comfort zones' and develop, manage and lead projects over extensive time frames in a way that brings others with them on the journey.

JAMIESON A. COPSEY is Director of Training for the Conservation Planning Specialist Group of the International Union for Conservation of Nature Species Survival Commission (IUCN SSC). Prior to this he was Head of Learning and Development for the Durrell Wildlife Conservation Trust. His research interests include island species conservation, invasive species management and conservation planning, management and leadership.

SIMON A. BLACK is a member of the Durrell Institute of Conservation and Ecology in the School of Anthropology and Conservation at the University of Kent, UK. His research and practice covers both conservation science and conservation management including performance measurement and evaluation. He is a trustee of Wildwood, the British wildlife conservation charity which is working at the forefront of species re-introduction and re-wilding in the United Kingdom.

JIM J. GROOMBRIDGE is Professor of Biodiversity Conservation at the Durrell Institute of Conservation and Ecology in the School of Anthropology and Conservation at the University of Kent. His research interests include the conservation genetics and ecology of small populations, evolutionary genetics, phylogenetics and biogeography.

CARL G. JONES is Chief Scientist at the Durrell Wildlife Conservation Trust and Scientific Director of the Mauritian Wildlife Foundation. In 2016 he won the prestigious Indianapolis Prize for Conservation. He has developed and led many programmes enabling some of the most striking animal population recoveries in the world, including the Mauritius kestrel, pink pigeon, echo parakeet and the Rodrigues warbler.

ECOLOGY, BIODIVERSITY AND CONSERVATION

The world's biological diversity faces unprecedented threats. The urgent challenge facing the concerned biologist is to understand ecological processes well enough to maintain their functioning in the face of the pressures resulting from human population growth. Those concerned with the conservation of biodiversity and with restoration also need to be acquainted with the political, social, historical, economic and legal frameworks within which ecological and conservation practice must be developed. The new Ecology, Biodiversity and Conservation series will present balanced, comprehensive, up-to-date and critical reviews of selected topics within the sciences of ecology and conservation biology, both botanical and zoological and both pure and applied. It is aimed at advanced final-year undergraduates, graduate students, researchers and university teachers, as well as ecologists and conservationists in industry, government and the voluntary sectors. The series encompasses a wide range of approaches and scales (spatial, temporal and taxonomic), including quantitative, theoretical, population, community, ecosystem, landscape, historical, experimental, behavioural and evolutionary studies. The emphasis is on science related to the real world of plants and animals rather than on purely theoretical abstractions and mathematical models. Books in this series will, wherever possible, consider issues from a broad perspective. Some books will challenge existing paradigms and present new ecological concepts, empirical or theoretical models and testable hypotheses. Other books will explore new approaches and present syntheses on topics of ecological importance.

Ecology and Control of Introduced Plants
Judith H. Myers and Dawn Bazely

Invertebrate Conservation and Agricultural Ecosystems
T. R. New

Risks and Decisions for Conservation and Environmental Management
Mark Burgman

Species Conservation

Lessons from Islands

Edited by

JAMIESON A. COPSEY

IUCN SSC Conservation Planning Specialist Group

SIMON A. BLACK

Durrell Institute of Conservation and Ecology

JIM J. GROOMBRIDGE

Durrell Institute of Conservation and Ecology

CARL G. JONES

Durrell Wildlife Conservation Trust

CAMBRIDGE
UNIVERSITY PRESS

CAMBRIDGE
UNIVERSITY PRESS

University Printing House, Cambridge CB2 8BS, United Kingdom

One Liberty Plaza, 20th Floor, New York, NY 10006, USA

477 Williamstown Road, Port Melbourne, VIC 3207, Australia

314–321, 3rd Floor, Plot 3, Splendor Forum, Jasola District Centre,
New Delhi – 110025, India

79 Anson Road, #06–04/06, Singapore 079906

Cambridge University Press is part of the University of Cambridge.

It furthers the University's mission by disseminating knowledge in the pursuit of
education, learning, and research at the highest international levels of excellence.

www.cambridge.org
Information on this title: www.cambridge.org/9780521899390
DOI: 10.1017/9781139030243

First published 2018

Printed in the United Kingdom by TJ International Ltd. Padstow Cornwall

A catalogue record for this publication is available from the British Library.

Library of Congress Cataloging-in-Publication Data
Names: Copsey, Jamieson A., 1971– editor. | Black, Simon A., 1968– editor. |
Groombridge, James J., 1970– editor. | Jones, Carl G., editor.
Title: Species conservation : lessons from islands / edited by Jamieson A.
Copsey, Simon A. Black (Durrell Institute of Conservation and Ecology at
the University of Kent), James J. Groombridge, Carl G. Jones (Durrell Wildlife
Conservation Trust).
Description: Cambridge : Cambridge University Press, 2018. | Series: Ecology,
biodiversity, and conservation | Includes bibliographical references and index.
Identifiers: LCCN 2017058249 | ISBN 9780521899390 (alk. paper)
Subjects: LCSH: Island animals – Conservation. | Island plants – Conservation. | Wildlife
conservation. | Biodiversity.
Classification: LCC QL111 .S64 2018 | DDC 591.680914/2–dc23
LC record available at https://lccn.loc.gov/2017058249

ISBN 978-0-521-89939-0 Hardback
ISBN 978-0-521-72819-5 Paperback

Contents

Colour plates are to be found between pp. 204 and 205.

Contributors

PATRICK MOLDOWAN
Department of Ecology and Evolutionary Biology, University of Toronto, Canada

SIMON A. BLACK
Durrell Institute of Conservation and Ecology, United Kingdom

PATRICIA BREKKE
Institute of Zoology, Zoological Society of London, United Kingdom

PAUL BUTLER
Rare, Arlington, VA, United States

STEFANO CANESSA
Faculty of Veterinary Medicine, Ghent University, Merelbeke, Belgium

ALIÉNOR L. M. CHAUVENET
Centre for Biodiversity and Conservation Science, University of Queensland, Australia

NIK C. COLE
Durrell Wildlife Conservation Trust, Republic of Mauritius

JAMIESON A. COPSEY
IUCN SSC Conservation Planning Specialist Group, Minneapolis, MN, United States

OLIVIA COPSEY
ISLANDS Project of the Indian Ocean Commission, Republic of Mauritius

JOHN G. EWEN
Institute of Zoology, Zoological Society of London, United Kingdom

DEBORAH J. FOGELL
Institute of Zoology, Zoological Society of London and Durrell Institute of Conservation and Ecology, United Kingdom

CHARLIE GARDNER
Durrell Institute of Conservation and Ecology, United Kingdom

STEVEN GREEN
Centre for Applied Zoology, Cornwall College, Newquay, United Kingdom

JIM J. GROOMBRIDGE
Durrell Institute of Conservation and Ecology, United Kingdom

DAN HEATH
Duke University Center for the Advancement of Social Entrepreneurship (CASE), Durham, NC, United States

CARL G. JONES
Durrell Wildlife Conservation Trust, Jersey, British Channel Islands

GILLIAN KEY
GB Non-Native Species Secretariat, London, United Kingdom

HANNAH MOUNCE
Maui Forest Bird Recovery Project, Makawao, HI, United States

JOHN PARKES
Kurahaupo Consulting, Christchurch, New Zealand

CLAIRE RAISIN
Chester Zoo, Chester, United Kingdom

SAMUEL T. TURVEY
Institute of Zoology, Zoological Society of London, United Kingdom

ALAN TYE
International Union for the Conservation of Nature (IUCN), Republic of Mauritius

RICHARD YOUNG
Durrell Wildlife Conservation Trust, Jersey, British Channel Islands

TIM WRIGHT
Durrell Wildlife Conservation Trust, Jersey, British Channel Islands

Foreword

Islands in the Life of Gerald Durrell

Islands punctuated the life of British author and conservationist, Gerald Durrell. Although born in India, he often said that his life began on Corfu, an enchanting Greek island where he lived as a boy with his family in the 1930s. Gerry passed away on the island of Jersey in 1995, hailed around the world as an 'icon of nature conservation of the 20th century' (Gerald Durrell, personal communication).

Islands shaped Gerry's work, both literary and in conservation. As a youngster, he explored every nook and cranny of Corfu, seeking out wildlife, from earwigs to eagle owls, to nourish his growing passion for the animal kingdom. Here he met his mentor, Dr Theodore Stephanides, a Corfiot doctor whose eclectic interests in the natural world broadened and deepened the boy's view of nature. His most enduring and, some say, most endearing book described this magical childhood.

Gerry became an animal collector for zoos, travelling in West Africa and South America, but he became unhappy with the profligate attitude of zoos of the day towards the animals in their care, summed up by the phrase 'there are always more where they came from'. He determined to have his own zoo, one devoted to the conservation of wild species and their habitats.

In 1959, Gerry settled on Jersey in the British Channel Islands, where both he and his modest zoo were warmly welcomed by the Islanders. The zoo found a niche in the budding tourism industry, and it flourished under the management of a charitable trust, now called the Durrell Wildlife Conservation Trust. Jersey Zoo became the standard-bearer for zoo conservation that Gerry had envisioned since his animal-collecting days, and the Trust began to undertake conservation action around the world from its headquarters in Jersey.

Its early efforts derived from Gerry's visits to the island of Mauritius in the 1970s. Mauritius was like a magnet to Gerry, because he had chosen the extinct dodo for the Trust's emblem, the large, flightless bird endemic to the island, which had perished at the hands of humankind. For

Gerry, the dodo symbolised the fragility and vulnerability of species when encountering *Homo sapiens*, and he vowed that no species the Trust chose to help would follow the dodo to oblivion. He and his team brought about the recovery of several endangered Mauritian species when many other conservationists would have given up on them. The Trust developed a 'conservation toolbox' of techniques – breeding, research, training, community conservation and restoration of wild populations and habitats. Using the appropriate tools, the Trust continues to revive species and rebuild habitats around the world.

Gerry himself was profoundly inspired by islands, and his legacy owes much to them. Corfu kindled his devotion to the natural world, Jersey sustained his first tangible ideas for protecting it and Mauritius gave full rein to his vision that it is indeed possible to reverse the ecological havoc caused by our own species.

It is no coincidence that, two decades after Gerry died, I am writing these words from the deck of a ship on a voyage around the islands of the Indian Ocean. The itinerary did not include Mauritius this time, but we have visited many other islands – Madagascar, Anjouan in the Comoros Archipelago, Aldabra and Aride, both in the Seychelles – which reflect the full range of themes in this book.

Madagascar, lying in splendid isolation for nearly a hundred million years, rejoices in great biodiversity and endemism yet reveals many taxonomic gaps, as most islands do. The nearby Comoros are volcanic islands only a few million years old, sustaining far fewer species and more taxonomic gaps. People arrived on both Madagascar and the Comoros within the last 2,000 years, and the hand of humanity lies heavy on their species and habitats.

On remote Aldabra, in contrast, human intervention has been relatively light, with few visitors and fewer settlers. Although the endemic giant tortoise was nearly wiped out in the nineteenth century, exploitation of the flora and fauna has long been curtailed, and the eradication of invasive species is nearly complete. Aldabra now represents 'a superlative example of an oceanic island ecosystem in which evolutionary processes are active within a rich biota', according to World Heritage Site Criterion IX. It is also an utter delight to visit, to watch dainty Aldabra rails mince among the great moving boulders of giant tortoises and the occasional coconut crab doing the best it can to scuttle along, not easy for the largest land invertebrate.

On the spectrum of island isolation in time and space and of human intervention, Aride lies in the middle. As a granitic island, it is many millions of years old but is tiny (only 68 hectares) and appeared on no charts until the eighteenth century, when it was described as 'a pile of rocks covered with a few bushes'. Occupied in the next century by a leper colony and covered with coconut palms and vegetable and fruit plots, its vast seabird populations were plundered for meat and eggs. Aride could have become a wasteland, but thanks to timely conservation action, it is now a natural paradise, reminiscent of the Galapagos, with much of its fauna and flora restored and functioning as a natural island community should.

Islands expose the worst of our deeds and display the best of our endeavours, proving that it is possible for us not only to learn from our mistakes but also to rectify them. The research, training and conservation undertaken on islands, substantially presented here by the practitioners themselves in a readable mix of theory and case studies, offer hope for the future of the special and precious biota of islands. If islands can be construed as microcosms of the wider world, then there is also hope for the planet.

LEE DURRELL

Gerald Durrell providing supplementary food for a wild Mauritius kestrel *Falco punctatus* (*c.* 1987). A species brought back from four known individuals to 300–400 free-living birds. (From C. G. Jones, M. D. Burgess, J. J. Groombridge et al. 2013. Mauritius kestrel *Falco punctatus*, in R. J. Safford and A. F. A. Hawkins (eds.), The Birds of Africa, vol. VIII: The Malagasy Region. Christopher Helm, London. *Photo credit:* John Hartley.)

Preface

'I want to know what you're going to *do* for me?', Carl Jones asked me as I sat next to him on his sofa in Wales, with one eye on daytime TV; this was definitely one of my weirdest and most memorable job interviews! I must have done all right, as the next thing I knew I was winging my way to Mauritius, fresh out of university, to volunteer for the Mauritius kestrel recovery team during the 1993–94 breeding season. So began my conservation career and a life to date unconsciously devoted to helping in some small way the recovery of threatened tropical island species. Mauritius taught me many things, the most significant one being that fieldwork was not my passion, but working with people was. Subsequently, I was delighted to realise that conservation requires a cross-disciplinary approach, increasingly recognising the value of anthropological, socio-economic, managerial and leadership skills, as well as those focused on developing our biological understanding of species, threats to their existence and how to support them. Everyone can find a significant role to play within the conservation community.

As a conservation trainer and facilitator, I have the opportunity to work and become friends with an eclectic mix of conservation professionals, each an expert in his or her respective field and some of whom have kindly contributed to the development of this book. My job has been to gather this expertise and direct it where it is most needed to help build capacity for conservation. Fortunately for me, the organisation to which I have dedicated much of my working life – the Durrell Wildlife Conservation Trust – prioritised tropical islands as their focus for conservation action and capacity building. This has meant that I've had the enviable task of bringing together friends and colleagues from across the conservation community to travel to locations such as Hawaii, the Galapagos Islands, Samoa, Fiji, the Philippines, St Lucia, Seychelles and, of course, Mauritius to work with individuals and organisations to help them save species from extinction. It was during a trip to the Galapagos Islands to run a training course on island species conservation that I sat down with Carl and my good friend Jim Groombridge, and we hatched a plan to write this book.

It was clear to us that members of the conservation community working to save threatened island species were missing a golden opportunity to learn from each other and avoid 'reinventing wheels'. In our travels, we witnessed fantastic examples of species recovery work, ranging from captive breeding of 'Extinct in the Wild' rails in Guam, to the restoration of multiple species and habitats in the Seychelles and Mauritius and to successful engagement of local communities in St Lucia resulting in the recovery of the island's national bird, the St Lucia parrot *Amazona versicolor*. Much of the knowledge that could be gleaned from these projects was not easily accessible through existing published literature, some of it sitting in internal reports and often just in certain people's heads! At the same time, we could see new projects starting up and long-running projects faltering when they could have been greatly helped by knowing more about what others were doing. The parallels between these projects in terms of biogeographic and socio-economic context were clear. It seemed to us that we could help in some small way by capturing this knowledge and providing some shared insights into how species conservation projects function and what we can learn from others' success as well as failure. Going further, we hoped that by pulling this together we might also provide some 'food for thought' for species conservation projects happening worldwide, creating another point of connection between islands and how they continue to inform our understanding of life on Earth and how to manage it long term.

Since these initial thoughts, we have worked with a broader set of experts with deep knowledge of life on islands to help pen this book. Our aim has been to provide some personal insights, backed up with appropriate theory, and evidence from conservation action to save some of the world's most threatened species, which we hope will inform future conservation efforts on islands and beyond. We have not tried to provide a comprehensive overview of all the elements that could go into a species recovery project. For example, we do not unpick the complexities of climate change and how they are likely to impact island life, nor do we discuss in any detail human-induced habitat destruction, overkill or secondary extinctions. Instead, we take readers on a journey, from an understanding of the past history of life on islands to the present and how we prioritise, plan, manage and lead conservation projects in a way that enables us to learn as we go and improve our practice.

The authors that contribute to this book have been selected based on their interest in and work on islands. I've had the pleasure of getting to know and learn from almost all of them during the various training courses Durrell has delivered over the last ten or so years. Their expertise ranges from understanding small–population biology and genetics, to the development of ecological histories and population monitoring, to invasive species management, to project planning and leadership, to species recovery, habitat restoration and public engagement in conservation action. Where possible, we have developed threads between the chapters, drawing readers' attention to related chapters where we can within the text.

The generation time for this book has been almost as long as that for an Aldabran giant tortoise! However, we hope that it will be received as a useful contribution to our understanding of life on islands and how to conserve it and go some way towards improving our effectiveness in recovering the growing raft of threatened species globally and saving more species from extinction.

JAMIESON A. COPSEY

Acknowledgements

The authors thank Mourant & Co. Trustees, Ltd., as Trustees of the Amazon Trust, for their initial funding to transport a number of us to some of the most stunning islands in the world to deliver island species conservation training and to subsequently begin to pen this book. We also thank Ellen Chalmers, a faithful Durrell supporter, for her additional funding to help complete this book. We are eternally grateful to the numerous individuals and organisations with which we have had the pleasure of working through our travels to islands across the world for their hospitality, wisdom and knowledge, all of which we hope has infused the text.

Specifically, we thank Charlotte Causton, Lori Colin, Birgit Fessl, Joel Miles, Shyama Pagad and John Parkes for information and leads to literature for Chapter 4 and John Parkes specifically for commenting on early drafts of that chapter. We also want to draw readers' attention to the following publication from which we drew heavily in the development of Chapter 11: J. Ervin, P. Butler, L. Wilkinson, M. Piper and S. Watkins. 2010. *Inspiring Support and Commitment for Protected Areas through Communication, Education and Public Awareness Programs: A Quick Guide for Protected Area Practitioners* (Quick Guide Series), ed. J. Ervin. Rare, Arlington, VA. We also thank the various friends and colleagues who commented on or reviewed various chapters, in particular, Peter Vaughan, Daniel Hayden, Kevin Green, Brian Day, Paul Antion and Dr Eric Jensen.

A number of us give a special thank you to Professor Carl Jones, MBE, who has been a first-rate mentor and friend and whose wisdom has greatly influenced us in our lives and careers in this wonderful, dynamic and challenging profession we call species conservation. Professor Michael Usher – as Series Editor – has been a guiding light throughout the process of finalising this book, which was for a number of us a new experience! Finally, we cannot end without making mention of Gerald Durrell, who inspired the Durrell Wildlife Conservation Trust: the organisation that we have all in some way been connected with over the years and that continues to set a benchmark for others to aim for.

1 · *Species Conservation*
Lessons from Islands

JAMIESON A. COPSEY AND SIMON A.
BLACK

1.0 Introduction

Islands and the species they support have provided the inspiration for some of the most important concepts in the theory and practice of conservation biology. Evolutionary biology, biogeography, small–population biology and genetics all owe much to islands for their development. Islands have demonstrated all too clearly the impacts of anthropogenic change on global biodiversity. In particular, island ecosystems have been significantly degraded by the spread of invasive alien species, in part facilitated by human population growth, human demand for local resources and the movement of people and trade goods across the globe. As a counter-narrative, islands are now showing us how a suite of conservation interventions at species to ecosystem levels can buck global trends and provide a more long-term future for small, threatened populations and the habitats on which they depend. Furthermore, they are providing rare examples of how people can be engaged more effectively in conserving threatened species through their direct involvement in conservation projects or indirectly by modifying existing human behaviour. In this introductory chapter, we set the scene for the chapters to follow. We illustrate the importance of islands as centres of learning about life on Earth and our place within it, their role as indicators of the negative impacts of human-induced change and, most importantly, as sentinels of hope for what is possible with appropriate intervention and management.

1.1 Islands and the Development of Biological Thought

In 1772, Johann Reinhold Forster accompanied Captain Cook on his expedition to New Zealand and Tahiti. He noted one of the most fundamental relationships in biogeography: that the number of species found within a given area is in part at least a function of the size of the area; larger land areas support more species. Decades later, Alfred Russel Wallace, during his year-long exploration of the Malay Archipelago (1854–62), began to document patterns in species distribution and design which he linked to varying environmental pressures, paralleling Charles Darwin's work to define natural selection as a guiding force in shaping the structure and function of species within systems. Darwin is now widely recognised as one of the founding fathers of biology, for his fundamental explanation of evolutionary processes, Wallace being credited as one of the pioneers in the development of biogeography as a scientific discipline. Both Wallace and Darwin derived their inspiration from islands.

In 1967, mathematician Robert MacArthur and evolutionary biologist and natural philosopher E. O. Wilson published their landmark book, *The Theory of Island Biogeography* (MacArthur and Wilson 1967). The theory provided a model to explain why any given island supports a particular number of species at a particular point in time, based on the premise that species number on islands increases with island area but decreases with isolation (see Section 2.2). While the theory has been criticised as being over-simplistic (see Whitakker and Fernández-Palacios 2007 for review), the Equilibrium Theory of Island Biogeography has been one of the most important catalysts for research into minimum viable populations, minimum viable areas and small–population biology, meta-population dynamics and the relative importance of deterministic (e.g. anthropogenic impacts) relative to stochastic (e.g. climatic fluctuations) effects on extinction rates. It has also informed the developing science of ecological restoration (Walker et al. 2007) and the design and development of protected area systems to determine how best to conserve maximum biodiversity. The theory has provided a foundation for global change research, informing hypotheses as to how ecosystems will respond to climate change. For example, the predicted shift of montane woodlands in the south-western United States to higher elevations as the climate warms is expected to result in the loss of up to 62 per cent of the small mammal species currently utilising these habitats (Brown 1995). In Mauritius – a recurring ecological, geographic and historical reference point for this book – climate change appears to result in delayed egg-laying in the Mauritius kestrel and the possibility of reducing chick survival due to heavy rainfall and the start of the cyclone season (Pearce-Higgins and Green 2014).

It was the birdlife of the south-western Pacific, and in particular New Guinea and the Solomon Islands, that inspired Ernst Mayr (1904–2005) to develop the 'biological species concept' ('groups of interbreeding natural populations that are reproductively isolated from other such groups'), a fundamental unit of measurement within conservation biology. Mayr was recognised as 'the Darwin of the 20th Century' (Nevo 2006), doing much to raise the status of biology as a scientific discipline in its own right, not simply a derivative of the physical sciences. Mayr went on to fuse Darwinian evolutionary thought with new developments in molecular biology and genetics to challenge our understanding of species and how they evolve (Box 1.1 for a classification of the lemur species, Madagascar, and Figure 1.1).

Box 1.1 *Lemurs of Madagascar*

The likely origin of the primates of Madagascar is from a single colonisation by an ancestral strepsirrhine from mainland Africa (Stevens and Heesy 2006), although there is some evidence for an Asian origin (Marivaux et al. 2001). This dispersal event is estimated to have occurred 55 to 60 million years ago, shortly after the first primates evolved and significantly earlier than the proposed origins of Madagascar's other terrestrial mammals. The dispersal mechanism responsible for these colonisations has long been controversial. Simpson (1940) famously proposed 'sweepstakes dispersal' by vegetation mats rafting across the Mozambique Channel, although the probabilities of this happening successfully have been considered small (Masters et al. 2006). However, Ali and Huber (2010) provide evidence that during the period (~60–20 million years ago (Mya)) the ocean currents were quite different and would have allowed these rafting events to occur.

While no one can deny the diversity of lemurs – from the recently extinct gorilla-sized Archaeoindris to the world's smallest primate, Berthe's mouse lemur *Microcebus berthae* – the number of extant species is hotly disputed. Largely as a result of molecular genetics, the number of proposed taxa doubled between 1994 and 2010. Mittermeier et al. (2010) recognise 101 distinct taxa. A further 17 species and three entire families of extinct lemurs have been identified from sub-fossil remains (Godfrey and Jungers 2003). This taxonomic upheaval has been particularly acute amongst mouse and sportive lemurs and is certainly not universally accepted (Tattersall 2007). Disagreement is likely to continue until a consensus is reached on the definition of a 'species'.

Lemurs are thought to have radiated into so many unique forms for a number of reasons. Firstly, they have had 55 to 60 million years of relatively low predation and competition pressures. For the first half of this time, there were no other terrestrial mammals, so competition and predation were even lower. Extant lemurs are subject to relatively few predators, primarily the fossa *Cryptoprocta ferox* and several snakes and birds of prey. However, it should be remembered that significantly larger predators of lemurs have existed until recently, for example, the 'giant fossa' *C. spelea* (Burney 2003). It has been suggested that changing predation pressures may also have contributed towards the evolution of cathemerality in some lemurs, although this is disputed (Curtis 2006). Many of Madagascar's ecosystems and therefore ecological niches are different to those found elsewhere, and this is likely to have contributed to the unique forms seen amongst lemurs. The absence of large ungulates has been cited as one contributing factor to the unique ecological landscape (Goodman et al. 2003).

Figure 1.1 The aye-aye *Daubentonia madagascariensis* of Madagascar. Madagascar supports 21 per cent of the world's primate genera and 36 per cent of primate families, making it the highest priority for primate conservation globally. (Mittermeier et al. 2010; *photo credit*: Georgia Dicks). (A black–and–white version of this figure will appear in some formats. For the colour version, please refer to the plate section.)

Islands have provided the intellectual stimulus for the development of new disciplines and sub-disciplines of biological thought. R. A. Rappaport, for example, played an important role in the emergence of ecological anthropology (study of the relationship between humans and the natural environment) as a discrete branch of anthropology in the early twentieth century. Rappaport's research was based largely on his work with the Tsembaga Maring people of Papua New Guinea. His work focused on the link between culture and economy and the role that ritual plays within this interchange. American anthropologist Julian Steward developed the related field of cultural ecology, placing cultural change within the context of adaptation to the environment. His Puerto Rica research project was the first attempt to study the human cultures of an entire area, considering the economic, political and ecological relationships that existed. This island-based project involving multiple researchers also launched the careers of many eminent anthropologists of the twentieth century.

In later life, E. O. Wilson has promoted the idea of 'biophilia', or the inbuilt urge that living things – including humans – have to associate or to interact with other organisms (Wilson 1984). This perspective came at least in part as a culmination of his studies on island biodiversity and its inescapable link with human life. Finally, one of the greatest impacts that humans have had on the natural world that has subsequently backfired has been the result of species introduced to new lands by people and (sometimes) for people. It was one of the founding fathers of ecology, Charles S. Elton, who developed the sub-discipline invasion ecology – how introduced species become established and can drive others to extinction. In Elton's book, *The Ecology of Invasions by Animals and Plants* – first published in 1958 and subsequently republished multiple times (Elton 2000) – he used examples from oceanic islands (Hawaii, New Zealand, Guam, etc.) to highlight the potential devastation of invasive introduced species as they outcompete and consume native fauna and flora (see Section 4.2).

Islands have therefore provided some of the greatest thinkers in the multidisciplinary field of conservation biology with an experimental playground, a chance to test out 'what if?', to look retrospectively at correlations between events (see Section 5.6) and to theorise about the future fate of life on Earth.

1.2 Islands as a Window onto Global Species Decline

Although islands span only approximately three per cent of the world's surface, they support a disproportionate amount of its plant and animal diversity (Kier et al. 2009). However, this rich diversity is rapidly disappearing. Within the last 500 years, more than 75 per cent of recorded vertebrate extinctions and two-thirds of plant extinctions globally have been from islands (Glen et al. 2013; Box 1.2). Future projections point to a shift in the scale of extinction risk, with one prediction suggesting that we are set to lose more than three times the number of vertebrate species than have gone extinct over the last 500 years (Rickets et al. 2005). Thirty-nine per cent of the species facing imminent extinction are island species (Rickets et al. 2005). When corrected for surface area,

---

Box 1.2 *A Tale of Two Extinctions: The Dodo and the Solitaire*

The dodo *Raphus cucullatus* on Mauritius and the solitaire *Pezophaps solitaria* on the neighbouring island of Rodrigues are believed to have evolved from the ancestors of the modern-day Nicobar pigeon *Caloenas nicobarica* (Grihault 2007). They diverged from this original pigeon stock around 43 million years ago when these birds moved south from the Nicobar Islands along a series of oceanic mountain ridges until they reached the islands of Mauritius and Rodrigues and evolved into two distinct species. Following arrival on their respective mammalian predator–free islands, each species lost the power of flight, there being no selective advantage to maintain this energetically costly means of movement. Without the need to fly, they were able to grow in size – an evolutionary trend in many island species. The solitaire would have been larger than a modern-day turkey, the dodo being slightly smaller at the size of a goose. This increase in size conferred important advantages on the species, likely increasing their life span, increasing their ability to tolerate extreme fluctuations in temperature and enabling them to go for extended periods without food (Livezey 1993).

Within 100 years of the arrival of the Dutch in 1598 (Cheke and Hume 2008), the dodo was extinct on Mauritius. On Rodrigues, the solitaire had all but disappeared within 70 years of the arrival of the French in 1691 (Grihault 2007). Prior to settlement on Mauritius in 1638, the Dutch introduced monkeys (macaques), goats, cattle and pigs. Rats had already been introduced by sporadic voyagers who made landfall on the island. However, as the dodos seemed to still be plentiful on the arrival of the Dutch, it seems unlikely that the rats in this instance had much of an impact. The dodo was initially hunted by the early settlers for food, it being a large bird and relatively easy to catch, and habitat destruction for timber extraction also would have taken its toll. However, it seems likely that the most significant factor causing the decline of the dodo was predation of the young and eggs by pigs.

It is less clear what caused the demise of the solitaire on Rodrigues. Pigs again are likely to have predated on eggs and young, potentially also competing with the birds for fruits and seeds. Cats may well have taken hatchlings, and sailors are likely to have hunted the birds for food, too. It appears that the remaining solitaires retreated to the less-populated south-west of the island where, by chance, a fire may have overtaken them and killed off the remnant population (Grihault 2007).

Relatives of the solitaire and dodo are alive today, in the forms of the crowned pigeon *Goura victoria* of New Guinea and Samoa's tooth-billed pigeon *Didunculus strigirostris*, as well as its closest extant relative, the Nicobar pigeon. However, populations of all three of these island pigeon species are in decline.

island species are 14 times more likely to be critically endangered than continental species (Tershy et al. 2015), highlighting the pressing need to scale up efforts to reverse population trends on islands. However, the overall shift in extinction risk towards the continents in future years, where the majority of biodiversity remains, and in particular to species experiencing restricted range distributions, should provide the impetus to reach out to islands to understand how certain threats drive population declines.

Alongside habitat loss and over-exploitation (Figure 1.2), the spread of invasive alien species has been a principal driver of species extinction on islands to date and remains a primary threat to many island species and ecosystems (see Chapter 4). Work on islands has shed light on the diverse impacts that invasive species can have, from directly predating on endemic species to disrupting gene flows, altering population dynamics, impacting community composition and function and compromising ecosystem-level processes (e.g. nutrient cycles). Invasion studies on islands are also highlighting how climate change may provide the catalyst for the further spread of invasive species. In South Georgia,

Figure 1.2 Deforestation in the Comoros. Thirty of the 45 once-permanent rivers on the Comorian island of Anjouan alone now only flow intermittently in large part as a consequence of deforestation. (ECDD 2012; *photo credit:* @Dahari.)

the melting ice sheets could facilitate the movement of rats *Rattus norvegicus* into new, previously inaccessible areas important for breeding seabirds (Petit and Prudent 2008). Such spreading presents a threat not only to species but also to human lives and livelihoods (see Section 4.3). Feral cats *Felis catus* have been implicated in the extinction of 14 per cent of birds, mammals and reptiles globally (Medina et al. 2011). They also represent a threat to human health via the disease toxoplasmosis (Dabritz and Conrad 2010), leading to increased likelihood of schizophrenia (Webster et al. 2006). We therefore need to recognise invasive alien species as a clear and present danger to global biodiversity and of relevance to human lives and livelihoods (see Section 4.3). Lessons from islands are also now showing us that we can begin to do something to control or eradicate this threat, helping to inform conservation projects on other islands and mainland systems where invasive species are threatening restricted-range species.

1.3 Islands as Beacons of Hope

In 1979, Norman Myers wrote, 'We might abandon the Mauritius kestrel to its all but inevitable fate', as a consequence of its extreme plight in the wild (Jachowski and Kesler 2009, cover image). From a known wild population of four birds (see Section 3.2.1), the population has now been increased to 300 to 400 individuals (Jones et al. 2013) (see Box 3.2). This example illustrates that even the most threatened of species can be brought back from the brink of extinction through intensive management. The Mauritius echo parakeet *Psittacula eques*, pink pigeon *Nesoenas mayeri*, Mallorcan midwife toad *Alytes muletensis*, Cayman blue iguana *Cyclura lewisi* and California Channel Islands fox *Urocyon littoralis* (e.g. Coonan et al. 2010) are a small selection of the species of island fauna that have been recovered from critically low numbers to a position where they now have a long-term future (Table 1.1).

Islands have been the testing ground for new and innovative techniques for understanding population declines through to managing species recovery. Our understanding of the biology of small populations and genetics (Chapters 2 and 3), invasive species ecology (Chapter 4) and the development of ecological histories to better monitor and understand population declines (Chapter 5) has benefitted from work conducted on islands. Through the development of invasive species management techniques (Chapter 7), captive breeding, translocation biology (Chapter 9), restoration ecology (Chapter 10) and human behaviour change (Chapter 11), we are beginning to learn how to more effectively mitigate threats and encourage species recovery and ecological function. Behind these actions, more effective management, leadership (Chapter 8) and planning of conservation projects (Chapter 6) are contributing to growing conservation success. Ultimately, islands have taught us that we should never give up on a species or the habitat on which it and others depend. This book seeks to illustrate how species recovery efforts on islands can inform our understanding of threatened species and habitat recovery and provide lessons for conservation work globally.

1.4 Rationale for Chapter Development

In this book we do not seek to provide a comprehensive overview of species recovery projects on islands. Instead, we wish to illustrate through examples what we believe to be helpful guiding principles and practices that can inform our conservation efforts. Species conservation projects operate, like other conservation work, within complex systems involving biological, ecological, geophysical and,

Table 1.1 *Example Vertebrate Species' Recovery Success on Islands*

Species	Location	Population change in the wild (lowest known population size (year) to most recent population size (year) or IUCN Red List status change)	Example texts for further reading
Mauritius pink pigeon *Nesoenas mayeri*	Mauritius, Indian Ocean	9 (1990) to 446 (2011)	Swinnerton 2001; Swinnerton et al. 2004; Young et al. 2014
Echo parakeet *Psittacula eques*	Mauritius, Indian Ocean	12–25 (1990s) to >500 (2010)	Kundu et al. 2012; Jones 2004
Rodrigues warbler *Acrocephalus rodericanus*	Rodrigues, Indian Ocean	c. 17 (1979) to 3,000+ (2010)	Showler et al. 2002
Rodrigues fody *Foudia flavicans*	Rodrigues, Indian Ocean	10–12 (1968) to 8,000 (2010)	Impey et al. 2002; Ricketts et al. 2005
Seychelles magpie robin *Copsychus sechellarum*	Seychelles, Indian Ocean	12–15 (1965) to 200 (2009)	Norris and Mcculloch 2003; Burt et al. 2016
Mallorcan midwife toad *Alytes muletensis*	Mallorca, Mediterranean	Cr[b] (1994) to Vu (2004) (increasing)	Griffiths and Pavajeau 2008; Young et al. 2014
Cayman blue iguana *Cyclura lewisi*	Cayman Islands, Caribbean	25 (2002) to 443 (2012)	Goodman et al. 2005; Burton 2010
Kakapo[a] *Strigops habroptila*	New Zealand	18 (1976) to 126 (2014)	Clout and Merton 1998; Robertson et al. 2006
California Channel Islands fox *Urocyon littoralis*	California Channel Islands	Cr (2004) to NT (2013)	Coonan et al. 2013

[a] Extinct in the wild (EW) in 1994 according to the International Union for Conservation of Nature (IUCN) Red List.

[b] Cr, Vu and NT are abbreviations of Critically Endangered (an extremely high risk of extinction in the wild), Vulnerable (high risk of extinction in the wild) and Near Threatened (likely to qualify for a threatened category in the near future), respectively, according to the IUCN (see www.iucnredlist.org for further details) (IUCN 2012).

where humans have an impact, sociological processes. To influence these systems, we must understand the underlying drivers of species decline, be equipped with a suite of intervention techniques to reverse the situation and appreciate how we organise and manage the resources at our disposal – the most significant one being people – to achieve success. This final point is expanded upon in this book to help us appreciate how we can influence our own practice and that of others with whom we work. We draw upon Beckhard's organisational design model (Beckhard 1972) to provide what we see as a helpful structure on which to hang our understanding of how threatened species recovery projects function (see Figure 12.1). The model contends that projects are composed of five elements: *purpose* (a long-term view as to why we do what we do), *goals* (the quantitative or qualitative descriptions that focus our work and by which we assess whether we are succeeding), the clarity of *roles* that people play within projects, the *processes* (namely, our activities and the organised order and flow of those activities) that we apply to get the work done, and finally, the *relationships* between the people involved. Each chapter either explicitly or implicitly considers one or more of the elements of this model through a conservation lens, with Chapter 12 revisiting the model and highlighting examples drawn from the book. The chapters are designed to capture knowledge from diverse disciplines and sub-disciplines ranging from the biology of small populations and genetics to invasion ecology, project management and planning and thereafter to social marketing and behavioural change. Throughout we refer to examples of either good or misguided practice, drawing on lessons from islands.

In Chapter 2, we begin by identifying some of the defining characteristics of island species developed as a consequence of evolution in isolation. We explore the development of evolutionary theory driven by studies on islands and end with a reflection on how this understanding can inform our appreciation of how to manage threatened small populations. This narrative is developed further in Chapter 3, where we consider how small, restricted populations can be influenced by genetic factors. We look at how these factors operate under emerging threats such as disease outbreaks and climate change and conclude by describing some of the practical implications of genetic management in the conservation of small, threatened populations. Chapter 4 brings us up to date with the topic of invasion ecology and the rationale for continuing to take the threat posed by invasive species seriously, exploring some of the multifaceted impacts they have on species, systems and human communities. We draw out what is known about the invasion process that can help to inform how we might intervene from a management perspective. We go on to reflect on some of the characteristics of islands that may predispose them to invasion and end by emphasising that far from considering invasive species as a threat that has passed, it has possibly only just begun.

Chapter 5 takes a step back from internal and external threats facing small populations to consider how we understand the process of population decline and distribution change from a historical perspective. We begin with a critical review of techniques used to help us reconstruct ecological histories for currently threatened (or extinct) species, such as the analysis of sub-fossil remains and the use of travellers' notebooks and maps. We consider how these approaches can help to inform our understanding of the cause(s) of population decline and so identify what remedial actions we may take. We review the range of methods used today to monitor current or recent population declines, touching on citizen science as well as more sophisticated monitoring techniques that account for imperfect detection. We summarise the components of an effective monitoring programme and end with a reflection on some of the steps we can take to infer or identify the causes behind the current status of threatened species.

In Chapter 6 we begin our analysis of how people within conservation projects can be better managed to enable them to be more effective in their work. We highlight the importance of considering upfront foreseeable issues that can undermine project outcomes and the need for regular monitoring and review. We introduce a range of project management tools to equip conservation managers with a kit to help manage the work, the people and the processes that enable the project to be completed. Finally, we reflect on methods for evaluating project outcomes, focusing on one particular model that provides a structure for examining project function. Given the importance of invasive species management in the recovery of threatened species worldwide, Chapter 7 takes some time to identify some of the key steps involved in planning for the eradication of sustained control, with a particular focus on invasive alien mammals. By the end of the chapter, we hope for readers to be clearer about key points to consider if faced with an invasive vertebrate management project. Chapter 8 devotes much-needed time to our understanding of leadership as a core discipline within species conservation. We provide a synopsis of central leadership theories and stress the importance of how to create, manage and motivate teams under what are often tiring and stressful conditions. We recognise that projects have natural high and low points and place emphasis on the value of 'systems thinking' as a helpful way of viewing projects from a leadership perspective. We end with consideration of 'project champions' and their important role in providing both leadership and encouragement throughout the process.

In Chapter 9 we focus in on the intensive species management approaches, often developed first on islands, that have led to the recovery of some of the world's most enigmatic species. The chapter draw heavily on our experience working on islands in New Zealand and the Mascarenes, experience that we feel is relevant to the process of species recovery worldwide and in particular for highly threatened species. We present a general approach used to evaluate new recovery opportunities and how we make decisions on which course of action to take. Chapter 10 reflects on how we should view species and their recovery within the context of their role within ecosystems. We consider the extent to which we can restore historical systems through habitat management and the recovery or replacement of threatened or lost species. We summarise some fundamental stages in habitat restoration, recognising the order in which we can put back the pieces of the puzzle and, where necessary, create new pieces that fit the space. We spend some time introducing the controversial concept of 'ecological replacement' and reflect on the fact that the *introduction* of novel species to systems may become more common practice as we seek to restore functioning ecosystems, more resilient to future shocks.

Throughout we draw on lessons from islands to inform our thinking as to how to achieve our conservation goals. Where helpful, we draw readers' attention to related text, examples or figures in other chapters. We include a range of case-study boxes to illustrate points raised in the chapters or to introduce approaches that we think are helpful in better understanding how to apply the principles in practice. We hope that readers find the topics covered within this book useful in developing their own thinking about how we understand, plan and deliver on conservation projects. In some small way, we hope that this book contributes to reversing the global trend in biodiversity loss that we are experiencing and, true to the mission of the Durrell Wildlife Conservation Trust, 'saving species from extinction'.

References

Ali, J. R. and Huber, M. (2010). Mammalian biodiversity on Madagascar controlled by ocean currents. *Nature* 463: 653–56.

Beckhard R. (1972). Optimizing team building effort. *Journal of Contemporary Business* 1(3): 23–32.

Brown, J. H. (1995). *Macroecology*. University of Chicago Press, Chicago, IL.

Burney, D. A. (2003). Madagascar's prehistoric ecosystems, pp. 47–51 in S. M. Goodman and J. P. Benstead (eds.), *The Natural History of Madagascar*. University of Chicago Press, Chicago, IL.

Burt, A. J., Gane, J., Olivier, I. et al. (2016). *The History, Status and Trends of the Endangered Seychelles Magpie-Robin Copsychus Sechellarum* (pp. 1–19). Bird Conservation International, Cambridge.

Burton, F. J. (2010). *The Little Blue Book: A Short History of the Grand Cayman Blue Iguana*. International Reptile Conservation Foundation, Tucson, AZ.

Cheke, A. and Hume, J. (2008). *Lost Land of the Dodo: An Ecological History of Mauritius, Réunion, and Rodrigues*. T & AD Poyser, London.

Clout, M. N. and Merton, D. V. (1998). Saving the kakapo: the conservation of the world's most peculiar parrot. *Bird Conservation International* 8(3): 281–96.

Coonan, T J., Schwemm, C. A. and Garcelon, D. K. (2010). *Decline and Recovery of the Island Fox: A Case Study for Population Recovery*. Cambridge University Press, Cambridge.

Coonan, T., Ralls, K., Hudgens, B., Cypher, B. and Boser, C. (2013). *Urocyon littoralis*. The IUCN Red List of Threatened Species 2013: e.T22781A13985603. Available at http://dx.doi.org/10.2305/IUCN.UK.2013–2.RLTS.T22781A13985603.en (last accessed 2 February 2017).

Curtis, D. J. (2006). Cathemerality in lemurs, pp. 133–57 in L. Gould and M. L. Sauther (eds.), *Lemurs: Ecology and Adaptation*. Springer, New York, NY.

Dabritz, H. A. and Conrad, P. A. (2010). Cats and *Toxoplasma*: implications for public health. *Zoonoses Public Health* 57: 34–52.

ECDD (2012). Déboisement et tarissement des rivières à Anjouan. Etude bibliographique, Engagement Communautaire pour le Développement Durable report. Available at http://km.chm-cbd.net/biodiversite/ecosystemes/document-chm.pdf (last accessed 5 May 2017).

Elton, C. S. (2000). *The Ecology of Invasions by Animals and Plants*. University of Chicago Press, Chicago, IL.

Glen, A. S., Atkinson, R., Keitt, B. S. et al. (2013). Eradicating multiple invasive species on inhabited islands: the next big step in island restoration? *Biological Invasions* 15: 2589–603.

Godfrey, L. R. and Jungers, W. L. (2003). Subfossil lemurs, pp. 1247–52 in S. M. Goodman and J. P. Benstead (eds.), *The Natural History of Madagascar*. University of Chicago Press, Chicago, IL.

Goodman, S. M., Ganzhorn, J. U. and Rakotondravony, D. (2003). Introduction to the mammals, pp. 1159–86 in S. M. Goodman and J. P. Benstead (eds.), *The Natural History of Madagascar*. University of Chicago Press, Chicago, IL.

Goodman, R. M., Echternacht, A. C. and Burton, F. J. (2005). Spatial ecology of the endangered iguana, *Cyclura lewisi*, in a disturbed setting on Grand Cayman. *Journal of Herpetology* 39(3): 402–8.

Griffiths, R. A. and Pavajeau, L. (2008). Captive breeding, reintroduction, and the conservation of amphibians. *Conservation Biology* 22(4): 852–61.

Grihault, A. (2007). *Solitaire: The Dodo of Rodrigues Island*. Andrew Isles, Prahran.

Impey, A. J., Côté, I. M. and Jones, C. G. (2002). Population recovery of the threatened endemic Rodrigues fody (*Foudia flavicans*) (Aves, Ploceidae) following reforestation. *Biological Conservation* 107(3): 299–305.

IUCN (2012). *IUCN Red List Categories and Criteria: Version 3.1*, 2nd edn. Cambridge: IUCN.

Jachowski, D. S. and Kesler, D. C. (2009). Allowing extinction: should we let species go? *Proceedings of the National Academy of Sciences USA* 105: 2919–22.

Jones, C. G. (2004). Conservation management of endangered birds, pp. 269–302 in William J. Sutherland, Ian Newton and Rhys Green (eds.), *Bird Ecology and Conservation: A Handbook of Techniques*, vol. 1. Oxford University Press, Oxford.

Jones, C. G., Burgess, M. D., Groombridge, J. J. et al. (2013). Mauritius kestrel *Falco punctatus*, pp. 262–319 in R. J. Safford and A. F. A. Hawkins (eds.), *The Birds of Africa*, vol. VIII: *The Malagasy Region*, Christopher Helm, London.

Kier, G., Kreft, H., Lee, T. M. et al. (2009). A global assessment of endemism and species richness across island and mainland regions. *Proceedings of the National Academy of Sciences USA* 106: 9322–27.

Kundu, S., Faulkes, C. G., Greenwood, A. G. et al. (2012). Tracking viral evolution during a disease outbreak: the rapid and complete selective sweep of a circovirus in the endangered Echo parakeet. *Journal of Virology* 86(9): 5221–29.

Livezey, B. C. (1993). An ecomorphological review of the dodo (*Raphus cucullatus*) and solitaire (*Pezophaps solitaria*), flightless columbiformes of the Mascarene Islands. *Journal of Zoology* 230(2): 247–92.

MacArthur, R. H. and Wilson, E. O. (1967). *The Theory of Island Biogeography* Princeton University Press, Princeton, NJ.

Marivaux, L., Welcomme, J.-L., Antoine, P.-O. et al. (2001). A fossil lemur from the Oligocene of Pakistan. *Science* 294: 587–91.

Masters, J. C., de Wit, M. J. and Asher, R. J. (2006). Reconciling the origins of Africa, India and Madagascar with vertebrate dispersal scenarios. *Folia Primatologica* 77: 399–418.

Medina, F. M., Bonnaud, E., Vidal, E. et al. (2011). A global review of the impacts of invasive cats on island endangered vertebrates. *Global Change Biology* 17(11): 3503–10.

Mittermeier, R. A., Louis Jr, E. E., Richardson, M. et al. (2010). *Lemurs of Madagascar* (Tropical Field Guide Series), 3rd edn. Conservation International, Arlington, VA.

Nevo, E. (2006). Ernst Mayr (1904–2005): evolutionary leader, protagonist, and visionary. *Theoretical Population Biology* 70(2): 105–10.

Norris, K. and Mcculloch, N. (2003). Demographic models and the management of endangered species: a case study of the critically endangered Seychelles magpie robin. *Journal of Applied Ecology* 40(5): 890–99.

Pearce-Higgins, J. W., Green, R. E. and Green, R. (2014). *Birds and Climate Change: Impacts and Conservation Responses.* Cambridge University Press, Cambridge.

Petit, J. and Prudent, G. (2008). *Climate Change and Biodiversity in the European Union Overseas Entities.* International Union for Conservation of Nature (IUCN), Gland.

Ricketts, T. H., Dinerstein, E., Boucher, T. et al. (2005). Pinpointing and preventing imminent extinctions. *Proceedings of the National Academy of Sciences USA* 102(51): 18497–501.

Robertson, B. C., Elliott, G. P., Eason, D. K., Clout, M. N. and Gemmell, N. J. (2006). Sex allocation theory aids species conservation. *Biology Letters* 2(2): 229–31.

Showler, D. A., Côté, I. M. and Jones, C. G. (2002). Population census and habitat use of Rodrigues warbler *Acrocephalus rodericanus*. *Bird Conservation International* 12(3): 211–30.

Simpson, G. G. (1940). Mammals and land bridges. *Journal of the Washington Academy of Sciences* 30: 137–63.

Stevens, N. J. and Heesy, C. P. (2006). Malagasy primate origins: phylogenies, fossils, and biogeographic reconstructions. *Folia Primatologica* 77: 419–33.

Swinnerton, K. (2001). Ecology and conservation of the pink pigeon *Columba mayeri* on Mauritius. *Dodo* 37: 99–100.

Swinnerton, K., Groombridge, J. J., Jones, C. G., Burn, R. W. and Mungroo, Y. (2004). Inbreeding depression and founder diversity among captive and free-living populations of the endangered pink pigeon *Columba mayeri*. *Animal Conservation* 7: 353–64.

Tattersall, I. (2007). Madagascar's lemurs: cryptic diversity or taxonomic inflation? *Evolutionary Anthropology* 16: 12–23.

Tershy, B. R., Shen, K. W., Newton, K. M., Holmes, N. D. and Croll, D. A. (2015). The importance of islands for the protection of biological and linguistic diversity. *BioScience* 65(6): 592–97.

Walker, L. R., Walker, J. and Hobbs, R. J. (2007). *Linking Restoration and Ecological Succession* (pp. 1–18). Springer, London.

Webster, J., Lamberton, P., Donnelly, C. and Torrey, E. (2006). Parasites as causative agents of human affective disorders? The impact of anti-psychotic, mood-stabilizer and anti-parasite medication on *Toxoplasma gondii*'s ability to alter host behaviour. *Proceedings of the Royal Society B* 273: 1023–30.

Whittaker, R. J. and Fernández-Palacios, J. M. (2007). *Island Biogeography: Ecology, Evolution, and Conservation.* Oxford University Press, Oxford.

Wilson, E. O. (1984). *Biophilia.* Harvard University Press, Cambridge, MA.

Young, R. P., Hudson, M. A., Terry, A. M. R. et al. (2014). Accounting for conservation: using the IUCN Red List Index to evaluate the impact of a conservation organization. *Biological Conservation* 180: 84–96.

2 · *Evolution on Islands*
Peculiarities and Implications for Species Conservation

JIM J. GROOMBRIDGE, STEPHEN E. W. GREEN AND SAMUEL T. TURVEY

2.0 Introduction

Species or populations endemic to islands (from here on referred to as 'island endemics') have evolved among their bewildering diversity of forms a number of traits that appear to be distinctive to island environments and driven by the properties of insular ecosystems. The study of these ecological traits, observed across a wide taxonomic scale, paved the way for the development of a variety of models to explain the very different mechanisms of evolution observed on islands. The study of island systems has generated a number of classic examples of insular evolution that have informed our wider understanding of how species change through time and in relation to their environments. In their role as so-called 'species-engines', island systems provide 'stepping-stones' to speciation within and between island groups but can also act as 'highways' between continental land masses. Advances in molecular genetics have revolutionised how we can interpret these patterns and measure evolutionary distinctiveness and their application to island and continental systems. They have also raised the level of precision in our knowledge of how island endemics have evolved. However, despite these advances, the challenge remains to apply our increasing awareness of how island endemics and island systems have evolved in such a way as to enhance conservation efforts to maintain and restore them.

This chapter is divided into three interrelated sections. We begin with an introductory summary of the types of characteristics which appear to be shared by island endemics and which subsequently mark them as distinct. We continue with an overview of a variety of models of evolution that have been developed to describe the different mechanisms that appear to drive evolutionary diversity on island systems. This section is followed by a review of both iconic and less well-known studies of evolution on islands and the evolutionary importance of islands as stepping-stones to speciation. Lastly, this chapter discusses how island species conservation programmes can be enhanced by understanding the evolutionary history of the endangered populations which they seek to conserve.

2.1 Peculiarities of Island Endemics

Islands and island systems have played a central role in our understanding of evolution, a fortunate circumstance that has been fuelled by our fascination and obsession with the evolutionary curiosities that islands can produce. For example, popular interest for two centuries in the dodo *Raphus cucullatus*, a flightless bird once found on the island of Mauritius (Box 1.2), not only helped to develop modern conservation conscious-ness but also focused a spotlight on the curious and unusual traits of island endemics in comparison to their continental or mainland equivalents. Island endemics, whatever their taxonomic status, appear to share a set of characteristics that sets them apart ecologically from their mainland counterparts. The most fundamental change that is often observed is a change or shift in 'ecological niche', the specific habitat and conditions under which the species exists and survives most favourably. A change in niche is typically associated with an adaptive morphological change in island colonists, with similar patterns of morphological change often seen repeated between different island taxa.

Change in body size (i.e. gigantism or dwarfism/nanism) is one characteristic feature commonly associated with island endemics. A perceived 'general rule' of change in body size on islands is supported by a relatively small number of well-known examples. Iconic examples of extant island species showing this trait include the giant tortoises of the Galapagos Islands and Aldabra, although similar species (a 'forgotten megafauna'; Hansen and Galetti 2009) are also known to have occurred during the Late Quaternary on Madagascar, the Mascarenes, the Greater and Lesser Antilles and the South American and African continents. Changes in body size have been observed in island taxa across a variety of modern groups, most notably perhaps in mammals where, upon island colonisation, small-bodied mammals typically become larger (85 per cent of island rodents are larger than their mainland sister taxa; Foster 1964; Lomolino 1985) and large-bodied mammals typically become smaller

(Damuth 1993). These reciprocal changes appear to be responses to either the predator-free nature of islands (small mammals evolve to become larger; Adler and Levins 1994) or selection pressures on islands where resources are limited (large mammals evolve to become smaller; Damuth 1993).

Some of the most striking examples of gigantism and dwarfism are shown in the Late Quaternary fossil record. The Mediterranean islands formerly contained multiple species of dwarfed elephants, hippopotami and deer (Reyment 1983; Lister 1993; Schüle 1993), whereas the islands of the Caribbean contained a giant rodent that weighed up to 210 kg (*Amblyrhiza inundata*), together with dwarfed sloths (e.g. *Neocnus dousman, N. toupiti*) (McFarlane et al. 1998; MacPhee et al. 2000); one dwarf sloth, *Bradypus pygmaeus*, still survives in the insular Caribbean (Anderson and Handley 2002). Changes such as these are traditionally thought to be associated with a shift from r selection to k selection, whereby intraspecific competition becomes an increasingly important factor in predator-free island systems, pushing insular species to evolve larger body sizes and invest more heavily in a smaller number of offspring so as to be at a greater competitive advantage against conspecifics. However, more recent work across a variety of taxa suggests that island carrying capacity plays a role and that these general rules do not apply consistently (Simard et al. 2008; Sinclair and Parkes 2008; Meiri et al. 2011; Raia and Meiri 2011).

Another frequently observed adaptive change shown by island colonists is a loss of dispersal ability, such as reduced wings in birds and insects and changes in morphology in plant seed dispersal propagules. This trait is not unique among island endemics, and several studies have shown how for some taxa such adaptations can occur outside of insular systems (e.g. for birds and insects; Roff 1991, 1994). However, many of the best-known examples of reduced dispersal ability are shown by island taxa, such as reduced wings in beetles from Tristan de Cunha (Williamson 1981) and the evolution of flightlessness in rails on oceanic islands (Diamond 1991), in the kakapo *Strigops habroptilus* (the only extant flightless parrot) and many other extant and extinct bird species from New Zealand, as well as, of course, in the dodo from Mauritius (Hume 2006; Cheke and Hume 2008). In plants, classic examples include patterns of lost or reduced hooks and barbs in dispersing seeds of Pacific island species of *Bidens* ('Spanish Beard', Asteraceae) (Carlquist 1974; Ehrendorfer 1979) and changes in seed size and dispersal ability in *Lactuca muralis* (Asteraceae), a wind-dispersing species which Cody and

Overton (1996) studied on 200 islands in Barkley Sound, Canada. The latter example illustrates beautifully how dispersal ability can become significantly reduced in time periods as short as a decade or less with increasing island isolation. Loss of dispersal ability in island taxa was noted by Darwin (1859) and has since undergone much debate regarding underlying explanations (Williamson 1981; Roff 1991). The two major theories for driving this adaptation are selection against highly dispersive taxa (especially for plants and insects) and reduced selective advantage for maintaining energetically expensive flight structures (e.g. powerful flight musculature) in typically predator-free insular environments (especially for birds).

Different evolutionary mechanisms may be responsible for explaining different instances of reduced dispersal ability in island taxa, but this trait appears to be closely associated with insular ecosystems and illustrates the strength of the evolutionary response to the alternative selection pressures operating in island environments. When considering what selection pressures may have shaped an island species, two points need to be borne in mind. First, it is important not to forget that island systems, especially faunal assemblages, are typically 'imbalanced' in that they have often only been colonised by certain representatives of mainland taxa. For example, among mammals, bats and rodents are the most frequent colonisers, with other groups such as carnivores rarely colonising offshore islands. Therefore, these biased assemblages also contribute to the unusual ecological properties and alternative selective pressures that operate on islands. Second, one adaptive trait may appear to be associated with another. For example, reduction in dispersal ability leading to the evolution of flightlessness in island birds can appear to be associated with gigantism, the extinct moas of New Zealand being one example (see Section 5.1.1). However, an increase in size can reduce flight ability anyway, irrespective of whether there is a separate selective advantage in becoming flightless (e.g. due to an absence of predators).

Consideration of both molecular and geological data has enabled approximate estimates of how long these size changes took to evolve, revealing some to be relatively rapid. For example, woolly mammoths from the Californian Channel Islands appear to have shrunk appreciably in body size in as little as 6,000 years (Tikhonov et al. 2003; see also Vartanyan et al. 1993). Elsewhere, on Isla de Escudo near Panama, the pygmy sloth *Bradypus pygmaeus* has been isolated from its mainland ancestor *B. variegatus* for about 9,000 years since sea levels rose at the start of the Holocene, resulting in a 40 per cent reduction in body mass in the insular form (Anderson and Handley 2002). However, changes in body size for some island endemics can be difficult to interpret from geological history alone, particularly if those changes are suspected to be comparatively recent. One example is the dwarfed Hog Island boa *Boa constrictor imperator* endemic to the Cayos Cochinos Archipelago off the coast of Honduras, for which a recent molecular genetic study has shed new light on when and how their dwarfism may have evolved (Box 2.1).

One of the best-known traits of island endemics is their susceptibility to predation compared to continental populations. This phenomenon

---

Box 2.1 *Evolution of Dwarfism in Hog Island Boas*

The Hog Island boa *Boa constrictor imperator* is endemic to two small islands in the Cayos Cochinos Archipelago, located off the northern coast of Honduras (Figure 2.1). Although traditionally considered to be the same subspecies that occurs throughout mainland Central America, these boas display a remarkable level of phenotypic divergence from boas on the adjacent mainland and nearby Bay Islands (see Figure 2.1). Hog Island boas are dramatically dwarfed in size, with adults averaging approximately 1 m in snout–vent length (SVL), representing around a 50 per cent reduction in body size compared to neighbouring populations. In addition to their small body size, Hog Island boas are also hypomelanistic, a genetic trait that causes a reduction in the production of the skin pigment melanin, leading to their distinctive light and often 'salmon pink' colouration.

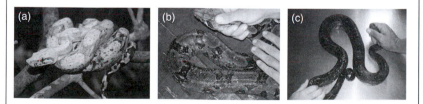

Figure 2.1 Phenotypic variation of boa constrictors between the Cayos Cochinos, Bay Islands and mainland Honduras. (a) Hog Island boa from the Cayos Cochinos Archipelago; (b) Bay Island boa from the island of Utila; and (c) mainland Honduran boa. (*Photo credit:* Stephen Green.) (A black–and–white version of this figure will appear in some formats. For the colour version, please refer to the plate section.)

Like many islands along the coasts of Central America, the Cayos Cochinos are geologically quite 'young', having only been isolated from the mainland by rising sea levels at the end of the last ice age glaciation less than 10,000 years ago (McCranie et al. 2005). It was assumed, therefore, that the Hog Island boa must share a relatively recent common ancestor with mainland boas and that the dramatic evolutionary shifts observed in the Cayos Cochinos populations must have taken place rapidly since the recent isolation of the islands. However, analysis of the Cayos Cochinos and Bay Island populations, using two mitochondrial genes (Green 2011), suggests that the dwarfed Hog Island boas from the Cayos Cochinos and the larger mainland-like boas found on the Bay Islands actually form a monophyletic group that diverged from the mainland boas approximately 2 Mya.

The results of the genetic analysis indicate that the common ancestor of the Cayos Cochinos and all Bay Island boas was most likely isolated on Roatan and/or Guanaja shortly after these islands were cut off from the mainland by rising sea levels in the early Pleistocene (Figure 2.2). Roatan and Guanaja, which lie off the continental shelf and which are surrounded by much deeper waters than the Cayos Cochinos or Utila, would not have been reconnected to the mainland by subsequent Pleistocene sea level fluctuations (Wilson and Hahn 1973; McCranie et al. 2005). In contrast, the Cayos Cochinos and Utila, which lie on the continental shelf, would have been repeatedly isolated from and subsequently reconnected to the mainland multiple times by changing seas levels during this period. It appears that since their most recent isolation from the mainland around 10,000 years ago, the Cayos Cochinos and Utila islands have been colonised by boas from Roatan and/or Guanaja rather than from the mainland (however, some evidence also exists for limited gene flow from the mainland to Utila and warrants further investigation).

Therefore, it appears that the original interpretation of the unique Hog Island boa phenotype having been brought about by rapid evolutionary shifts on the Cayos Cochinos was correct. These changes must have occurred over a remarkably short time frame since the newly isolated Cayos Cochinos Islands were colonised by boas from one or more of the Bay Islands. However, assumptions

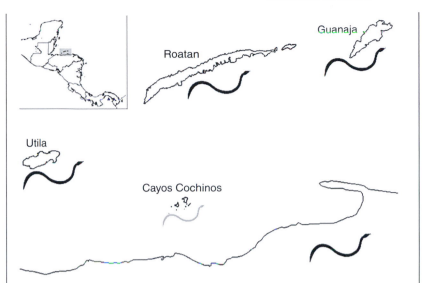

Figure 2.2 Map of the Bay Islands (Utila, Roatan and Guanaja) and Cayos Cochinos Archipelago off the northern coast of Honduras. Large black snakes signify populations of *Boa constrictor imperator* that display large body size and dark mainland-like colouration. Small grey snake signifies dwarfed populations of *B. c. imperator* known as the 'Hog Island boa' (see Figure 2.1).

about the evolutionary relationship of Hog Island boas to mainland boas have proven to be incorrect. Having been isolated from the mainland for approximately two million years, it would appear that the Cayos Cochinos and Bay Island populations represent an 'evolutionarily significant unit' (ESU) and are of greater conservation 'value' than previously recognised. This somewhat counter-intuitive result would not have been apparent without the use of molecular techniques.

unfortunately can be illustrated easily by the numerous documented cases of island populations that have been driven to extinction following accidental or deliberate anthropogenically mediated introduction of a mainland predator (see Section 4.2). Well-known examples include the disappearance or endangerment of countless island populations of birds on both small and large islands. Across the Pacific islands, recent extinctions of island birds have been widely attributed to anthropogenic introduction of invasive mammals such as rats (*Rattus* spp.), cats

Felis catus and mongoose *Herpestes auropunctatus* (Blackburn et al. 2004, 2005) (see Chapters 4 and 5 for further examples), in addition to recent habitat conversion (Didham et al. 2005). Interest in the late Holocene wave of bird extinctions across the Pacific islands (see Section 5.1) has played an important part in the current debate on whether the observed general pattern of high extinction rates among island endemics is due to their ecological traits (Jamieson et al. 2006; Jamieson 2007), genetic factors associated with their evolutionary histories of island isolation (Frankham 1997, 1998, 2005; Frankham et al. 2002; Spielman et al. 2004) or a combination of the two (Groombridge 2007) (see Chapter 3).

The characteristic relative naivety to predation shown by island endemics is displayed in a variety of forms among animals and plants. In the same way that many plant species can be shown to have lost their dispersal mechanisms upon colonising an island, many others have lost anti-herbivore defences such as toxins and defensive structures. However, such traits can just as readily become acquired by island endemics as a consequence of opposite evolutionary pressures. A classic example of this response is seen among the lobelioid plants found across the Hawaiian Islands. Species of *Cyanea* have not only famously co-evolved alongside their endemic forest bird pollinators (Box 2.2), but some have also developed extensive prickles, a common evolutionary defence against herbivores that is frequently observed on islands and continents alike. Although there are no surviving native large browsers in the Hawaiian fauna, the pre-human Late Quaternary fauna contained a radiation of large-bodied browsing geese, the moa-nalo, which became extinct following Polynesian colonisation in the late Holocene. Reconstruction of the phylogenetic history of the Hawaiian lobelioids using molecular

---

Box 2.2 *Adaptive Radiation of Hawaiian Forest Birds*

Few iconic examples of rapid evolutionary adaptation on islands surpass that of the Hawaiian honeycreepers. This endemic group of birds has caught the attention of evolutionary biologists since Victorian times, when historical naturalists explored the impenetrable forests of the volcanic island chain and were able to describe and collect specimens of honeycreeper species, many of which have since become extinct. The Hawaiian Islands comprise a string of volcanoes that arose sequentially as oceanic plates moved over a weak spot in the Earth's crust, creating a system whereby each island increases in geological age from east (youngest) to west (oldest). During this geological process, the islands were colonised by what is believed to have been a single songbird lineage, initially considered to have originated from South America and which subsequently radiated across the islands, rapidly evolving into new forms to fill a diverse range of ecological niches.

This explosive radiation of Hawaiian honeycreepers is best known for the remarkable morphological adaptations in bill shape, illustrating how speciation within this group of island birds has been driven by adaptations in feeding ecology. This evolutionary process led to the formation of myriad feeding types, from seed-eating generalists to insectivores and nectivores, as well as highly specialised feeding strategies such as mollusc-eating species, delicate long-billed nectivores and larvae-eating excavators. Advances in DNA sequencing technology have meant that it is now possible to sequence large numbers of genes from blood/tissue samples from modern populations of those species that survive today, as well as from 100- to 200-year-old museum specimens of skins of extinct species that were collected by past naturalists. Recent work by Lerner et al. (2011) places the radiation of Hawaiian honeycreepers as starting around 5.7 Mya ago and that most of the lineages that gave rise to distinctive morphologies diverged after the island of Oahu was formed, around 3.7–4.0 Mya. From a conservation perspective, one of their most striking findings was the phylogenetic placement of the po'ouli *Melamprosops phaeosoma*, a species that became extinct very recently despite intensive conservation efforts (Groombridge et al. 2004; VanderWerf et al. 2006; Groombridge 2009). Although the po'ouli was always considered to be highly evolutionarily distinct based on morphology and its unique feeding preference for native snails, the extent of distinctiveness only became clear from the phylogenetic work by Lerner et al. (2011), who show the po'ouli to be the most evolutionarily distinct of all the Hawaiian honeycreepers, having diverged as an ancestral form 7.24 Mya. This extraordinary result is a clear example of loss of a large amount of phylogenetic diversity within a single modern-day extinction event.

data suggests that prickles evolved independently multiple times on different Hawaiian Islands in response to this browsing pressure (Givnish et al. 1994).

Colonisation of an island also appears to trigger changes in other fundamental aspects of a population's biology, including changes in breeding system, perhaps the central mechanism that defines any population. One often-cited example of this trait in plants is the evolution of 'woodiness' (arborescence) in insular plant species. Darwin noted this phenomenon in his observations of tree sun-flowers in the Galapagos Islands (Darwin 1859), which subsequently spawned a number of competing theories among early naturalists to explain why herbaceous plant species appear to have frequently evolved tree-like habits on islands. Darwin (1859) argued that acquiring an ability to grow taller offered a competitive advantage over other plant colonists for scarce island resources. Alfred Russel Wallace (1878) suggested that with woodiness came the ability to extend an individual's lifespan and that this longevity offered a greater possibility of achieving sexual reproduction on islands where natural pollinators might be scarce.

These early observations and ideas have since been augmented by molecular studies, which have brought renewed clarity and interpretation to remarkable examples of the evolution of arborescence. Such examples include the silverswords and lobelioids of the Hawaiian Islands (Figure 2.3) (Givnish et al. 1994), the tree lettuces of Macaronesia and the tree cabbages of St Helena (Carquist 1974), the latter two being comparable to examples of the evolution of gigantism in island faunas. Many of these molecular studies have produced time-calibrated phylogenies that can identify chronology and estimate depth of divergence, showing how, in line with Victorian ideas, evolutionary processes can be closely tied to geology but also just how rapidly radiations can occur on islands. In other taxa, an island life without predators can produce somewhat comparable effects on a species' life history, such as slower maturation rates. For example, periods of growth to enable bird species to reach skeletal maturity are apomorphically shortened to less than a year in living birds. However, evidence from annual growth marks in the cortical bone of extinct moa in New Zealand suggests that they took at least several years to achieve skeletal maturity (Turvey et al. 2005), which may reflect the lack of mammalian predators there to prey on juvenile moa.

Figure 2.3 Silversword *Argyroxiphium sandwicense* subsp. *macrocephalum* on the crater of Haleakalā Volcano, Maui. (*Photo credit:* Jim J. Groombridge.)

Taken together, the series of traits commonly observed in plant and animal populations endemic to islands have contributed to our interest in and fascination with insular ecosystems and, consequently, our wish to conserve them. Studies of the unique and seemingly endless varieties of island endemic species, however, have shown them to be the product of specific mechanisms that lie at the heart of understanding evolutionary processes on islands.

2.2 Models of Evolution on Island Systems

The concept of speciation underpins our understanding of evolution and is the mechanism by which two or more species evolve from a single ancestral form. The mechanics of speciation are largely built upon the concept of reproductive isolation. Here an ecological or behavioural trait (or traits) arises within a subset of individuals in a population, and this leads to a reduction in gene flow across the population, eventually leading to complete reproductive isolation between the two forms. The evolutionary genetic processes of natural selection (see Section 3.1.3) and random genetic drift (see Section 3.1.1) are the key processes acting within populations to drive this divergence of populations towards eventual speciation. This over-simplified and brief general description belies the diversity of micro-evolutionary mechanisms and the complexity of interactions involved. However, island systems offer a level of simplicity in their geographic isolation and ecological transparency that has allowed us to observe and comprehend these different processes. Consequently, our knowledge of speciation has become naturally intertwined with studies of island systems.

Several important distinctions are helpful in understanding how populations endemic to islands have evolved. One important realisation is that the endemic biodiversity we see on islands must be viewed within the context of a snapshot in evolutionary time and that different island systems will have different geological and evolutionary histories, providing very different means by which endemism can arise. For example, reduction in sea level during an island's evolutionary history (especially during the recent Late Quaternary glacial–interglacial cycles) can form temporary land bridges with nearby mainland regions, enabling colonisation of an island before sea level subsequently rises again. Extinction of the mainland population (or neighbouring island population) can leave a specific island population as a 'pseudo-endemic', whereas more commonly a colonising island population evolves *in situ* to become a true endemic. What this distinction illustrates is that the endemic biodiversity we observe on island systems can be products of very different events through time.

Our understanding of the evolutionary processes responsible for shaping biodiversity on islands has for a long time benefitted from our knowledge of biogeography. An important landmark contribution was MacArthur and Wilson's book *The Theory of Island Biogeography* (1967), which set out the general principles that could explain how biological systems on islands work and what governs the evolutionary processes that operate within them. These two pioneers of island biogeography developed the theoretical understanding to explain the extent and rate at which species colonise islands and identified a set of core factors, including island size, degree of geographic isolation, island age and the prevailing climate and habitats of the island. MacArthur and Wilson (1967) demonstrated eloquently how the number of species that go extinct on an island per unit time increases as a function of the number on the island because more species exist there to go extinct. Alongside this, the number of species that colonise the island through time decreases as a function of the number on the island because an increasing number of those species or lineages on the mainland already exist on the island (or their niches are already filled on the island). These two processes operate together to reach an equilibrium, whereby the number of extinctions is offset by the number of new arrivals.

Other pivotal studies at around this time also examined the prevalence of endemism on islands. Mayr (1965) demonstrated that larger islands appear to contain a larger number of endemic species than small islands, an observation that he suggested was because larger islands allowed populations to persist for long enough (i.e. at larger population sizes) to become evolutionarily differentiated to the level of a different species compared to small islands. Diamond (1980) showed that isolated islands in the Pacific contained proportionally more endemics than islands in close proximity to mainland continents, an observation that he suggested was explained by lowered extinction rates due to reduced competition on generally species–poor isolated islands.

More recent studies focusing on island endemism in birds have refined our understanding of evolution on islands. For example, numbers of endemic bird species have been shown to be positively correlated with both island area and isolation for both Indian Ocean and Pacific Ocean birds. Very different natural island systems, involving invertebrates such as snails, emphasise other island attributes. For example, work by Cowie and Holland (2006) points to the importance of dispersal mechanisms in accounting for the high diversity of Pacific island snails. As the complexities of these diverse natural island systems become unravelled, more advanced general theories of island biogeography can be developed. One example is the general dynamic model of oceanic island biogeography advocated by Whittaker et al. (2008), which combines the key dynamic biological processes of migration, speciation and extinction as developed by MacArthur and Wilson

(1967) but integrates them alongside evolutionary and geological time scales that describe the life cycle of oceanic islands. Taken together, these observed patterns imply that the more remote islands of the world may be a powerful evolutionary source for the production of island endemic species. However, it should be noted that rates of extinction can vary through time and, in particular, that anthropogenically driven extinctions of island faunas have left most surviving island faunas depauperate in comparison to their recent levels of pre-human species richness, thus complicating how today's observed island diversity patterns should be interpreted (Turvey 2009; see also Chapter 5).

Whether or not island systems truly are speciation machines, rapidly 'cranking out' new species, the broad mechanisms of speciation on islands can be categorised into allopatric (or geographic) speciation, sympatric (or competitive) speciation and polyploidy. The first mechanism is underpinned by geography, the second by ecological opportunity and the third by a change in chromosome number. Allopatric speciation arises when a geographic barrier restricts gene flow within a sexually reproducing species. The isolated subpopulations then evolve in separation for a time, becoming sufficiently differentiated to be called separate species. In an island setting, the starting point ('geographic barrier') is the arrival of a founding population of colonists from a geographically isolated source population (either a continental mainland or another island). The critical mechanism is the restriction of gene flow between the two, which for remote islands might mean no gene flow at all. Consequently, the founding population contains only a subset of the collective gene pool, a circumstance known as the 'founder effect' and which is similar in its effect to a population undergoing a genetic bottleneck (see Chapter 3). The resulting population, if it persists through evolutionary time, evolves in its newly isolated island setting to form a new species. This mechanism of speciation is perhaps the most common on islands, and rejoining of islands with neighbouring islands or the mainland through repeated changes in sea level (particularly within island archipelagos) can allow for repeated opportunities for allopatric speciation.

In contrast to allopatric speciation, sympatric speciation requires no physical barrier or isolation, but instead an unexploited ecological niche within the same environment as the original source population. In the context of an island setting, a colonising species expands its niche range to occupy an empty niche, with pioneering individuals expanding into the available niche as a consequence of a reduction in competition with the original species. The differentiation into two separate species is then driven by decreased competitive pressure between the individuals of each population best able to thrive in the two different niches. Island systems may contain endemic species that have arisen by either allopatric or sympatric speciation. Indeed, it is difficult to assess the proportion of speciation events that occur by each mechanism. However, ecological isolation leading to reproductive isolation is the key ingredient for either mechanism.

Finally, speciation through polyploidy arises when individuals of a species evolve an increase in chromosome number and automatically establish a population that is genetically isolated from the original species. This mechanism of speciation is largely found in plants and invertebrates. Studies of flora on different islands give an idea of how variable the frequency of polyploidy can be. None of the plant species of the Juan Fernandez Islands appear to be polyploid (Stuessey et al. 2006), whereas polyploidy appears to have occurred in approximately 25 per cent of plant species on the Canary Islands and between 0 and 63 per cent in the New Zealand flora depending on taxonomic group. As a mechanism of speciation for producing island endemics, polyploidy remains a relatively little-known phenomenon and one which does not appear to play a dominant role among most well-documented radiations of island plant species.

Island endemics on some island systems appear to show little evidence of evolutionary radiation and diversification from their mainland relatives despite considerable periods of time since island colonisation. This is known as 'anagenesis', describing a lineage that has not undergone evolutionary radiation to produce a diversity of different forms but which may still have undergone considerable morphological differentiation from its original ancestral population. A clear example of anagenesis is found on Ullung Island off the coast of Korea, where 88 per cent of endemic plants appear to have arisen involving very few divergence and speciation events despite their colonisation of these islands approximately two million years ago (Stuessy et al. 2006).

Conversely, many island endemic groups have diverged extensively, and often remarkably rapidly, from their mainland ancestor. Iconic examples of this include the radiation of Darwin's finches on the Galapagos Islands, where today's 14 species of finch (which have diverged by means of micro-evolutionary changes in beak morphology and behaviour) are thought to have evolved in just 5 million years following the islands' colonisation by a single finch-like ancestor from South America. Other classic examples include the explosive radiation of *Partula* land snails and the co-evolutionary radiation of the lobelioid plants of the Hawaiian Islands and the endemic Hawaiian forest birds that evolved alongside them and which serve as their pollinators (Box 2.2). Such cases are examples of adaptive radiation, the sympatric diversification of a single ancestral lineage into multiple descendant taxa morphologically differentiated from each other through adaptation for different niches. Adaptive radiation is the most commonly known mode of evolution on islands and is responsible for driving some of the major evolutionary diversifications known on island systems.

Classic examples of adaptive radiation include divergence in beak morphology in Darwin's finches in the Galapagos Islands, where, among many such instances, populations of the ground finches *Geospiza fortis* and *G. fuliginosa* have evolved divergent beak depths where they are resident on the same island but similar beak depths on islands where only one or the other occurs (Lack 1947; Schluter 1988). The Galapagos Islands and the diversity of endemic finch populations that have evolved there have also produced classic examples of other types of evolutionary response, including 'ecological release', or niche expansion. This response is a phenomenon whereby taxa that colonise an environment with multiple vacant niches, characteristic of an island system that does not contain the full complement of mainland taxonomic groups, may expand their range of habitats, modes of feeding or types of behaviours in response to the absence on islands of constraints imposed by competitors. A widely cited example is the Darwin's finch of Cocos Island *Pinaroloxias inornata*, one of the more remote Galapagos Islands. This species has diversified behaviourally into a very wide range of individual feeding behaviours; while showing very little accompanying variation in morphology, these differing behavioural patterns appear to be very stable from one generation to the next (Werner and Sherry 1987). Another type of response is 'character displacement' (or 'divergence of character', as described by Darwin in 1859). This is a process that often includes changes in both body size and other components of morphology (Brown and Wilson 1956). In its simplest form, the phenomenon of character displacement is driven by competition between two initially allopatric (i.e. geographically separate) species. Competition causes divergence in particular characteristics that allow the two species to exploit different resources and therefore coexist as sympatric (i.e. geographically overlapping) populations. Some of the best examples are found in the tree-dwelling populations of *Anolis* lizards on Caribbean Islands, where divergence in characteristics such as perch height are thought to have evolved to reduce competition among sympatric populations.

'Taxon cycles' represent an additional model of evolution on islands and one that brings together the processes of colonisation, natural selection, specialisation and extinction. This term describes a cyclical process of speciation whereby a population (usually considered to be a generalist species) colonises an island and via differentiation into different available niches gradually evolves to produce divergent and highly specialised species. These species are then gradually out-competed by subsequent colonisations of generalists and eventually become extinct, leaving open an available niche to be refilled by later colonisations. Continual arrival of new colonist species and competitive interaction with later arrivals are believed to drive these niche shifts, leading to cycles of speciation and extinction. Taxon cycles have been postulated to occur largely within island archipelagos, where regular re-colonisation among islands could occur. Examples of natural systems where taxon cycles have been proposed include the cyclical evolution of Melanesian ants, Caribbean birds and Galapagos finches. These studies, fuelled by a quest to understand biogeographic and ecological theory (and to some extent by repeated surveys of remote archipelagos), have maintained a spotlight on island systems.

The advent of molecular genetic techniques has not only revolutionised our understanding of the natural world but also allowed us to view in an entirely new light the ecological and evolutionary processes that have shaped biodiversity on islands (see Section 5.1.4). While molecular methods at the individual and population levels have enabled direct measurement of evolutionary processes such as gene flow and migration, the rapidly developing field of molecular phylogenetics has changed how evolutionary biologists observe the mechanisms that underpin speciation and extinction, with profound implications for the conservation of island biodiversity. With regard to the study of how island endemics evolve, the ability to generate DNA sequence data for particular genes for different individuals, populations and species has provided an alternative to more traditional approaches using morphological characteristics for reconstructing a phylogenetic history between different mainland and island forms. Alongside these genetic advances, methods of phylogenetic reconstruction have also progressed to incorporate knowledge of how different genes evolve. Large, taxonomically comprehensive DNA sequence data sets can now be applied to a variety of evolutionary questions. The ability to do this has fuelled important debates on how modern phylogenetic approaches should be used to inform priority setting in conservation, both at the population and at the species levels (Crozier 1992, 1997; Moritz 2002; Purvis et al. 2005). This new wealth of knowledge from molecular research has allowed many of the classic and most spectacular examples of evolution in natural island systems to be refined and has also enabled evolutionary processes to be examined in detail for obscure taxonomic groups and their island systems.

2.3 New Insights from DNA

Perhaps the most iconic example of an island species is the dodo (Box 1.2), and no book chapter on the evolution of island species would be complete without it. The dodo, a large, extinct flightless bird from Mauritius, has both confounded and enthralled biologists seeking to determine its evolutionary history and to explain the unusual morphology of this most charismatic species. Perhaps more has been written about the dodo than any other species, and yet, paradoxically, relatively little scientific evidence for the species now exists due to the scarcity of preserved skins and fossil material. A great deal of information has been extracted from analyses of artists' impressions (Fuller 2003; Hume 2006), morphologic analysis of subfossil remains and reconstructed skeletons (Strickland and Melville 1848; Kitchener 1993; Hume and Prys-Jones 2005; Rijsdijk et al. 2009), as well as a variety of interpretations of direct and indirect reports of the species and its subsequent cultural history (Cheke and Hume 2008; Turvey and Cheke 2008). Many who have studied the dodo have referred to this species as an example of an 'evolutionary dead-end' (Bergman 2005), although it should be noted that the species was fully adapted to its island environment until the arrival of European colonists and a series of invasive mammals.

Over the centuries, the dodo, together with its presumed sister-species, the extinct solitaire *Pezophaps solitaria* from the neighbouring island of Rodrigues, has been attributed to a variety of bird taxa ranging from ratites to raptors, although most commentators have agreed that it was some sort of pigeon (Strickland and Melville 1848; Janoo 1996, 2005). DNA analysis of dodo and solitaire remains and phylogenetic reconstruction identified the most recent common living ancestor of these species as the Nicobar pigeon *Caloenas nicobarica* from the Nicobar Islands and nearby South-east Asia, with broader affinities to the crowned pigeons within the Columbiformes. By making assumptions about the rate at which the genes used in this study evolve through time, Shapiro and co-workers were able to estimate that the dodo–solitaire lineage diverged from its closest living relatives approximately 42 Mya and that the dodo and solitaire diverged from each other 25 Mya (Shapiro et al. 2002). These dates predate the geological ages of Mauritius and Rodrigues (7 and 1.5 million years, respectively), implying that geologically transient island 'stepping stones' may have existed in the Indian Ocean prior to the eventual colonisation of Mauritius and Rodrigues. These types of inferences would not have been possible without DNA sequence data.

The radiation of Darwin's finches on the Galapagos and Cocos islands has contributed more to our understanding of evolution than perhaps any other species group. Not surprisingly, then, the application of molecular methods has seen a large number of genetic studies focus on Darwin's finches. Analysis of mitochrondrial DNA (mtDNA) sequence data has helped to confirm many of the initial morphology-based relationships. For instance, it has been shown that Darwin's finches are indeed monophyletic (in other words, they are an evolutionary group, or clade, in which all species share a common ancestor and are each other's closest relatives). The geographically isolated Cocos finch is in fact closely related to the tree finches, and the warbler–like finches were among the first to speciate from the original colonising form. Indeed, these molecular data have allowed Darwin's own classification of these finches to be refined. Darwin grouped the warbler finch with the American warblers, whereas molecular evidence indicates that its warbler-like appearance is simply morphological convergence (i.e. the independent evolution of two separate evolutionary lineages which share a very similar morphology). The group's adaptive characters have masked its true evolutionary origin on the Galapagos Islands.

This reconstruction of the phylogenetic history of Darwin's finches was soon followed by further studies using additional data and different molecular tools, and together they have proved possible to address some of the finer evolutionary details of this spectacular adaptive radiation. For example, molecular data have identified the most closely related living ancestor of Darwin's finches to be a South American grassquit *Tiaris obscura*, and molecular dating has placed the arrival of the original finch colonist on the Galapagos Islands at around 2.3 Mya. Other studies have made further sense of the details by examining genetic differences within and between finch populations and species, identifying the role of hybridisation as a mechanism for speciation on islands and refining our understanding of how natural selection shapes both the genetic and morphological architecture of species on islands.

Because the study of Darwin's finches has provided such a wealth of knowledge, this natural system has since been used to help define our wider understanding of evolutionary processes. The Galapagos Archipelago also supports other iconic examples of adaptive evolution. (Box 2.3).

Box 2.3 *Evolution of Galapagos Giant Tortoises*

The giant land tortoises that inhabit the islands of the Galapagos Archipelago contributed to the development of Darwin's theory of natural selection, and studies of their different island populations over the past century from morphological, ecological and molecular genetic perspectives have provided one of the most engaging examples of island evolution. Up to 15 species or subspecies of Galapagos tortoise have been described, most corresponding to single island taxa, except on the largest island of Isabela, whose five volcanic domes are each home to different tortoise subspecies (the southern two volcanos share more than two different races). The morphology of each subspecies differs most prominently in the shape of the carapace (either being 'dome shaped' or 'saddle backed'; Figure 2.4) and in the relative length of the neck and limbs, although some of these characteristics overlap to some extent between different subspecies (Fritts 1984).

Several decades before the widespread availability of molecular techniques, the Galapagos tortoises featured in a variety of different evolutionary studies. These included experimental tests on the germination of native and non-native tomato seedlings that

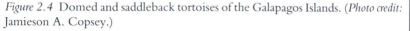

Figure 2.4 Domed and saddleback tortoises of the Galapagos Islands. (*Photo credit:* Jamieson A. Copsey.)

indicated how tortoises may have played an important ecological role as seed propagators due to the beneficial effect of their unique gut chemistry (Rick and Bowman 1961). However, molecular markers have provided much of the evolutionary framework upon which morphological and ecological information can be interpreted. Analysis of DNA sequence data and calibration against a molecular clock indicate that tortoises colonised the eastern Galapagos Islands from South America 2–3 Mya and subsequently radiated westwards across the archipelago, with some of the most recently diverged forms found on Isabela, the most westerly of the main islands (Caccone et al. 1999, 2002).

This already complex pattern of phylogeographic history, driven by sequential colonisation of neighbouring islands and tempered by patterns of ocean currents among the islands, is further complicated by the possible effects of recent translocations of tortoises between islands by early sailors. More detailed analysis of genetic variability within each of the island populations shows a pattern broadly consistent with the east–west colonisation of these animals as they radiated from old to younger islands (Beheregaray et al. 2003, 2004). These and other studies have since applied different molecular markers at the population level to address important taxonomic and conservation issues (Ciofi et al. 2006). For example, the last representative of the subspecies *Geochelone nigra abingdoni* from the isolated island of Pinta, an individual tortoise better known as 'Lonesome George', who died in 2012, has been shown from analysis of its DNA to have most likely originated from Española or San Cristobal. This finding implies an unlikely path of radiation given the location of much-nearer islands. Such an event appears more plausible when ocean currents are considered. Prevailing currents surge north-west from San Cristobal towards Pinta Island, and it is thought these could have easily influenced the direction of travel by floating tortoises caught in the tide (Caccone et al. 1999).

As is the case with most studies of biological systems, answers to questions lead to yet more questions, and the giant tortoises of the Galapagos are likely to shed further light on the intricacies of evolution. These tortoises feed largely on native *Opuntia* cacti, and there is evidence that the phenology and anti-herbivore mechanisms of these huge cacti may have co-evolved alongside the foraging habits of the various tortoise island forms. Differences in tortoise neck length broadly correspond to differences in the extent of spines in short juvenile cacti and the morphology of adult cacti. More recently, similar genetic approaches have been applied to other island populations of giant tortoises on Aldabra. Microsatellite DNA markers have revealed the tortoise population there to be structured according to geographic and ecological barriers hindering tortoise movement (Balmer et al. 2010). Recent interest in evolutionary studies, fuelled by the increasing ease with which DNA sequence information can be generated for almost any biological taxon, has stimulated an explosion of studies focusing on species- and population-level DNA-based phylogenies, bringing a new level of precision to priority setting in island species conservation.

2.4 Evolutionary History Contributions to Species Conservation

Rapid developments in molecular genetics have revolutionised our ability to learn new insights about the evolutionary history of island biotas and have seen an ever-expanding application of these techniques to species conservation. However, for many threatened species, an understanding of their evolutionary history and unique distinctiveness has not saved them from eventual extinction, in many cases despite considerable conservation effort. One example is the po'ouli *Melamprosops phaeosoma*, a Hawaiian forest bird species endemic to the island of Maui that was only discovered in 1973 (Figure 2.5; Box 5.3). When the species was discovered by undergraduate members of

Figure 2.5 Po'ouli *Melamprosops phaeosoma*, one of the most evolutionarily distinct Hawaiian honeycreepers and once one of the world's rarest birds, prior to its recent extinction. (*Photo credit:* Jim J. Groombridge.) (A black-and-white version of this figure will appear in some formats. For the color version, please refer to the plate section.)

a University of Hawaii expedition, only nine individuals of this species could be found, of which two were subsequently taken as voucher specimens. The number of known individuals slowly dwindled to three birds by 1997, after which a last-ditch attempt at translocation to create a wild breeding pair failed in 2002 (Groombridge et al. 2004; VanderWerf et al. 2006). Sadly, the po'ouli was last seen in the wild in 2004 and is now classified as extinct.

When this unusual-looking bird was first discovered, its distinctive appearance earned the species its own monotypic genus *Melamprosops* (Casey and Jacobi 1974), a status that helped set the po'ouli apart from other Hawaiian honeycreepers (Pratt 1979, 1992, 2001; Berger 1981). Two *Xestospiza* honeycreepers most closely resemble the po'ouli, but both species are known only from subfossil bones (James and Olson 1991). The extreme rarity of the po'ouli generated considerable interest in how distinctive it might be in relation to other Hawaiian forest birds. Pratt (1992) performed a detailed study of plumage pattern, tongue morphology and the presence or absence of a distinctive odour that is shared by almost all drepanids. He declared the po'ouli to be phenotypically very different from any drepanid, stating that it 'does not look, smell, act, or sound like a Hawaiian honeycreeper' (Pratt 1992:179), a finding which he subsequently corroborated by analysis of a wider selection of phenotypic characters (Pratt 2001). In contrast, analyses of osteological characters and molecular DNA sequences by Fleischer et al. (2001) provided a very different perspective, placing the po'ouli firmly within the drepanidine clade. Importantly, Fleischer et al. (2001) were able to quantify the amount of genetic distinctiveness contributed by each species to the honeycreeper group as a whole, revealing that the po'ouli contributed more evolutionary diversity to the clade than any other member. This genetic information contributed to the po'ouli being earmarked as a high priority for conservation efforts, but by then the species was at the brink of extinction. The po'ouli is an example where realisation of a species' evolutionary history came too late.

Examples where a lack of knowledge of evolutionary history leads directly to the failure of conservation programmes and species extinction are not just restricted to island systems. On the US continent, the seaside sparrow *Ammodramus maritimus* occurs along the coastal marshes between Texas and New England. The dusky seaside sparrow *A. m. nigrescens*, which once inhabited parts of Florida, has been considered both a subspecies and a separate species of seaside sparrow. During the 1960s and 1970s, the dusky seaside sparrow was the focus of intensive conservation efforts, but its available habitat and population size continued to decline, and by 1980, the captive population had dwindled to just five males and no known females (Walters 1992). Hybridisation between dusky breeding males and the most evolutionarily closely related subspecies seemed to be the only option if the remnants of 'dusky' genetic diversity were not to be lost forever. Hybridisation was subsequently initiated with captive individuals of Scott's seaside sparrow *A. m. peninsulae* from the Gulf Coast population, believed then to be the closest relative of the dusky seaside sparrow based on morphological similarity. These last–ditch attempts failed to produce a viable hybrid population (Walters 1992). Subsequently, molecular analyses of the evolutionary history of seaside sparrows showed that Scott's seaside sparrow was not the most appropriate candidate for interbreeding and that more closely related subspecies might have yielded better results due to their closer evolutionary affinities (Avise and Nelson 1989; O'Brien and Mayr 1991; but see Zink and Kale 1995).

Cases such as the dusky seaside sparrow serve to illustrate how conservation programmes can make better, more informed management decisions when armed with knowledge of the evolutionary affinities of the species they are working to restore. While molecular studies were applied too late to assist the sparrow's recovery, evolutionary genetic studies are now frequently carried out prior to the onset of species conservation initiatives or soon after, to confirm or refine conservation priorities. An example that illustrates this increasingly common practice is work on the tuatara *Sphenodon*, an unusual reptile endemic to New Zealand that is the last remaining representative of an ancient evolutionary lineage that diverged from other reptiles about 230 Mya (Hay et al. 2008; Rest et al. 2003). This island endemic therefore comprises a significant proportion of global reptilian biodiversity. The surviving populations are now restricted to many offshore islands in the Cook Strait and north of the North Island. Among these islands, two species or subspecies are currently recognised, the more common *S. punctatus*, which exists both on offshore islands above North Island and islands in Cook Strait, and *S. guntheri*, which exists as a single island population on North Brother Island in Cook Strait.

These island populations appeared initially to show very little genetic differentiation between them, which contributed to issues regarding conservation prioritisation (Daugherty et al. 1990). This molecular research identified substantial species-level differences among a group of reptiles that had until then all been regarded as conspecifics. This revelation precipitated a wider call for improving how measurement of taxonomic distinctiveness is combined with measures of abundance and geographic distribution. Much of the reason for the observed low genetic diversity in tuatara is probably due to their unusually protracted range contractions and population declines. Despite the close affinities between their island populations, sufficient variability was later detected (by combining genetic data from a number of different genes) to identify phylogenetic relationships between them and to propose three distinct evolutionarily significant units to be conserved separately: western Cook Strait *S. punctatus*, northern *S. punctatus* and *S. guntheri* on North Brother Island (Hay et al. 2003).

All the tuatara populations have been the focus of considerable conservation efforts for many years (Cree and Butler 1993; Nelson et al. 2002), and ongoing application of molecular techniques continues to influence the direction of conservation efforts as new methods and new DNA markers become available. More recently, microsatellite DNA markers have shown substantial population structure among some of the different islands as well as evidence for substantial inbreeding in the single population of S. *guntheri* on North Brother Island (MacAvoy et al. 2007). Conservation geneticists have since reviewed all available genetic information and reassessed the taxonomic status of tuatara, now advocating a single species, but which contains distinctive and important geographic variants for conservation management (Hay et al. 2010).

In some instances, molecular genetics data have shed new light on island species once thought to be relatively obscure to reveal their true evolutionary significance. One example of this is the sooglossid frog family, endemic to the islands of the Seychelles. These populations of island frogs belong to their own family, containing four species, some of which are among the smallest frogs in the world. All are listed as Vulnerable by the International Union for the Conservation of Nature (IUCN) on the basis of their restricted ranges. *Sooglossus sechellensis* and S. *gardineri* inhabit leaf litter, whereas S. *pipilodryas* is arboreal, and *Nesomantis thomasseti* inhabits rock overhangs. The Seychelles Islands are granitic and have a continental rather than oceanic origin, consisting of an ancient Gondwanan fragment that split off from the Indian continent approximately 47–67 Mya and that has been isolated ever since. More recently, the islands are likely to have been connected to each other at various points due to sea-level changes during the last glaciation.

The evolutionary origin of the frogs that occur here came to light upon the very unusual discovery in India of a burrowing frog *Nasikabatrachus sahyadrensis* whose morphology was clearly distinct from all other anurans. A molecular study to determine its origins identified the sooglossid frogs of the Seychelles as the closest relatives and estimated from genetic data that the Seychelles and Indian species diverged from each another approximately 131 Mya (Biju and Bossuyt 2003). The Indian species is believed to be the sole living representative of its own family, Nasikabatrachidae; its sister taxa, the Seychelles sooglossid frogs, make up a considerable portion of this highly evolutionarily distinct cluster of anuran biodiversity and on this basis form a very worthy focus for conservation efforts. Further molecular work has refined the evolutionary relationships between the Seychelles Island populations (Van der Meijden et al. 2007). Sooglossid frogs were until recently thought only to exist on two of the Seychelles Islands, Mahé and Silhouette. However, in 2009, a previously overlooked population of sooglossid frogs was discovered on Praslin Island (Gerlach 2010; Taylor et al. 2012), opening the door to possibilities that other potentially distinct populations may also exist on some of the smaller outer islands within the Seychelles Archipelago.

Lastly, there is growing evidence, both theoretical and experimental, to suggest that island endemics have evolved reduced resistance to pathogens (and therefore increased susceptibility to disease), through both geographic isolation of mainland pathogens and reduced likelihood of long-term pathogen persistence in relatively small host populations on islands, making insular taxa more prone to novel outbreaks. A heightened risk of susceptibility to disease as a consequence of evolutionary history is an important consideration for conservationists tasked with recovering island endemics. Examples of this condition are known from the Galapagos Archipelago (Wikelski et al. 2004), the Hawaiian Islands (Warner 1968) and the Mascarenes (Swinnerton et al. 2005), where immune systems of island endemics are likely to have evolved with little immunological defence against large suites of pathogens. Rather than there being selection for a reduced immune function in island endemics, it may be that there has instead been a 'reorganisation' of immune function, with a possible evolutionary trade-off between the two main components of the immune system resulting in an enhanced innate (i.e. inherited) immune response at the cost of reduced acquired (i.e. learnt) immunity (Matson 2006).

2.5 Summary

Key points from this chapter:

- Studies of evolutionary processes on islands have illustrated the relative rapidity of evolutionary change.
- Speciation is at the heart of our understanding of evolution, driven by reproductive isolation and occurring as a consequence of geographic, ecological or genetic barriers, the latter through the development of additional chromosomes.

- Island systems appear to function as 'speciation engines' where evolutionary processes work in particular ways to produce novel variations.
- Island species have evolved traits that distinguish them from continental relatives and make them worthy of conservation attention.
- Molecular studies can now reveal relationships between (and within) species that both inform our understanding of evolutionary processes and help inform conservation priorities.

References

Adler, G. H. and Levins, R. (1994). The island syndrome in rodent populations. *Quarterly Review of Biology* 69: 473–90.

Anderson, R. P. and Handley, C. O., Jr. (2002). Dwarfism in insular sloths: biogeography, selection, and evolutionary rate. *Evolution* 56: 1045–58.

Avise, J. C. and Nelson, W. S. (1989). Molecular genetic relationships of the extinct dusky seaside sparrow. *Science* 243: 646–48.

Balmer, O., Ciofi, C., Galbraith, D. A. et al. (2010). Population genetic structure of Aldabra giant tortoises. *Journal of Heredity* 102(1): 29–37.

Beheregaray, L. B., Gibbs, J. P., Havill, N. et al. (2004). Giant tortoises are not slow: rapid diversification and biogeographic consensus in the Galapagos. *Proceedings of the National Academy of Sciences USA* 101: 6514–19.

Beheregaray, L. B., Ciofi, C., Caccone, A., Gibbs, J. P. and Powell, J. R. (2003). Genetic divergence, phylogeography and conservation units of giant tortoises from Santa Cruz and Pinzon, Galapagos Islands. *Conservation Genetics* 4: 31–46.

Bergman, J. (2005). The history of the dodo bird and the cause of its extinction. *Perspectives on Science and Christian Faith* 57: 221–29.

Berger, A. J. (1981). *Hawaiian Birdlife*. 2nd edn. University of Hawaii Press, Honolulu, HI.

Biju, S. D. and Bossuyt, F. (2003). New frog family from India reveals an ancient biogeographical link with the Seychelles. *Nature* 425: 711–14.

Blackburn, T. M., Cassey, P., Duncan, R. P., Evans, K. L. and Gaston, K. J. (2004). Avian extinction and mammalian introductions on oceanic islands. *Science* 305: 1955–58.

Blackburn, T. M., Cassey, P., Duncan, R. P., Evans, K. L. and Gaston, K. J. (2005). Response to comment on 'Avian extinction and mammalian introductions on oceanic islands'. *Science* 307: 1412.

Brown, W. L., Jr. and Wilson, E. O. (1956). Character displacement. *Systematic Zoology* 7: 49–64.

Caccone, A., Gibbs, J. P., Ketmaier, V., Suatoni, E. and Powell, J. R. (1999). Origin and evolutionary relationships of giant Galapagos tortoises. *Proceedings of the National Academy of Sciences USA* 96: 13223–28.

Caccone, A., Gentile, G., Gibbs, J. P. et al. (2002). Phylogeography and history of giant Galapagos tortoises. *Evolution* 56: 2052–66.

Carlquist, S. 1974. *Island Biology*. Columbia University Press, New York, NY.

Casey, T. L. C. and Jacobi, J. D. (1974). A new genus and species of bird from the island of Maui, Hawaii (Passeriformes: Drepanididae). *Occasional Papers of the B.P. Bishop Museum* 24: 215–26.

Ciofi, C., Wilson, G. A., Berherebaray, L. B. et al. (2006). Phylogeographic history and gene flow among giant Galapagos tortoises on Southern Isabel Island. *Genetics* 172: 1727–44.

Cheke, A. S. (1987). An ecological history of the Mascarene Islands, with particular reference to extinctions and introductions of land vertebrates, pp. 5–89 in A. W. Diamond (ed.), *Studies of Mascarene Island Birds*. Cambridge University Press, Cambridge.

Cheke, A. S. and Hume, J. (2008). Lost land of the dodo, in A. S. Cheke and J. Hume (eds.), *An Ecological History of Mauritius, Reunion and Rodrigues*. T & AD Poyser, London.

Collen, B., Turvey, S. T., Waterman, C. et al. (2011). Investing in evolutionary history: implementing a phylogenetic approach for mammal conservation. *Philosophical Transactions of the Royal Society B* 366: 2611–22.

Cody, M. L. and Overton, J. M. (1996) Short-term evolution of reduced dispersal in plant populations. *Journal of Ecology* 84: 53–61.

Cowie, R. H. and B. S. Holland. (2006). Dispersal is fundamental to biogeography and the evolution of biodiversity on oceanic islands. *Journal of Biogeography* 33: 193–98.

Cree, A. and D. Butler (1993). *Tuatara recovery plan (Sphenodon spp.)*. Threatened Species Recovery Plan No. 9. Threatened Species Unit, New Zealand Department of Conservation, Wellington.

Crozier, R. H. (1992). Genetic diversity and the agony of choice. *Biological Conservation* 61: 11–15.

Crozier, R. H. (1997). Preserving the information content of species: genetic diversity, phylogeny and conservation worth. *Annual Review of Ecology and Systematics* 28: 243–68.

Damuth, J. (1993). Cope's rule, the island rule and the scaling of mammalian population density. *Nature* 365: 748–50.

Darwin, C. (1859). *On the Origin of Species by Means of Natural Selection*. J. Murray, London.

Daugherty, C. H., Cree, A., Hay, J. M. and Thompson, M. B. (1990). Neglected taxonomy and continued extinctions of tuatara (*Sphenodon*). *Nature* 347: 177–79.

Diamond, J. M. (1980). Species turnover in island bird communities. *Proceedings of the 17th International Ornithological Congress* 2: 777–82.
    (1991). A new species of rail from the Solomon Islands and convergent evolution of insular flightlessness. *The Auk* 108: 461–70.

Didham, R. K, Ewers, R. M. & Gemmell, N. J. (2005). Comment on 'Avian extinction and mammalian introductions on oceanic islands'. *Science* 307: 1412.

Duncan, R. P. & Blackburn, T. M. (2004). Extinction and endemism in the New Zealand avifauna. *Global Ecology and Biogeography* 13: 509–17.

Ehrendorfer, E. (1979). Reproductive biology in island plants, pp. 293–306 in D. Bramwell (ed.), *Plants and Islands*. Academic Press, London.

Fleischer, R. C., Tarr, C. L., James, H. F., Slikas, B. and McIntosh, C. E. (2001). Phylogenetic placement of the po'ouli, *Melamprosops phaeosoma*, based on mitochondrial DNA sequence and osteological characters. *Studies in Avian Biology* 22: 98–103.

Foster, J. B. (1964). Evolution of mammals on islands. *Nature* 202: 234–35.

Frankham R., (2005). Genetics and extinction. *Biological Conservation* 12: 131–40.

(1997). Do island populations have less genetic variation than mainland populations? *Heredity* 78: 311–27.

(1998). Inbreeding and extinction: island populations. *Conservation Biology* 12: 665–75.

Frankham, R., Ballou, J. D. and Briscoe, D. D. (eds.). (2002). Introduction, in *Introduction to Conservation Genetics*. Cambridge University Press, Cambridge.

Fritts, T. H. (1984). Evolutionary Divergence of Giant Tortoises in Galapagos. *Biological Journal of the Linnean Society* 21: 165–76.

Fuller, E. (2003). *Dodo: From Extinction to Icon*. Universe Publishers, New York.

Gerlach, J. (2010). Status of the Sooglossidae and an action plan for their conservation. Newsletter of the IUCN/SSC Amphibian Specialist Group, London, pp. 4–7.

Givnish, T. J., Sytsma, K. J., Smith, J. F., and Hahn, W. J. (1994). Thorn-like prickles and heterophylly in Cyanea: adaptations to extinct avian browsers on Hawaii? *Proceedings of the National Academy of Sciences USA* 91: 2810–14.

Green, S. (2011). Evolutionary Biology and Conservation of the Hog Island Boa Constrictor. Unpublished PhD thesis, University of Kent, United Kingdom.

Groombridge, J. J. (2009). Po'o-uli, pp. 487–98 in T. K. Pratt, B. L. Woodworth, C. T. Atkinson, J. Jacobi and P. Banko (eds.), *Conservation Biology of Hawaiian Forest Birds: Implications for Insular Avifauna*. New Haven, CT: Yale University Press.

(2007). Genetics and extinction of island endemics: the importance of historical perspectives. *Animal Conservation* 10: 147–48.

Groombridge, J. J., Massey, J. G., Bruch, J. C. et al. (2004). An attempt to recover the po'ouli by translocation and an appraisal of recovery strategy for bird species of extreme rarity. *Biological Conservation* 118: 365–75.

Hansen, D. M. and Galetti M. (2009). The forgotten megafauna. *Science* 324: 42–43.

Hay, J. M., Daugherty, C. H., Cree, A. and Mason, L. R. (2003). Low genetic divergence obscures phylogeny among populations of *Sphenodon*, remnant of an ancient reptilian lineage. *Molecular Phylogenetics and Evolution* 29: 1–19.

Hay, J. M., Subramanian, S., Miller, C. D., Mohandesan, E. and Lambert, D. M. (2008). Rapid molecular evolution in a living fossil. *Trends in Genetics* 24: 106–9.

Hay, J. M., Sarre, S. D., Lambert, D. M., Allendorf, F. W. and Daiugherty, C. H. (2010). Genetic diversity and taxonomy: a reassessment of species designation in tuatara (Sphenodon: Reptilia). *Conservation Genetics* 11: 1063–81.

Hume, J. P. (2006). The history of the dodo *Raphus cucullatus* and the penguin of Mauritius. *Historical Biology* 18: 65–89.

Hume, J. P. and Prys-Jones, R. P. (2005). New discoveries from old sources, with reference to the original bird and mammal fauna of the Mascarene Islands, Indian Ocean. *Zoologische Mededelingen* 79(8): 85–95.

Hutchinson, G. E. (1957). Concluding remarks. *Cold Spring Harbour Symposia on Quantitative Biology* 22: 415–27.

Isaac, N. J. B., Turvey, S. T., Collen, B., Waterman, C. and Baillie, J. E. M. (2007). Mammals on the EDGE: conservation priorities based on threat and phylogeny. *PLoS ONE* 2(3): e296.

Jamieson, I. G. (2007). Has the debate over genetics and extinction of island endemics truly been resolved? *Animal Conservation* 10: 139–44.

Jamieson I. G., Wallis, G. P. and Briskie, J. V. (2006). Inbreeding and endangered species management: is New Zealand out of step with the rest of the world? *Conservation Biology* 20: 38–47.

James, H. F. and Olson, S. L. (1991). Descriptions of thirty-two new species of birds from the Hawaiian Islands: II. Passeriformes. *Ornithological Monographs* 46: 1–88.

Janoo, A. (2005). Discovery of isolated dodo bones [*Raphus cucullatus* (L.), Aves, Columbiformes] from Mauritius cave shelters highlights human predation, with a comment on the status of the family Raphidae Wetmore, 1930. *Annales de Paléontologie* 91: 167–80.

Kitchener A. (1993). On the external appearance of the dodo, *Raphus cucullatus* (L., 1758). *Archives of Natural History* 20: 279–301.

Lack, D. (1947). *Darwin's Finches: An Essay on the General Biological Theory of Evolution.* Cambridge University Press, Cambridge.

Lerner H. R., Meyer, M., James, H. F., Hofreiter, M. and Fleischer, R. C. (2011) Multilocus resolution of phylogeny and timescale in the extant adaptive radiation of Hawaiian honeycreepers. *Current Biology* 21: 1838–44.

Lister, A. M. (1993). Mammals in miniature. *Nature* 362: 288–89.

Lomolino, M. V. (1985). Body size of mammals on islands: the island rule re-examined. *American Naturalist* 125: 310–16.

MacArthur, R. H. and Wilson, E. O. (1967). *The Theory of Island Biogeography.* Princeton University Press, Princeton, NJ.

MacAvoy, E. S., McGibbon, L. M., Sainsbury, J. P. et al. (2007). Genetic variation in island populations of tuatara (*Sphenodon* spp.) inferred from microsatellite markers. *Conservation Genetics* 8: 305–18.

MacPhee, R. D. E., White, J. L. and Woods, C. A. (2000). New megalonychid sloths (Phyllophaga, Xenarthra) from the Quaternary of Hispaniola. *American Museum Novitates* 3303: 1–32.

Matson, K. D. (2006). Are there differences in immune function between continental and insular birds? *Proceedings of the Royal Society B: Biological Sciences* 273: 2267–74.

May, R. M. (1990) Taxonomy is destiny. *Nature* 347: 129–30.

Mayr, E. (1965). Avifauna: turnover on islands. *Science* 150: 1587–88.

Meiri, S., Raia, P. and Phillimore, A. B. (2011).Slaying dragons: limited evidence for unusual body size evolution on islands. *Journal of Biogeography* 38: 89–100.

McCranie, J. R., Wilson, L. D. and Köhler, G. (2005). *Amphibians and Reptiles of the Bay Islands and Cayos Cochinos, Honduras.* Bibliomania, Salt Lake City, UT.

McFarlane, D. A., MacPhee, R. D. E. and Ford, D. C. (1998). Body size variability and a Sangamonian extinction model for *Amblyrhiza*, a West Indian megafaunal rodent. *Quaternary Research* 50: 80–89.

Moritz, C. (2002). Strategies to protect biological diversity and the evolutionary processes that sustain it. *Systematic Biology* 51: 238–54.

Nelson, N. J., Keall, S. N., Brown, D. and Daugherty, C. H. (2002). Establishing a new wild population of tuatara (*Spenodon guntheri*). *Conservation Biology* 16: 887–94.

O'Brien, S. J. and Mayr, E. (1991). Bureacratic mischief: recognizing endangered species and subspecies. *Science* 251: 1187–88.

Pratt, H. D. (2001). Why the Hawaii creeper is an *Oreomystis*: what phenotypic characters reveal about the phylogeny of Hawaiian honeycreepers. *Studies in Avian Biology* 22: 81–97.

(1992). Is the po'ouli a Hawaiian honeycreeper? (Drepanidinae). *Condor* 94: 172–80.

(1979). A Systematic Analysis of the Endemic Avifauna of the Hawaiian Islands. PhD thesis, Louisiana State University, Baton Rouge, LA.

Purvis, A. P., Gittleman, J. L. and Brooks, T. (eds.). (2005). *Phylogeny and Conservation*. Cambridge University Press, Cambridge.

Raia, P. and Meiri, S. (2011). The tempo and mode of evolution: body sizes of island mammals. *Evolution* 65: 1927–34.

Rest, J. S., Ast, J. C., Austin, C. C. et al. (2003). Molecular systematics of primary reptilian lineages and the tuatara mitochondrial genome. *Molecular Phylogenetics and Evolution* 29: 289–97.

Reyment, R. A. (1983). Palaeontological aspects of island biogeography: colonisation and evolution of mammals on Mediterranean islands. *Oikos* 41: 299–306.

Rick, C. M. and Bowman, R. L. (1961). Galapagos tomatoes and tortoises. *Evolution* 15: 407–17.

Rijsdijk, K. F., Hume, J. P., Bunnik, F. et al. (2009). Mid-Holocene vertebrate bone concentration-Lagerstätte on oceanic island Mauritius provide a window into the ecosystem of the dodo (*Raphus cucullatus*). *Quaternary Science Reviews* 28: 14–24.

Roff, D. A. (1991). The evolution of flightlessness in insects. *Ecological Monographs* 60: 389–421.

(1994). The evolution of flightlessness: is history important? *Evolutionary Ecology* 8: 639–57.

Schluter, D. (1988). Character displacement and the adaptive divergence of finches on islands and continents. *American Naturalist* 131: 799–824.

Schüle, W. (1993). Mammals, vegetation and the initial human settlement of the Mediterranean islands: a palaeoecological approach. *Journal of Biogeography* 20: 399–411.

Shapiro, B., Sibthorpe D., Rambaut A., Austin J., Wragg G., Bininda-Emonds O., Lee, P. Cooper, A. (2002). Flight of the Dodo. *Science* 295: 1683.

Simard, M. A., Côté, S. D., Weladji, R. B. and Huot, L. J. (2008) Feedback effects of chronic browsing on life-history traits of a large herbivore. *Journal of Animal Ecology* 77: 678–86.

Sinclair, A. R. E. and Parkes, J. P. (2008). On being the right size: food-limited feedback on optimal body size. *Journal of Animal Ecology* 77: 635–37.

Spielman, D., Brook, B. W., Briscoe, D. A. and Frankham, R. (2004). Does inbreeding and loss of genetic diversity decrease disease resistance? *Conservation Genetics* 5: 439–48.

Steadman, D. W. (2006). An extinct species of tooth-billed pigeon (*Didunculus*) from the Kingdom of Tonga, and the concept of endemism in insular landbirds. *Journal of Zoology* 268: 233–41.

Strickland, H. E. and Melville, A. G. (1848). *The Dodo and Its Kindred*. Reeve, Benham and Reeve, London.

Stuessy, T. F., Jakubowsky, G., Gómez, R. A. et al. (2006). Anagenetic evolution in island plants. *Journal of Biogeography* 33: 1259–65.

Swinnerton, K. J., Groombridge, J. J., Jones, C. G., Burn, R. W. and Mungroo, Y. (2004). Inbreeding depression and founder diversity among captive and free-living populations of the endangered pink pigeon *Columba mayeri*. *Animal Conservation* 7: 1–12.

Swinnerton, K. J., Greenwood, A. G., Chapman, R. E. and Jones, C. G. (2005). The incidence of the parasitic disease trichonomiasis and its treatment in reintroduced and wild pink pigeons *Columba meyeri*. *Ibis* 147: 772–82.

Taylor, M. L., Bunbury, N., Chong-Seng, L. et al. (2012). Evidence for evolutionary distinctiveness of a newly discovered population of sooglossid frogs on Praslin Island, Seychelles. *Conservation Genetics* 13: 557–66.

Tikhonov, A., Agenbroad, L. and Vartanyan, S. (2003). Comparative analysis of the mammoth populations on Wrangel Island and the Channel Islands. *Deinsea* 9: 415–20.

Towns, D. R., Daugherty, C. H. and Cree, A. (2001). Raising the prospects for a forgotten fauna: a review of 10 years of conservation effort for New Zealand reptiles. *Biological Conservation* 99: 3–16.

Turvey, S. T. (2009). *Holocene Extinctions*. Oxford University Press, Oxford.

Turvey, S. T. and Cheke, A. S. (2008). Dead as a dodo: the fortuitous rise to fame of an extinction icon. *Historical Biology* 20: 149–63.

Turvey, S. T., Green, O. R. and Holdaway, R. N. (2005). Cortical growth marks reveal extended juvenile development in New Zealand moa. *Nature* 435: 940–43.

Van der Meijden, A., Boistel, R., Gerlach, J. et al. (2007). Molecular phylogenetic evidence for paraphyly of the genus *Sooglossus*, with the description of a new genus of Seychellean frogs. *Biological Journal of the Linnean Society* 91: 347–59.

VanderWerf, E. A., Groombridge, J. J., Fretz, J. S. and Swinnerton, K. J. (2006). Decision-analysis to guide recovery of the po'ouli, a critically endangered Hawaiian honeycreeper. *Biological Conservation* 129: 383–92.

Vartanyan, S. L., Garutt, V. E. and Sher, A. V. (1993). Holocene dwarf mammouths from Wrangel Island in the Siberian Arctic. *Nature* 362: 337–40.

Wallace, A. R. (1878). *Tropical Nature and Other Essays*. Macmillan, London.

Walters, M. J. (1992). *A Shadow and a Song: The Struggle to Save an Endangered Species*. Chelsea Green, White River Junction, VT.

Warner, R. E. (1968). The role of introduced diseases in the extinction of the endemic Hawaiian avifauna. *Condor* 70: 101–20.

Werner, T. K. and Sherry, T. W. (1987). Beahvioural feeding specialisation in *Pinaroloxias inornata*, the 'Darwin's finch' of Cocos Island, Coasta Rica. *Proceedings of the National Academy of Sciences USA* 84: 5506–10.

Whittaker, R. J., Triantis, K. A., and Ladle, R. J. (2008). A general dynamic theory of oceanic island biogeography. *Journal of Biogeography* 35: 977–94.

Wikelski, M., Foufopoulos, J., Vargas, H. and Snell, H. (2004). Galápagos birds and diseases: invasive pathogens as threats for island species. *Ecology and Society* 9 (1): 5.

Williamson, M. H. (1981). *Island Populations.* Oxford University Press, Oxford.

Wilson, L. D. and Hahn, D. E. (1973). The herpetofauna of the Islas de la Bahìa, Honduras. *Bulletin of the Florida State Museum* 17: 93–150.

Zink, R. M. and Kale, H. W. (1995). Conservation genetics of the extinct dusky seaside sparrow *Ammodramus maritimus nigrescens*. *Biological Conservation* 74: 69–71.

3 · *Island Populations*
Genetic Factors Driving Declines

JIM J. GROOMBRIDGE, CLAIRE RAISIN
AND PATRICIA BREKKE

3.0 Introduction

Island endemic populations are 'closed' (i.e. with limited immigration or emigration), often founded by just a few colonising individuals, commonly exposed to frequent reductions in population size ('population bottlenecks'), and are usually restricted in size by the physical confines of their island distribution. These traits are shared by populations of many threatened species, whether free living or in captivity, and consequently, endemic island species provide important model systems as well as a popular focus in the field of conservation genetics. Within the current biodiversity crisis and the ensuing challenge presented by global climate change, it is now more important than ever before that threatened and restored populations are managed in such a way as to retain their ability to evolve.

This chapter examines the genetic factors associated with island endemic populations and considers how these could be managed to enhance recovery of endangered island species. First, we explain the relevant population genetics processes required to understand and manage populations. Second, we draw on genetic case studies of island taxa that illustrate how genetic processes operate in the wild and work under emerging threats such as disease outbreaks and climate change. Third, we consider the dilemmas commonly faced by conservation managers when evaluating the importance and practical implementation of genetic management for conserving endemic species.

3.1 Genetic Variation and the Preservation of Evolutionary Potential

Genetic variation is the raw material for natural selection, enabling adaptation and allowing populations to evolve to cope with environmental change. This simple statement is a primary reason why the International Union for the Conservation of Nature (IUCN) recognises the need to conserve genetic variation within populations, as well as the need to conserve species and ecosystems (IUCN 2008). Given that populations endemic to islands are largely unable to disperse to more favourable environments, island endemics must evolve in situ to survive changing conditions. Species must retain 'evolutionary potential' through the genetic variation within their populations.

Genetic variation ultimately arises from the process of 'mutation' (the sudden genetic change in a portion of the genetic makeup, or genome, of an organism, which produces new genetic variants, or alleles, in that individual within a population). Alleles are distributed through the population by inheritance during successive breeding generations to produce new combinations of alleles, or genotypes, among individuals within the population. While it takes a very long time (an evolutionary time scale) for mutations to arise and for genetic variation (i.e. new alleles) to accumulate in a population, most large, naturally out-breeding populations can be expected to maintain high levels of genetic variation. As a consequence, large populations are theoretically able to adapt to their environment via the process of natural selection. In addition to such directional evolutionary forces, gene flow (through immigration) and stochasticity (the random change in allele frequencies from one generation to the next, called 'genetic drift') also play a part in determining gain and loss of genetic variation in a population.

Not all genetic variation has a direct effect on fitness or adaptation through natural selection. From a conservation genetics standpoint, our goal should be to measure and conserve variation at adaptive sites within the genome, ensuring that the genetic material maintained can confer adaptive opportunities for the species (Soulé 1985). Measuring adaptive genetic variation, however, is often difficult, as it requires a substantial quantity of longitudinal (i.e. temporal) data for quantitative genetic analysis (e.g. offspring–parent regression or half-sibling analysis), which are rarely available for wild populations. Adaptive genetic variation can now be measured using a range of molecular tools, although this is technically and conceptually demanding and relatively costly (Ouborg et al. 2010). Instead, most conservation studies on island endemics have measured genetic variation at neutral sites (e.g. microsatellite loci, mito-chondrial DNA), namely, areas on the genome that do not code for protein construction in cells of the organism so are neither beneficial nor detrimental in the organism's ability to reproduce. Inferences on adaptive variation from neutral molecular markers should be treated with caution because the relationship between neutral and adaptive variation is very complex (Reed and Frankham 2001). This problem is further exacerbated by the constraints of relatively small numbers of loci in most species-focused, conservation-based studies (Reed 2010). Despite this issue, measures of neutral genetic variation are extremely useful in understanding other population-level genetic parameters such as genetic drift.

3.1.1 Genetic Drift

Unlike the processes of mutation and migration, genetic drift leads to the loss of genetic variation, particularly in small populations (Lacy 1987). In each generation, the alleles inherited by offspring are a subsample of those found in the parental generation, the net effect of which is known as 'random genetic drift' (or 'genetic drift') and is particularly acute in small populations. Some alleles, in particular, rare alleles, can be lost from one generation to the next, which changes the resulting allele frequencies in the population, leading to a reduction in allelic abundance and heterozygosity (i.e. degree to which individuals have a mixture of alleles for a single trait). Eventually, genetic drift will lead to all except one allele being lost (a frequency of 0) and the remaining allele being fixed (Wright 1931). Since genetic drift is not driven by environmental or adaptive processes, beneficial, neutral or negative alleles can become fixed. If random genetic drift predominates in small populations, the effect of selection on allelic frequencies generally becomes negligible. This scenario means that genetic drift can also constrain adaptive evolution since, by random chance, drift could either decrease the frequency of adaptive alleles or increase the frequency of detrimental recessive alleles (Kimura M. 1968).

3.1.2 Inbreeding and Inbreeding Depression

Inbreeding occurs when close relatives mate and is an unavoidable by-product of small, closed island populations. Inbreeding increases the likelihood of sharing the same alleles by descent than mating with non-related individuals. Most individuals carry some recessive deleterious alleles, but offspring from inbred mating have more homozygous genotypes (i.e. individuals in a population which have only one version of an allele for a single trait), which rapidly increase the chances of rare deleterious alleles being expressed. Loss of heterozygosity due to mating between relatives ('true inbreeding') and genetic drift are both referred to as 'inbreeding'. Inbreeding and genetic drift have differing effects on the subpopulations' genotypic frequencies. Inbreeding increases the frequency of both homozygotes, while genetic drift increases the frequency of only one homozygote's frequency as only one allele increases in frequency towards fixation. Despite these differences, the phenotypic expression of inbreeding and genetic drift is similar and can lead to an increase in frequency of deleterious recessives expressed in homozygote individuals (Kimura M. 1968).

The expression of deleterious recessive alleles decreases fitness, an effect called 'inbreeding depression'. Inbreeding depression has been found to vary across traits, populations, life-history stages and environmental conditions (Keller and Waller 2002). Generally, inbreeding depression is thought to be more severe in traits closely associated with fitness (e.g. survival and reproduction; DeRose and Roff 1999), under natural (Crnokrack and Roff 1999; Keller et al. 2002) and/or stressful conditions (e.g. extreme weather changes, disease outbreaks, pollution; Armbruster and Reed 2005). However, evidence for the impact of environmental stress on the magnitude of inbreeding is not conclusive (Keller and Waller 2002); some studies show higher levels of inbreeding depression in stressful environments (Keller et al. 2002; Armbruster and Reed 2005; Fox et al. 2011a), while others report lower levels (Fox et al. 2011b). An empirical study in plants has suggested that this discrepancy could be explained if the variance observed in a trait sets an upper limit to the expression of inbreeding depression (Waller et al. 2008). Therefore, inbreeding depression may be more pronounced in environments that promote variation in fitness traits. Small island populations exposed to both inbreeding and highly variable environmental conditions are therefore particularly likely to be at risk (Hedrick 1994), which may affect their long-term persistence (Bijlsma et al. 2000).

Measuring inbreeding at the individual level in wild populations can be difficult, as it requires large sample sizes, long-term data sets and the ability to accurately measure fitness (Keller and Waller 2002). However, several studies on island endemics achieved this with a mixture of pedigrees (Ewing et al. 2008; Grueber et al. 2008; Jamieson 2011; Brekke et al. 2015) and molecular tools (Brekke et al. 2010; Townsend and Jamieson 2013). These studies were enabled by advances in molecular techniques and priorities placed on long-term monitoring of threatened wild populations (see Sections 5.1.4 and 5.2). Molecular techniques enable more ready access to genetic information, for example, to assign paternity and build reliable pedigrees (Kruuk et al. 2008; Pemberton 2008).

3.1.3 Selection

Natural selection shapes a population's genetic makeup to best suit its environment by selecting out individuals that inherit deleterious mutations which reduce individuals' fitness while favouring individuals with mutations that confer an advantage. Importantly, mutations vary in their 'selective value'. Natural selection acts to either decrease or increase a mutation's frequency in the population. Whether mutational alleles increase or decrease in frequency depends on whether they appear outside of functional genes (and therefore confer no change in fitness, so-called neutral mutations) or within functional genes (in which case they will be predominantly deleterious or mildly deleterious and seldom advantageous).

From what we know of mutations in model organisms, approximately 90 per cent are deleterious, 10 per cent are neutral (or nearly neutral) and perhaps as few as 1–2 per cent are advantageous (Lande 1995). Deleterious mutations exist in large out-bred populations as well as small inbred ones but in large out-bred populations these deleterious mutations can be expected to occur at low frequency as a consequence of natural selection. Depending on the selective value of a deleterious allele, natural selection becomes less effective at reducing the frequency of deleterious alleles as they become rarer in the population. Over evolutionary time, through interplay between production of deleterious alleles by mutation or removal of them by selection, all large, out-breeding populations will contain a proportion of deleterious mutations at any one time, maintained at low frequency by selection. This form of genetic variation is known as the 'mutational load'. Large out-breeding populations are likely to 'carry' large numbers of deleterious alleles, but each at very low frequency. Of course, when a large, out-bred population declines to small size, then this mutational load becomes a problem, as deleterious alleles may drift to higher frequency and subsequently, via inbreeding, become expressed in their homozygous form (Figure 3.1).

Figure 3.1 The kakapo *Strigops habroptilus* from New Zealand. One Critically Endangered species that is being recovered from a severe bottleneck and the possibility that inbreeding depression is being expressed through reduced hatching success. (*Photo credit:* Jake Osborne.)

3.1.4 Purging

It has been suggested that the robustness of endemic island populations arises from a history of small population size that allows populations to shed much of their genetic load, a process referred to as 'purging'. Purging is thought to occur when increased homozygosity due to inbreeding exposes recessive deleterious alleles to selection. Individuals harbouring deleterious alleles become selected out of the population, thereby reducing the genetic load (Hedrick 1994). As the frequency of deleterious alleles decreases, the population's reduced genetic load may enable a rebound in fitness. It has therefore been suggested that purging may be a useful conservation management tool to deal with the negative consequences of inbreeding (Templeton and Read 1984). While there is general agreement that purging may act efficiently to filter out lethal and semi-lethal alleles via selection, mildly deleterious alleles are considered more difficult to purge because of their smaller, subtler negative effects on fitness. Consequently, the effectiveness of purging in rejuvenating island populations remains open to debate (Lynch et al. 1995; Lande 1999; Keller and Waller 2002).

The island avifauna endemic to New Zealand has been of particular focus in this discourse. The kakapo *Strigops habroptilis* (Figure 3.1) and the black robin *Petroica traverse* (Jamieson et al. 2006) are among several New Zealand endemics that are cited as examples of recovered populations which appear relatively impervious to the effects of inbreeding and genetic impoverishment (Craig 1994; Pain 2002). However, the use of purging as a management tool to reduce the inbreeding load (i.e. the portion of genetic load attributable to inbreeding) of island endemic populations is unlikely to be effective and is not recommended for a number of reasons (Frankham et al. 2001; Keller et al. 2012). Firstly, in small island populations, genetic drift is stronger than selection. Selection can only remove very harmful alleles and is not effective against mildly deleterious alleles, which constitute a high proportion of inbreeding load (Charlesworth and Willis 2009). Secondly, harmful alleles may accumulate over time and remain 'hidden' until an individual that carries them is exposed to novel conditions (e.g. novel disease or climate change). Individuals carrying alleles that make them more susceptible should experience a reduction in fitness, but if they are never exposed to the pathogen or changed environment, that increased susceptibility will never be expressed (Bijlsma et al. 2000; Bijlsma and Loeschcke 2012).

3.1.5 Effective Population Size

The concept of 'effective population size' N_e ties together most of the genetic processes described earlier. N_e is responsible for the rate of genetic drift, loss of diversity of neutral alleles and the increase in inbreeding experienced by a population (Waples 2002). N_e is defined as the size of an ideal population that would be affected by genetic drift at the same rate as the actual population (Wright 1931, 1938; Crow and Kimura 1970; Box 3.1; Figure 3.2). At its simplest interpretation, N_e is a reflection of the number of breeding adults contributing to the next generation. In an ideal population, N_e would equal N (the population census size), but in most populations, N_e is reduced by a number of factors, including unequal sex ratio, fluctuations in population size, overlapping generations and variation in reproductive success (family size). This clearly has ramifications when considering risks to threatened populations since the actual number of adults contributing to the next generation may be

Box 3.1 *Rate of Loss of Genetic Variation and Rate of Inbreeding in Small Populations*

The extent to which the size of a population N or, more specifically, the effective population size N_e underpins loss of genetic variation and rate of inbreeding can be most easily described by the simple equation $1/(2N)$ or $1/(2N_e)$. Equation 3.1 (Figure 3.2) describes the proportion of heterozygosity that is lost by a population in a single generation. For example, if a population experiences a 'population bottleneck' of $N = 25$, in a single generation, 2 per cent of heterozygosity is lost as a consequence. Loss of genetic variation normally arises from sustained periods of small population size (i.e. prolonged bottlenecks of several/ many generations) rather than single-generation bottlenecks, so this equation can be applied across successive generations (Equation 3.2, t = number of generations, Figure 3.2).

Effective population size N_e will more accurately determine the extent of loss of genetic variation than the population census size N. N_e is defined as the size of an idealised population that would lose genetic variation (or become inbred) at the same rate as the actual population. Thus, N_e is a measure of the genetic behaviour of a population relative to that of an idealised population, and commonly the N_e is considerably smaller than the census population size N. Of course, what is usually of more interest is the proportion of genetic variation that we can expect to be retained by a population following a particular generational history of population size, and this can be calculated from Equation 3.3 (Figure 3.2). For example, for a population with $N_e = 25$, the proportion of heterozygosity retained after 50 generations at that size will be 0.364 (36.4 per cent); consequently, this population will lose 64 per cent of its initial heterozygosity.

These equations also describe the extent and accumulation of the level of inbreeding in populations. As populations decline in size, inbreeding and its effects become a problem. The level of inbreeding F in a population increases at a rate of $1/(2N_e)$ per generation (Equation 3.1), and the increment in inbreeding per generation equals the loss of heterozygosity per generation. Consequently, the overall effect is that inbreeding accumulates over time and does so more rapidly as population size declines. Beyond the theoretical basis just described, there is now overwhelming evidence from molecular genetics studies that levels of genetic variation are closely related to population size.

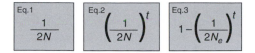

Figure 3.2 Equations 3.1 to 3.3 describing the proportion of genetic material lost across a single generation (Eq. 3.1), across multiple generations (Eq. 3.2) and retained within a population following a particular generational history of population size (Eq. 3.3) (see Box 3.1 for details).

considerably less than the total population estimate. In large populations, the effect of genetic drift on allele frequencies is relatively minimal (i.e. the effect is ever present but is inversely proportional to N_e) and is overridden by the evolutionary force of natural selection, which ensures that the population evolves in concert with changes in the environment.

One important consideration is that N_e can be defined in two ways (Crow 2010): inbreeding effective population size N_{eI} and variance effective population size N_{eV}. N_{eI} is related to the rate of increase in inbreeding and N_{eV} to the rate of change in allele frequency (Crow and Kimura 1970). These two parameters are generally similar in populations with random mating and constant population size from one generation to the next (Frankham 1995). However, in changing populations, for example, those experiencing a bottleneck (declining) or recovering (growing), N_{eI} and N_{eV} are decoupled. During a bottleneck with rapid decline in population size, N_{eV} reflects this change immediately, while the change in N_{eI} lags a generation. The decline will have an immediate impact on allele frequencies since frequency depends completely upon the number of individuals in the progeny generation. In contrast, a bottleneck will not have an immediate effect on N_{eI} because the probability of identity by descent (IBD) in the progeny generation is determined by the size of the parental generation (e.g. Ewing et al. 2008).

The effects on inbreeding will only become apparent in the successive generations (Waples 2002). Hence, population bottlenecks have less effect on measures of heterozygosity, but a very large impact on allelic richness and loss of rare alleles. In a declining population N_{eI} will be substantially higher than N_{eV}, but in a recovering (growing) population $N_{eI} < N_{eV}$. N_{eV} will recover faster than N_{eI} to pre-bottleneck levels (Waples 2002). N_{eI}

and N_{eV} can be measured in wild populations using pedigrees and molecular markers, but molecular methods tend to be less reliable at estimating N_{eI} (Keller et al. 2012).

3.2 Genetic Developments and the Management of Species Recovery

3.2.1 Documenting Shifts in Genetic Variation

Prior knowledge that a species has experienced a recent dramatic reduction in effective population size can allow managers to anticipate the problems associated with inbreeding depression, such as lowered reproductive fitness, reduced survival and increased susceptibility to disease (Madsen et al. 1999; Keller et al. 2002; Swinnerton et al. 2004). With the increasing use of molecular genetics methods, it has become possible to analyse genetic variation not only in contemporary populations but also in historical samples from museum specimens. Often this approach can help to clarify a species' recent demographic history by revealing instances of loss of genetic variation that indicate previously undetected population bottlenecks. A clear understanding of the recent population history is an important part of a species' ecological history (see Chapter 10) and can be vital for managing future recovery (Matocq and Villablanca 2001).

An example that illustrates the value of this approach is a comparison of historical genetic profiles for two island endemic kestrel species, the Mauritius kestrel *Falco punctatus* and the Seychelles kestrel *F. araea*. The Mauritius kestrel population was reduced to just four known birds in the wild in 1974 before a dramatic recovery to several hundred pairs through intensive conservation management (Jones et al. 1995). Genetic studies characterised substantial loss of genetic diversity as a consequence of this population crash and also revealed the Seychelles kestrel to be equally genetically impoverished. Analysis of historical levels of genetic diversity from museum specimens has characterised the bottleneck profiles for both of these island species and has provided a new perspective on their respective population recoveries (Box 3.2; Figure 3.3).

Routine collections of tissue or blood samples from target species allow tracking of the impact of conservation interventions on the genetic health of these populations. In the case of the Mauritius echo parakeet *Psittacula echo*, routine blood samples taken throughout the decades

Box 3.2 *Historical Genetic Profiles in Two Island Endemic Birds, the Mauritius and Seychelles kestrels.*

For endemic island species, current genetic impoverishment could be due to either a recent population crash or an evolutionary history of sustained isolation and small effective population size. Unravelling an island species' ecological history can be further complicated by incomplete or contradictory evidence from historical field surveys that might suggest a very different demographic profile. The Seychelles kestrel *F. araea*, a species of small falcon endemic to the Seychelles Archipelago, was previously listed as critically endangered but is now relatively common (Cook 1960; Collar 1985; Kay et al. 2002, 2004). A set of 11 microsatellite DNA markers were used to quantify genetic variation in blood samples taken from the contemporary population and in samples taken from museum specimens of Seychelles kestrels that were collected by Victorian naturalists 100–150 years ago.

Genetic analysis using a Bayesian method (Beaumont 2003) estimated the temporal change in effective population size N_e and revealed evidence for a recent and severe population crash since the 1940s to an N_e of approximately eight individuals, before the population recovered to its current size (Figure 3.3; Groombridge et al. 2009). This finding is surprising in light of the minimal intervention required for this species to recover (Watson 1989). This contrasts with the 25-year-long intensive conservation management required to restore the population of the Mauritius kestrel *F. punctatus*, a closely related island endemic species that was recovered from a single breeding pair in 1974 to the current size of 300–400 birds today (Groombridge et al. 2001, 2004; Nichols et al. 2001; Jones et al. 2013). This evidence of a recent population bottleneck and current genetic impoverishment in the Seychelles kestrel highlights the long-term exposure that even temporary small population size can bring to island endemic species, particularly in terms of exposure due to reduced long-term evolutionary potential. More encouragingly, this case study illustrates that not every rare island species requires extensive conservation intervention to recover from severely small population sizes.

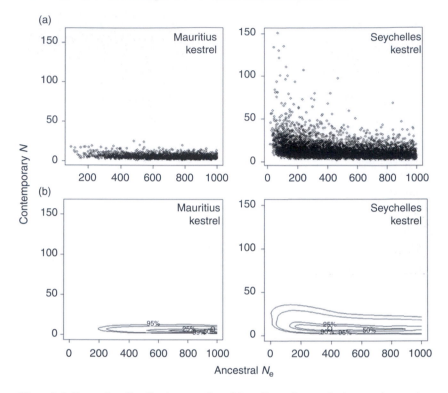

Figure 3.3 Posterior distribution produced by a Bayesian analysis to estimate the ancestral and contemporary effective population size N_e of the Seychelles and Mauritius kestrels, following the methods of Beaumont (2003). (A) The density of points is proportional to the probability density of population size at the two different times; hence, an off-diagonal distribution indicates a change in N_e (*note:* the *y*-axis extends only to 150). (B) Between 25 and 95 per cent higher posterior density limits of the posterior distribution. The joint mode is plotted as a single open circle.

spanning the conservation programme enabled subsequent genetic studies to quantify temporal changes in the degree of population structure as well as the extent of loss of genetic diversity. These molecular studies revealed genetic homogenisation of the restored population as a consequence of the years of intensive management alongside significant loss of genetic diversity (Raisin et al. 2012; Tollington et al. 2013; Figure 3.4). Together these findings (Box 3.3; Figure 3.5) illustrate the impact that field management programmes (see Chapter 9) can have on genetic diversity.

Figure 3.4 Field teams on Mauritius that worked with critically endangered species on the brink of extinction required a particular sense of humour. (*Image credit:* Wayne Page.) (A black-and-white version of this figure will appear in some formats. For the colour version, please refer to the plate section.)

Box 3.3 *Genetic Homogenisation and Loss of Genetic Diversity in the Endangered Mauritius Parakeet*

Historical records suggest the Mauritius parakeet *P. echo* inhabited most of the heavily forested island of Mauritius before human colonisation in the 1600s (Cheke and Hume 2010). Habitat-based estimates suggest an ancestral population in excess of 15,000 birds (Raisin 2010). Subsequent land clearance by settlers dramatically reduced native forest, with less than 2 per cent surviving today. Reduced availability of mature native trees with natural cavity nest sites contributed to the Mauritius parakeet's steep decline. By the 1980s, the population was reduced to an estimated 20 individuals before an intensive management programme enabled recovery to over 500 birds by 2010 (Figure 3.4). Blood samples routinely collected from birds throughout this conservation programme provided a DNA archive for two studies: (1) to quantify temporal changes in the population structure across the decades spanning conservation management and (2) to characterise the genetic trajectories of subpopulations and their genetic differentiation relative to reintroduction strategies applied during intensive management.

Raisin et al. (2009) used 18 microsatellite DNA markers developed for the parakeet to genotype 504 individuals sampled from 1995 to 2008, spanning the species' conservation history across three phases: (1) pre–intensive management, (2) intensive management (between 2000 and 2005) and (3) post–intensive management. This temporal framework enabled an assessment of the extent of genetic structure before and after intensive management to reveal how interventions might have affected spatial patterns of genetic diversity. While average levels of heterozygosity and allelic richness were not observed to decrease significantly from pre– to post–intensive management, the extent of genetic structure was markedly higher in the pre–intensive management period (Raisin et al. 2012). The reduction in genetic structure can be closely tied to the release programme and the movement of birds between sites during intensive management (see Chapter 9).

Tollington et al. (2013) extended this temporal genetic study and examined net loss of genetic diversity for the recovering population alongside the extent of differentiation between subpopulations (Figure 3.5). The study provided evidence for genetic homogenisation across subpopulations as a result of translocated or reintroduced individuals entering the breeding population. The management-induced genetic homogenisation has benefitted the population by redistributing rare alleles and slowing the rate of loss of genetic diversity.

3.2.2 Informing Conservation Decision-Making

The increasing accessibility of modern molecular genetics techniques to conservation managers has led to more readily obtainable information on the genetic characteristics of a population or species of concern alongside standard demographic, population and ecological information provided by field studies. Many different types of molecular genetic markers exist for identifying and quantifying genetic variation (Table 3.1).

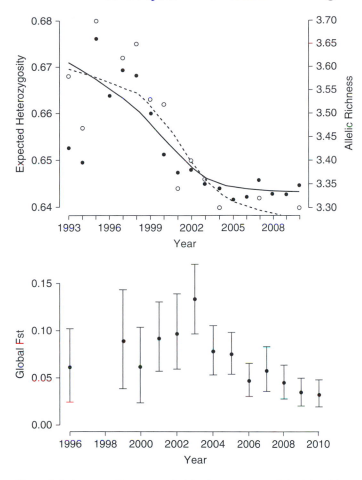

Figure 3.5 Across a 17-year period in the recovery of the Mauritius parakeet, both allelic richness and average heterozygosity decreased significantly; the slower rate of decline in the latter years is most likely a consequence of a period of substantial population growth leading to increased population size and reduction in the effects of genetic drift (upper panel). Annual measures of global F_{ST} across the three main subpopulations reveal a consistent reduction in genetic differentiation since 2003, most likely an effect of management-enhanced and natural gene flow via dispersal of individuals between sites (lower panel).

The application of these technical developments to conservation projects can help to inform decisions over how best to conserve a species or population. A good example of this application lies with the land iguanas of the Galapagos Islands. The Galapagos land iguanas diverged from the

Table 3.1 *Comparison of Different Types of Genetic Markers and Practical Considerations for Their Use*

Marker type	Process	Application	Development time/cost	Reproducibility/examples
Randomly amplified polymorphic DNA markers (RAPDs)	Use of random primers to amplify random segments of DNA; produces a multi-locus fingerprint	Population genetics questions such as average levels of genetic variation between individuals and subpopulations	Generic marker sets available for many taxa; generally low cost	Poor, e.g. two limpet species (Wood and Gardner 2007)
Single-nucleotide polymorphisms (SNPs)	Location in the genome of a species where at least two different nucleotide bases can occur; information on these point mutations are then harnessed on a large scale throughout the genome	Genomic analysis such as linkage; assessment of genetic variation and relate genetic measures to phenotypic traits, etc.	Currently requires high investment of resources but is a rapidly developing field	Good, e.g. Tasmanian devil (*Sarcophilus harrisii*; Miller et al. 2011; Wright et al. 2015)
Short tandem repeats (STRs) such as microsatellites and mini-satellites	A locus within the DNA sequence where a short tandem repeat, such as AC or GATC in microsatellites, is repeated a variable	Population genetics questions such as average levels of genetic variation, population structure, parentage analysis,	Existing marker sets for some taxa can be cross-amplified in closely related taxa; otherwise, development of	Good, e.g. hihi/stitchbird (*Notiomystis cincta*; Brekke et al. 2010, 2011, 2015), Floreana mockingbird (*Mimus*

Marker/Method	Description	Application	Notes/Limitations	Examples
	number of times within a population; this variation is then measured within and between individuals and between populations	estimation of level of inbreeding	species-specific markers can be costly	trifasciatus; Hoeck et al. 2009)
Mitochondrial DNA markers	Maternally inherited, whole genes (or the whole mtDNA genome) is sequenced and nucleotide differences compared between individuals, populations and species/genera	Evolutionary distinctiveness at the species and subspecies or population level	Generic markers are available for a large proportion of taxa for certain frequently used genes; targeting hypervariable regions of the mtDNA such as the non-coding control region may require design of specific markers	Good, e.g. Azorean bat (*Nyctalus azoreum*; Salgueiro et al. 2004), pink pigeon (*Columba mayeri*; Swinnerton et al. 2004)
Sequencing of specific functional genes	Requires targeted effort to isolate and characterise specific genes of interest	Analysis of quantitative traits, such as sequencing of MHC genes to assess individual-level variation at these immune function genes and relate this	Can require high level of investment except when working on species for which markers are already available for closely related taxa	Good, e.g. a number of threatened island endemic birds (Grueber et al. 2013, 2015), Seychelles warbler (*Acrocephalus sechellensis*; Wright et al. 2015)

Table 3.1 (cont.)

Marker type	Process	Application	Development time/cost	Reproducibility/examples
		information to evolutionary history of the population and to traits such as disease or parasite load		Good, e.g. Tasmanian devil (*Sarcophilus harrisii*; Murchison et al. 2012), aye-aye (*Daubentonia madagascariensis*; Perry et al. 2012)
Whole-genome sequencing	The complete nucleotide sequence for all chromosomes, usually for only one individual of the species, using shotgun sequencing	Population structure, adaptive genetic variation, identify genetic basis of inbreeding, hybridisation and demography	Currently requires high investment of resources, and conservation application still limited	

Galapagos marine iguanas 10–20 Mya and comprise a single endemic genus, *Conolophus*, which contains two recognised species, *C. subcristatus*, which is found naturally on five islands and has been translocated to three additional islands of the Galapagos Archipelago, and *C. pallidus*, which is found only on the island of Santa Fé (Snell et al. 1984, 1996). Morphologic analysis of the island populations suggests three distinct clusters that reflect differences in island age across the archipelago, from the oldest island (Santa Fé) in the east to the youngest (Isabella and Fernandina) in the west (Snell et al. 1984). Most of the iguana populations have suffered anthropogenic impacts including predation by humans and impacts associated with introduced animals such as competition for food and loss of habitat. Almost all island populations have experienced substantial population declines in recent times. Some of the island populations have been or have come close to being extirpated within the last 70 years, only to be reintroduced through timely conservation translocations and captive-breeding and reintroduction efforts.

Tzika et al. (2008) used nine microsatellite DNA markers to survey levels of genetic diversity among 703 land iguanas sampled across the different island populations. The genotype data showed that levels of genetic diversity for the different island populations increased from east to west, with the lowest diversity on Santa Fé and the highest diversity on the islands of Isabela and Fernandina. Most strikingly, an analysis of genetic structure across the archipelago grouped the six island populations into five distinct clusters, one comprising the single island population of *C. pallidus* on Santa Fé and three other clusters – one comprising Plaza Sur; one comprising the islands of Isabela, Fernandina and Baltra; and another comprising Santa Cruz. On Isabela, the largest island of the Galapagos Archipelago and made up of at least six adjoining volcanic cones, there are two genetically distinct iguana populations. One population comprises individuals from the most northern part of the island which share a unique phenotype of a pink colouration known as the 'rosada' form; further molecular work subsequently revealed this form to be a separate species (Gentile et al. 2009).

Tzika et al. (2008) advocated separate management of the five genetically identified iguana populations as distinct conservation units given the high levels of genetic differentiation between them. In several cases, demographic history explained the marked differences in levels of genetic diversity among the island populations; for example, the least genetically diverse population occurred on Santa Fé, one of the few island populations not to have been restored by reintroduction of individuals from captive-breeding programmes. Overall, this and subsequent studies (Gentile et al. 2009) provide straightforward guidance regarding genetic delineation of the different island populations of land iguanas which can inform future management plans (see Chapter 6), as well as identifying genetically impoverished island populations that could benefit from augmentation via captive stock or translocation of individuals.

3.2.3 Challenging Our Perception of What to Conserve

A frequent challenge in conservation is how to interpret evidence of genetic differentiation derived either from molecular DNA studies or morphology between two or more fragmented populations of a species to determine whether the differences reflect truly different evolutionary trajectories for each population or are a consequence of recent genetic drift. Choosing between these alternatives has a direct impact on conservation management. Maintenance of different evolutionary trajectories requires each population to be managed separately, whereas a diagnosis of a single evolutionary unit affected by recent genetic drift may call for managed gene flow between them to ameliorate genetic problems associated with small population size. This dilemma is based upon our uncertainty regarding how we define 'a species' and the concept of 'evolutionary significant units' (ESUs), a topic widely debated in conservation biology (Ryder 1986; Moritz 1994; Templeton 1998; Crandall et al. 2000).

The St Lucia whiptail lizard *Cnemidophorus vanzoi* is considered to be a single species and is found on two small islets (Maria Major and Maria Minor) off the south-east coast of the main island of St. Lucia (Baskin and Williams 1966), plus a third reintroduced population on Praslin Island formed by translocation of individuals from Maria Major (Dickinson and Fa 2000). Initial indications of morphologic and genetic differences between the two source populations of Maria Major and Maria Minor (Buley et al. 1997; Rowe et al. 2002) were subsequently confirmed by detailed morphometric analysis, mitochrondrial DNA (mtDNA) sequencing and microsatellite DNA genotyping of a sample of lizards from both islands (Funk and Fa 2006). Significant morphologic differences were observed in body size alongside small but fixed differences in mtDNA between the two island populations. Microsatellite DNA genotypes revealed low diversity within each population (mean number of alleles 3.00 ± 1.15 on Maria Major, 1.14 ± 0.38 on Maria Minor) but very high levels of genetic differentiation between them (Funk and Fa 2006). Although the morphologic differences were somewhat equivocal, requiring further studies to test for evidence of ecological non-exchangeability (Crandall et al. 2000), the genetic data indicated that the two island populations represent distinct ESUs with different evolutionary trajectories and close to the species boundary. Subsequent field surveys by Young et al. (2006) estimated population sizes of 335 lizards in the reintroduced population on Praslin, 1,985 lizards on Maria Major and just 29 on Maria Minor. Young et al. (2006) advocated maintaining the latter two source populations as separate entities while the possibility of a heritable basis for the observed morphologic differences is explored, but noting the high risk of the smallest population going extinct in the meantime.

3.2.4 Immune Function and Response to Infectious Disease

The management of infectious disease is becoming an increasingly common feature within species recovery projects. Introduced disease has been demonstrated as a threat to island species endemic to the Galapagos (Wikelski et al. 2004), Christmas Island (Wyatt et al. 2008), Tasmania (Hawkins et al. 2006), the islands of New Zealand (Crump et al. 2001) and the US Channel Islands (Crooks et al. 2001, 2004), as well as the devastating effects of chytridiomycosis on amphibian populations worldwide (Pounds et al. 2006). Inbreeding and loss of genetic variation are believed to reduce the ability of populations to cope with disease, presenting important implications for the conservation of small, bottlenecked populations. Given the insular nature of endemic island populations, infectious disease therefore poses a considerable and insidious threat.

The link between loss of variation and reduced resistance to disease has been shown experimentally in *Drosophila* populations (reduced resistance in inbred lines; Spielman et al. 2004) and in house finches (genetically diverse individuals mounted stronger immune responses and developed less severe symptoms when experimentally infected; Hawley et al. 2005). In the case of endemic island species, studies are emerging that illustrate the potential duel impacts of genetic problems associated with small population size, low genetic variation and susceptibility to disease. Managers of endangered island endemics should be aware of the growing body of evidence that suggests a close relationship between pathogenic causes of population decline and the genetic issues associated with small population size that have already been outlined in this chapter. The amount and type of genetic variation have been shown to be important in studies of disease or levels of immune response in island populations of song sparrows (Reid et al. 2003), Galapagos hawks (Whiteman et al. 2006), New Zealand parakeets and robins (Hale and Briskie 2007; Tompkins et al. 2006). What remains clear is that the challenges ahead will continue to require managers to minimise the impacts of disease while at the same time ensuring that strategies for genetic management are not compromised – a difficult balance to strike.

One immediate concern facing restored populations is how to maintain genetic variation at genes that are known to be important for immune function. The major histocompatibility complex (MHC) is a family of genes whose products are crucial components of the vertebrate adaptive immune response (Klein 1986). The interaction between the MHC and pathogen infection drives natural selection for polymorphisms at these loci (Potts and Sley 1995). Numerous studies in mammals, fish and birds have shown evidence of an association between the presence of specific MHC alleles and either the presence, extent or lethality of infection (Hill et al. 1991; Harf and Sommer 2005; Westerdahl et al. 2005; Kjoglum et al. 2006; Siddle et al. 2010). Inbreeding and genetic impoverishment, a characteristic common to island endemics, have been shown to decrease resistance to pathogens (Acevedo-Whitehouse et al. 2003), and consequently, there has been an increasing interest in genetic variation at such functional loci within endangered island populations, such as the Seychelles warbler *Acrocephalus sechellensis* (Richardson and Westerdahl 2003) and Tasmanian devil *Sarcophilus harrisii* (McCallum 2008). However, more work is needed on the MHC within conservation biology because observed patterns of genetic variation at the MHC are not clear; for instance, some studies document low MHC polymorphism in apparently viable populations (Murray et al. 1995; Hoelzel et al. 1999), whereas others reveal high MHC variation in species in apparent decline due to susceptibility to disease (Gutierrez-Espeleta et al. 2001) or despite evidence of a genetic bottleneck (Jarvi et al. 2004).

What is becoming increasingly clear is that interpretations based on neutral DNA markers ideally should be augmented by data on non-neutral variation. For example, the San Nicolas Island fox *Urocyon littoralis dickeyi* is believed to be the most genetically monomorphic sexually reproducing animal species documented to date, based on genetic data derived using neutral DNA markers, but levels of MHC variation remain high due to the effects of strong balancing selection (a form of natural selection which results in genetic variation being maintained at selectively important genes; Aquilar et al. 2004). A comprehensive review by Sommer (2005) of the importance of conserving MHC variation in small and endangered populations high-lights the importance of the potential functional role of background genes (i.e. non-MHC genes) in disease resistance, both for individual fitness and for long-term population persistence. Beyond the MHC, other functional loci are becoming available for use in conservation genetics, including development of markers for surveying genetic variation at the Toll-like receptor genes (Grueber and Jamieson 2013). Therefore, the picture emerging as the future focus of conservation genetic studies is the need for multi-marker studies that embrace genome-wide genetic variation, alongside recognition of the importance of variation at functional loci for ensuring maximum evolutionary potential in recovering populations.

3.2.5 Monitoring for Population Recovery

Long-term genetic monitoring of island populations is increasingly popular and is now strongly advocated. Tracking and sampling indivi-duals in small island populations have become more commonplace as molecular methods are becoming less expensive, more reliable and, with the aid of non-invasive sampling methods, can be applied to species that are cryptic, dangerous and/or rare (e.g. Brekke et al. 2011). Genetic monitoring techniques can provide three main sources of information. Firstly, they can be used to identify genetically important individuals, populations and species, which allows conservation managers to prioritise their efforts, as well as providing associated information on sex ratio, hybridisation and disease emergence. Secondly, they can be used to directly monitor changes in key genetic parameters such as genetic variation, inbreeding, effective population size, population structure and migration (Schwartz et al. 2006). Thirdly, used in combination with more traditional monitoring techniques such as the collection of breeding and census data, molecular techniques can provide invaluable insight into a species' life-history traits (see Chapter 5), for example, their mating system and dispersal behaviour. Furthermore, combining genetic and demographic information enables the deploy-ment of more sophisticated analytical techniques such as quantitative genetics from pedigree reconstruction. Quantitative genetic techniques provide valuable information on how a population might respond to selection in the face of, for example, climate change or disease outbreaks, a predictive power that is rarely achieved with other molecular techniques.

3.3 Future Genetics: The Genomics Era

Long-term genetic monitoring efforts can provide immediate results and an invaluable resource for future work. For this purpose, it is vital to preserve and catalogue samples to enable the application of future genetics techniques. With this in mind, some exciting developments in genetics have the potential to revolutionise the field with the advent of the genomics era (Avise 2010; Ouborg et al. 2010; Shafer et al. 2015). Most of the work in conservation has been based on neutral genetic variation and the assumption that it reflects detrimental and adaptive genetic variation. However, changes in the level of neutral and adaptive genetic variation rarely correlate, making it extremely difficult to understand the impact of loss of genetic variation on population viability and adaptive potential. Genomics allows not only the targeting of functional loci such as those involved in immune function (e.g. MHC genes and Toll-like receptor genes) but also the development of much larger sets of markers (from tens to thousands) and new marker types (e.g. SNPs or SNiPs; see Table 3.1), which can substantially increase reliability. Conservation genomics can address the factors discussed earlier and many more, such as migration, adaptation, N_e, demographic history (e.g. bottleneck events), genetic rescue, disease susceptibility and resistance, hybridisation, inbreeding and out-breeding depression in much more detail (Steiner et al. 2013). For example, they may allow us to go beyond estimating overall migration rates – possibly using neutral genetic markers – to assessing rates of gene flow specific to particular adaptive genes (Allendorf et al. 2010).

The development of genomics techniques, such as next-generation sequencing, whole-genome scans and gene expression pattern analysis, will enable a much better understanding of adaptive genetic variation directly. The ability to apply these new technologies to threatened island species is becoming increasingly possible with the development of new ultra-high-throughput sequencing, and these techniques, used in conjunction with traditional monitoring, will become powerful tools for conservation (see Miller et al. 2011; Murchison et al. 2012; Perry et al. 2013; Wright et al. 2014).

3.4 Chapter Summary

Key points from this chapter:

- Genetic variation is the raw material upon which natural selection acts. Preserving this variation within populations is necessary to retain their evolutionary potential and adaptation to future environmental challenges.
- Island endemic populations are usually closed populations, often founded by just a few colonising individuals, commonly exposed to frequent population bottlenecks and are restricted in size by the physical confines of their island distribution.
- Natural selection acts on new mutations and causes the frequency of these alleles to change depending on the extent of their deleterious or advantageous effects on individual-level fitness within the population. The net effect of deleterious mutations within a population – genetic load – can have detrimental consequences when a large out-bred population becomes reduced in size.
- In small populations, the stochastic effects of random genetic drift have an increasing effect on changing genetic variation within the population, while natural selection becomes less effective.
- Inbreeding in small populations can result in inbreeding depression (reduction in fitness) as a consequence of increased levels of homozygosity and the expression of deleterious recessive mutations in their homozygous form.
- The increasing availability of molecular DNA markers means that levels of genetic variation can be monitored spatially and through time to reveal the genetic effects of population management and help conservation managers make informed conservation decisions.
- While molecular DNA markers that quantify neutral genetic variation are valuable for observing population genetic processes, there is an increasing need for the development and wider application of non-neutral markers in order to quantify levels of adaptive genetic variation at functional loci.

References

Acevedo-Whitehouse, K., Gulland, F., Greig, D. and Amos, W. (2003). Inbreeding: disease susceptibility in California sea lions. *Nature* 422(6927): 35.

Aguilar, A., Roemer, G., Debenham, S. et al. (2004). High MHC diversity maintained by balancing selection in an otherwise genetically monomorphic mammal. *Proceedings of the National Academy of Sciences USA* 101(10): 3490–94.

Allendorf, F. W., Hohenlohe, P. A. and Luikart, G. (2010). Genomics and the future of conservation genetics. *Nature Reviews Genetics* 11(10): 697–709.

Armbruster, P. and Reed, D. H. (2005). Inbreeding depression in benign and stressful environments. *Heredity* 95(3): 235–42.

Avise, J. C. (2010). Perspective: conservation genetics enters the genomics era. *Conservation Genetics* 11(2): 665–69.

Baskin, J. N. and Williams, E. E. (1966). The Lesser Antillean ameiva. *Studies on the Fauna Curacao and Other Caribbean Islands* 89: 143–76.

Beaumont, M. A. (2003). Estimation of population growth or decline in genetically monitored populations. *Genetics* 164(3): 1139–60.

Bijlsma, R., Bundgaard, J. and Boerema, A. C. (2000). Does inbreeding affect the extinction risk of small populations?: predictions from *Drosophila*. *Journal of Evolutionary Biology* 13(3): 502–14.

Bijlsma, R. and Loeschcke, V. (2012). Genetic erosion impedes adaptive responses to stressful environments. *Evolutionary Applications* 5(2): 117–29.

Brekke, P., Bennett, P. M., Wang, J., Pettorelli, N. and Ewen, J. G. (2010). Sensitive males: inbreeding depression in an endangered bird. *Proceedings of the Royal Society of London B: Biological Sciences* 277: 3677–684.

Brekke, P., Bennett, P. M., Santure, A. W. and Ewen, J. G. (2011). High genetic diversity in the remnant island population of hihi and the genetic consequences of reintroduction. *Molecular Ecology* 20(1): 29–45.

Brekke, P., Ewen, J. G., Clucas, G. and Santure, A. W. (2015). Determinants of male floating behaviour and floater reproduction in a threatened population of the hihi (*Notiomystis cincta*). *Evolutionary Applications* 8(8): 796–806.

Buley, K. R., Prior, K. A. and Gibson, R. C. (1997). In search of the St. Lucia racer *Liophis ornatus*, with further observations on the reptile fauna of the Maria Islands, St. Lucia, West Indies. *Dodo – Journal of the Wildlife Preservation Trusts* 33: 104–17.

Charlesworth, D. and Willis, J. H. (2009). The genetics of inbreeding depression. *Nature Reviews Genetics* 10(11): 783–96.

Cheke, A. and Hume, J. P. (2010). *Lost Land of the Dodo: The Ecological History of Mauritius, Réunion and Rodrigues*. Bloomsbury Publishing, London.

Collar, N. J. and Stuart, S. N. (1985). *Threatened Birds of Africa and Related Islands*. International Council for Bird Preservation, London.

Craig, J. L. (1994). Meta-populations: is management as flexible as nature?, pp. 50–66 in P. J. S. Olney, G. M. Mace and A. T. C. Feistner (eds.), *Creative Conservation, Interactive Management of Wild and Captive Animals*. Chapman & Hall, London.

Crandall, K. A., Bininda-Emonds, O. R., Mace, G. M. and Wayne, R. K. (2000). Considering evolutionary processes in conservation biology. *Trends in Ecology and Evolution* 15(7): 290–95.

Crnokrak, P. and Roff, D. A. (1999). Inbreeding depression in the wild. *Heredity* 83(3): 260–70.

Crook, J. H. (1960). The present status of certain rare land birds of the Seychelles islands. *Government Bulletin* 1060: 1–5.

Crooks, K. R., Scott, C. A. and Van Vuren, D. H. (2001). Exotic disease and an insular endemic carnivore, the island fox. *Biological Conservation* 98(1): 55–60.

Crooks, K. R., Garcelon, D. K., Scott, C. A. et al. (2004). Ectoparasites of a threatened insular endemic mammalian carnivore: the island spotted skunk. *American Midland Naturalist* 151(1): 35–41.

Crow, J. F. (2010). Wright and Fisher on inbreeding and random drift. *Genetics* 184 (3): 609–11.

Crow, J. F. and Kimura, M. (1970). An introduction to population genetics theory, in *An Introduction to Population Genetics Theory*. Harper & Row, New York.

Crump, J. A., Murdoch, D. R. and Baker, M.G. (2001). Emerging infectious diseases in an island ecosystem: the New Zealand perspective. *Emerging Infectious Diseases* 7(5): 767.

DeRose, M. A. and Roff, D. A. (1999). A comparison of inbreeding depression in life-history and morphological traits in animals. *Evolution* 53: 1288–92.

Dickinson, H. C. and Fa, J. E. (2000). Abundance, demographics and body condition of a translocated population of St. Lucia whiptail lizards (*Cnemidophorus vanzoi*). *Journal of Zoology* 251(2): 187–97.

Ewing, S. R., Nager, R. G., Nicoll, M. A. et al. (2008). Inbreeding and loss of genetic variation in a reintroduced population of Mauritius kestrel. *Conservation Biology* 22(2): 395–404.

Fox, C. W. and Reed, D. H. (2011). Inbreeding depression increases with environmental stress: an experimental study and meta-analysis. *Evolution* 65(1): 246–58.

Fox, C. W., Stillwell, R. C., Wallin, W. G., Curtis, C. L. and Reed, D. H. (2011). Inbreeding-environment interactions for fitness: complex relationships between inbreeding depression and temperature stress in a seed-feeding beetle. *Evolutionary Ecology* 25(1): 25–43.

Frankham, R. (1995). Effective population size/adult population size ratios in wildlife: a review. *Genetics Research* 66(2): 95–107.

Frankham, R., Gilligan, D. M., Morris, D. and Briscoe, D. A. (2001). Inbreeding and extinction: effects of purging. *Conservation Genetics* 2(3): 279–84.

Frankham, R., Briscoe, D. A. and Ballou, J. D. (2002). *Introduction to Conservation Genetics*. Cambridge University Press, Cambridge.

Funk, S. M. and Fa, J. E. (2006). Phylogeography of the endemic St. Lucia whiptail lizard *Cnemidophorus vanzoi*: conservation genetics at the species boundary. *Conservation Genetics* 7(5): 651–63.

Gentile, G., Fabiani, A., Marquez, C. et al. (2009). An overlooked pink species of land iguana in the Galápagos. *Proceedings of the National Academy of Sciences USA* 106(2): 507–11.

Groombridge, J. J., Dawson, D. A., Burke, T. et al. (2009). Evaluating the demographic history of the Seychelles kestrel (*Falco araea*): genetic evidence for recovery from a population bottleneck following minimal conservation management. *Biological Conservation* 142(10): 2250–57.

Groombridge, J. J., Nicoll, M. A., Jones, C. G. and Watson, J. (2004). Associations of evolutionary and ecological distinctiveness amongst Indian Ocean kestrels, pp. 679–92 in R. D. Chancellor and B.-U. Meyburg (eds.), *Raptors Worldwide, Proceedings of the VI World Conference on Birds of Prey and Owls*. Mauritian Wildlife Foundation, Mauritius.

Groombridge, J. J., Bruford, M. W., Jones, C. G. and Nichols, R. A. (2001). Evaluating the severity of the population bottleneck in the Mauritius kestrel *Falco punctatus* from ringing records using MCMC estimation. *Journal of Animal Ecology* 70(3): 401–9.

Grueber, C. E. and Jamieson, I. G. (2008). Quantifying and managing the loss of genetic variation in a free-ranging population of takahe through the use of pedigrees. *Conservation Genetics* 9(3): 645–51.

(2013). Primers for amplification of innate immunity toll-like receptor loci in threatened birds of the Apterygiformes, Gruiformes, Psittaciformes and Passeriformes. *Conservation Genetics Resources* 5(4): 1043–47.

Grueber, C. E., Knafler, G. J., King, T. M. et al. (2015). Toll-like receptor diversity in 10 threatened bird species: relationship with microsatellite heterozygosity. *Conservation Genetics* 16(3): 595–611.

Gutierrez-Espeleta, G. A., Hedrick, P. W., Kalinowski, S. T., Garrigan, D. and Boyce, W. M. (2001). Is the decline of desert bighorn sheep from infectious disease the result of low MHC variation?. *Heredity* 86(4): 439–50.

Hale, K. A. and Briskie, J. V. (2007). Decreased immunocompetence in a severely bottlenecked population of an endemic New Zealand bird. *Animal Conservation* 10(1): 2–10.

Harf, R. and Sommer, S. (2005). Association between major histocompatibility complex class II DRB alleles and parasite load in the hairy-footed gerbil, *Gerbillurus paeba*, in the southern Kalahari. *Molecular Ecology* 14(1): 85–91.

Hawkins, C. E., Baars, C., Hesterman, H. et al. (2006). Emerging disease and population decline of an island endemic, the Tasmanian devil *Sarcophilus harrisii*. *Biological Conservation* 131(2): 307–24.

Hawley, D. M., Sydenstricker, K. V., Kollias, G. V. and Dhondt, A. A. (2005). Genetic diversity predicts pathogen resistance and cell-mediated immunocompetence in house finches. *Biology Letters* 1(3): 326–29.

Hedrick, P. W., 1994. Purging inbreeding depression and the probability of extinction: full-sib mating. *Heredity* 73(4): 363–72.

Hill, A. V., Allsopp, C. E., Kwiatkowski, D. et al. (1991). Common West African HLA antigens are associated with protection from severe malaria. *Nature* 352 (6336): 595–600.

Hoeck, P. E., Beaumont, M. A., James, K. E. et al. (2009). Saving Darwin's muse: evolutionary genetics for the recovery of the *Floreana* mockingbird. *Biology Letters* 6: 212–15.

Hoelzel, A. R., Stephens, J. C. and O'Brien, S. J. (1999). Molecular genetic variation and evolution at the MHC DQβ locus in four species of pinnipeds. *Molecular Biology and Evolution* 16: 291–96.

International Union for Conservation of Nature (2008). *Red List of Threatened Species*. IUCN Species Survival Commission, IUCN, Cambridge.

Jamieson, I. G. (2011). Founder effects, inbreeding, and loss of genetic diversity in four avian reintroduction programs. *Conservation Biology* 25(1): 115–23.

Jamieson, I. G., Wallis, G. P. and Briskie, J. V. (2006). Inbreeding and endangered species management: is New Zealand out of step with the rest of the world?. *Conservation Biology* 20(1): 38–47.

Jarvi, S. I., Tarr, C. L., Mcintosh, C. E., Atkinson, C. T. and Fleischer, R. C. (2004). Natural selection of the major histocompatibility complex (MHC) in Hawaiian honeycreepers (Drepanidinae). *Molecular Ecology* 13(8): 2157–68.

Jones, C. G., Burgess, M. D., Groombridge, J. J. et al. (2013). Mauritius kestrel *Falco punctatus*, in R. J. Safford and A. F. A. Hawkins (eds.), *The Birds of Africa,* vol. VIII: *The Malagasy Region*, Christopher Helm, London.

Jones, C. G., Heck, W., Lewis, R. E. et al. (1995). The restoration of the Mauritius kestrel *Falco punctatus* population. *Ibis* 137: S173–80.

Kay, S., Millet, J., Watson, J. and Shah, N. J. (2002). Status of the Seychelles kestrel *Falco araea*: a reassessment of the populations on Mahé and Praslin 2001–2002, in *Report by BirdLife Seychelles, Victoria*. Republic of Seychelles, Mahé.

(2004). Status of the Seychelles kestrel *Falco araea* on Praslin: an assessment of a re-introduced population on Praslin 2002–2003, in *Report by BirdLife Seychelles, Victoria*. Republic of Seychelles, Mahé.

Keller, L. F. and Waller, D. M. (2002). Inbreeding effects in wild populations. *Trends in Ecology and Evolution* 17(5): 230–41.

Keller, L. F., Grant, P. R., Grant, B. R. and Petren, K. (2002). Environmental conditions affect the magnitude of inbreeding depression in survival of Darwin's finches. *Evolution* 56(6): 1229–39.

Keller, L. F., Biebach, I., Ewing, S. R. and Hoeck, P. E. (2012). The genetics of reintroductions: inbreeding and genetic drift. *Reintroduction Biology: Integrating Science and Management* 9: 360.

Kimura, M. (1968). Evolutionary Rate at the Molecular Level. Nature. 217: 624–6.

Kjøglum, S., Larsen, S., Bakke, H. G. and Grimholt, U. (2006). How specific MHC class I and class II combinations affect disease resistance against infectious salmon anaemia in Atlantic salmon (*Salmo salar*). *Fish & Shellfish Immunology* 21(4): 431–41.

Klein, J., 1986. *Natural History of the Major Histocompatibility Complex*. Wiley, New York, NY.

Kruuk, L. E., Slate, J. and Wilson, A. J. (2008). New answers for old questions: the evolutionary quantitative genetics of wild animal populations. *Annual Review of Ecology, Evolution, and Systematics* 39: 525–48.

Lacy, R. C. (1987). Loss of genetic diversity from managed populations: interacting effects of drift, mutation, immigration, selection, and population subdivision. *Conservation Biology* 1(2): 143–58.

Lande, R. (1999). *Extinction Risks from Anthropogenic, Ecological and Genetic Factors*, pp. 1–22 in I. F. Landweber and A. P. Dobson (eds.), *Genetics and the Extinction of Species*. Princeton University Press, Princeton, NJ.

(1995). Mutation and conservation. *Conservation Biology* 9(4): 782–91.

Lynch, M., Conery, J. and Burger, R. (1995). Mutation accumulation and the extinction of small populations. *American Naturalist* 146(4): 489–518.

Madsen, T., Shine, R., Olsson, M. and Wittzell, H. (1999). Conservation biology: restoration of an inbred adder population. *Nature* 402(6757): 34–35.

Matocq, M. D. and Villablanca, F. X. (2001). Low genetic diversity in an endangered species: recent or historic pattern? *Biological Conservation* 98(1): 61–68.

McCallum, H. (2008). Tasmanian devil facial tumour disease: lessons for conservation biology. *Trends in Ecology and Evolution* 23(11): 631–37.

Miller, W., Hayes, V. M., Ratan, A. et al. (2011). Genetic diversity and population structure of the endangered marsupial *Sarcophilus harrisii* (Tasmanian devil). *Proceedings of the National Academy of Sciences USA* 108(30): 12348–53.

Moritz, C. (1994). Defining 'evolutionarily significant units' for conservation. *Trends in Ecology and Evolution* 9(10): 373–75.

Murchison, E. P., Schulz-Trieglaff, O. B., Ning, Z. et al. (2012). Genome sequencing and analysis of the Tasmanian devil and its transmissible cancer. *Cell* 148 (4): 780–91.

Murray, B. W., Malik, S. and White, B. N. (1995). Sequence variation at the major histocompatibility complex locus DQ beta in beluga whales (*Delphinapterus leucas*). *Molecular Biology and Evolution* 12(4): 582–93.

Nichols, R. A., Bruford, M. W. and Groombridge, J. J. (2001). Sustaining genetic variation in a small population: evidence from the Mauritius kestrel. *Molecular Ecology* 10(3): 593–602.

Ouborg, N. J., Pertoldi, C., Loeschcke, V., Bijlsma, R. K. and Hedrick, P. W. (2010). Conservation genetics in transition to conservation genomics. *Trends in Genetics* 26: 177–87.

Pain, S. (2002). No dodo. *New Scientist*, June: 32–37.

Pemberton, J. M. (2008). Wild pedigrees: the way forward. *Proceedings of the Royal Society of London B: Biological Sciences* 275(1635): 613–21.

Perry, G. H., Louis, E. E., Ratan, A. et al. (2012). Aye-aye population genomic analyses highlight an important center of endemism in northern Madagascar. *Proceedings of the National Academy of Sciences USA* 110(15): 5823–28.

Potts, W. K. and Slev, P. R. (1995). Pathogen-based models favouring MHC genetic diversity. *Immunological Reviews* 143(1): 181–97.

Raisin, C. (2010). Conservation genetics of the Mauritius parakeet. PhD thesis, University of Kent, United Kingdom.

Raisin, C., Dawson, D. A., Greenwood, A. G., Jones, C. G. and Groombridge, J. J. (2009). Characterization of Mauritius parakeet (*Psittacula eques*) microsatellite loci and their cross-utility in other parrots (Psittacidae, Aves). *Molecular Ecology Resources* 9(4): 1231–35.

Raisin, C., Frantz, A. C., Kundu, S. et al. (2012). Genetic consequences of intensive conservation management for the Mauritius parakeet. *Conservation Genetics* 13 (3): 707–15.

Reed, D. H. (2010). Albatrosses, eagles and newts, Oh My!: exceptions to the prevailing paradigm concerning genetic diversity and population viability? *Animal Conservation* 13(5): 448–57.

Reed, D. H. and Frankham, R. (2001). How closely correlated are molecular and quantitative measures of genetic variation?. A meta-analysis. *Evolution* 55(6): 1095–103.

Reid, J. M., Arcese, P. and Keller, L. F. (2003). Inbreeding depresses immune response in song sparrows (*Melospiza melodia*): direct and inter-generational effects. *Proceedings of the Royal Society of London B: Biological Sciences* 270(1529): 2151–57.

Richardson, D. and Westerdahl, H. (2003). MHC diversity in two *Acrocephalus* species: the outbred Great reed warbler and the inbred Seychelles warbler. *Molecular Ecology* 12(12): 3523–29.

Rowe, G., Dickinson, H. C., Gibson, R., Funk, S. M. and Fa, J. E. (2002). St Lucia whiptail lizard *Cnemidophorus vanzoi* (Sauria: Teiidae) microsatellite primers. *Molecular Ecology Notes* 2(2): 124–26.

Ryder, O. A. (1986). Species conservation and systematics: the dilemma of subspecies. *Trends in Ecology and Evolution* 1(1): 9–10.

Salgueiro, P., Coelho, M. M., Palmeirim, J. M. and Ruedi, M. (2004). Mitochondrial DNA variation and population structure of the island endemic Azorean bat (*Nyctalus azoreum*). *Molecular Ecology* 13(11): 3357–66.

Shafer, A. B., Wolf, J. B., Alves, P. C. et al. (2015). Genomics and the challenging translation into conservation practice. *Trends in Ecology and Evolution* 30(2): 78–87.

Siddle, H. V., Marzec, J., Cheng, Y., Jones, M. and Belov, K. (2010). MHC gene copy number variation in Tasmanian devils: implications for the spread of a contagious cancer. *Proceedings of the Royal Society of London B: Biological Sciences* 277(1690): 2001–6.

Snell, H. L., Snell, H. M. and Tracy, C. R. (1984). Variation among populations of Galapagos island iguanas (*Conolophus*): contrasts of phylogeny and ecology. *Biological Journal of the Linnean Society* 21(1–2): 185–207.

Snell, H. M., Stone, P. A. and Snell, H. L. (1996). A summary of geographical characteristics of the Galapagos Islands. *Journal of Biogeography* 23(5): 619–24.

Sommer, S. (2005). The importance of immune gene variability (MHC) in evolutionary ecology and conservation. *Frontiers in Zoology* 2(1): 16.

Soulé, M. E. (1985). What is conservation biology?. *BioScience* 35(11): 727–34.

Spielman, D., Brook, B. W., Briscoe, D. A. and Frankham, R. (2004). Does inbreeding and loss of genetic diversity decrease disease resistance?. *Conservation Genetics* 5(4): 439–48.

Steiner, C. C., Putnam, A. S., Hoeck, P. E. and Ryder, O. A. (2013). Conservation genomics of threatened animal species. *Annual Review Of Animal Bioscience* 1(1): 261–81.

Swinnerton, K. J., Groombridge, J. J., Jones, C. G., Burn, R. W. and Mungroo, Y. (2004). Inbreeding depression and founder diversity among captive and free-living populations of the endangered pink pigeon *Columba mayeri*. *Animal Conservation* 7(4): 353–64.

Templeton, A. R. (1998). Species and speciation: geography, population structure, ecology, and gene trees, pp. 32–43 in D. J. Howard and S.A. Berlocher (eds.), *Endless Forms: Species and Speciation*. Oxford University Press, New York, NY.

Templeton, A. R. and Read, B. (1984). Factors eliminating inbreeding depression in a captive herd of Speke's gazelle (*Gazella spekei*). *Zoo Biology* 3(3): 177–99.

Tollington, S., Jones, C. G., Greenwood, A. et al. (2013). Long-term, fine-scale temporal patterns of genetic diversity in the restored Mauritius parakeet reveal genetic impacts of management and associated demographic effects on reintroduction programmes. *Biological Conservation* 161: 28–38.

Tompkins, D. M., Mitchell, R. A. and Bryant, D. M. (2006). Hybridization increases measures of innate and cell-mediated immunity in an endangered bird species. *Journal of Animal Ecology* 75(2): 559–64.

Townsend, S. M. and Jamieson, I. G. (2013). Molecular and pedigree measures of relatedness provide similar estimates of inbreeding depression in a bottlenecked population. *Journal of Evolutionary Biology* 26(4): 889–99.

Tzika, A. C., Rosa, S. F., Fabiani, A. et al. (2008). Population genetics of Galapagos Islands iguana (genus *Conolophus*) remnant populations. *Molecular Ecology* 17 (23): 4943–52.

Waller, D. M., Dole, J. and Bersch, A. J. (2008). Effects of stress and phenotypic variation on inbreeding depression in *Brassica rapa*. *Evolution* 62(4): 917–31.

Waples, R. S. (2002). Definition and estimation of effective population size in the conservation of endangered species, pp. 147–48 in S. R. Beissinger and D. R. McCullough (eds.), *Population Viability Analysis*. Chicago, IL: University of Chicago Press.

Watson, J. (1989). Successful translocation of the endemic Seychelles kestrel *Falco araea* to Praslin, pp. 363–67 in B.-U. Meyburg and R. D. Chancellor (eds.), *Raptors in the Modern World*. World Working Group on Birds of Prey and Owls, Berlin.

Westerdahl, H., Waldenström, J., Hansson, B. et al. (2005). Associations between malaria and MHC genes in a migratory songbird. *Proceedings of the Royal Society of London B: Biological Sciences* 272(1571): 1511–18.

Whiteman, N. K., Matson, K. D., Bollmer, J. L. and Parker, P. G. (2006). Disease ecology in the Galapagos hawk (*Buteo galapagoensis*): host genetic diversity, parasite load and natural antibodies. *Proceedings of the Royal Society of London B: Biological Sciences*, 273(1588): 797–804.

Wikelski, M., Foufopoulos, J., Vargas, H. and Snell, H. (2004). Galapagos birds and diseases: invasive pathogens as threats for island species. *Ecology and Society* 9(1): 5.

Wood, A. R. and Gardner, J. P. A. (2007). Small spatial scale population genetic structure in two limpet species endemic to the Kermadec Islands, New Zealand. *Inter-Research, Marine Ecology Progress Series* 349: 159–70.

Wright, S. (1931). Evolution in Mendelian populations. *Genetics* 16: 97–159.
    (1938). Size of population and breeding structure in relation to evolution. *Science* 87(2263): 430–31.

Wright, D. J., Spurgin, L. G., Collar, N. J. et al. (2014). The impact of translocations on neutral and functional genetic diversity within and among populations of the Seychelles warbler. *Molecular Ecology* 23(9): 2165–77.

Wright, B., Morris, K., Grueber, C. E. et al. (2015). Development of a SNP-based assay for measuring genetic diversity in the Tasmanian devil insurance population. *BMC Genomics* 16: 791.

Wright, D. J., Brouwer, L., Mannarelli, M.-E. et al. (2015). Social pairing of Seychelles warblers under reduced constraints: MHC, neutral heterozygosity, and age. *Behavioral Ecology* 27: 295–303.

Wyatt, K. B., Campos, P. F., Gilbert, M. T. P. et al. (2008). Historical mammal extinction on Christmas Island (Indian Ocean) correlates with introduced infectious disease. *PloS ONE* 3(11): e3602.

Young, R. P., Fa, J. E., Ogrodowczyk, A. et al. (2006). The St Lucia whiptail lizard *Cnemidophorus vanzoi*: a conservation dilemma?. *Oryx* 40(3): 358–61.

4 · *Threats to Islands*

Invasive Species and Their Impacts

ALAN TYE, GILLIAN KEY AND JAMIESON
A. COPSEY

4.0 Introduction

For centuries, humans have introduced a common suite of 'alien' species, deliberately or by accident, to islands across the globe. Many of these species have become established and have begun to dilute and eliminate the unique faunas and floras that existed before humans arrived; in other words, they have become invasive. Some of these invasive species have had a catastrophic impact on many endemic life forms, preying upon them, out-competing them, hybridising with them and spreading introduced parasites and pathogens. If we are to prevent more species from going extinct as a consequence of such invasions, we need first to understand the process by which invaders become such a problem.

This chapter begins by examining what is meant by invasion and why it is a problem. We detail a range of impacts of invasive species, highlighting both socio-economic and environmental concerns. We then analyse the steps of the invasion process and the hurdles that species must overcome if they are to establish and then further be classed as invasive. We go on to examine the characteristics that predispose a species to 'invasiveness' and the characteristics of islands that make them vulnerable to invasion. Finally, we explore the concern that far from having passed through the main period of invasion, it may be just beginning.

4.1 What Is 'Invasion' and Why Is It Now a Problem?

'Invasion' is usually termed 'colonisation' when the process is not mediated by humans. Without it, there would be no life on most oceanic islands in the first place, as they have never been connected by land to continents. Their terrestrial species have somehow had to cross an ocean barrier to get there. On the Galapagos Islands, on average, one plant species has established naturally every 10,000 years (Porter 1983; Tye 2006). This slow colonisation, followed by many crossings between islands and evolution on those islands, is enough to produce, over several millennia, the remarkable island endemic flora that we know and value (see Chapter 2).

To a degree, then, invasions are essential to island life, providing the source material on which evolution can operate (see Chapter 2). The problem now is not the fact that species reach new lands but the increasing rate at which they are taken there. For example, since their discovery in 1535, at least 750 plant species have been introduced to the Galapagos Islands: this human-mediated introduction rate is about 1.6 species per year, or more than 15,000 times the natural rate (Tye 2006; Guézou et al. 2010). Similarly, for vertebrates, natural arrivals to Galapagos are estimated at one species every 50,000 years, while post-1535 rates are one species every 16–20 years (Snell et al. 2002). It is estimated that in total more than 400,000 species may have been transported outside of their natural ranges by humans in the last 10,000 years (Pimentel et al. 2001).

4.2 Biodiversity Impacts of Invasive Species

Loss of island species is particularly heavy through predation (e.g. of island birds; Blackburn et al. 2004; Hilton and Cuthbert 2010) and is well documented for many predators, notably rats, cats, monkeys, snakes (Box 4.1a; Figure 4.1), ants and snails (Lever 1994; Davis 2009). Invasive rodents (rats and the house mouse *Mus musculus*) are probably responsible for the majority of island species extinctions to date (Courchamp et al. 2003; Towns et al. 2006). Atkinson (1985) listed 15 species of birds known to be predated upon by the Pacific rat *Rattus exulans*, 39 species by the black rat *Rattus rattus* and at least 53 by the brown rat *Rattus norvegicus*, and these numbers have since greatly increased. These three rat species are among the largest contributors to seabird extinction and endangerment worldwide (Jones et al. 2008). The Pacific rat probably also caused many invertebrate extinctions in New Zealand (Gibbs 2009), and rats are probably a principal cause of the many declines and extinctions among the exceptionally rich endemic snail faunas of islands (Hadfield and Saufler 2009). In New Zealand, 25 native species of plants, 15 species of invertebrates, two amphibians, 10 reptiles, 13 birds and two mammals have been affected

Box 4.1 *The Invasion of Guam*

a. **Brown Tree Snakes.** The brown tree snake *Boiga irregularis* is believed to have been introduced to the northern Pacific island of Guam in about 1949 (Savidge 1987; Figure 4.1). Its impacts on the avifauna of Guam constitute perhaps the most sobering demonstration of the damage an invasive can do to island biodiversity and the extreme rapidity with which native populations can decline once an introduced species becomes established: most of Guam's native and endemic breeding birds were extinct or nearly so within 35 years of the snake's arrival (Wiles et al. 2003). The snake eradicated eight of the island's 11 endemic forest-living birds and 12 non-forest birds and caused population declines of over 90 per cent in eight others (Wiles et al. 2003).

It is likely that the snake was originally transported from the Solomon Islands to Guam on the undercarriage of military aircraft (Rodda et al. 1992). Worryingly, stray snakes have been picked up on or near airfields on many islands with US military bases, including Hawaii, Kwajalein and Okinawa in the Pacific, and Diego Garcia in the Indian Ocean (Engeman et al. 1998). These present a risk over a period of time of sufficient numbers getting through to allow the species to establish, in which case it would devastate the wildlife on these islands as it has done on Guam.

b. **Compounding Impacts.** The effects of multiple near-simultaneous invasions can be especially striking, where a single invader might not have caused such a problem. In 2003, the cycad scale insect *Aulacaspis yasumatsui*, originally from Southeast Asia, was introduced to Guam, probably on ornamental plants from Hawaii or Florida. It began to attack Guam's endemic cycad *Cycas micronesica*. Infested leaves are dropped, and most plants on the island died, although they can sprout new leaves and recover if scale infestation is reduced by introduced biological control agents (Marler and Lawrence 2012). However, in 2005, the cycad blue butterfly *Chilades pandava*, previously introduced to the nearby Northern Mariana Islands and whose caterpillars feed on young cycad leaves, arrived on Guam through self-dispersal down the island chain (Moore et al. 2005), and another introduced cycad pest insect (*Erechtites* sp.) was also found on the island (Marler and Muniappan 2006). The cycads are therefore now under triple attack from invasive alien insects, making it very difficult for the plants to recover and reproduce (Marler and Lawrence 2012).

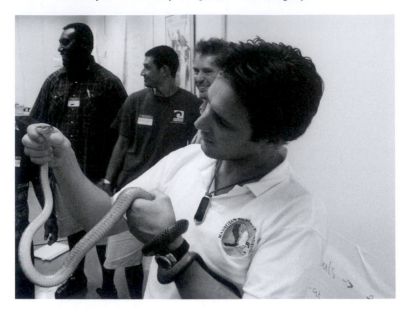

Figure 4.1 Lead editor (J. Copsey) with brown tree snake *Boiga irregularis*, Guam, Pacific Ocean. The establishment and subsequent invasion of this species resulted in the loss of at least 20 bird species on the island. (*Photo credit:* Jamieson A. Copsey.)

by these three rats species, with at least 35 of these species driven to local extinction (Towns et al. 2006). Many of the worst invasive mammalian predators are opportunistic and can take advantage of novel food sources. Rats' dietary flexibility enables them to adapt to new conditions and to attack different species at different times and in different places; e.g. black rats introduced to Surprise Island, New Caledonia, switch to preying on sea turtle hatchlings outside the sea-bird nesting season (Caut et al. 2008).

Among the most voracious invasive predators to have been introduced deliberately by humans to islands throughout the world are the domestic cat *Felis catus* and the small Indian mongoose *Urva auropunctatus* (Medina et al. 2011; Morley and Winder 2013). Cats have been implicated as the major cause of extinction of many ground-living island birds, with at least 12 species driven to extinction on the New Zealand island of Mangere alone (Bell 1978). On Australian islands, the extinction of native mammals has been closely correlated with the presence of introduced cats, particularly on dry islands, which better suit their ecology (Burbridge and Manly 2002). In 1998, a single cat extirpated the Angel de la Guarda deer mouse *Peromyscus guardia* from Estanque Island in the Gulf of California (Álvarez-Castañeda and Ortega-Rubio 2003), and a lone cat was also believed to have caused the extinction of the endemic wren *Xenicus lyalli* on Stephens Island, New Zealand (Greenway 1967). It has been estimated that within a five-month period, cats in the British Isles could have consumed ~92 million prey items, including roughly 57 million mammals, 27 million birds and 5 million reptiles and amphibians (Woods et al. 2003).

Introduced monkeys function like 'super rats', predating eggs, chicks, fruit and seeds and changing the composition of vegetation (Carter and Bright 2002; Kemp and Burnett 2003). The crab-eating macaque *Macaca fascicularis*, introduced to previously monkey-free islands, has caused rapid declines in the populations of lizards, arboreal mammals and tree-nesting birds, as on Papua (Indonesia), Angaur Island (Palau) and Mauritius (Cheke and Hume 2008; Parkes and Fisher 2011): Angaur now has the lowest bird population of any major island in Palau (VanderWerf 2007), while 83 to 95 per cent of observed nesting failures for the endemic Mauritius fody *Foudia rubra* were put down to predation from the macaque or the black rat (Safford 1997). The main cause of the extermination of the dodo on Mauritius (Box 1.2; see Section 2.3) was probably introduced predators, including pigs *Sus scrofa* and the macaque; hunting was only a secondary cause (Cheke and Hume 2008).

Lesser known vertebrate predators with serious impacts on islands include some surprising species. In the Scottish Outer Hebrides, the introduced hedgehog *Erinaceus europaeus* has been the principal factor driving resident shorebird numbers down by an average of 39 per cent (Jackson et al. 2004) as it eats their eggs.

Species loss through competition or displacement is less well documented, probably because it happens more slowly and is less dramatic (Sax and Gaines 2008), but evidence of its effects is now accumulating from the recovery of island ecosystems after the successful management of invasive species, as well as from detailed investigations of species interactions. For example, black rats compete with endemic rice rats *Nesoryzomys swarthii* on Santiago Island in the Galapagos, the black rat dominating during wetter years and the rice rats during dry ones (Gregory and MacDonald 2009; Harris and MacDonald 2007). The invasive ant *Technomyrmex albipes* prevents access to the endemic plant *Roussea simplex* by the pollinating and seed-dispersing endemic blue-tailed gecko *Phelsuma cepediana* in Mauritius (Hansen and Muller

2009). The introduced house gecko has caused the catastrophic decline of the endemic night gecko *Nactus durrelli* in the Mascarene Islands by displacing it from favoured positions (Cole et al. 2005). Competition and displacement are probably the major impacts of invasive plants, but the effects are subtle, not leading quickly to extinction but causing declines in native species richness and major changes to ecosystem functions (Jäger et al. 2007, 2009; Gaertner et al. 2009).

The mechanisms by which ecosystem change occurs following invasion are often so subtle that they are far from being fully understood. For example, invasive plants may alter the structure of rainforests (Asner et al. 2008) and change light regimes (Reinhart et al. 2006) or soil chemistry (Raizada et al. 2008), which may affect native plants and other organisms as much as does direct competition for space (Jäger et al. 2007, 2009, 2013). In Hawaii, the nitrogen-fixing fire tree *Myrica faya* not only outcompetes native trees but changes the nutrient balance in the soil, making it unsuitable for native forest regeneration (Vitousek et al. 1987). Invasive grasses can accumulate dense mats of dry leaves which change the fire cycle of the ecosystem and consequently vegetation composition (D'Antonio 2000). By altering plant community structure, invasive plants may have impacts on organisms higher up the food chain. For example, in Hawaiian forests, another introduced nitrogen-fixing tree, *Falcataria moluccana*, increases the abundance of introduced leaf-litter amphipods and isopods by 400 per cent and predatory ants by 200 per cent (Tuttle et al. 2009). Some invasive species, particularly generalists such as fast-breeding omnivores, can have multiple effects: in New Zealand, the Pacific rat not only caused many invertebrate extinctions but also suppressed the recruitment of at least 11 species of plants, many invertebrates, reptiles and small seabirds, and modified the forest composition (Towns and Broome 2003).

Since plants usually form the biological structure of most habitats, major habitat change can also be caused by herbivory, the equivalent for plants of predation. The Pacific rat may have caused the complete collapse of native palm forests in Hawaii (Athens 2009). Ebenhard (1988) reported that at least 40 per cent of all mammal introductions caused shifts in native animal and plant abundance, and of 95 herbivore introductions on oceanic islands, 93 caused habitat change. The rabbit has inflicted catastrophic impacts on island flora and fauna, causing cascading multiple impacts (Table 4.1). One of the reasons for the difficulty in estimating the true impact of invasive species is that their effects are often subtle, indirect or compound. It might seem unlikely

Table 4.1 *Some of the Many Impacts of Introduced Rabbits on Island Biodiversity*

Impact	Location
Approximately 10 per cent of Hooker's sea lion pups suffocate in rabbit burrows.	Enderby and Rose islands, New Zealand
Overgrazing reduced plant cover for nesting seabirds, reducing reproductive success.	Meeuw Island, South Africa
Overgrazing increased competition for food between granivorous and insectivorous birds.	Meeuw Island, South Africa
Disturbance led to abandonment of breeding grounds by birds.	Meeuw Island, South Africa
Reduced the area of substrate suitable for nesting by seabirds.	Islands off Western Australia
Increased predation levels on native species by providing alternative prey for native and introduced predators.	Macquarie Island, Australia
Eliminated tussock grassland almost completely.	Macquarie Island, Australia
Eliminated the Kerguelen cabbage *Pringlea antiscorbutica*.	Kerguelen Island, Indian Ocean
Overgrazing eliminated 26 plant species, leading to loss of three bird species.	Laysan Island, Hawaii
Removal of plants reduced invertebrate and insectivorous lizard abundance, causing extinction of at least one species of snake.	Round Island, Mauritius
Native palms declined, reducing the island's ability to withstand the impact of cyclones.	Round Island, Mauritius
Overgrazing and burrowing led to elevated soil erosion.	Round Island, Mauritius
Soil erosion inhibited plant regeneration following catastrophes, e.g. fire.	Rabbit Island, Australia

Sources: Courchamp et al. (2003) and Long (2003).

that herbivorous rabbits could contribute to reducing native gecko populations in New Zealand, but they achieved this by changing the vegetation composition, resulting in the loss of plant hosts for a scale insect whose honeydew was the major energy source for the gecko (Towns 2002). The brushtail possum *Trichosurus vulpecula* similarly demonstrates the multiple levels at which an introduced species can alter ecosystems. Introduced into New Zealand in the late nineteenth century for a fur industry and as pets, by the 1950s it was considered

Figure 4.2 Male Lesser Antilles iguana *Iguana delicatissima* displaying. Hybridisation with the introduced *Iguana iguana* is threatening the species across its Caribbean range. (*Photo credit:* Gerardo Garcia.) (A black-and-white version of this figure will appear in some formats. For the colour version, please refer to the plate section.)

a pest, owing to the great damage caused to the native forest, including reduced fruit and flower availability, which, in turn, hindered forest regeneration and removed an important food supply for native birds (Courchamp et al. 2003). Possums also compete for nest holes with kiwis *Apteryx* spp., prey on the eggs and chicks of threatened birds and transmit bovine tuberculosis to cattle and deer, with economic repercussions (Clout and Sarre 1997).

   Invasive species can cause genetic loss and destruction of an endemic species by hybridising with it, and introduced plants can do this while present only in cultivation, i.e. without even being 'invasive' in the usual sense of the word. Released or escaped green iguanas *Iguana iguana*, a popular pet species, are threatening in this way the native Lesser Antilles iguana *I. delicatissima* on Guadeloupe and Martinique (Powell and Henderson 2005; Figure 4.2). Elimination by hybridisation has been documented for several island birds, such as the New Zealand grey duck *Anas superciliosa* and the Hawaiian duck *A. wyvilliana*, both now threatened through mating with the widely introduced mallard *A. platyrhynchos* (Rhymer and Simberloff 1996).

Among disease agents, West Nile virus, avian influenza and the parasitic *Batrachochytrium* fungi that kill frogs and salamanders (Martel et al. 2014) are all causing major species declines of various vertebrate taxa around the world, having been spread by humans. In Hawaii, diseases introduced in exotic birds are among the main reasons why 53 of 71 endemic bird species and subspecies there are either extinct or endangered (Kilpatrick 2006; also see Section 3.2.4). Other introduced invertebrates cause mortality through parasitism. A muscid fly *Philornis downsii* – native to Central and South America – whose larvae live in bird nests and parasitise the nestlings, has been introduced to the Galapagos Islands within the last 50 years. It now causes over 60 per cent mortality in Darwin's finches (Dudaniec and Kleindorfer 2006) and poses a significant threat to the survival of the critically endangered mangrove finch *Camarhynchus heliobates* (Fessl et al. 2010).

While these examples clearly illustrate the negative impacts of invasive alien species on global biodiversity (and in particular on islands), their impacts ramify further into the realms of public health, livelihoods and food security (Pimentel et al. 2005; Murphy and Cheesman 2006; Pejchar and Mooney 2009).

4.3 Socio-economic Impacts of Introduced Species

Worldwide, it has been estimated that 67,000 pest species attack crops (9,000 insects and mites, 50,000 pathogens and 8,000 weeds), of which between 20 and 70 per cent are not native to the area they affect, together reducing global food production by up to 40 per cent (Oerke et al. 1994; Oerke 2006). The agricultural and forestry production-based economies typical of many small islands are highly vulnerable to such impacts, and rural communities on islands often report significant production losses from invasive species and higher costs because of the extra labour needed to manage them (e.g. McGregor and Bishop 2011; Daigneault et al. 2013).

Attempts to quantify national economic impacts of invasive species, e.g. Pimentel et al. (2001, 2005) for Australia, Brazil, India, the United Kingdom and the United States and Williams et al. (2010) for Great Britain, produce figures in the billions of dollars per country, but these are to varying degrees anecdotal and difficult to use for comparative purposes. There are no similar total estimates for oceanic islands, but the economic costs of invasive species on islands, especially on small-island developing states, likely represent a much higher proportion of their gross domestic product (GDP) than they do for continental countries (Mwebaze et al. 2010). Some partial estimates exist for islands: e.g. the cost of four invasive mammal species in the Seychelles was estimated at US$21 million per year (Mwebaze et al. 2010).

In any case, most published cost estimates are incomplete, as they omit impacts on ecosystem services, which are hard to value and which include provisioning (e.g. food, timber, water), supporting-regulating (e.g. nutrient cycling, climate, floods, erosion, disease, pollination, water purification) and cultural (e.g. recreation, aesthetics, spirituality) services (Charles and Dukes 2007; Pejchar and Mooney 2009; Vilà et al. 2010). The cost impacts on provisioning can be relatively easy to calculate for individual invasive species in particular places, such as losses in rice production caused by the golden apple snail *Pomacea canaliculata* in the Philippines, estimated at US$12–18 million per year in 1990 (Naylor 1996), and losses caused to village economies in Fiji by the invasive *Merremia peltata* vine, tulip tree *Spathodea campanulata*, taro beetle *Papuana uninodis*, red-vented bulbul *Pycnonotus cafer* and small Indian mongoose (Daigneault et al. 2013). Net economic losses due to damage by feral cattle, comprising wild meat and tourism revenue losses after taking into account cattle management costs, were estimated at US$214,000 per year in one Montserrat forest, thus confirming that cattle management is economically worthwhile (Peh et al. 2015). But it is difficult to estimate the total costs of even a well-studied invader such as the brown tree snake on Guam (see Box 4.1a), where the direct costs of power cuts caused by snakes and of snake management have been estimated, but there is no easy way to measure the indirect effects, such as the losses caused to businesses by the power cuts or losses to tourist revenues caused by the presence of snakes (Kahl et al. 2012). In general, impacts on regulatory processes or cultural values are difficult to estimate and have rarely been quantified, although some examples exist, such as the reduced property values of homes in parts of Hawaii invaded by coqui frogs *Eleutherodactylus coqui* owing to the frogs' unwanted nocturnal noise (Kaiser and Burnett 2006).

In some cases, the costs of a 'useful' invasive can be compared with its benefits. For example, the invasive tree *Melaleuca* in Florida contributes $15 million to honey production annually, but removing this species would prevent some 10 times greater current and future tourism dollar losses that are accruing as the species invades the Everglades (Pejchar and Mooney 2009). The costs and benefits of invasive species are often distributed differently: those who benefit do not pay the costs, and those who lose are not compensated. In Mauritius, the government considered introducing biological control agents to prevent dieback of the invasive *Leucaena leucocephala* caused by an introduced sap-sucking insect, *Heteropsylla cubana*, because *Leucaena* has perceived value as a fodder crop. In such cases, an economic counter-argument is probably the best way to convince decision-makers to take an environmentally favourable course of action. Although estimates of the economic costs of invasive species are imprecise, those that exist indicate that the costs are enormous, clearly add up to a powerful argument for decision-makers and provide a reason to understand the invasion process more fully.

4.4 The Steps to Invasion

To determine how best to prevent further invasions of introduced species onto our islands or to eradicate or manage those that are already present, it is helpful to understand the steps, or filters, that a species must pass through to become invasive (Cassey et al. 2004). We can then consider the points in the process at which we might intervene to deal with an invasion (see Chapter 7). In order to be considered invasive, species must first be transported from their place of origin to a new location, then they must become established (including escape from captivity or cultivation) and finally they must spread into natural or semi-natural habitats and/or cause noticeable ecological or other impacts. Although these stages are a continuum, rather than truly discrete (Richardson et al. 2000), at each step there is a probability that a species will not pass.

Ambiguity in the definition of 'invasive', with the word used to mean either just spread or spread-plus-significant-impact, has led plant ecologists to develop the term 'transformer' for introduced plants that both spread and cause significant ecological impacts (Richardson et al. 2000); this allows 'invasive' to be used more broadly, in a similar sense to the non-technical use of the word, to mean simply spreading into natural habitats. According to either of these definitions, invasive species are non-native (alien); that is, they have been introduced from somewhere else through human-mediated activities. Sometimes a native species can become invasive in the sense of suddenly spreading rapidly or causing damage in some way. This usually happens when humans cause environmental changes, such as clearing forest or changing nutrient flows, which favour a particular species and allow it to increase unexpectedly; for example, both native and non-native species of algae can cause blooms in Hawaii (Shluker 2003). However, in this book, our discussion is restricted to 'invasive alien species', since introduction is the principal feature of the invasion problem on islands.

4.4.1 Pathways of Introduction

Introductions by human-mediated pathways can be deliberate or unintentional (Table 4.2). These two processes differ in many ways, including the kinds of species introduced by them, their means of introduction and their success of establishment. The vehicle or actual mechanism of transfer is called the 'vector', and examples include goods, food, ballast water, boat hulls, horticultural products, forest products, live animals and animal products. Apart from commensals such as rats, unintentional introductions are often contaminants such as beetles (Coleoptera) in timber or weed seeds in grain, or hitchhikers, such as organisms in ballast water or hull-fouling on ships (Siguan 2003). Terrestrial invertebrates, non-useful plants and marine organisms are thus primarily accidental introductions. Species that frequently accompany human transport are often termed 'tramp' species.

Over time, there has been a change in dispersal patterns due to changes in the nature of both pathways and vectors (Andow 2003). For example, up to the early 1800s, most insect pests transferred were beetles infesting wood, stored products and soil ballast, moving slowly around the world on wooden sailing ships. By the mid-1800s, sap-sucking bugs (Homoptera) had become the main pests moved, as faster ships more easily carried around the live plants on which they lived. In the 1900s, there was another switch to wasps (Hymenoptera), as biological control agents were deliberately transferred around the world. For vertebrates and plants, the pet and horticultural trades became predominant from the mid–twentieth century (Kraus 2003; Kowarik 2005; Tye 2006).

The rate at which new species are delivered by the various pathways is difficult to estimate, particularly for unintentional pathways, because only the species that successfully establish tend to get noticed, whereas the many that fail to survive the journey or do not find suitable conditions on arrival and just die remain unrecorded. However, the few figures available suggest that delivery rates are high; for example, during

Table 4.2 *Pathways (or Reasons, in the Case of Deliberate Introductions) for Introduction*

	Pathway
Intentional introductions direct to the wild	• Birds, mammals released for hunting (on inhabited islands) or as a food source for sailors (on uninhabited islands) • Fishery releases to stock natural waters • Releases to 'enrich' the native flora and fauna (e.g. by acclimatisation societies) • Biological control • Re-wilding with ecological analogues to replace extinct species or populations • Introductions of threatened species to conservation refuges
Deliberate introductions with no particular concern for containment	• Plants (including germplasm) introduced for agriculture, forestry or soil improvement, including by development aid programmes • Ornamental plants, pets and aquarium organisms that are deliberately released into the wild or escape
Introductions to containment that subsequently escape	• Escapes of farmed animals, including aquaculture and mariculture • Escapes from zoos, botanical gardens and research facilities
Unintentional introductions	• Seeds, invertebrates, parasites and pathogens in animals, plants and seed traded for agriculture, forestry, aquaculture and mariculture • Seed, invertebrate and pathogen contaminants of agricultural, forestry, aquaculture and mariculture produce • Seed, invertebrate and pathogen contaminants of nursery plants and cut flowers • Soil-inhabiting species transported in soil • Organisms on machinery, equipment and vehicles, including military • Organisms adhering to passenger/tourist luggage and equipment • Organisms in or on packing materials • Hitchhikers in or on cargo, including shipping containers • Hitchhikers in or on planes • Organisms in dry ballast, ballast water and ballast tank sediment in ships • Boat hull-fouling organisms • Organisms in or on synthetic marine debris

Source: Amended from Wittenberg and Cock (2001) with additions.

a technical audit of inspections carried out at an airport in Hawaii during 20 weeks in 2000–1, 45 per cent of the insect species (279 species) and 34 per cent of the plant species (47 species) detected were new to Hawaii (Lodge et al. 2009).

International trade is one of the main drivers behind the recent surge in the rate of both deliberate and unintentional introductions (McGeoch et al. 2010). Since the 1950s, world trade has increased 14-fold (Hayes 2003; Ruiz and Carlton 2003), world merchandise and commercial services trade has increased by about 7 per cent per year on average since 1980 and developing economies raised their share of world imports from 29 to 42 per cent (WTO 2013). For a number of decades, world trade has grown on average nearly twice as fast as production, reflecting the increasing international supply chains (WTO 2013). As a result, more species and more individuals of each species are transferred, more quickly and more often, to more locations (Ruiz and Carlton 2003). Numbers of introduced plant species correlate more strongly with GDP for island states than for continents, reflecting the greater proportion of imports to islands (Hulme 2009). In Japan, the only islands with no records of insect introduction were those that lacked international airports and seaports (Kiritani and Yamamura 2003). A new addition to the threat from invasive species in trade comes from online trade, which is poorly regulated and difficult to monitor and control (Derraik and Phillips 2010).

International tourism has also risen (and is still growing) and now generates almost 10 per cent of total world GDP, employing almost 10 per cent of the global workforce (WTTC 2014). In the Caribbean, tourism accounts for 70 per cent of GDP per island on average (except Cuba), and 55 per cent of the Caribbean labour force works in the tourism sector (Waugh 2009). The Caribbean hosted 21 million visitors in 2004, a 35 per cent increase since 1994 and a 520 per cent increase since 1970; in addition, 19 million cruise ship passengers visited in 2004 (Waugh 2009). Tourism to the Galapagos Islands increased from roughly 2,000 visitors per year in the 1960s to over 120,000 in 2005 and has continued to rise at a similar rate since; this fuelled an 8 per cent per year increase in the local population (mostly by immigration) over the same period (Epler 2007), although the immigration rate has since declined (INEC 2016). The number of commercial flights into the islands almost tripled from 2001 to 2006; surveys in the first six months of 2006 indicated that, on average, 0.71

invertebrates arrived per flight (Causton 2008), or more than 1,500 per year. Aside from the introductions of insects and seeds on flights, tourism promotes further introductions because tourist facilities require imported materials, including ornamental plants, which frequently are invasive or carry invasive pests (Waugh 2009). Another significant pathway is created by the establishment of military outposts on strategically important islands, such as the US bases on Guam and Hawaii (Pacific Ocean) and Diego Garcia (Indian Ocean), military ships and planes providing regular opportunities for species to hitch-hike between distant locations (see Box 4.1a).

Most invasive plants were introduced deliberately, until recently mostly for food or medicine or as forestry species. Nowadays, ornamentals form an increasing proportion, probably the majority, of deliberately introduced invaders (Kowarik 2005; Tye 2006). It has been estimated that ~25,000 species of flowering plant are currently available through the nursery trade, many of which can be bought over the Internet with no controls (Mack 2003).

Invasive vertebrate species have been introduced for food (e.g. rabbits, goats *Capra aegagrus*, pigs), sport (e.g. red fox *Vulpes vulpes*, pheasants *Phasianus* spp.), poorly planned biological control (e.g. mongooses, cane toad *Bufo marinus*, myna birds *Acridotheres* spp.), pets (eg hamsters Cricetinae, snakes, red-eared terrapin *Trachemys scripta*, iguanas) and various other purposes (e.g. reindeer *Rangifer tarandus*). Deliberate releases of exotic species were important in the newly colonised Americas, New Zealand and Australia in the late nineteenth and early twentieth centuries, where many 'acclimatisation' societies were formed explicitly to import European species to the colonists' new homes as well as take exotic species back to Europe (Long 1981). Many species now considered major pests were lovingly brought in and carefully established, often at considerable effort and expense. More than 400 bird introduction events were recorded worldwide during the European diaspora of 1850–1930 (Blackburn and Duncan 2001). Birds were mostly introduced to islands, with 77 per cent of all bird introductions made to countries and islands colonised by the British. Approximately 21 per cent of the bird species that now have populations established outside their natural range originate from the Palaearctic, even though this region only supports 14 per cent of the birds of the world (Blackburn et al. 2009). Despite growing awareness of the problems, this still goes on; recently, over 12 species of bird were deliberately introduced to Mauritius and released from a local bird park (C. Jones, personal communication), and more bird introductions were proposed in 2017.

Most invasive invertebrates were accidentally introduced (Box 4.2); the notable exceptions are the deliberately introduced biological

---

Box 4.2 *Invasive Ants*

Invasive ants are a major threat to islands. Around 200 species of ants have been introduced outside their native range, with six particularly widespread and harmful species: red imported fire ant *Solenopsis invicta*, tropical fire ant *S. geminata*, yellow crazy ant *Anoplolepis gracilipes*, Argentine ant *Linepithema humile*, little fire ant *Wasmannia auropunctata* and African big-headed ant *Pheidole megacephala*. These reduce growth or survival of vertebrates, including 19 species of birds, 13 mammals and more than 15 reptiles and amphibians (Plentovich et al. 2008). In Hawaii, where there are no native ants, there are now more than 44 introduced species, three of which are implicated in bird nest failure and injuries (Plentovich et al. 2008); the big-headed ant has decimated the endemic insect fauna of the lowlands, as it predates or displaces a wide variety of insects that are important food for most native insectivorous Hawaiian birds (Wetterer 2007).

Oceanic islands tend to be poor in native ant species, although ants are among the dominant arthropods in ecosystems worldwide, capable of shaping them by redirecting energy flow, turning soil and interacting with other arthropods through predation and competition. As a consequence, some invasive ants have had serious impacts on island plant and animal communities. On Christmas Island (Indian Ocean), the yellow crazy ant killed between 10 million and 15 million red land crabs *Gecarcoidea natalis*, thereby removing the dominant native omnivore from the system (O'Dowd et al. 2003). As a result, native seedling recruitment, litter breakdown and invertebrates have all been affected. It has also been argued that *G. natalis* may have helped to prevent the establishment of newly arrived non-native plants and molluscs through predation; decimation of this species may therefore facilitate invasion of the island by other alien species. Finally, the mutualistic relationship that the ant forms with honeydew-secreting scale insects appears to cause tree canopy dieback, further impeding native forest regeneration. This tendency for invasive ants to care for other invertebrates as a food supply illustrates the complexity of non-native species favouring each other and working together.

control agents. Early attempts at biological control, such as the mongooses mentioned earlier, often produced invasive species because the effects of the introductions were not well understood or predicted, and many early attempts involved opportunistic predators. The subsequent havoc they have caused has given biological control a bad name. However, the increasingly successful use of very host-specific biological control agents such as hymenopteran parasitoids and fungal strains, accompanied by proper risk assessment, is an entirely different matter and now makes biological control an attractive and relatively safe management option for many invasive invertebrate and plant species (see Chapter 7).

4.4.2 Becoming Established

Based on data on plants, Williamson (1996) proposed what has become known as the 'tens rule' as a guide to the proportion of species that will pass through two filters: this states that for every 100 species that are transported, roughly 10 are likely to establish, and of these, one may go on to become invasive (in the sense of spread-plus-impact). However, this 'rule' appears to be a gross underestimate for animals. In different groups of introduced reptiles and amphibians, 33 to 76 per cent of introductions worldwide have become established, as have 43 per cent of introduced birds (Kraus 2003). In New Zealand, 32 of 55 documented mammal introductions have become established, a success rate of 58 per cent (Courchamp et al. 2003). For islands, the proportions that pass both filters appear to be higher than on continents (e.g. Kraus 2003; Jeschke and Strayer 2005: fig. 2) and often much higher than the tens rule would predict. This trend appears to be true even for plants; e.g. 40 per cent of introduced plants in Galapagos have naturalised (Tye 2006).

However, all these estimates of the proportion that establish are affected by the fact that establishment is more likely to be documented than are introduction events, many of which go undetected or unreported (Kraus 2003). Since our knowledge about introduction rates is not particularly reliable, all the percentages just cited should probably be regarded as maxima, with the words 'up to' placed before them. Where introduction rates are more carefully measured, establishment rates have sometimes been found to be lower than 10 per cent; e.g. if the 279 insect species detected at one airport in Hawaii in 20 weeks during 2000–1 are extrapolated to a whole year and to other ports of entry, then the 20 to 30 new invertebrates that are estimated to establish in Hawaii each year are a tiny proportion of the introductions (Lodge et al. 2009). In the field of biological control, the data are more precise, because species are deliberately introduced and monitored. It has been estimated that some 34 per cent of biological control agents establish (Kiritani and Yamamura 2003), although one would expect the proportion to be high in such cases because considerable effort is put into supporting their establishment. On St Helena Island (South Atlantic), deliberate introductions of 16 species of parasitoid wasps were made between 1972 and 1975 to control common crop pests (Lepidoptera), but few individuals were introduced, no care was provided after release and all failed to establish. Subsequent introductions of six further parasitoids in 1999–2000, with a programme of intensive breeding, monitoring and public awareness to restrict the use of pesticides in the release sites, all established (Key 2000). These figures indicate the great difference in establishment success between deliberate and accidental introductions and the big difference that caring for newly introduced species can make.

4.4.3 Spreading and Causing Damage or Biding Their Time?

The invasion process can take many decades (Box 4.1a). Williamson (2001) observed that about a third of the established introduced birds in Australia are still spreading, in some cases up to 100 years after release. In 1949, five cats were introduced to Marion Island in the sub-Antarctic (Bester et al. 2000) to control the feral house mouse (Watkins and Cooper 1986). In 1965, the cat population was considered not large enough to be having any serious impact on the bird populations but fulfilling its role as a mouse control agent (Bester et al. 2002). By 1975, however, there were an estimated 2,139 cats on the island killing approximately 450,000 burrowing seabirds every year (Van Aarde 1978). This case highlights three features of introduced species of concern to conservationists: they can become established from relatively few founding individuals (see Section 4.5.2 for evidence of genetic consequences), their effects can take a while to be seen, but once they do take hold, their impacts can be devastating.

Such apparent 'lag phases' are common. Studies of invasive insects in Japan revealed an average lag period between estimated date of introduction and detection in the wild of around 11.8 years but varying from 0.5 to 80 years (Kiritani and Yamamura 2003). Long delays between the known introduction date and a species being considered invasive have been reported for many plants and have led some to suppose that some 'threshold' or barrier has to be overcome before a plant becomes invasive. However, among 23 invasive plant species in the Hawaiian Islands, Daehler (2009) found an average lag of only 14 years between initial planting and first recorded escape for woody invaders and 5 years for herbaceous ones. An apparent lag is more likely a simple consequence of the exponential population growth that is characteristic of a newly established population: invasions are just not noticed or do not have significant impacts until the population reaches the steep climb phase of the exponential increase (Daehler 2009). Even where severe impacts occur very quickly after a new invasion, they may not be noticed or understood for some time. In line with this, species with shorter generation times (e.g. insects, fish) average shorter latency periods than those with longer generation times (e.g. plants, mammals) (Jeschke and Strayer 2005; Ding et al. 2008).

The time needed to disperse into favourable habitat from suboptimal introduction sites may also contribute to some latency periods (Cox 2004). Or a previously benign population may become invasive following a change in the environment that suddenly favours it; such changes can be natural (e.g. cyclone damage) or human mediated, such as bush fires, forest clearance, changes in agricultural practices or global climate change. Invasive species management itself can also create new problems by opening up areas for invasion that were previously dominated by the managed species (see Section 7.5). In a few cases, an initial population may not have the necessary evolutionary adaptations to permit invasion and may require time for genetic reorganisation. This may, for example, take the form of selection for earlier flowering, as preceded the population explosion of the ragwort *Senecio inaequidens* introduced into Europe (Cox 2004). Similarly, hybridisation between multiple successive introductions of the same species could eventually introduce enough genetic variability for a population to become suddenly invasive (Ellstrand and Schierenbeck 2000).

Whatever the cause, a long presence of a new species, without spreading widely or without obvious impacts, should not be taken as a sign that the species will always remain harmless, as illustrated in Boxes 4.1 and 4.2. We should apply the precautionary principle: always carry out risk assessment before deliberate introductions (discussed below), assume that every species that arrives unintentionally has the potential to become invasive and remove it before it has the chance to become established. Rapid response to new invasions is particularly important given the high cost and difficulty of the alternatives: eradicating once established (see Section 7.5) or accepting permanent impacts and costs.

Once a new species has arrived on one island of an archipelago, its chances of reaching other nearby islands are greatly increased, as the smaller distances open up more pathways. These secondary pathways may or may not differ from the one that brought it to the first island, as in the case of the cycad blue butterfly in the Mariana Islands (Box 4.1b). Brown tree snakes may have been carried from Guam to other islands of the Marianas chain (Wiles et al. 2003) not by military air transport but by boat or civil aeroplane, and many insects are transported between islands in Galapagos when they are attracted to tour ship lights (Roque-Albelo et al. 2009). Spread to nearby islands is especially likely if they are part of the same country, since inter-island biosecurity measures within a single country are mostly non-existent or weak.

Since it is true that usually only a small proportion of introduced species become problematic, and the prevention of introduction and establishment (the earlier steps in the invasion process) is much cheaper than managing an established invasion, an important question for conservation managers is, which species should we be concerned about, among all the potential introductions and already-introduced but not yet established species (see Section 7.2)? Knowing this, we can take action at earlier stages in the invasion process. Since many introduced species are important to human livelihoods, one cannot apply a blanket prohibition on introductions. These considerations highlight the importance of 'risk assessment' both before undertaking any deliberate introduction and in order to assess risks associated with unintentional transport.

In order to assess risk, we need to understand the great variation observed in rates of introduction and establishment in different taxa and locations. The reasons for this variation include both intrinsic features of the species, such as dispersal ability, and the human contributions that favour the transport or establishment of certain species. Many of these factors contribute to one common feature of successful introductions: propagule pressure. But first we consider the intrinsic characteristics of a species that contribute to making it a successful invader.

4.5 What Makes an Invasive Species?

4.5.1 Intrinsic Factors

There are invasive species among all higher taxa, plants, animals, fungi and microorganisms, but some species share features that increase their likelihood of becoming invasive (Table 4.3). Many of these can be grouped into three main factors that favour successful invasion and which are intrinsic to a species:

- High dispersal ability and therefore often with large native range from which to be spread (Andow 2003); includes being useful to or associated with humans
- High reproductive rate (r-strategy) or long life (K-strategy)
- Great adaptability (ecological, phenotypic or evolutionary)

This combination neatly describes the typically opportunistic nature of many invasive species ('weedy' characteristics). For plants, the

Table 4.3 *Some Characteristics of Invasive Species*

Intrinsic factors
- Good disperser (may have large native range)
- Association with humans (useful, commensal, associated with disturbed areas, etc.)
- Ability to self-fertilise: parthenogenetic or hermaphroditic species (e.g. many plants, some insects)
- Vegetative reproduction (plants)
- Ability to use local pollinators or seed dispersers (plants)
- K-Strategists: longer lifespan, large size, big seeds
- r-Strategists: higher rate of reproduction (e.g. large clutch size, long flowering), small size
- Generalists: adaptable to many habitats (plants) or generalist feeders (animals)
- Has 'aggressive' physical or chemical characteristics or can change ecosystem processes
- Rapid evolution
- Taxonomically close to other invasive species

Extrinsic factors
- Propagule pressure
- Climate match
- Positive interaction between invasive species

Sources: Partly based on Drake et al. (1989), Cox (2004), and Pyšek and Richardson (2007).

combination of factors that is associated with high likelihood of becoming established and invasive includes dispersal by people or wind, self-fertilisation, and one of two life-history patterns: on the one hand the *r*-strategists (many seeds, small seeds, extended flowering period) and on the other the *K*-strategists (large, long-lived, few large seeds; Pyšek and Richardson 2007). Since these traits are evolutionarily selected, they tend to occur together in groups of closely related organisms. This explains the observation that the invasive potential of a species correlates with its having invasive relatives.

In animal species, parthenogenetic reproduction can facilitate invasiveness. For example, in the little fire ant, queens can produce more queens parthenogenetically (Fournier et al. 2005). A few vertebrates, mainly reptiles, are also parthenogenetic, such as many whiptail lizards *Cnemidophorus* (Reeder et al. 2002) and the mourning gecko *L. lugubris*, in which males are unknown and which has been introduced to islands all around the tropics. In plants, self-fertilising species have a similar advantage in that a single seed arriving on an island can produce a colonising population.

However, if asexual or self-fertilising reproduction does not occur, then enough individuals have to arrive at the same time or have to survive long enough to meet later arrivals so that they can find suitable mates. On the one hand, therefore, long-lived species such as trees and some reptiles and fish might be favoured, while, on the other hand, small organisms of which large numbers are likely to be introduced together are also likely candidates for establishment. In general, good invaders may be species that 'try harder' than the native species, being either better *K*-strategists (those that invest in persistence) such as larger, longer-lived species and (in plants) those with bigger seeds or, at the other extreme, better *r*-strategists (investing in reproductive output) such as small, rapidly maturing, prolifically reproducing species (Andow 2003; Pyšek and Richardson 2007); 'pioneer' plant species are thus good candidates for invasion. Obviously, of these two strategies, invasion by *r*-strategists is likely to run faster and become damaging earlier. One pair of *r*-strategic rats arriving on an island with plentiful food and few predators could theoretically produce a population of 17 million individuals within three years. Something like this may have caused the ecological collapse on Rapa Nui (Easter Island), where archaeological evidence suggests that the island may have supported several million rats within a few years of human arrival around AD 1200 (Hunt 2007).

An introduced species, particularly an *r*-strategist, may evolve rapidly to adapt to its new habitat, such as changing its life-history features or prey type. Introduction to a new area frequently means leaving predators, parasites and diseases behind, allowing the organism to divert resources from defence to reproduction and growth. Newly introduced plants may evolve to produce more flowers and seeds than the ancestral population (Cox 2004). The effects of rapid evolution can be unexpected. For example, the 100 cane toads that were introduced to Australia in 1935, as control agents for sugar cane pests, rapidly established and started to spread. But 70 years later the invasion front was advancing at 27–50 km/year, three times faster than when the invasion speed was first measured, partly because the toads along the front line had evolved significantly longer legs than those at the point of origin (Phillips et al. 2006).

While the preceding generalisations are helpful in identifying likely invasive species, there are exceptions. Not all invasive species have large native ranges: even species endemic to a single island, such as the coqui frog, can become invaders. Similarly, the relatively slow growth and reproduction of the brown tree snake would not have indicated that it would become so quickly invasive on Guam. This highlights the need for more investigation of the ecology and life history of new arrivals, as well as the ecology of the islands at risk. But prediction of invasiveness will never be perfect, and the extreme impacts of some species that do become invasive add to the argument for following the precautionary principle: any species should be assumed likely to be invasive unless a thorough risk assessment indicates otherwise.

4.5.2 Extrinsic Factors: The Human Factor

The more individuals released at a time (sometimes termed 'propagule size' but since this term is also used for seed size, we prefer to call it 'propagule number') and the more introduction events that take place ('propagule frequency'), the higher is the likelihood that the species will become established (Simberloff 1989; Blackburn et al. 2009; Drake and Jerde 2009). The combined force of propagule number and frequency generates the 'propagule pressure': the total number of individuals released at a given location (Williamson 1996). For example, establishment rates for deliberately introduced plants are related to the period of time that the species was sold, varying from 2 per cent establishment for species sold for only one year up to 69 per cent for species sold for over 30 years (Myers and Bazely 2003). Similarly, the establishment success of birds introduced to New Zealand and Australia is strongly correlated with the number of introductions, the number of introduction sites and the total number of individuals introduced (Duncan 1997; Duncan et al. 2001). There are clear parallels here with the principles for translocation of threatened species (see Sections 9.4.1 and 9.4.2). However, propagule pressure is not the only factor involved in introduction success, e.g. climate match also correlates with bird establishment in Australia (Duncan et al. 2001), and recall the other factors listed in Table 4.3, so there is no simple overall relationship between propagule pressure and establishment probability; when other factors are favourable, the numbers of individuals required for successful establishment can be very small (Hulme 2009; Moulton et al. 2011).

There is a need for better information on the human activities that lead to the repeated introduction of larger quantities of a species into islands; trends in choice of pets or in cultural traditions involving the use of wildlife demand understanding if we are to prevent new species from being imported. For example, on Taiwan, followers of Buddhism and Taoism release approximately 200 million wild animals per year as a means of accruing merit (Agoramoorthy and Hsu 2007). In 1996, 6 per cent of the birds available on the island for sale for release during prayers were of introduced species, while even larger proportions of other prayer animals (turtles and fish) were non-native. Such activities over extended periods of time increase the likelihood that introduced species become established. Among the impacts of such species, the endemic Styan's bulbul *Pycnonotus taivanus* is now threatened with extinction through hybridisation with the commonly released Chinese bulbul *P. sinensis* (Severinghaus and Chi 1999).

The number of founders influences the severity of the initial genetic bottleneck that occurs at low population sizes (see Section 3.1.5). In most cases, an introduced population is small and would consequently be expected to show founder effects, i.e. reduction of genetic variability and shifts in average character state, compared with the population of origin. For example, just 29 reindeer were introduced to St Matthew Island in the Bering Sea (Courchamp et al. 2003), five domestic cats to Marion Island in the South Atlantic (van Aarde and Robinson 1980), a single pair of Himalayan thar *Hemitragus jemlahicus* to South Africa (Ehrlich 1989) and perhaps a single pregnant female brown tree snake to Guam in the Pacific (Rodda and Savidge 2007).

Such population bottlenecks leave genetic evidence in invasive species. The European starling *Sturnus vulgaris* in North America is derived from around 100 individuals and is now continent-wide, but it lacks about 42 per cent of alleles compared with the European source population (Cox 2004). However, levels of genetic heterogeneity in invasive species are very variable (Cox 2004), and one cannot assume that low levels are a problem for the species or might help management. For example, the Argentine ant *Linepithema humile* is invasive in California, where DNA microsatellite techniques found that the populations have only 47 per cent of the variability of Argentine populations and 9 per cent heterozygosity as opposed to 30 per cent in Argentina. In its native range, the ant is less abundant and nest colonies show aggression to each other, whereas in California, as a result of the genetic homogeneity of the introduced population, they show little aggression and form super-colonies over big areas (Cox 2004): low genetic variability is in this case aiding invasion. In contrast, a recent study of introduced aquatic species found that their population genetic diversity was much greater than expected, probably at least partly due to the high numbers of founders involved, such as of planktonic larvae in ballast water (Roman and Darling 2007).

Introduced species do not become invasive in isolation. Interactions between them, such as when one introduced species alters the environment structurally or in terms of resource availability in a way that favours another, can promote invasion (Box 4.2). For example, grazing deer open the under-storey and facilitate possum invasion in New Zealand, and introduced rats disperse seeds of introduced plants (Davis 2009). In the Galapagos Islands, the black rat, introduced about AD 1600, is being displaced by the brown rat, first recorded in the late 1980s and since dispersed to four islands in the archipelago. Where they occur together, the black rat becomes more arboreal and the brown rat becomes the only species to be found in houses. These two species force each other into more specialised niches, so their combined impact becomes greater (Key and Heredia 1994; Key and Woods 1996). Permanent populations of introduced prey can facilitate the establishment of an introduced predator or can maintain introduced predator populations over the lean season so that there are high numbers of them present whenever native prey increase, such as when seabirds return to breed.

In addition to threatening native species by hybridising with them, hybridisation with another invader or with a native species may also enable an invader to gain genetic variability and ecological vigour: the invasive saltmarsh grass *Spartina anglica*, which arose as a hybrid between an introduced and a native species, is a classic case of this (Ellstrand and Schierenbeck 2000; Cox 2004).

4.6 Why Are Islands More 'Invasible'?

Islands appear to be more vulnerable to invasion than continents (Kraus 2003; McGeoch et al. 2010), and island ecosystems seem more likely to suffer impacts from introductions partly because of their high proportions of endemic species with small populations. Island characteristics that make them susceptible to invasion include endemics that evolved in isolation (therefore naive to predators and competitors), few species (fewer competitors, so new arrivals can get a 'foot in the door') and ecological release, where introduced species are freed from the factors (predation, competition) that controlled their numbers in their native range (Cronk and Fuller 1995). These three intertwined factors contribute to the vulnerability of islands to invasions, even after controlling for propagule pressure (Pyšek and Richardson 2006). They are compounded by the high human population densities on islands, whose heavy modification of the landscape provides the disturbance and food that many new arrivals need: 14 of the top 20 most densely populated countries and territories in the world are islands (Cronk and Fuller 1995), and fragmented and disturbed habitats are more likely to be invaded (Andow 2003; Myers and Bazely 2003).

4.7 Are We Past the Worst?

Invasive species have had a devastating impact on island ecosystems in the past and continue to do so. The proportion of continental animals and plants already introduced to somewhere else averages less than 10 per cent (Jeschke and Strayer 2005), so there are plenty of new candidates for invasive species. Although there are signs that some introduction rates are declining, e.g. for a few vertebrate groups (Kraus 2003; Jeschke and Strayer 2005), in many more taxa this is not the case, and the highest introduction rates recorded are mostly those of the last 30 years.

The evidence also suggests that the rate at which species are being moved around and introduced has increased significantly in recent times. For example, in French Polynesia, the number of plant species introduced in the last 250 years (>1,700) is more than 20 times greater than the number (c. 80) introduced in the preceding 2,500 years (Meyer 2003; Fourdrigniez and Meyer 2008). Worldwide, the accidental introduction rates of amphibians and reptiles have increased greatly since 1983, and new introductions to islands via the pet trade are also likely to increase (Kraus 2003). Where measured, the rate of introduction of plants to islands has mostly been linear, with no sign of a decrease in recent years (Tye 2006; Sax and Gaines 2008); the recent high rates are primarily of ornamentals, of which many potential invaders are already present in cultivation on islands, thousands more species exist in trade and thousands more could become adopted or fashionable (e.g. Tye 2006; Meyer et al. 2008). The rate of establishment of marine invasive species in many seas appears to be exponential (Boudouresque et al. 2005). The world is still nowhere near homogeneous, and these patterns suggest that many more invasive species will become established on islands in the future (Kueffer et al. 2010).

The numbers of invasive species documented in most countries are clearly underestimates, and intensive surveys can double the previously known numbers (e.g. Guézou et al. 2010). Impacts on biodiversity are also likely to have been underestimated, at least in part owing to delays between recognising an invasive and documenting its impacts (McGeoch et al. 2010). So, as data quality increases, the known scale of the problem will also increase. In addition to simply improving knowledge about them, the impacts of invasive species on threatened species are genuinely increasing too, and where information on trends is available, it seems that the threat has increased steadily, with no sign of levelling off (McGeoch et al. 2010). An important difference between the effects of a new invasion and some other catastrophic environmental events such as fire or pollution is that the impact starts small and gets progressively worse, whereas the others start large and diminish over time. Consequently it may be more difficult to detect the multiple impacts of invasive species, until it is too late.

The impact of invasions on islands is higher than it might otherwise be, because island biodiversity is already stressed by human population pressures: habitat destruction, over-exploitation and climate change.

These stressors are also increasing, making islands progressively more vulnerable to invasion, rather than less so. Island habitat diversity, species abundance and distribution are all likely to change as a consequence of climate change, which is likely to contribute to habitat disturbance, making island systems even more vulnerable. For example, Madagascar is projected to lose 11–50 per cent of its remaining natural habitat (Hannah et al. 2008). Declines in precipitation in the Caribbean and other islands may lead to the migration of drier, lowland forests to higher altitudes and complete loss of high altitude rainforests. Conversely the distribution of the laurel forests of Macaronesia is likely to shift to lower altitudes as a consequence of a predicted drop in trade winds and lowering of the cloud-line (Sperling et al. 2004). Such habitat shifts may provide additional opportunities for invasive species. In any case, an increase in the spread of invasive species and diseases is a likely consequence of climate change, since most successful invasives are naturally adaptable species, and changing conditions favour adaptable species. Temperature and precipitation changes are likely to aid the spread of emerging infectious diseases, such as chytridiomycosis in amphibians. Diseases and their vectors will not only move between islands but also up existing islands as climate warms at higher altitudes. The current avian malaria ceiling on Hawaii's high islands may rise, threatening the survival of their remaining endemic birds. Climate change may enable a new set of invasive species to take hold of our island systems as environmental conditions shift in their favour.

On the other hand, many conservation successes (as measured by red-listed species moving from higher to lower categories of threat) result from effective management of invasive species that threaten endemic or native species (McGeoch et al. 2010), which highlights the potential of invasive species management as an effective biodiversity conservation tool (see Chapter 7). The prospects for habitat improvement and restoration (see Chapter 10) through invasive species management are excellent, and restoration plans are becoming both more ambitious and more confident (e.g. Hutton et al. 2007). Island conservationists can use these successes in arguments to persuade decision-makers to increase resources for invasive species management.

However, at present, the resources devoted to invasive species management are minuscule in proportion to the size of the problem, so the situation is rapidly getting worse. There is little sign of change in the pattern of resource allocation towards conservation, either by island nations or globally, on a scale that would enable the invasive species threat to island biodiversity to be adequately tackled. The prognosis at the moment is therefore poor, and fundamentally this cannot change until human values change (see Chapter 11).

4.8 Summary

Key points from this chapter:

- The arrival of species on new islands is an essential component of evolution. Current concern over invasive species stems from the exponentially increasing rate at which introductions are now occurring.
- Introduced species that become invasive cause loss of biodiversity through a range of forces and can also pose significant socioeconomic threats to human communities. Identifying which species may become invasive when introduced is important for prevention, the most cost-effective form of management.
- The intrinsic characteristics of a species that correlate with 'invasiveness' are dispersal mechanisms, reproduction and life-history traits, ecology and evolutionary potential.
- While our understanding of the impacts of invasive species has grown in recent years, there is little sign that the rate of their spread is decreasing. They are likely to become more of a global threat with climate change.

References

Agoramoorthy, G. and Hsu, M. J. (2007). Ritual releasing of wild animals threatens island ecology. *Human Ecology* 35: 251–54.
Álvarez-Castañeda, S. T. and Ortega-Rubio, A. (2003). Current status of rodents in the Gulf of California. *Biological Conservation* 109: 157–63.
Andow, D. A. (2003). Pathways-based risk assessment of exotic species invasions, Chapter 17 in G. M. Ruiz and J. T. Carlton (eds.), *Invasive Species: Vectors and Management Strategies*. Island Press, Washington, DC.
Asner, G. P., Hughes, R. F., Vitousek, P. M. et al. (2008). Invasive plants transform the three-dimensional structure of rain forests. *Proceedings of the National Academy of Sciences USA* 105: 4519–23.
Athens, J. S. (2009). *Rattus exulans* and the catastrophic disappearance of Hawaii's native lowland forest. *Biological Invasions* 11: 1489–501.
Atkinson, I. A. E. (1985). The spread of commensal species of *Rattus* to oceanic islands and their effect on island avifaunas, pp. 35–81 in P. J. Moors (ed.), *Conservation of Island Birds*. International Council for Bird Preservation, Cambridge.

Bell, B. D. (1978). The big South Cape Islands rat irruption, pp. 33–45 in P. R. Dingwall, I. A. E. Atkinson and C. Hay (eds.), *The Ecology and Control of Rodents in New Zealand Nature Reserves*. Information Series No. 4, Department of Lands and Survey, Wellington.

Bester, M. N., Bloomer, J.P., Bartlett, P.A. et al. (2000). Final eradication of feral cats from sub-Antarctic Marion Island, southern Indian Ocean. *South African Journal of Wildlife Research* 30: 53–57.

Bester, M. N., Bloomer, J. P., Aarde, R. J. V. et al. (2002). A review of the successful eradication of feral cats from sub-Antarctic Marion Island, southern Indian Ocean. *South African Journal of Wildlife Research* 32: 65–73.

Blackburn, T. M. and Duncan, R. P. (2001). Determinants of establishment success in introduced birds. *Nature* 414: 195–97.

Blackburn, T. M., Cassey, P., Duncan, R. P., Evans, K. L. and Gaston, K. J. (2004) Avian extinction and mammalian introductions on oceanic islands. *Science* 305: 1955–58.

Blackburn, T. M., Lockwood, J. L. and Cassey, P. (2009). *Avian Invasions: The Ecology and Evolution of Exotic Birds*. Oxford University Press, Oxford.

Boudouresque, C. F., Ruitton, S. and Verlaque, M. (2005). Large-scale disturbances, regime shift and recovery in littoral systems subject to biological invasions, pp. 85–101 in V. Velikova and N. Chipev (eds.), *Unesco-Roste/Bulgarian Academy of Sciences Workshop on Regime Shifts*, 14–16 June 2005, Varna.

Burbridge, A. A. and Manly, B. F. J. (2002). Mammal extinctions on Australian islands: causes and conservation implications. *Journal of Biogeography* 29: 465–73.

Carter, S. P. and Bright, P. W. (2002). Habitat refuges as alternatives to predator control for the conservation of endangered Mauritian birds, pp. 71–78 in C. R. Veitch and M.N. Clout (eds.), *Turning the Tide: The Eradication of Invasive Species*. IUCN, Gland.

Cassey, P., Blackburn, T. M., Russell, G., Jones, K. E. and Lockwood, J. L. (2004). Influences on the transport and establishment of exotic bird species: an analysis of the parrots (Psittaciformes) of the world. *Global Change Biology* 10: 417–26.

Causton, C. (2008). Risks associated with current and proposed air routes to the Galapagos Islands, pp. 55–59 in *Galapagos Report 2006–2007*. Charles Darwin Foundation, Puerto Ayora.

Caut, S., Angulo, E. and Courchamp, F. (2008). Dietary shift of an invasive predator: rats, seabirds and sea turtles. *Journal of Applied Ecology* 45: 428–37.

Charles, H. and Dukes, J. S. (2007). Impacts of invasive species on ecosystem services, pp. 217–37 in W. Nentwig (ed.), *Biological Invasions* (Ecological Studies Vol. 193). Springer, Berlin.

Cheke, A. and Hume, J. (2008) *Lost Land of the Dodo*. T & AD Poyser, London.

Clout, M. N. and Sarre, S. D. (1997). Model marsupial or menace? A review of research on brushtail possums in Australia and New Zealand. *Wildlife Society Bulletin* 25: 168–72.

Cole, N. C., Jones, C. G. and Harris, S. (2005). The need for enemy-free space: the impact of an invasive gecko on island endemics. *Biological Conservation* 125: 467–74.

Courchamp, F, Chapuis, J. L. and Pascal, M. (2003). Mammal invaders on islands: impact, control and control impact. *Biological Reviews* 78: 347–83.

Cox, G. W. (2004). *Alien Species and Evolution*. Island Press, Washington, DC.

Cronk, Q. C. B. and Fuller, J. L. (1995). *Plant Invaders: The Threat to Natural Ecosystems*. Springer, Berlin.

Daehler, C. C. (2009). Short lag times for invasive tropical plants: evidence from experimental plantings in Hawaii. *PLoS ONE* 4(2): e4462.

Daigneault, A., Brown, P., Greenhalgh, S. et al. (2013). *Valuing the Impact of Selected Invasive Species in the Polynesia-Micronesia Hotspot*. Landcare Research New Zealand, Lincoln.

D'Antonio, C. M. (2000). Fire, plant invasions and global changes, Chapter 4 in H. A. Mooney and R. J. Hobbs (eds.), *Invasive Species in a Changing World*. Island Press, Washington, DC.

Davis, M. A. (2009). *Invasion Biology*. Oxford University Press, Oxford.

Derraik, J. G. B. and Phillips, S. (2010). Online trade poses a threat to biosecurity in New Zealand. *Biological Invasions* 12: 1477–80.

Ding, J., Mack, R. N., Lu, P., Ren, M. and Huang, H. (2008). China's booming economy is sparking and accelerating biological invasions. *BioScience* 58: 317–24.

Drake, J. A., Mooney, H.A., di Castri, F. et al. (1989). *Biological Invasions: A Global Perspective*. Wiley, New York, NY.

Drake, J. M. and Jerde, C. L. (2009). Stochastic models of propagule pressure and establishment, pp. 83–102 in *Bioeconomics of Invasive Species: Integrating Ecology, Economics, Policy, and Management*. Oxford University Press, Oxford.

Dudaniec, R. Y. and Kleindorfer, S. (2006). The effects of the parasitic flies *Philornis* (Diptera: Muscidae) on birds. *Emu* 106: 13–20.

Duncan, R. P. (1997). The role of competition and introduction effort in the success of passeriform birds introduced to New Zealand. *American Naturalist* 149: 903–15.

Duncan, R. P., Bomford, M., Forsyth, D. M. and Conibear, L. (2001). High predictability in introduction outcomes and the geographical range size of introduced Australian birds: a role for climate. *Journal of Animal Ecology* 70: 621–32.

Ebenhard, T. (1988). Introduced birds and mammals and their ecological effects. *Swedish Wildlife Research* 13: 1–107.

Ehrlich, P. (1989). Attributes of invaders and the invading process: vertebrates, Chapter 13 in J. A. Drake, H. A. Mooney, F. di Castri et al. (eds.), *Biological Invasions: A Global Perspective*. Wiley, New York, NY.

Ellstrand, N. C. and Schierenbeck, K. A. (2000). Hybridization as a stimulus for the evolution of invasiveness in plants? *Proceedings of the National Academy of Sciences USA* 97: 7043–50.

Engeman, R. A., Rodriquez, D. V., Linnell, M. A. and Pitzler, M. E. (1998). A review of the case histories of the brown tree snakes (*Boiga irregularis*) located by detector dogs on Guam. *International Biodeterioration and Biodegradation* 42: 161–65.

Epler, B. (2007). *Tourism, the Economy, Population Growth, and Conservation in Galapagos*. Charles Darwin Foundation, Puerto Ayora.

Fessl, B., Young, H. G., Young, R. P. et al. (2010). How to save the rarest Darwin's finch from extinction: the mangrove finch on Isabela Island. *Philosophical Transactions of the Royal Society of London B: Biological Sciences* 365: 1019–30.

Fourdrigniez, M. and Meyer, J.-Y. (2008). Liste et caractéristiques des plantes introduites naturalisées et envahissantes en Polynésie française. Contribution à la Biodiversité de Polynésie française No. 17. Délégation à la Recherche, Pape'ete.

Fournier, D., Estoup, A., Orivel, J. et al. (2005). Clonal reproduction by males and females in the little fire ant. *Nature* 435(7046): 1230–34.

Gaertner, M., Den Bree, A., Hui, C. and Richardson, D. M. (2009). Impacts of alien plant invasions on species richness in Mediterranean-type ecosystems: a meta-analysis. *Progress in Physical Geography* 33: 319–38.

Gibbs, G. W. (2009). The end of an 80-million-year experiment: a review of evidence describing the impact of introduced rodents on New Zealand's 'mammal-free' invertebrate fauna. *Biological Invasions* 11: 1587–93.

Guézou, A., Trueman, M., Buddenhagen, C. E. et al. (2010). An extensive alien plant inventory from the inhabited areas of Galapagos. *PLoS One* 5(4): e10276.

Greenway, J. C., Jr. (1967). *Extinct and Vanishing Birds of the World*. Dover, New York, NY.

Gregory, S. D. and Macdonald, D. W. (2009). Prickly coexistence or blunt competition? Opuntia refugia in an invaded rodent community. *Oecologia* 159: 225–36.

Hadfield, M. G. and Saufler, J. E. (2009). The demographics of destruction: isolated populations of arboreal snails and sustained predation by rats on the island of Moloka'i 1982–2006. *Biological Invasions* 11: 1595–609.

Hannah, L., Dave, R., Lowry, P. P. et al. (2008). Climate change adaptation for conservation in Madagascar. *Biology Letters* 4: 590–94.

Hansen, D. M. and Muller, C. B. (2009). Invasive ants disrupt gecko pollination and seed dispersal of the endangered plant *Roussea simplex* in Mauritius. *Biotropica* 41: 202–8.

Harris, D. B. and Macdonald, D. W. (2007). Interference competition between introduced black rats and endemic Galapagos rice rats. *Ecology* 88: 2330–44.

Hayes, K. R. (2003). Biosecurity and the role of risk assessment, Chapter 15 in G. M. Ruiz and J. T. Carlton (eds.), *Invasive Species: Vectors and Management Strategies*. Island Press, Washington, DC.

Hilton, G. M. and Cuthbert, R. J. (2010). The catastrophic impact of invasive mammalian predators on birds of the UK Overseas Territories: a review and synthesis. *Ibis* 152: 443–58.

Hulme, P. E. (2009). Trade, transport and trouble: managing invasive species pathways in an era of globalization. *Journal of Applied Ecology* 46: 10–18.

Hunt, T. (2007). Rethinking Easter Island's ecological catastrophe. *Journal of Archaeological Science* 34: 485–502.

Hutton, I., Parkes, J. P. and Sinclair, A. R. E. (2007). Reassembling island ecosystems: the case of Lord Howe Island. *Animal Conservation* 10: 22–29.

INEC (2016). *Principales resultados, Censo de Población y Vivienda de Galápagos 2015*. Instituto Nacional de Estadísticas y Censos, Quito, Ecuador.

Jackson, D. B., Fuller, R. J. and Campbell, S. T. (2004). Long-term population changes among breeding shorebirds in the Outer Hebrides, Scotland, in relation to introduced hedgehogs (*Erinaceus europaeus*). *Biological Conservation* 117: 151–66.

Jäger, H., Tye, A. and Kowarik, I. (2007). Tree invasion in naturally treeless environments: impacts of quinine (*Cinchona pubescens*) trees on native vegetation in Galapagos. *Biological Conservation* 140: 297–307.

Jäger, H., Kowarik, I. and Tye, A. (2009). Destruction without extinction: long-term impacts of an invasive tree species on Galapagos highland vegetation. *Journal of Ecology* 97: 1252–63.

Jäger, H., Alencastro, M. J., Kaupenjohann, M. and Kowarik, I. (2013). Ecosystem changes in Galapagos highlands by the invasive tree *Cinchona pubescens*. *Plant and Soil* 371(1–2): 629–40.

Jeschke, J. M. and Strayer, D. L. (2005). Invasion success of vertebrates in Europe and North America. *Proceedings of the National Academy of Sciences USA* 102: 7198–202.

Jones, H. P., Tershy, B. R., Zavaleta, E. et al. (2008). Severity of the effects of invasive rats on seabirds: a global review. *Conservation Biology* 22: 16–26.

Kahl, S. S., Henke, S. E., Hall, M. A. and Britton, D. K. (2012). Brown treesnakes: a potential invasive species for the United States. *Human–Wildlife Interactions* 6: 181–203.

Kaiser, B. and Burnett, K. (2006). Economic impacts of *E. coqui* frogs in Hawaii. *Interdisciplinary Environment Review* 8: 1–11.

Kemp, N. J. and Burnett, J. B. (2003). *A Biodiversity Risk Assessment and Recommendations for Risk Management of Long-Tailed Macaques (Macaca fascicularis) in New Guinea*. Indo-Pacific Conservation Alliance, Washington, DC.

Key, G. E. (2000). St. Helena crop pests and diseases, in *An IPM Guide to Their Control*. IPM Project, Jamestown.

Key, G. E. and Heredia, E. M. (1994). Distribution and current status of rodents in the Galapagos islands. *Noticias de Galápagos* 53: 21–24.

Key, G. E. and Woods, R. D. (1996). Spool-and-line studies on the behavioural ecology of rats (*Rattus* spp.) in the Galapagos Islands. *Canadian Journal of Zoology* 74: 733–37.

Kilpatrick, A. M. (2006). Facilitating the evolution of resistance to avian malaria in Hawaiian birds. *Biological Conservation* 128: 475–85.

Kiritani, K. and Yamamura, K. (2003). Exotic insects and their pathways for invasion, Chapter 3 in G. M. Ruiz and J. T. Carlton (eds.), *Invasive Species: Vectors and Management Strategies*. Island Press, Washington, DC.

Kowarik, I. (2005). Urban ornamentals escaped from cultivation, pp. 97–121 in J. Gressel (ed.), *Crop Ferality and Volunteerism*. CRC Press, Boca Raton, FL.

Kraus, F. (2003). Invasion pathways for terrestrial vertebrates, Chapter 4 in G. M. Ruiz and J. T. Carlton (eds.), *Invasive Species: Vectors and Management Strategies*. Island Press, Washington, DC.

Kueffer, C., Daehler, C. C., Torres-Santana, C. W. et al. (2010). A global comparison of plant invasions on oceanic islands. *Perspectives in Plant Ecology, Evolution and Systematics* 12: 145–61.

Lever, C. (1994). *Naturalized Animals: The Ecology of Successfully Introduced Species*. T & AD Poyser, London.

Lodge, D. M., Lewis, M. A., Shogren, J. F. and Keller, R. P. (2009). Introduction to biological invasions: biological, economic, and social perspectives, Chapter 1 in R. P. Keller, D. M. Lodge, M. A. Lewis and J. F. Shogren (eds.), *Bioeconomics of Invasive Species: Integrating Ecology, Economics, Policy, and Management.* Oxford University Press, Oxford.

Long, J. L. (1981). *Introduced Birds of the World.* David & Charles, London.

(2003). *Introduced Mammals of the World: Their History, Distribution and Influence.* Centre for Agriculture and Bioscience International (CABI), London.

Mack, R. N. (2003). Global plant dispersal, naturalization and invasion: pathways, modes and circumstances, Chapter 1 in G. M. Ruiz and J. T. Carlton (eds.), *Invasive Species: Vectors and Management Strategies.* Island Press, Washington, DC.

Marler, T. E. and Lawrence, J. H. (2012). Demography of *Cycas micronesica* on Guam following introduction of the armoured scale *Aulacaspis yasumatsui. Journal of Tropical Ecology* 28: 233–42.

Marler, T. E. and Muniappan, R. (2006). Pests of *Cycas micronesica* leaf, stem, and male reproductive tissues with notes on current threat status. *Micronesica* 39: 1–9.

Martel, A. M., Blooi, C., Adriaensen, P. et al. (2014). Recent introduction of a chytrid fungus endangers Western Palearctic salamanders. *Science* 346(6209): 630–31.

McGeoch, M. A., Butchart, S. H. M., Spear, D. et al. (2010). Global indicators of biological invasion: species numbers, biodiversity impact and policy responses. *Diversity and Distributions* 16: 95–108.

McGregor, A. M. and Bishop, R. V. (2011). *A Technical Assessment of the Current Agricultural Conditions of Angaur Island Palau: With Recommendations for the Sustainable Use of the Island's Natural Resources.* GIZ, Koror.

Medina, F. M., Bonnaud, E., Vidal, E. et al. (2011). A global review of the impacts of invasive cats on island endangered vertebrates. *Global Change Biology* 17: 3503–10.

Meyer, J. Y. (2003). French Polynesia, pp. 22–28 in C. Shine, J. K. Reaser and A. T. Gutierrez (eds.), *Invasive Alien Species in the Austral Pacific Region: National Reports and Directory of Resources.* Global Invasive Species Programme, Cape Town.

Meyer, J. Y., Lavergne, C. and Hodel, D. R. (2008). Time bombs in islands: invasive ornamental palms in tropical islands, with emphasis on French Polynesia (Pacific Ocean) and the Mascarenes (Indian Ocean). *Palms* 52 (2): 71–82.

Moore, A., Marler, T., Miller, R. H. and Muniappan, R. (2005). Biological control of cycad aulacaspis scale on Guam. *Cycad Newsletter* 28: 6–8.

Morley, C. G. and Winder, L. (2013). The effect of the small Indian mongoose (*Urva auropunctatus*), island quality and habitat on the distribution of native and endemic birds on small islands within Fiji. *PLoS ONE* 8(1): e53842 (doi:10.1371/journal.pone.0053842).

Moulton, M. P., Cropper, W. P. and Avery, M. L. (2011). A reassessment of the role of propagule pressure in influencing fates of passerine introductions to New Zealand. *Biodiversity and Conservation* 20: 607–23.

Murphy, S. T. and Cheesman, O. D. (2006). The Aid Trade: International Assistance Programs as Pathways for the Introduction of Invasive Alien

Species. A Preliminary Report. World Bank Environment Department Papers No. 109, Washington, DC.

Mwebaze, P., MacLeod, A., Tomlinson, D., Barois, H. and Rijpma, J. (2010). Economic valuation of the influence of invasive alien species on the economy of the Seychelles Islands. *Ecological Economics* 12: 2614–23.

Myers, J. H. and Bazely, D. R. (2003). *Ecology and Control of Introduced Plants.* Cambridge University Press, Cambridge.

Naylor, R. L. (1996). Invasions in agriculture: assessing the cost of the golden apple snail in Asia. *Ambio* 25: 443–48.

O'Dowd, D. J., Green, P. T. and Lake, P. S. (2003). Invasional meltdown on an oceanic island. *Ecology Letters* 6: 812–17.

Oerke, E. C. (2006). Crop losses to pests. *Journal of Agricultural Science* 144: 31–43.

Oerke, E. C., Dehne, H. W., Schonbeck, F. and Weber, A. (1994). *Crop Production and Crop Protection: Estimated Losses in Major Food and Cash Crops.* Elsevier, Amsterdam.

Parkes, J. and Fisher, P. (2011). *Feasibility of eradicating long-tailed macaques (Macaca fascicularis) from the islands of Palau.* Landcare Research New Zealand, Lincoln.

Peh, K. S. H., Balmford, A., Birch, J. C. et al. (2015). Potential impact of invasive non-native species on ecosystem services provided by a forested ecosystem: a case study from Montserrat. *Biological Invasions* 17: 461–75.

Pejchar, L. and Mooney, H. A. (2009). Invasive species, ecosystem services and human well-being. *Trends in Ecology and Evolution* 24: 497–504.

Phillips, B. L., Brown, G. P., Webb, J. K. and Shine, R. (2006). Invasion and the evolution of speed in toads. *Nature* 439: 803.

Pimentel, D., McNair, S., Janecka, J. et al. (2001). Economic and environmental threats of alien plant, animal and microbe invasions. *Agriculture, Ecosystems and Environment* 84: 1–20.

Pimentel, D., Zuniga, R. and Morrison, D. (2005). Update on the environmental and economic costs associated with alien-invasive species in the United States. *Ecological Economics* 52: 273–88.

Plentovich, S., Hebshi, A. and Conant, S. (2008). Detrimental effects of two widespread invasive ant species on weight and survival of colonial nesting seabirds in the Hawaiian Islands. *Biological Invasions* 11: 289–98.

Porter, D. M. (1983). Vascular plants of the Galapagos: origins and dispersal, pp. 33–96 in R. I. Bowman, M. Berson and A. E. Leviton (eds.), *Patterns of Evolution in Galapagos Organisms.* American Association for the Advancement of Science, San Francisco, CA.

Powell, R. and Henderson, R. W. (2005). Conservation status of Lesser Antillean reptiles. *Iguana* 12: 62–77.

Pyšek, P. and Richardson, D. M. (2006). The biogeography of naturalization in alien plants. *Journal of Biogeography* 33: 2040–50.

    (2007). Traits associated with invasiveness in alien plants: where do we stand?, pp. 97–125 in W. Nentwig (ed.), *Biological Invasions* (Ecological Studies 193). Springer, Berlin.

Raizada, P., Raghubanshi, A. S. and Singh, J. S. (2008). Impact of invasive alien plant species on soil processes: a review. *Proceedings of the National Academy of Sciences India Section B: Biological Sciences* 78: 288–98.

Reeder, T., Dessauer, H. C. and Cole, C. J. (2002). Phylogenetic relationships of whiptail lizards of the genus *Cnemidophorus* (Squamata, Teiidae): a test of monophyly, reevaluation of karyotypic evolution, and review of hybrid origins. *American Museum Novitates* 3365: 1–61.

Reinhart, K., Gurnee, O. J., Tirado, R. and Callaway, R. M. (2006). Invasion through quantitative effects: intense shade drives native decline and invasive success. *Ecological Applications* 16: 1821–31.

Rhymer, J. M. and Simberloff, D. (1996). Extinction by hybridization and introgression. *Annual Review of Ecological Systems* 27: 83–109.

Richardson, D. M., Pysek, P., Rejmánek, M. et al. (2000). Naturalization and invasion of alien plants: concepts and definitions. *Diversity and Distributions* 6: 93–107.

Rodda, G. H. and Savidge, J. A. (2007). Biology and impacts of Pacific invasive species: 2. *Boiga irregularis*, the brown tree snake (Reptilia: Colubridae). *Pacific Science* 61(3): 307–24.

Rodda, G. H., Fritts, T. H. and Conry, P. J. (1992). Origin and population growth of the brown tree snake, *Boiga irregularis*, on Guam. *Pacific Science* 46: 46–57.

Roman, J. and Darling, J. A. (2007). Paradox lost: genetic diversity and the success of aquatic invasions. *Trends in Ecology and Evolution* 22: 454–64.

Roque-Albelo, L., Lomas Chauca, E. and Castillo Gaona, O. (2009). Dispersal of insect species attracted to ship lights: conservation implications for Galapagos, pp. 107–9 in *Galapagos Report 2007–2008*. Charles Darwin Foundation, Puerto Ayora.

Ruiz, G. M. and Carlton, J. T. (eds.) (2003). *Invasive Species: Vectors and Management Strategies*. Island Press, Washington, DC.

Safford, R. J. (1997). Nesting success of the Mauritius fody *Foudia rubra* in relation to its use of exotic trees as nest sites. *Ibis* 139: 555–59.

Savidge, J. A. (1987). Extinction of an island forest avifauna by an introduced snake. *Ecology* 68: 660–68.

Sax, D. F. and Gaines, S. D. (2008). Species invasions and extinction: the future of native biodiversity on islands. *Proceedings of the National Academy of Sciences USA* 105(1): 11490–97.

Severinghaus, L. L. and Chi, L. (1999). Prayer animal release in Taiwan. *Biological Conservation* 89: 301–4.

Shluker, A. D. (2003). *State of Hawaii Aquatic Invasive Species Management Plan*. Department of Land and Natural Resources, Division of Aquatic Resources, Honolulu, HI.

Siguan, M. A. R. (2003). Pathways of biological invasions of marine plants, Chapter 8 in G. M. Ruiz and J. T. Carlton (eds.), *Invasive Species: Vectors and Management Strategies*. Island Press, Washington, DC.

Simberloff, D. (1989). Which insect introductions succeed and which fail?, Chapter 3 in J. A. Drake, H. A. Mooney, F. di Castri et al. (eds.), *Biological Invasions: A Global Perspective*. Wiley, New York, NY.

Snell, H. L., Tye, A., Causton, C. E. and Bensted-Smith, R. (2002). The status of and threats to terrestrial biodiversity, pp. 30–47 in R. Bensted-Smith (ed.), *A Biodiversity Vision for the Galapagos Islands*. Charles Darwin Foundation, Puerto Ayora.

Sperling, F. N., Washington, R. and Whittaker, R. J. (2004). Future climate change of the subtropical North Atlantic: implications for the cloud forests of Tenerife. *Climatic Change* 65: 103–23.

Towns, D. R. (2002). Interactions between geckos, honeydew scale insects and host plants revealed on island in northern New Zealand, following eradication of introduced rats and rabbits, pp 329–35 in C. R. Veitch and M.N. Clout (eds.), *Turning the Tide: The Eradication of Invasive Species*. IUCN, Gland.

Towns, D. R. and Broome, K. G. (2003). From small Maria to massive Campbell: forty years of rat eradications from New Zealand islands. *New Zealand Journal of Zoology* 30: 377–98.

Towns, D. R., Atkinson, I. A. E. and Daugherty, C. H. (2006). Have the harmful effects of introduced rats on islands been exaggerated?. *Biological Invasions* 8: 863–91.

Tuttle, N. C., Beard, K. H. and Pitt, W. C. (2009). Invasive litter, not an invasive insectivore, determines invertebrate communities in Hawaiian forests. *Biological Invasions* 11: 845–55.

Tye, A. (2006). Can we infer island introduction and naturalization rates from inventory data? Evidence from introduced plants in Galapagos. *Biological Invasions* 8: 201–15.

Van Aarde, R. J. (1978): Reproduction and population ecology in the female house cat *Felis catus* on Marion Island. *Carnivora Genetics Newsletter* 3: 288–316.

Van Aarde, R. J. and Robinson, T. J. (1980). Gene frequencies in feral cats on Marion Island. *Journal of Heredity* 71: 366–68.

VanderWerf, E. (2007). *2005 Bird Surveys in the Republic of Palau*. US Fish and Wildlife Service, Honolulu, HI.

Vilà, M., Basnou, C., Pyšek, P. et al. (2010). How well do we understand the impacts of alien species on ecosystem services? A pan-European, cross-taxa assessment. *Frontiers in Ecology and Environment* 8: 135–44.

Vitousek, P. M., Walker, L. R., Whiteaker, L. D., Mueller-Dombois, D. and Matson, P. A. (1987). Biological invasion by *Myrica faya* alters ecosystem development in Hawaii. *Science* 238: 802–4.

Watkins, B. P. and Cooper, J. (1986). Introduction, present status and control of alien species at the Prince Edward Islands. *South African Journal of Antarctic Research* 16: 86–94.

Waugh, J. (2009). *Trade and Invasive Species in the Caribbean: A Universe of Risk.*, IUCN, Gland.

Wetterer, J. K. (2007). Biology and impacts of Pacific Island invasive species: 3. The African big-headed ant, *Pheidole megacephala* (Hymenoptera: Formicidae). *Pacific Science* 61: 437–56.

Wiles, G. J., Bart, J., Beck, R. E. and Aguon, C. F. (2003). Impacts of the brown tree snake: patterns of decline and species persistence in Guam's avifauna. *Conservation Biology* 17: 1350–60.

Williams, F., Eschen, R., Harris, A. et al. (2010). *The Economic Cost of Invasive Non-Native Species on Great Britain*. CABI, Wallingford, CT.

Williamson, M. (1996). *Biological Invasions*. Chapman & Hall, London.

   (2001). Can the impacts of invasive species be predicted?, Chapter 3 in R. H. Groves, F. D. Panette and J. G. Virtue (eds.), *Weed Risk Assessment*.

Commonwealth Scientific and Industrial Research Organisation (CSIRO), Canberra.

Wittenberg, R. and Cock, M. J. W. (eds.) (2001). *Invasive Alien Species: A Toolkit of Best Prevention and Management Practices*. CAB International, Oxford.

Woods, M., McDonald, R. A. and Harris, S. (2003). Predation of wildlife by domestic cats *Felis catus* in Great Britain. *Mammal Review* 33: 174–88.

WTO (2013). *World Trade Report 2013*. World Trade Organisation, Geneva.

WTTC (2014). *Economic Impact of Travel and Tourism 2014 Annual Update: Summary*. World Travel and Tourism Council, London.

5 · *Documenting Change on Islands*
Measuring and Diagnosing Species Decline

RICHARD P. YOUNG, JAMIESON A.
COPSEY AND SAMUEL T. TURVEY

5.0 Introduction

In order to decide when and how to act to save species threatened with
extinction, we need to understand the current size and distribution of
populations and, most importantly, why they are in decline or what is
limiting their recovery. However, to truly understand the status of
species and why they are threatened, it is important, where possible, to
look back and consider their ecological histories in order to set any
conservation decisions within a long-term context.

This chapter begins with a critical review of the approaches used to
reconstruct population histories in order to understand past ecological
baselines and help diagnose causes of decline, drawing on examples from
islands. We consider the use of qualitative data and diverse information
sources to reach further back in time and reconstruct ecological histories.
We then review the various methods and approaches available today for
surveying and monitoring species to build up our understanding of
population changes, from citizen science to sophisticated monitoring
techniques that account for imperfect detection. In this section we then
review the attributes of effective monitoring programmes to help scientists
and practitioners design schemes that are likely to meet their research or
management goals and that can be sustained. Finally, we discuss how
causes of threatened species decline can be identified or inferred.

5.1 Reconstructing Species Population Histories

Human impacts on island faunas and floras are not restricted to the recent
past. Instead, anthropogenic activities have affected island species and

ecosystems throughout much of the Late Quaternary, following prehistoric human arrival on different island groups during the Late Pleistocene and Holocene from ~40,000 years onwards (Turvey 2009). The recent fossil/subfossil record (representing non-anthropogenic or 'natural' bone deposition) and zooarchaeological record (representing anthropogenically mediated bone deposition) together provide ample evidence that the Late Quaternary island ecosystems encountered by the first colonists and settlers were typically drastically different to what we see today, with human arrival almost always leading to major changes in insular biodiversity and ecosystem processes (Worthy and Holdaway 2002; Steadman 2006a; Cheke and Hume 2008; Turvey 2009).

The majority of research into past human-caused extinctions in island faunas has focused on describing now-extinct species and attempting to reconstruct their extinction chronologies in relation to the past timing of different putative threat factors. This research is still nowhere near complete for many island systems; for example, extrapolation-based estimates suggest that as many as 8,000 bird species or discrete island populations, including 2,000 flightless rails, may have become extinct across the insular tropical Pacific following Polynesian expansion across this region during the Late Holocene (Steadman 1995). These estimates were based on extrapolation from the number of extinct or locally extirpated bird species identified from subfossil remains on seven islands within the central Pacific. Assuming that 10 species became extinct on each of the Pacific's 800 major islands (50 per cent of the number found to have become extinct or locally extirpated from the seven sampled islands), Steadman (1995) was able to arrive at the figure of 8,000 species lost, which represents roughly 80 per cent of the current total number of bird species identified globally. While this figure may well represent an overestimate (see Turvey (2009) for further discussion), it highlights both the potential scale of biodiversity loss experienced historically on island systems, and the value of the subfossil record as a source of unique information on the magnitude and potential causes of species declines that we only see the results of today.

5.1.1 The Fossil and Zooarchaeological Records

There is increasing awareness among both palaeontologists and conservation practitioners that the recent fossil and zooarchaeological records represent important sources of data for evidence-based conservation, as

Figure 5.1 Abbott's booby *Papasula abbotti*, a species known from subfossil remains distributed across the Indian and Pacific oceans but currently restricted to Christmas Island (Indian Ocean). (*Photo credit:* Alan Tate.)

they can provide a unique long-term perspective on past patterns of biodiversity change that can potentially be integrated into modern-day environmental management (e.g. Lauwerier and Plug 2004; Jackson and Hobbs 2009; Louys 2012). In particular, the spatial distribution of fossil and zooarchaeological remains can provide novel insights into past patterns of species decline that are unavailable from other contexts. For example, Abbott's booby *Papasula abbotti* (Figure 5.1) today occurs only on Christmas Island in the Indian Ocean, where it is threatened by deforestation and invasive species, although it was described from a specimen collected in the nineteenth century from Assumption Island (also in the Indian Ocean), where it has now been extirpated (Steadman 2006a). On the basis of recent historical data alone, it would appear that Abbott's booby still survives across 50 per cent of its former range. However, relatively recent skeletal remains of this species are also known from Holocene fossil deposits on Mauritius and Rodrigues, which supports seventeenth- and eighteenth-century historical accounts of birds resembling Abbott's booby from the Mascarenes (Cheke and Hume 2008), as well as from pre-European Holocene archaeological sites on Tikopia (Santa Cruz Group, Solomon Islands) and Efate

(Vanuatu); the bones of an extinct subspecies *P. abbotti costelloi* have also been reported from similar sites on Tahuata, Hiva Oa and Ua Huka (Marquesas) (Steadman 2006a). These records therefore provide the only evidence that Abbott's booby once had an extremely wide range across the tropical Indian and Pacific oceans until human arrival across this region and that its current-day distribution is greatly reduced and relictual. Many other island bird species have similarly relictual distributions today, often restricted to just one or two small islands, but were much more widespread at the time of regional first human arrival; this phenomenon is referred to as 'pseudo-endemism' (Steadman 2006b).

Spatial information about recent fossil sites can provide unique insights into the ecology as well as the geography of past population declines, with important implications for modern-day conservation management. For example, the takahe *Porphyrio hochstetteri* is a flightless New Zealand bird that is extremely vulnerable to predation by introduced mammalian predators. The only surviving wild population occurs above the tree line of the South Island's Southern Alps, and this distribution led some researchers to consider that the species was a grassland-feeding specialist adapted to the alpine region (Mills et al. 1984). Takahe are relatively abundant in New Zealand's Holocene fossil record, but their remains are instead predominantly found at low-elevation sites characterised by a habitat mosaic of forest, shrub and grassland, indicating that their current-day distribution represents a relict population surviving in suboptimal habitat (Trewick and Worthy 2001).

In addition to providing data on spatial patterns of decline, the recent fossil and zooarchaeological records can also provide some insights into past rates and drivers of decline, although such data can be harder to interpret. This is in part because of the substantial variation in rates of species decline in relation to different anthropogenic threats and different ecological conditions (Diamond 1989). If past population declines are rapid and closely correlated temporally with the appearance of a novel anthropogenic process in the recent fossil or zooarchaeological record, then it can often be relatively straightforward to identify likely drivers of the decline. As an example, moa (giant ratites) are often extremely common in pre-human Holocene fossil sites and are also present in the earliest archaeological layers associated with Maori occupation of New Zealand, whereas abundant later pre-European archaeological sites lack any evidence of moa. Radiocarbon dating of prehistoric Maori sites with and without moa remains, coupled with population modelling, indicates that moa probably disappeared within 100 years of first Maori arrival in New Zealand as a result of unsustainably high levels of overexploitation for food (Holdaway and Jacomb 2000). Similar patterns of rapid extinction following first human arrival can also be reconstructed from the Holocene record for other species, such as the giant meiolaniid horned turtles of Vanuatu (White et al. 2010). Megafaunal species on other islands, such as the giant lemurs and elephant birds of Madagascar, instead persisted for a millennium or more following first regional human arrival, as demonstrated by available radiocarbon dates (Burney et al. 2004), indicating that different insular megafaunas displayed considerable variation in extinction dynamics on different island systems. Persistence of several now-extinct species into the recent European historical era can also often be demonstrated on the basis of co-occurrence of extinct species with historically introduced black rats *Rattus rattus* in cave deposits (MacPhee and Flemming 1999).

Data from the recent fossil record can also provide important new insights into other aspects of conservation management for many island systems, notably by identifying former ecosystem processes and defining environmental baselines for restoration ecology (see Chapter 10). A good example of this is the use of recent fossil data to inform introduction of non-native extant giant tortoises to Round Island in the Mascarenes to restore plant–tortoise interactions disrupted following the human-caused extinction of the region's endemic giant tortoises (Griffiths et al. 2011). However, it is important to recognise that even the recent fossil record is highly incomplete and so cannot provide useful data on many aspects of past species declines. Reconstruction of spatial declines is usually restricted to identifying changes in the extent of occurrence rather than the area of occupancy, i.e. overall range contraction rather than any accompanying range fragmentation (see IUCN 2001), due to poor data resolution. Determining past distributions can also be confused by prehistoric translocations of species between different islands as long ago as the Late Pleistocene (e.g. *Thylogale* forest pademelon populations between islands in the New Guinea Archipelago; Macqueen et al. 2011).

Bayesian analysis of radiocarbon dates has been used to try to identify the magnitude and duration of population declines as well as final extinction dates. Attempts to reconstruct past declines using data from the fossil and zooarchaeological records are typically restricted to temporal correlation between first decline or final disappearance of a specific taxon and appearance of a new anthropogenic threat process, even when rigorous Bayesian approaches are employed (e.g. Holdaway et al. 2002). Even last-occurrence dates for charismatic, well-studied taxa such as large carnivores in the United Kingdom (e.g. lynx, *Lynx lynx*; Hetherington 2010) remain poorly understood, and it is usually not possible to develop a meaningful understanding of any changes in population abundance that have occurred since recent prehistory for species of conservation concern. The abundance of different species varies markedly in the fossil record, but this is strongly influenced by secondary taphonomic (preservation and excavation) processes (e.g. how habitat type in which an individual organism dies will influence long-term preservation) rather than the original composition of source communities. Indeed, factors such as body mass, specific ecological conditions and past patterns of human exploitation typically play a more important role in determining likelihood of preservation than original population abundance (Turvey and Blackburn 2011).

5.1.2 Historical Accounts

The more recent historical record, representing a diverse series of data sources such as eyewitness accounts, museum specimens and bounty records, has the potential to provide higher-resolution and more accurate information for establishing baselines for population monitoring and understanding patterns of species declines. Extensive data sets on associated human pressures to island environments, such as historical levels and patterns of deforestation, are also often available for this period. For example, detailed records of changing environmental conditions during recent centuries are available for the West Indies, as islands were progressively cleared for sugarcane plantations (Watts 1987; Funes Monzote 2008).

In some cases, the historical record has been able to provide a useful source of quantitative data that has permitted detailed understanding of past declines and extinction dynamics. Tasmanian government bounty statistics for Tasmanian tiger or thylacine *Thylacinus cynocephalus* from 1888–1908 have been used to develop an integrated bio-economic model by Bulte et al. (2003), which suggested that this level of persecution on its own was very unlikely to have driven thylacines to extinction. Conversely, population modelling using available hunting data demonstrated that overexploitation alone was responsible for the extremely rapid extinction of the final relict populations of Steller's sea cow *Hydrodamalis gigas* around Bering and Copper islands, with no need to invoke further ecosystem cascades driven by the additional removal of sea

Figure 5.2 Hispaniolan solenodon *Solenodon paradoxus*, one of Hispaniola's only two surviving non-volant land mammals. (*Photo credit:* Jose Nuñez-Miño.)

otters from inshore marine ecosystems (Turvey and Risley 2006). Statistical approaches for inferring extinction dates, notably optimal linear estimation (a technique based on the temporal spacing of historical sighting records), have also been applied to understand extinction events in island faunas (Roberts and Solow 2003; Solow 2005).

Unfortunately, the historical record often fails to provide data that are much more robust or informative for understanding past population declines than can be provided by the recent fossil or zooarchaeological records. Older historical accounts in particular can be very hard to interpret or integrate into modern conservation management and can often present challenges even in terms of identifying which threatened or possibly extinct species are being referred to, especially when names are used without any accompanying description. For example, the sixteenth-century Spanish chronicler Oviedo described four land mammal species on Hispaniola, the *hutia, quemi, mohuy* and *cori* (Miller 1929), although Hispaniola today has only two surviving native non-volant land mammals, making this historical account of potential importance for understanding the timing of extinction for other representatives of the island's formerly diverse mammal fauna (Box 5.2; Figure 5.2). However, the animals reported by Oviedo cannot easily be identified to species level, and were discussed largely in terms of how good they were to eat rather than more useful diagnostic or ecological characteristics. Further complications in interpreting historical records at face value are caused by simultaneous use of the same name for different species, and name transfer. A well-known example of this latter phenomenon is the use of the word 'dodo' or its derivative forms to refer to the unrelated but equally flightless Mauritius red hen *Aphanapteryx bonasia* by contemporary local observers following the decline and extinction of the 'real' dodo *Raphus cucullatus* (Cheke 2006; see Box 1.2). Further problems for using historical data to understand population declines are caused by unavoidable variation in past survey effort, which can lead to considerable but largely unquantifiable biases in detection probability over time. Any interpretation of historical data at face value in this way, for example in optimal linear estimation, cannot overcome these persistent problems of variable data quality and potential misidentification.

More recent historical records can often provide more accurate and potentially detailed data on past distributions of threatened species, permitting reconstruction of spatial changes in species distributions during recent centuries. However, even relatively recent records are still usually unable to provide quantitative data on past species abundances. Historical accounts by Western observers into the twentieth century typically refer to species abundances using relative terms such as 'rare' or 'common' (e.g. Chouteau et al. 2012), providing opportunities for only coarse calibration of past changes in abundance patterns for species of interest or conservation concern. Similar problems can make it difficult or impossible to accurately interpret supposedly quantitative data even for studies from recent decades. The challenges of using such data are illustrated by attempts to understand patterns of population decline in the Hainan gibbon *Nomascus hainanus*, today the world's rarest and most threatened primate species. Nineteenth- and early twentieth-century reports merely refer to the species as being 'very rare' (e.g. Beddard 1905). The first quantitative estimate of gibbon population numbers was made by Liu et al. (1984), who stated that during the early 1950s, there had been 2,000 gibbons left on Hainan but did not give any explanation for the basis of this population estimate. Further studies during the 1980s and 1990s (e.g. Liu et al. 1989; Zhang and Sheeran 1993; Zhou et al. 2005) provided varying estimates of the number of both gibbons and gibbon social groups left in Bawangling National Nature Reserve, the final refuge for the species on Hainan.

Figure 5.3 Anonymous engraving of Dutch activity on Mauritius in 1598 from Het Tvveede. Note early engraving of a dodo (centre left), suggesting that the species once occupied coastal habitats. (*Photo credit:* Julian Pender Hume, private collection.)

They provided little or no information on key parameters such as survey method or effort, meaning that the accuracy, assumptions and biases of all these studies and their conclusions cannot be evaluated; their usefulness for informing ongoing recovery efforts for the Hainan gibbon is therefore unfortunately reduced.

Contemporary pictorial or sculptural reconstructions can also be useful in understanding the morphology and ecology of extinct taxa (Figure 5.3). An examination of early illustrations and a sculpture of the extinct raven parrot *Lophopsittacus mauritianus* from Mauritius and comparison with extant parrots demonstrated that this species had a well-developed alula and short, rounded wings, dispelling previous suggestions that it was flightless (Cheke 1987; Cheke and Hume 2008; Figure 5.4). This approach of using reconstructions to understand function is well developed in archaeology and can provide assistance in interpreting the morphology of extinct species. Insights into the ecological function of extinct species are particularly important for identifying modern-day analogues to occupy the former niches of such species (see Section 10.5).

Figure 5.4 The extinct raven parrot *Lophopsittacus mauritianus* of Mauritius, a species whose ecology and morphology have been hypothesised through examination of an early sculpture and sketches. (*Photo credit:* Julian Pender Hume.) (A black-and-white version of this figure will appear in some formats. For the colour version, please refer to the plate section.)

Finally, old maps can also help to assess broad changes in species ranges and habitats, as place names can give insights into past species distributions. For example, several small islands off Mauritius are named after the birds that once nested or roosted there, giving valuable information on the former marine and coastal bird community, e.g. Ile aux Aigrettes (dimorphic egret *Egretta dimorpha*), Ile aux Fouquets (wedge-tailed shearwater *Puffinus pacificus*), Roche des Fous (masked booby *Sula dactylatra*) and Ilot Marianne (brown noddy *Anous stolidus*) (Cheke and Hume 2008).

5.1.3 Traditional and Local Ecological Knowledge

Species that are very visible or vocal, have cultural significance or are harvested may be well known to local people using the same environments (Figure 5.5). Relevant information can represent either local ecological

Figure 5.5 Community-based data collection of local ecological knowledge, Haiti, 2007. (*Photo credit:* Samuel Turvey.)

knowledge, i.e. experiential knowledge derived from lived interactions with local environments and able to provide information about the contemporary status of target species and ecological resources, or traditional ecological knowledge, i.e. the cumulative body of ecological knowledge and belief passed down between generations by cultural transmission. Patterns and levels of interaction with local environments (e.g. occupation, time spent in forests), duration that they have lived in the local area, and cultural and/or ethnic background and accompanying traditions can all contribute to the value of untrained informants as sources of information for documenting past and present species status (Turvey et al. 2014) and how environmental change over time (e.g. climate change) may be influencing species status (see Section 11.6).

Asking people to recall former species occurrences, the timing of past species losses or other changes in diversity or wider environmental conditions through time is not without its biases. There are basic concerns around both the accuracy of species identification by untrained non-scientists, who may use ethnozoological classification systems that do not correspond with scientific taxonomies, and also accurate recall of the timing of past events. Informants may also consciously or unconsciously exaggerate or overestimate for a variety of reasons (e.g. to please the interviewer, possibly for perceived reward), and some socio-economic informant groups may have an increased tendency for such overestimation (Lunn and Dearden 2006). Conversely, informants may choose to underestimate abundance or underreport species encounters, particularly when activities associated with these counts are illegal (e.g. hunting particular species). However, under certain conditions at least, data on threatened species provided by untrained informants can be accurate and of importance for conservation management.

5.1.4 Genetic Approaches

The different approaches for reconstructing past declines that have been described so far all rely on using comparative data that were either collected by past observers or represent the remains of animals that existed in the past. However, novel insights into the magnitude and timing of past population declines can also be obtained through genetic analysis (see Section 3.2), in particular through the use of Bayesian statistical analysis of allelic distributions. This approach can permit the estimation both of different past and present population sizes and of the time (in generations) since demographic change in population size. For example, Goossens et al. (2006) used three complementary approaches for analysing the largest-ever set of genetic samples from wild orang-utan *Pongo pygmaeus* populations to detect, quantify and date population decline, revealing not only that orang-utans in north-eastern Borneo have decreased by more than 95 per cent but that this decline is largely attributable to habitat destruction experienced within the last few decades (Box 5.1). Ongoing advances in genetic analysis promise further novel applications for reconstructing and understanding the dynamics of past population declines. It should also be noted that as well as reconstructing past demographic change, genetic status (e.g. low levels of heterozygosity and high levels of inbreeding) can in itself compromise populations and potentially contribute to their decline (Frankham 1995; see Chapter 3).

5.2 Measuring Population Change

In most species conservation programmes, a significant effort will (or should) be invested in determining ongoing changes in population size or geographic range through monitoring. In this chapter, while we

Box 5.1 *Genetic Modelling of Population Decline and Likely Causes in Bornean Orang-utans*

Orang-utans are the only great apes found outside Africa. During the Pleistocene Epoch (~2.5 Mya to 11,700 years ago), they were distributed throughout south-east Asia from China to the islands of Sumatra, Java and Borneo, but today the three extant species, *Pongo abelii, P. pygmaeus* and *P. tapanuliensis*, are restricted to northern Sumatra and Borneo. Ongoing habitat fragmentation, forest loss and conversion of cleared land for oil palm plantations, together with illegal hunting and collection for the pet trade, threaten the survival of these species and continue to fragment populations. One estimate from Sumatra (Leuser area) suggests that between 1993 and 2000, 1,000 orang-utans were killed annually from a population of approximately 12,000 in the early 1990s (Robertson and van Schaik 2001; van Schaik et al. 2001; Wich et al. 2003).

What has remained unclear until recently is the original size of orang-utan populations, the magnitude of the current downward population trajectory, and its primary underlying causes and timing of initial decline. One extrapolation suggests that there were still more than 20,000 orang-utans as recently as the 1980s (Payne 1987), although this figure may be overoptimistic (Rijksen and Meijaard 1999). Other projections trace the start of the decline back to the arrival of the first hunter-gatherers in south-east Asia 40,000 years ago (Cribb 2000) and associated hunting of orang-utans over tens of millennia (Goossens et al. 2006). Climate change has also been implicated as a possible driver of the original decline, in addition to driving population changes in other Asian mammals (Warrens et al. 2001). By dating the start of the ongoing population decline, it will be possible to begin to understand the relative impacts of the shifting threats to orang-utans.

Goosens et al. (2006) collected faecal and hair samples from wild orang-utans along the Kinabatangan River, eastern Sabah (Borneo), and identified 200 different individuals from these samples using microsatellite data. Three complementary methods were used to detect, quantify and date the decline in orang-utan populations through the development of predictive models of population change. The first method looked at allelic frequencies based on the assumption that rare alleles will be lost or gained more rapidly than changes in heterozygosity depending on whether a population has gone through a bottleneck or has experienced demographic expansion. The extent to which allele frequencies differ from simulated mutation models is used to predict population decline or expansion. The other two methods used Bayesian statistics and genealogical modelling (Beaumont 1999; Storz and Beaumont 2002) and, using the full range of allelic distributions available in the samples collected, focused on the estimated difference between historical and present population size. The combination of these methods enabled prediction of both the extent of orang-utan population decline and the time frame over which it has occurred.

The results from these three genetic investigations provided evidence that the orang-utan populations studied have declined by more than 95 per cent, with the majority of this decline having occurred within the last few decades, coinciding with a recent massive regional increase in deforestation. Manipulations of the models to account for prehistoric change with the arrival of the first hunter-gathers or climate change failed to explain the genetic structure observed today. Additional genetic analysis revealed that levels of heterozygosity within the remaining populations in Kinabatangan remain high (again suggesting a recent rather than prolonged population crash), giving hope that if conservation action is taken swiftly to reconnect the isolated pockets of habitat, orang-utan populations can still be recovered.

This case study neatly illustrates the value of genetic analyses as a tool to inform our understanding of population change and its likely causes, complementing more direct field observations and inferences made from different information sources (for further details of the methods used, see Goossens et al. 2006).

recognise the distinction between surveillance and monitoring provided by Sutherland (2006), we treat monitoring in the broadest sense, i.e. repeated surveying of a population parameter of interest with respect to a target (i.e. the size or change in a population that is considered desirable) and in situations where no specific target is set (surveillance). Often long-term monitoring will be required to reliably detect and demonstrate population declines and understand their drivers. A good illustration of such long-term data collation is provided for native and introduced birds

Box 5.2 *Ancient Evolutionary Heritage of Caribbean Insular Mammals*

The Caribbean islands were formerly home to approximately 120 different endemic species of non-volant land mammals, comprising sloths, primates, rodents and lipotyphlan insectivores. However, this unique fauna has experienced a massive level of anthropogenically mediated extinction following Amerindian arrival around 6,000 years ago and subsequent European arrival around 500 years ago, with only a handful of endemic species persisting to the present (Turvey 2009). Only two of the region's four original solenodon species still survive, one on Hispaniola (*Solenodon paradoxus*, Figure 5.2, in Dominican Republic and Haiti) and the other on Cuba (*Atopogale cubana*).

These large insectivore species display unusual morphological features characteristic of ancient mammals, notably strongly grooved lower caniniform incisors which represent a unique dental venom delivery system comparable to that found in snakes and possibly also in basal eutherians (Fox and Scott 2005; Orr et al. 2007). Although past morphological studies have suggested phylogenetic affinities with tenrecs (Afrotheria) based largely on morphology of cheek teeth, genetic analysis has instead demonstrated that solenodons are part of the lipotyphlan radiation, sister to shrews, moles and hedgehogs. They diverged from other lipotyphlans as long ago as 76 million years during the Late Cretaceous, when the proto-Antillean block first broke away from continental North America; the Hispaniolan and Cuban solenodon lineages themselves probably diverged around 26 Mya, when the two islands themselves broke apart from each other, justifying their taxonomic assignment to separate genera (Roca et al. 2004).

In contrast, other insular Caribbean mammal groups reached the islands through subsequent over-water dispersal events, making the solenodons the oldest representatives of the region's mammal fauna. However, whereas two solenodon species have survived to the present, they are now threatened by both habitat destruction and predation by invasive species, notably dogs. This combination of high evolutionary distinctiveness and threat has led to solenodons recently being recognised as one of the highest global priorities for mammal conservation (Isaac et al. 2007; Collen et al. 2011). However, due to their relatively unassuming and non-charismatic status (Sitas et al. 2009), in common with many other threatened small mammal species, until recently they had been the focus of no conservation attention and almost no field research. This situation has now changed in Hispaniola, with *S. paradoxus* having become the focus of an international conservation programme (Turvey et al. 2008). It is hoped that not only will effective conservation management strategies be implemented for both solenodon species in order to ensure their continued survival into the future but also that the question of how they have already managed to survive for so long, when so many other endemic Caribbean land mammal species have become extinct, will be able to be answered.

on the Pacific island of Guam, across the time period of arrival and growth in the population of the introduced brown tree snake *Boiga irregularis* (see Boxes 8.2 and 4.1).

Two major factors need consideration during the design of any population monitoring programme, as they will inform the most appropriate monitoring approach to adopt:

1. *'Know your species'*. Knowledge of the target species' biology, behaviour and ecology is key to informing the most appropriate monitoring methods and design.
2. *'Know your purpose'*. Clarity on the specific aims of the monitoring programme, target audiences, and how the data will inform management of the species is vital in guiding the programme's design and how it operates.

An in-depth understanding of a species' breeding biology, ecology and behaviour – or those of a closely related species if the target species is poorly known – will inform the most appropriate monitoring plan to develop. Such 'basic' research may involve the use of information sources as described earlier in this chapter, but getting out into the field to make behavioural observations cannot be valued too highly. For example, initial concern that the Barbados leaf-toed gecko *Phyllodactylus pulcher* had recently become extinct on the main island of Barbados was soon dispelled through some simple but informed field observations (N. Cole, personal communication) achieved through logical predictions based on where (in rock crevices) and when (at night) related species are likely to be found. Potentially expensive and time-consuming work to assess whether the species was extinct was therefore avoided through basic fieldwork and sound understanding of species ecology and behaviour. Conducting an initial site visit prior to launching any monitoring plan will provide invaluable baseline data, highlight logistical issues and help to focus the research questions that the monitoring programme should aim to answer.

Clearly, understanding the purpose (see Sections 6.5 and 8.10) behind a monitoring plan is critical to its success. Knowing which stakeholders the monitoring programme is designed for (e.g. conservation managers, funders, the public, local authorities) will have an impact on which design is adopted. In many cases, the reason for monitoring will be to inform adaptive management of the species or the area where it occurs. Project managers typically also require information on the success of particular interventions to inform future developments, donors may want to see results in relation to predetermined project objectives, and local landowners might simply seek regular updates on progress made in a species recovery programme. In cases where diverse stakeholders are involved in the project, it is advisable to ask directly what they require rather than assuming that their needs have been met through a particular monitoring plan.

Developing well-considered research questions helps to clarify the purpose of the monitoring programme. Not only do they articulate what is to be found out, but they also inform the selection of sampling design and method. In relation to population monitoring, research questions should address measurable variables and so should be focused and specific. The main types of questions (modified from Gill and Daltry 2014) include

1. *Measuring changes through time* (e.g. How has the population size and range of a focal species changed over a 10-year period?)
2. *Comparing differences* (e.g. Does nesting success of a focal species differ between habitats of varying quality?)
3. *Quantifying the impacts of a threat or conservation action* (e.g. How does adult survival in a focal species change in the five years following the eradication of an invasive vertebrate compared with the prior five years?)

Once the programme's main objectives and primary research questions have been established and widely agreed on, it is then time to consider the most appropriate monitoring methods and sampling designs to employ.

5.3 Population Monitoring Methods and Sampling Design

Apart from the rare instances in which all the individuals within a population can be reliably counted – for example, with colonial nesting or roosting birds – monitoring populations of threatened species requires 'sampling' a population – in other words, collecting information from a representative sample of the population of the target species. Therefore, thinking very carefully about sampling design (the way that data are collected from the target species) is key, as it is easy to introduce biases into the monitoring data. While we do not address sampling design in any detail in this chapter, the following considerations in sampling design are important (modified from Gill and Daltry 2014):

1. *Type of sampling unit being monitored* (e.g. plot, line transect, point count, camera trap location)
2. *Size of each sampling unit* (e.g. length of each transect or dimensions of each plot)
3. *Number of samples* (the more samples being monitored, the more reliable are the results likely to be)
4. *Location of samples* (e.g. are samples located randomly or systematically?)
5. *When will the samples be visited* (this will be determined by the seasonal and daily activity patterns of the target species)
6. *How often will the sampling units be visited within a monitoring session* (repeat visits may be necessary to build up a 'detection history' of the target species)
7. *How many monitoring sessions are needed to fulfil the programme's objectives* (e.g. how many individual population size estimates are likely to be needed to detect trends of different magnitudes; depending on objectives and research questions, it may be preferable either to systematically visit the same plots or transects each year or to choose new ones)
8. *What types of data will be collected at each sampling unit* (e.g. collecting distance data along line transects will enable modelling of how detection probability varies with distance).

For useful and accessible guides on sampling design, see Bibby et al. (2000) with a focus on birds, Gill and Daltry (2014) with a focus on trees and Sutherland (2006) for a comprehensive review. Whatever decisions are made on sampling design, a pilot study (a short trial period) before implementation of the main monitoring programme will always be highly informative. Such a pilot study provides an opportunity to test out various practical considerations (e.g. field equipment, logistical arrangements, skills of field staff) and, most crucially, the preferred monitoring technique.

Threatened species are often elusive and cryptic, and therefore careful thought is required on the choice of monitoring technique in terms of maximising the chances of either observing the species directly or detecting the signs (e.g. droppings, footprints) that it leaves behind. With many species, the only realistic chance of gathering sufficient observational data for monitoring is to use remote detection devices such as video and still camera traps, hair traps, tracking stations, or drones. The range of technological solutions that are helping to improve monitoring of threatened species is increasing fast (e.g. Linchant et al. 2015; Pimm et al. 2015). A further consideration in the choice of monitoring technique is how to deal with the problem of 'imperfect detection', i.e. when individuals of a given species may be present at a particular sampling location but cannot be observed with certainty. Survey methods underpinned by statistical frameworks such as 'occupancy' and 'distance sampling' have been developed to account for such 'hidden' subsets of a given population. Guillera-Arroita et al. (2010) used an occupancy statistical framework and data from boat-based surveys of the Alaotran gentle lemur *Hapalemur alaotrensis* to produce reliable estimates of the proportion of the species' global range that is occupied. In another example in Madagascar, Young et al. (2008) used distance sampling along line transects to monitor giant jumping rat *Hypogeomys antimena* populations in a dry forest in Madagascar, and Green et al. (2014) used distance sampling from point counts to produce the first reliable population estimate of the Anjouan scops owl *Otus capnodes*.

One of the criteria for selecting the most appropriate technique will be the degree of prior skill required to apply it. Highly technical monitoring approaches can require scientific training and experience to use appropriately and so limit the range of people that can apply them. However, there is growing debate and evidence on both the effectiveness and cost-effectiveness of monitoring by non-scientists (e.g. Luzar et al. 2011), including citizens who have received very limited education (Danielsen et al. 2014). Growing interest in 'citizen science' and the engagement of the public in conservation research and action are encouraging the development of monitoring programmes in which non-scientists can collect meaningful data. The large geographic areas over which some monitoring projects operate (e.g. for migratory seabird populations or sea turtles) and the long time frames usually required to identify population trends can require reaching out beyond scientific circles. In addition, for certain species and systems, 'local' or indigenous people may possess greater biological knowledge than visiting scientists (Luzar et al. 2011). Danielsen et al. (2014) compared the relative quality of monitoring data collected by local communities and scientists across 63 taxa from four countries, including Madagascar and the Philippines. The results showed that where local communities were involved in selecting the natural resource to be monitored, they could collect observational data along line transects comparable in quality to those collected by trained scientists and so can represent a reliable source of information on population estimates and trends.

5.4 Developing Effective and Sustainable Monitoring Programmes

Designing and implementing a monitoring programme, even for restricted-range species on small islands, is often labour intensive, requires significant and sustained funding and is challenging to maintain over periods long enough to produce reliable data on population trends. Conservation scientists and practitioners should therefore carefully consider the establishment and ongoing running of monitoring programmes and understand what factors characterise successful monitoring programmes. A useful review of the key attributes of successful monitoring is provided by Pocock et al. (2015), who surveyed 52 UK conservation professionals experienced in design and management of monitoring programmes to identify and rank the importance of monitoring programme attributes (Table 5.1).

5.5 Diagnosing Causes of Decline

A common dilemma facing conservation managers is deciding how much information to collect before action is taken. This is particularly the case when trying to understand the scale of a population decline and its underlying causes. The examples of the Jamaican hutia *Geocapromys brownii* and po'ouli *Melamprosops phaeosoma* (Box 5.3) provide an illuminating reminder of what happens when action is carried out either

Table 5.1 *Ten Priority Attributes for Effective Monitoring Programmes for Threatened Species*

Monitoring programme attribute	Explanation
1. Monitoring objectives are agreed on and articulated.	Particularly important to ensure that all members of the team understand the goals of the monitoring programme, helping to sustain the programme and maintain consistency of data collection protocols and ultimately data quality.
2. Scientifically robust survey design (e.g. stratified or randomised site selection) is in place.	Seeking expert survey design advice from a statistician is essential to ensure that the monitoring programme has a good chance of meeting its objectives and will provide statistically robust results. This is particularly the case when imperfect detection of species needs to be accounted for in the survey design.
3. Standardised methodology and protocols to ensure consistency are used.	Increases the chances that valid temporal and spatial comparisons can be made with the monitoring data. The long-term feasibility of such monitoring methods necessitates careful thought from the outset over their design. There is also a trade-off to be made between methodological stability and incorporating more robust or relevant methods and technologies as they arise.
4. Sufficient specialist knowledge of the species exists within the monitoring team.	It is vital that the monitoring team has deep knowledge of the target species to ensure that the design of the programme is effective and that the observational data collected are reliable. The field specialists may not need to be scientists, as highlighted in Section 5.3.
5. Mentoring, training and support of monitoring team members are provided.	This point is further addressed in Chapter 6, recognising that team management and leadership require recognition of the individual needs within a team as well as an understanding of team dynamics and a focus on the task to be performed. Ongoing training and support of field staff are key to ensuring that data collection protocols are followed and therefore data are consistently of high quality.
6. Good staff retention occurs within the monitoring team.	Changes in staff and the subsequent shift in knowledge and skills can undermine the programme. Chapter 6 provides some useful pointers on how to create, manage and develop teams.
7. Suitable field identification guides are accessible.	In multi-species monitoring programmes, particularly involving taxa that are hard to identify, it is vital that the monitoring team has access to good-quality identification guides.

Table 5.1 *(cont.)*

Monitoring programme attribute	Explanation
8. Data management systems are in place for efficient data capture and storage.	Monitoring programmes generate large volumes of data that can be very difficult to access, analyse and generate results if not managed electronically in well-formatted spreadsheets or databases. It is important that monitoring data are routinely and frequently entered into a database and reviewed periodically during the survey to check on data quality and identify any problems.
9. Appropriate feedback is given to team on monitoring results and findings.	Ensuring that the field staff on the monitoring team receive regular feedback on findings is important in maintaining morale, aiding with interpretation of results and maintaining data quality.
10. Monitoring results are reported at appropriate intervals.	It is important to carefully consider the target audiences for monitoring results, the frequency with which they want to receive updates and reports and their preferred reporting format.

Source: Modified from Pocock et al. (2015).

too soon or too late. Interestingly, in both cases there was a failure to collect basic biological and ecological data on the target species, hindering efforts to monitor population change and identify likely causes of decline.

Conservation managers must make the best-informed decisions (based on a combination of scientific evidence, experience and 'gut feeling') to overcome the tension between a desire to act and a desire for data acquisition (Black and Copsey 2014; see also Chapter 8). With regard to understanding the causes of population decline, this requires managers to take actions informed by the best available data on the biology and ecology of the target species (or some 'good guesses' based on knowledge of similar species), but to do so in a way that encourages learning about the system the species inhabits. Through this process of trial and error or the development of empirical understanding informed by new information as it becomes available, conservation interventions can be modified through active, dynamic management for maximum impact (Black and Copsey 2014). A useful guide to help identify the combination of questions to be asked and actions to be taken to establish the magnitude of a population decline and diagnose its cause(s) is proposed in Table 5.2.

Table 5.2 *Systematic Approach to Diagnosing Population Declines*

Stage of diagnosing population decline	Potential questions to ask
1. Confirmation that the species or population has declined in abundance or distribution.	• Has the species declined throughout its range, or is the decline localised? • Is the decline in one area compensated by increases elsewhere? • When did the decline occur? • Could the decline be part of a natural fluctuation in population size, or is there reason to believe this is atypical?
2. Know your species – document what is known about its ecology, behaviour and life history.	• What habitat or microhabitat does it occupy? • What is its relationship with other species (predators, prey, parasites, pathogens, competitors)? • What are the main causes of mortality? • Do habitat or food preferences change throughout the year? • Where and how does it breed? • What is its social system?
3. List all possible causes of the decline.	• What human activities have occurred within the species' range? • Have exotic species become established? • Are there any signs of a disease outbreak? • Does exploitation occur? • Has the habitat been modified? • What factors have been important in the declines of similar species?
4. Correlate potential cause of the decline with the change in abundance or distribution.	• Does the timing of the decline correlate with increases in abundance/magnitude or distribution of possible threats (e.g. introduced invasive species, habitat loss)? • Are there related species elsewhere that have suffered similar declines from known causes? • Are other native species populations in its range changing, and if so, how? • Has harvesting of the species increased? • Is there interdependence with other native species in its range, and is there evidence for any change in their populations?
5. Test out the hypotheses for the cause of decline.	• How successful have conservation interventions been to support the recovery of related species elsewhere, and what can we learn from them to apply here?

Table 5.2 *(cont.)*

Stage of diagnosing population decline	Potential questions to ask
	• Does exclusion of certain introduced species lead to localised increases in abundance of the target species?
	• Does supplementary feeding increase population size and therefore indicate food shortage as an important threat?
	• What is the breeding success and survival rate, both for the species overall and for its different life stages?
	• Does the provision of artificial breeding sites increase productivity and so suggest a shortage of suitable habitat as a cause of decline?
	• Does habitat/community composition differ between areas where the population has declined and areas where it has not?

Sources: Modified from Caughley and Gunn (1996) and Sutherland (2006).

As threats overwhelm a species in one area, it may survive in another. As discussed earlier, just because a species is found to inhabit a certain landscape, it should not be assumed that this constitutes the most ecologically optimal or suitable environment for the species; instead, it may be the only place where the species can still survive, having been extirpated from more suitable habitats. Therefore, when analysing potential threats to target species, we should ask not only why is it found in some areas but also why is it *not* found elsewhere? For example, 53 of Hawaii's 71 avian taxa are extinct or threatened (Jacobi and Atkinson 1995; Scott et al. 2001), and many of those that remain are restricted to high-altitude forest more than 1,000 m above sea level. Superficial consideration might suggest that this is because the most suitable habitat for these species is found at or above this altitude. However, more thorough analysis would show that suitable habitat also occurs at lower elevations and that perhaps it is the establishment of numerous exotic, invasive bird species that are outcompeting or predating the natives that has restricted them to higher elevations. It is only when spatial abundance patterns of avian malaria-carrying *Culex* mosquitoes are superimposed onto this picture that a deeper understanding emerges. Mosquitoes are restricted to lower elevations, where temperatures are higher. Parasite prevalence is highest where introduced and endemic birds come into contact at the mosquito's upper altitudinal threshold. The introduced birds act as carriers of the disease, the mosquitoes provide the vector and the endemic birds are the unwilling recipients. With little immunity to avian malaria, the native Hawaiian birds are actually being restricted in their elevational distribution by the limits of the range of the malaria-carrying mosquito. A final twist is the presence of introduced pigs, which have a preference for the hearts of native tree ferns. By knocking them over and rooting around in the trunks, the pigs are creating ideal breeding grounds for mosquitoes, artificially raising their abundance in these forests and compounding the impact on the endemic birds. The reasons for species decline can be complex.

5.6 Correlation or Causation

Potential threats to a given species cannot be identified as definite drivers of decline until they have been investigated empirically in the field. Once the most likely causes of species decline have been identified, it is possible to generate a further list of hypotheses to test their validity. These tests may be comparative, such as trying to map spatial correlations between the distribution of potential threats with the presence or absence of the same or related species elsewhere. For example, by comparing the presence or absence of rats, cats and introduced tenrecs *Tenrec ecaudatus* on the abundance of native geckos on various islands in the Seychelles Archipelago, Gardner (1986) was able to question the importance of rats as the main cause of gecko decline and provide evidence for the impact of tenrecs.

Replicated, controlled experiments may also be possible to provide evidence for or against particular hypothesised causes of decline. In the late 1950s, Warner (1968) hypothesised that introduced diseases rather than habitat loss had restricted Hawaii's endemic birds to higher altitudes. To test his theory, he collected a group of 36 Laysan finches *Telespiza cantans* from mosquito-free Laysan Island and brought them to Kauai, one of Hawaii's smaller islands. Once the birds were settled, he exposed a third of them to the island's mosquitoes, the remaining birds being kept as a control behind mosquito-proof mesh. Within five nights the first bird within the experimental group died, and within two weeks, all 13 birds had perished. Post-mortem examination showed their blood to be full of the parasite that causes avian malaria. The experiment was repeated with other endemic Hawaiian passerines with similar results; after nine days of exposure to the mosquitoes, all individuals showed signs of avian malaria at varying stages of development. These simple trials neatly demonstrated the role of avian malaria as a cause of species decline in Hawaii's endemic avifauna.

When populations are critically low, conducting controlled experiments is unlikely to be sensible or even feasible, not only because of a lack of experimental subjects and/or financial or logistical constraints but also because of the imperative to act on the immediate threat rather than potentially endanger the limited number of surviving individuals. Instead, non-invasive field data can be interpreted in terms of 'before-and -after' intervention scenarios. For example, the impact of introduced feral cats *Felis catus* on the Seychelles magpie robin *Copsychus sechellarum* was inferred through the negative correlation between respective population sizes of cats and robins. In the 1930s, magpie robins were only found on two islands in the Seychelles island chain, Alphonse and Frigate (Vesey-Fitzgerald 1940). The introduction of cats to Alphonse in the 1950s led to the extirpation of robins on this island in 1959 (Caughley and Gunn 1996). The later establishment of cats on Frigate led to robins declining in the mid-1960s, only increasing again when cats were intensively hunted. While not conclusive evidence that cats were the primary or only cause of robin decline, such correlations do provide reasonable confidence that cats were a threat.

Management intervention, if conducted in a way that allows monitoring of impacts, not only can help to improve the survival of threatened species but also can help to develop a deeper understanding of the factors limiting population growth. A shortage of nest sites was thought to be one cause of decline in the Java sparrow *Padda oryzivora* (Kurniandaru 2008). To address this concern, researchers installed artificial nest boxes of different designs within the home range of the largest single population of the species on Java, totalling approximately 16 pairs. In subsequent years, sparrows began to use the nest boxes and fledge young from them, suggesting that nest-site availability was at least a factor limiting population growth in the species.

These examples serve to illustrate how a more systematic approach can be applied to help diagnose and treat the causes of population declines. However, we must not confuse the drive to improve the efficiency of management actions with an obligation to acquire scientifically robust evidence before we act. The risk of doing more than the most management-relevant research to direct our activities is that we may 'study species to extinction'. The po'ouli is arguably one of the most illustrative examples of a species for which action was delayed while awaiting more data, with disastrous results (Black et al. 2011) (Box 5.3).

Box 5.3 *A Tale of Two Extremes: The Jamaican Hutia and Po'ouli*

In the early 1970s, a large-scale captive breeding programme was established for the Jamaican hutia *Geocapromys brownii*, believed to be in imminent risk of extinction (Caughley and Gunn 1996). Agricultural expansion was assumed to be driving population decline. However, a more targeted ecological study in 1982 identified 16 sites on Jamaica where hutias still occurred; the nocturnal nature of the species and its increased elusiveness as a consequence of generations of hunting pressure had made it difficult to find, but it was apparently not in imminent danger of extinction. In this instance, action was taken prematurely, without sufficient – though still relatively simple – understanding of the species' ecology and biology.

At the other extreme, the po'ouli *Melamprosops phaeosoma* illustrates how species can be studied intensively while rapid declines are occurring, and yet critical questions around population trends or threats can still fail to be answered. Discovered in 1973, there were never more than a handful of individual po'ouli ever seen (Black et al. 2011). Population estimates suggested a decline from 76 birds per square kilometre in 1975 to eight birds per square kilometre in 1985 (Groombridge et al. 2004). Despite the species' apparent rarity and a potentially catastrophic population decline, direct conservation intervention did not begin until the 1990s, with the establishment of fenced areas to exclude feral pigs, a potential predator of nestlings and eggs. The Hanawī NAR reserve was established in 1986, but reserve management did not involve any direct protection of the species. In common with the hutia example given earlier, insufficient research efforts were directed at documenting the species' biology and ecology to gain a better understanding of likely population size or, crucially, clarity around threats (Black et al. 2011).

In the 1980s, a pair was observed laying multiple eggs, but only a single fledgling was raised despite two nesting attempts (Powell 2008). The subsequent death of this individual, probably due to poor weather causing the female to abandon the nest (Powell 2008), provided anecdotal evidence that the wet zone to which it was restricted may not have been its preferred habitat. It was not until 2002 that translocation was attempted, to create a pair from the remaining three known individuals. While this intervention did provide insights into the species' feeding ecology and suggested potential for captive breeding, the attempt failed (Groombridge et al. 2004). One of the three remaining birds (a male) was captured in 2004 and subsequently died in captivity before a female could be found (VanderWerf et al. 2006). The po'ouli is now presumed to be extinct.

5.7 Summary

Key points from the chapter:

- The fossil and zooarchaeological records constitute a significant source of information to help understand past population sizes, distributions and early causes of decline.
- Historical accounts, maps, museum specimens and traditional/local ecological knowledge can provide additional useful, if imperfect, information to understand changes in species status through time and possible threats.
- Genetic analyses are becoming increasingly useful in providing evidence of historical population declines.
- The design of contemporary population monitoring programmes requires clarity around their purpose. What specific question is the programme required to answer?
- Effective, long-term monitoring programmes rely not only on selection of the most appropriate monitoring techniques but also on timely feedback to those involved in collecting the data.
- Hypothesis-driven management interventions should be designed not only to halt or reverse population declines but also to build understanding of the causes of decline.

References

Beaumont, M. A. (1999). Detecting population expansion and decline using microsatellites. *Genetics* 153: 2013–29.
Beddard, F. E. (1905). *Natural History in Zoological Gardens*. Archibald Constable, London.

Bibby, C. J., Burgess, N. D., Hill, D. A. and Mustoe, S. H. (2000). *Bird Census Techniques*, 2nd edn. Academic Press, London.

Black, S. A. and Copsey, J. A. (2014). Does Deming's 'system of profound knowledge' apply to leaders of biodiversity conservation? *Open Journal of Leadership* 3 (2): 53–65.

Black, S. A., Groombridge, J. J. and Jones, C. G. (2011). Leadership and conservation effectiveness: finding a better way to lead. *Conservation Letters* 4: 329–39.

Bulte, E. H., Horan, R. D. and Shogren, J. F. (2003). Is the Tasmanian tiger extinct? A biological-economic re-evaluation. *Ecological Economics* 45: 271–79.

Burney, D. A., Burney, L. P., Godfrey, L. R. et al. (2004). A chronology for late prehistoric Madagascar. *Journal of Human Evolution* 47: 25–63.

Caughley, G. and Gunn, A. (1996). *Conservation Biology in Theory and Practice.* Blackwell Science, Oxford.

Cheke, A. S. (1987). An ecological history of the Mascarene Islands, with particular reference to extinctions and introductions of land vertebrates, pp. 5–89 in A. W. Diamond (ed.), *Studies of Mascarene Island Birds.* Cambridge University Press, Cambridge.

(2006). Establishing extinction dates: the curious case of the dodo *Raphus cucullatus* and the red hen *Aphanapteryx bonasia. Ibis* 148: 155–58.

Cheke, A. S. and Hume, J. P. (2008). *Lost Land of the Dodo: An Ecological History of Mauritius, Réunion and Rodrigues.* A&C Black, London.

Chouteau, P., Jiang, Z., Bravery, B. D. et al. (2012). Local extinction in the bird assemblage in the greater Beijing area from 1877 to 2006. *PLoS ONE* 7(6): e39859.

Collen, B., Turvey, S. T., Waterman, C. et al. (2011). Investing in evolutionary history: implementing a phylogenetic approach for mammal conservation. *Philosophical Transactions of the Royal Society B* 366: 2611–22.

Cribb, R. (2000). *Historical Atlas of Indonesia.* Curzon-New Asian Library, London.

Danielsen, F., Jensen, P. M., Burgess, N. D. et al. (2014). A multicountry assessment of tropical resource monitoring by local communities. *BioScience* 64: 236–51.

Diamond, J. M. (1989). Quaternary megafaunal extinctions: variations on a theme by Paganini. *Journal of Archaeological Science* 16: 167–75.

Fox, R. C. and Scott, C. S. (2005). First evidence of a venom delivery apparatus in extinct mammals. *Nature* 435: 1091–93.

Frankham, R. (1995). Effective population size/adult population size ratios in wildlife: a review. *Genetics Research* 66: 95–107.

Funes Monzote, R. (2008). *From Rainforest to Cane Fields in Cuba: An Environmental History since 1492.* University of North Carolina Press, Chapel Hill, NC.

Gardner, A. S. (1986). Morphological evolution in the day gecko *Phelsuma sundbergi* in the Seychelles: a multivariate study. *Biological Journal of the Linnean Society* 29: 223–44.

Gill, D. and Daltry, J. (2014). *How to Make a Monitoring Plan for Threatened Tree Species.* Global Trees Campaign, available at http://globaltrees.org/resources/resource-type/practical-guidance/.

Goossens, B., Chikhi, L., Ancrenaz, M. et al. (2006). Genetic signature of anthropogenic population collapse in orang-utans. *PLoS Biology* 4(2): e25.

Green, K. E., Daniel, B. M., Lloyd, S. P. et al. (2015). Out of the darkness: the first comprehensive survey of the critically endangered Anjouan scops owl *Otus capnodes*. *Bird Conservation International* 25: 322–34.

Griffiths, C. J., Hansen, D. M., Jones, C. G., Zuël, N. and Harris, S. (2011). Resurrecting extinct interactions with extant substitutes. *Current Biology* 21: 762–65.

Groombridge, J. J., Massey, J. G., Bruch, J. C. et al. (2004). An attempt to recover the po'ouli by translocation and an appraisal of recovery strategy for bird species of extreme rarity. *Biological Conservation* 118: 365–75.

Guillera-Arroita, G., Lahoz-Monfort, J. J., Milner-Gulland, E. J., Young, R. P. and Nicholson, E. (2010). Using occupancy as a state variable for monitoring the critically endangered Alaotran gentle lemur *Hapalemur alaotrensis*. *Endangered Species Research* 11: 157–66.

Hetherington, D. (2010). The lynx, pp. 75–82 in T. O'Connor and N. Sykes (eds.), *Extinctions and Invasions: A Social History of British Fauna*. Windgather Press, Oxford.

Holdaway, R. N. and Jacomb, C. (2000). Rapid extinction of the moas (Aves: Dinornithiformes): model, test and implications. *Science* 287: 2250–54.

Holdaway, R. N., Jones, M. D. and Beavan Athfield, N. R. (2002). Late Holocene extinction of Finsch's duck (*Chenonetta finschi*), an endemic, possibly flightless, New Zealand duck. *Journal of the Royal Society of New Zealand* 32: 629–51.

Isaac, N. J. B., Turvey, S. T., Collen, B., Waterman, C. and Baillie, J. E. M. (2007). Mammals on the EDGE: conservation priorities based on threat and phylogeny. *PLoS ONE* 2(3): e296.

IUCN (2001). *IUCN Red List Categories and Criteria*, Version 3.1. World Conservation Union, Gland.

Jackson, S. T. and Hobbs, R. J. (2009). Ecological restoration in the light of ecological history. *Science* 325: 567–69.

Jacobi, J. D. and Atkinson, C. T. (1995). Hawaii's endemic birds, pp. 376–81 in T. E. LaRoe, C. E. Puckett, P. D. Doran and M. J. Mac (eds.), *Our Living Resources: A Report to the Nation on the Distribution, Abundance and Health of U.S. Plants, Animals, and Ecosystems*. US Department of Interior, National Biological Service, Washington, DC.

Kurniandaru, S. (2008). Providing nest boxes for Java sparrows *Padda oryzivora* in response to nest site loss due to building restoration and an earthquake, Prambanan Temple, Java, Indonesia. *Conservation Evidence* 5: 62–68.

Lauwerier, C. G. M. and Plug, I. (eds.) (2004). *The Future from the Past: Archaeozoology in Wildlife Conservation and Heritage Management*. Oxbow Books, Oxford.

Linchant, J., Lisein, J., Semeki, J., Lejeune, P. and Vermeulen, C. (2015). Are unmanned aircraft systems (UASs) the future of wildlife monitoring? A review of accomplishments and challenges. *Mammal Review* 45: 239–25.

Liu, Z., Yu, S. and Yuan, X. (1984). Resources of the Hainan black gibbon and its present situation. *Chinese Wildlife* 6: 1–4.

Liu, Z., Zhang, Y., Jiang, H. and Southwick, C. (1989). Population structure of *Hylobates concolor* in Bawanglin Nature Reserve, Hainan, China. *American Journal of Primatology* 19: 247–54.

Louys, J. (2012). *Paleontology in Ecology and Conservation*. Springer-Verlag, Berlin.

Lunn, K. and Dearden, P. (2006). Monitoring small-scale marine fisheries: an example from Thailand's Ko Chang Archipelago. *Fisheries Research* 77: 60–71.

Luzar, J. B., Silvius, K. M., Overman, H. et al. (2011). Large-scale environmental monitoring by indigenous peoples. *BioScience* 61: 771–81.

MacPhee, R. D. E. and Flemming, C. (1999). Requiem æternam: the last five hundred years of mammalian species extinctions, pp. 333–371 in R. D. E. MacPhee (ed.), *Extinctions in Near Time: Causes, Contexts, and Consequences*. Kluwer Academic/Plenum, New York.

Macqueen, P., Goldizen, A. W., Austin, J. J. and Seddon, J. M. (2011). Phylogeography of the pademelons (Marsupialia: Macropodidae: *Thylogale*) in New Guinea reflects both geological and climatic events during the Plio-Pleistocene. *Journal of Biogeography* 38: 1732–47.

Miller, G. S., Jr. (1929). Mammals eaten by Indians, owls, and Spaniards in the coast region of the Dominican Republic. *Smithsonian Miscellaneous Collections* 82: 1–16.

Mills, J. A., Lavers, R. B. and Lee, W. G. (1984). The takahe: a relic of the Pleistocene grassland avifauna in New Zealand. *New Zealand Journal of Ecology* 7: 55–70.

Orr, C. M., Delezene, L. K., Scott, J. E., Tocheri, M. W. and Schwartz, G. T. (2007). The comparative method and the inference of venom-delivery systems in fossil mammals. *Journal of Vertebrate Paleontology* 27: 541–46.

Payne, J. (1987). Surveying orang-utan populations by counting nests from a helicopter: a pilot survey in Sabah. *Primate Conservation* 8: 92–103.

Pimm, S. L., Alibhai, S., Bergl, R. et al. (2015). Emerging technologies to conserve biodiversity. *Trends in Ecology & Evolution* 30: 685–96.

Pocock, M. J., Newson, S. E., Henderson, I. G. et al. (2015). Developing and enhancing biodiversity monitoring programmes: a collaborative assessment of priorities. *Journal of Applied Ecology* 52: 686–95.

Powell, A. (2008). *The Race to Save the World's Rarest Bird: The Discovery and Death of the Po'ouli*. Stackpole Books, Mechanicsburg, PA.

Rijksen, H. D. and Meijaard, E. (1999). *Our Vanishing Relative: The Status of Wild Orang-utans at the Close of the 20th Century*. Kluwer Academic Publishers, Dordrecht.

Roberts, D. L. and Solow, A. R. (2003). When did the dodo become extinct? *Nature* 426: 245.

Robertson, J. M. Y. and van Schaik, C. P. (2001). Causal factors underlying the dramatic decline of the Sumatran orang-utan. *Oryx* 35: 26–38.

Roca, A. L., Kahila Bar-Gal, G., Eizirik, E. et al. (2004). Mesozoic origin for West Indian insectivores. *Nature* 429: 649–51.

Scott, J. M., Conant, S. and Van Riper, C. (eds.) (2001). *Evolution, Ecology, and Management of Hawaiian Birds: A Vanishing Avifauna* (Studies in Avian Biology 22). Cooper Ornithological Society, Chicago, IL.

Sitas, N., Baillie, J. E. M. and Isaac, N. J. B. (2009). What are we saving? Developing a standardized approach for conservation action. *Animal Conservation* 12: 231–37.

Solow, A. R. (2005). Inferring extinction from a sighting record. *Mathematical Biosciences* 195: 47–55.

Steadman, D. W. (1995). Prehistoric extinctions of Pacific Island birds: biodiversity meets zooarchaeology. *Science* 267: 1123–31.
  (2006a). *Extinction and Biogeography of Tropical Pacific Birds*. University of Chicago Press, Chicago, IL.
  (2006b). An extinct species of tooth-billed pigeon (*Didunculus*) from the Kingdom of Tonga, and the concept of endemism in insular land birds. *Journal of Zoology* 268: 233–41.
Storz, J. F. and Beaumont, M. (2002). Testing for genetic evidence of population expansion and contraction: an empirical analysis of microsatellite DNA variation using a hierarchical Bayesian method. *Evolution* 56: 154–66.
Sutherland, W. J. (2006). *Ecological Census Techniques: A Handbook*. Cambridge University Press, Cambridge.
Trewick, S. A. and Worthy, T. H. (2001). Origins and prehistoric ecology of takahe based on morphometric, molecular, and fossil data, pp. 31–48 in W. G. Lee and I. G. Jamieson (eds.), *The Takahe: Fifty Years of Conservation Management and Research*. University of Otago Press, Dunedin.
Turvey, S. T. (ed.) (2009). *Holocene Extinctions*. Oxford University Press, Oxford.
Turvey, S. T. and Blackburn, T. M. (2011). Determinants of species abundance in the Quaternary vertebrate fossil record. *Paleobiology* 37: 537–46.
Turvey, S. T. and Risley, C. L. (2006). Modelling the extinction of Steller's sea cow. *Biology Letters* 2: 94–97.
Turvey, S. T., Meredith, H. M. R. and Scofield, R. P. (2008). Continued survival of Hispaniolan solenodon (*Solenodon paradoxus*) in Haiti. *Oryx* 42: 611–14.
Turvey, S. T., Fernández-Secades, C., Nuñez-Miño, J. M. et al. (2014). Is local ecological knowledge a useful conservation tool for small mammals in a Caribbean multicultural landscape? *Biological Conservation* 169: 189–97.
VanderWerf, E. A., Groombridge, J. J., Fretz, J. S. and Swinnerton, K. J. (2006). Decision analysis to guide recovery of the po'ouli, a critically endangered Hawaiian honeycreeper. *Biological Conservation* 129: 383–92.
van Schaik, C. P., Monk, K. A. and Robertson, J. M. Y. (2001). Dramatic decline in orang-utan numbers in the Leuser Ecosystem, Northern Sumatra. *Oryx* 35: 14–25.
Vesey-Fitzgerald, D. (1940). The birds of the Seychelles: 1. The endemic birds. *Ibis* 14: 482–89.
Warner, R. E. (1968). The role of introduced diseases in the extinction of the endemic Hawaiian avifauna. *Condor* 70: 101–20.
Warren, K. S., Verschoor, E. J., Langenhuijzen, S. et al. (2001). Speciation and intrasubspecific variation of Bornean orang-utans, *Pongo pygmaeus pygmaeus*. *Molecular Biology and Evolution* 18: 472–80.
Watts, D. (1987). *The West Indies: Patterns of Development, Culture and Environmental Change since 1492*. Cambridge University Press, Cambridge.
White, A. W., Worthy, T. H., Hawkins, S., Bedford, S. and Spriggs, M. (2010). Megafaunal meiolaniid horned turtles survived until early human settlement in Vanuatu, southwest Pacific. *Proceedings of the National Academy of Sciences USA* 107: 15512–16.
Wich, S. A., Singleton, I., Utami-Atmoko, S. S. et al. (2003). The status of the Sumatran orang-utan *Pongo abelii*: an update. *Oryx* 37: 49–54.

Worthy, T. H. and Holdaway, R. N. (2002). *The Lost World of the Moa*. Indiana University Press, Bloomington, IN.

Young, R. P., Toto Volahy, A., Bourou, R. et al. (2008). A baseline estimate of population size for monitoring the endangered Madagascar giant jumping rat *Hypogeomys antimena*. *Oryx* 42: 584–91.

Zhang, Y. and Sheeran, L. (1993). Current status of the Hainan black gibbon (*Hylobates concolor hainanus*). *Asian Primates* 3: 3.

Zhou, J., Wei, F., Li, M. et al. (2005). Hainan black-crested gibbon is headed for extinction. *International Journal of Primatology* 26: 453–65.

6 · *Conservation Project Organisation*

Planning for Recovery

SIMON A. BLACK

6.0 Introduction

A conservation project – defined here as the process of applying resources to achieve a clearly defined endpoint, such as the recovery of a threatened species – requires the leader, who we will hereafter describe as the 'project manager', to take on both the 'big picture' perspective of what he or she is aspiring to achieve alongside dealing with the necessary details to make sure that the work is successful. Managing a conservation project is not the same as planning, and planning is not the same as creating a project plan. It is not unheard of for a dedicated project working group to produce detailed species action plans that sit gathering dust on the shelves of conservation organisations. Similarly, without sufficient planning, conservation projects fail. While some projects have evolved over time without formal project planning, the disciplines of effective project management remain important. The link between effective planning and project management should be seamless – one informs the other. Successful restoration of threatened species that occur on islands and elsewhere requires a responsive planning process that generates results on the ground.

This chapter begins by considering how people within a project can be organised to improve clarity of roles and decision-making authority. We consider how to manage people within the project, and – using examples from islands – highlight important elements within any project plan to help everyone within it understand what the project is trying to achieve and how they will know they are moving in the right direction. We reflect on the importance of building-in from the outset steps that reduce the risk of foreseeable issues undermining project outcomes and recognise the importance of regular monitoring and review. Project management tools are introduced to provide managers with a kit they can use to help manage the task at hand, the people within the project and the work processes that enable the project to be completed. Finally, we reflect on methods for evaluating project outcomes, focusing on one particular model that provides a structure for examining projects to see how they are functioning as well as to see what results they've achieved.

6.1 Background on Project Planning in Conservation

Despite an encouraging number of conservation success stories worldwide (e.g. see Chapters 9 and 10), conservation effort has not yet halted the decline in global biodiversity. This is most starkly illustrated by the failure to meet the 2010 targets set at the 1990 Convention on Biological Diversity (Butchart et al. 2010). Many causes lie outside the conservationists' control, including human population growth and industrialisation of the emerging economies. Nevertheless, there are lessons to be learnt that would help conservation managers be more effective and efficient. Project management is a broad discipline involving planning, implementation and review. Too often conservation project managers mistakenly consider developing the plan as the purpose of their efforts. Some of the best examples of well-resourced and expertly devised planning processes in conservation are the species recovery plans associated with the US Endangered Species Act (ESA). An insightful review of ESA plans (Boersma et al. 2001) identified several common but unhelpful traits. Conservation plans can take too long to be developed and can be either too brief or painfully over-documented. Boersma et al.'s (2001) study identified that the lag between date of ESA listing and plan approval since 1990 was 5.1 years ± 0.5, with the size of planning documents ranging from 14 to 432 pages (mean 104 ± 7).

Planning is not the reason for the existence of a project; instead, the purpose and outcomes of the project must remain at the forefront of the project manager's mind. Put the species first. To transform a written plan into a practical scheme of activity, we suggest that several key principles need to be addressed: project governance, role clarity, decision-making authority, managing by exception, identifying and managing a team, stakeholder management, managing project timelines, plan protection and review and enhancement of the project plan.

6.2 Project Governance, Role Clarity and Managing by Exception

An effective conservation project relies on appropriate structures of governance – people knowing who is doing what and when. A few sensible structures need to be set in place to ensure that the people making decisions and doing the work have the appropriate mandate and supporting infrastructure. Overall project leadership should involve either an influential sponsor or a project board of senior managers and stakeholders. The project board are responsible for authorising the project manager to get work underway at the outset of the project and for the project manager to ensure the completion of each project stage. The sponsor leads the board and ensures that decisions are made in a timely manner. Along with the board, the sponsor should engage stakeholders and ensure that resources are available for the project to proceed. To enable this, it is often useful for the project board to include representatives of key stake-holders or user groups (including local communities) and technical experts (such as veterinarians). Nevertheless, it is also important to avoid unnecessary members in the board. Board members must be willing and able to make decisions and sign off each project stage (thereby allowing the next stage of work to be initiated) and even-tually to confirm completion of the project. They must also be ready to give authority and resources if exceptional circumstances for action arise. Overall governance of the project should allow the project manager to be responsible for day-to-day management (delegated by the project board). The project manager selects the team, develops plans and ensures the work is completed, using input and ideas from team members.

Sadly, there are too many occasions in conservation when neither a decision-making mandate nor available resources have been given to the project manager and the team. For example, in the attempted recov-ery of the po'ouli (Powell 2008; see also Box 5.3), field teams often had to wait weeks for permission to carry out routine conservation interventions due to an overly complex hierarchy of authority (Vanderwerfe et al 2006). It is important that the project manager and the project sponsor work together to agree at the outset on the level of authorisation across the project and how exceptions to this plan should be managed. Levels of authorisation need to be agreed by the project board, including the designation of project stages within which the project manager is given full authority to make decisions and take actions to achieve stage outcomes (within defined boundaries; see below). Thereafter, the project manager should be free to undertake actions and make decisions within these boundaries. If issues arise that lie outside these boundaries, the project manager needs to raise those exceptional items with the project board. This is the concept of 'managing by exception'. Boundaries for the project manager's responsibilities are set as 'tolerances' using measures of time, cost, quality, risk and scope. If activities progress within the agreed tolerances for a project stage, then the manager can proceed with some flexibility and without the need for permission from the project board. However, anything outside these tolerances is an 'exception' that requires decisions to be deferred upwards to the board, with an agreed decision process (e.g. via meeting, conference call, or email) including a minimum number of board participants to sanction the decisions.

6.3 Identifying and Managing the Team

Careful selection and formation of a project team (Figure 6.1) ensure that people working on the project can understand, support and participate in planning and implementation as well as being able to offer an increased contribution to problem solving, decisions and improvements. For

Figure 6.1 Project team in action, Hawaii. Teams such as these operate under challenging field conditions where relationships can sometimes be strained. Managers need to ensure clarity of roles and monitor the well-being of the individuals within the team, the effectiveness of the team itself and the progress of the task(s) that they are carrying out. (*Photo credits:* Maui Forest Bird Recovery Project, taken by Zach Pezzillo.)

people to fulfil their intended role of improving organisational effectiveness, it is critical that team members have a common purpose or reason for existing (see Chapter 8). An effective project team is likely to involve a mix of individuals with differing sets of skills and expertise. Many of the technical requirements for team membership will be evident at the outset of a project. It is also useful to get a mix of personal qualities across the team. There are also some generic personal characteristics that are worth looking for in potential team members, including curiosity, innovation, optimism, pro-activity, cheerfulness, conscientiousness and work ethic (Clayton 2012). Other traits may also be particularly useful in the resource-scarce conservation setting, including adaptability, resilience, willingness to ask questions constructively and readiness to take a lead on topics in support of the project manager (Westrum 1994). The project manager needs to be ready to select, induct, train and develop team members (Box 6.1). For some people, training will involve acquisition of technical or scientific skills, but for more mature team members, it may involve developing their ability to take responsibility and initiative.

Box 6.1 *Staff Induction within the Maui Forest Bird Recovery Project, Hawaii, USA, by Dr Hanna Mounce*

Maui Forest Bird Recovery Project (MFBRP) is responsible for the recovery of endemic bird species on Maui, Hawaii. The work involves a core management team supported by various technicians, mostly hired from mainland United States. One challenge for new staff is figuring out how MFBRP work fits into the larger Hawaiian conservation picture. Induction training used to consist of five days in the office to collect gear, watch videos and do shopping for the field. Induction now runs across the first couple of weeks and incorporates inputs from visiting speakers (e.g. from state of Hawaii, invasive species committees). New staff members get a clear idea of how MFBRP fits into conservation on Maui and how their work fits into recovering Hawaii as a whole.

It is important for everyone within MFBRP to be able to understand the project mission and its work. Now, during induction, not only does the team leader describe the mission and vision, but the team also runs a community outreach event during the first weekend of the crew's employment. As part of the design, the team discuss how to answer questions from the public. New staff work shifts at an outreach table alongside permanent staff. The experience of hearing what people ask and having to think about how to answer questions is really helpful: staff have to consider issues that they might otherwise not have formulated in their own minds.

The induction now includes a discussion about decision-making, including when the team will have input and when they won't. The leader also runs a group expectations exercise with the team split into small groups to brainstorm expectations they had, what they expect from their teammates and what they expect from their boss. This exercise is hugely beneficial for a couple of reasons. Firstly, it is useful to hear what team members expect and for the leader to have a written version of those expectations. Secondly, it gives team members the opportunity to each get in front of everyone for at least one of the questions and be listened to instead of 'talked to'.

The induction extends into the first few field trips. Previously, not everyone collected the correct quality of data, even after receiving the same training. The leader now collects personal field notebooks after the second field trip and gives each person feedback on missing elements, changes to approach and what they are doing effectively. While on the surface this seems like 'teacher with the red pen', the team really appreciate the feedback: doing this early eliminates problems and miscommunication later. The investment in time and effort has paid off: a motivated team that knows what they are doing, understands the background of MFBRP and appreciates its fit with wider conservation.

The 'purpose, goals, roles, processes, relationships framework' (Beckhard 1972) is useful for reviewing the root causes of team effectiveness. The project manager needs to monitor whether each of these five elements is effectively in place and whether they are clear to all team members, including the set of acceptable behaviours for working and cooperating together. The manager also needs to recognise that if a breakdown in working relationships occurs, it is most likely driven by the quality of effective implementation of the other four factors. Many teams verbalise the behavioural aspects as 'ground rules' to which everyone should adhere, including the leader. Common examples include respect, listening, punctuality, openness, honesty, supportiveness and responding to requests for help (Westrum 1994).

All expectations should be agreed clearly between the manager and the team: designated tasks, specific requests, objectives, job roles and working relationships (Covey 1989). Responsibilities should be clarified in clear job roles for team members, while permissions and delegation of tasks should be clarified before and during the progression of the project. This will vary with the development of team members' levels of competence and familiarity with the work and the species or ecosystems of concern (see Chapter 8). The project manager should keep an eye on this progression within the team and avoid people taking on responsibility by assumption. Regular team meetings and project reviews are a useful way of keeping up with this. A well-functioning team takes time to review its processes of decision-making, delegation and task assignment and discuss and agree on where any improvement is required.

A successful project manager will pay balanced attention to three factors: the task, the team and individual members (Box 6.2). The activities that surround each of these responsibilities are

---

Box 6.2 *'Task, Team and Individual' at Maui Forest Bird Recovery Project, by Dr Hanna Mounce*

An imbalance was noticed in the running of the Maui Forest Bird Recovery Project team when managing fieldwork patterns and staff time out of the field. The team (Figure 6.1) are housed in small huts, and people's field schedules (the 'task' process) are alternated to give people more personal space on their days off (the 'individual' process). The intention of this arrangement was to benefit each team member to improve overall morale (the 'team' process). However, this meant that everyone arrived at and departed from the field at different times, creating communication problems. Staff would hear different information from supervisors, or things told to part of the team were not relayed to the rest of the team.

The task schedule structure has since been changed to overcome this. Now all staff leave and return to the field, for the most part, at the same time. What might have been lost (e.g. data) by not having a constant presence in the field has been far surpassed by gains from better communication and team dynamics. The recovery project team now has a meeting involving everyone after each field trip; all staff members get the appropriate information about schedules and tasks. As an added advantage, the teams are now more cohesive as a unit. They work as one instead of previous sub-teams that only occasionally overlapped.

In this case, simple scheduling changes, consciously made in order to balance the task with team and individual needs, have played a major role in the improved functionality of the team.

intertwined as three types of processes: 'task core processes' (the work and the flow between tasks), 'team processes' (how team members interact and collaborate) and 'individual processes' (how each person develops and contributes). The manager needs to be clear on how these three processes are managed to enable a balance of activity across the duration of the project and to enable people to work effectively. Managers should provide clarity to their teams through coherent communication, straightforward expectations, alongside defined responsibilities, permissions and relevant delegation (Coppin and Barratt 2002). Effective communication is based upon listening to understand, which involves seeking mutual understanding before action and finding solutions together (a 'win-win' scenario). The project manager must deliver clear and concise messages using the right medium (e.g. conversation, letter, email, meeting) and language (e.g. use of formal/informal words, varying voice speed/pitch/volume/tone) so that other people can understand.

6.4 Stakeholder Management

For a small investment of time, it is usually very worthwhile for the project manager and team to spend some time considering the various people who have an interest (stake) in the project. 'Stakeholders' might have a positive or negative interest in the project because the project offers them benefits or, alternatively, might give them concerns (IFC 2007; see also Section 7.1). Either way, some proactive effort is worthwhile to identify how people or organisations should be managed. The key point to be aware of is that different types of stakeholders need to be managed in different ways. For example, (1) stakeholders in a position of power but with little interest in the project need only be kept informed of project progression but will require ongoing effort by the project manager to cultivate their support, to keep them up-to-date and to give them confidence in the success of the project; (2) other powerful players who also have a high degree of interest in the project will need to be engaged much more closely in the project and may take ownership for some aspects of the work; (3) people with high levels of interest but low power might need to be consulted on certain matters and generally kept up-to-date (e.g. through web feeds and newsletters); and (4) people with low interest and low involvement might only need general information (IFC 2007). By rating different stakeholders on a 1–10 scale for 'power' and 'interest' and plotting them onto a power-versus-interest chart, you can identify cohorts of stakeholders with whom you can communicate and who could be involved using common approaches. For example, diverse community groups could be invited to regular open days or town hall meetings at the same time.

6.5 Defining the Project and Setting Goals

The long-term purpose or 'reason for being' is an important focus for a project team (see Chapter 8). In conservation, maintaining a species or ecosystem demands that sustainable solutions are put in place by an otherwise short-term project. Intended outcomes often stretch beyond the horizons of the project itself. Specific project goals and objectives reside within the project's lifetime (e.g. three or five years) and set the expectations for achievement by the team. It is therefore very important to be clear about purpose, vision, goals and objectives (Figure 6.2). Common terms encountered in project management include

- **Purpose.** Why are we here? A clear, succinct statement understood and communicated by all.
- **Vision.** What will long-term success look like? Will it inspire people?
- **Goals.** What do we want (to achieve in this project)? (Analogous to 'fundamental objectives'; see Section 9.1,1)
- **Objectives.** What specific things do we need to achieve in our activities to attain our goals? (Analogous to 'means objectives'; see Section 9.1,1)
- **Scope.** How much do we want to get done (breadth and depth of the work)?

Figure 6.2 Cayman blue iguana: 'We envision a population of at least one thousand Grand Cayman blue iguanas, living freely within protected areas, reproducing naturally and continuing to evolve in step with their ever-changing natural environment.' By 2012, the population had risen to 750, resulting in a down-listing of the species from critically endangered to endangered. (*Photo credit:* John Binns.) (A black-and-white version of this figure will appear in some formats. For the colour version, please refer to the plate section.)

- **Strategy.** The broad approach(es) that the project will take to achieve its purpose and goals.
- **Plan.** Detail of how to attain the objectives: tasks, time scales, resource allocations
- **Measures.** Indicators to monitor progress (quality, quantity, time cost, behaviour)?

- **Activities.** The work that needs to be carried out by the team.
- **Milestones.** Checkpoints in the progress of the project to support monitoring.

It is useful to set clear criteria to measure the achievement of the project and to enable measurement of how the project is progressing towards its goals and overall purpose. These criteria are routinely called 'objectives'. An objective must be clear and precise so that its achievement can easily be recognised, or a failure to perform can be investigated and future improvement can be identified. Very often objectives are shared, which is the most useful way to instil collaboration, involvement, mutual interest and a team ethic. A useful framework to use when writing objectives is SMART (Doran 1981):

> **Specific.** Ensure that you describe the objective without ambiguity and avoiding generalities.
>
> **Measurable.** Use metrics of quantity, quality, time, cost, behaviour or other indicators of success.
>
> **Agreed.** The person who is assigned the objectives must be identified and must also buy into what is being set.
>
> **Realistic.** Is it achievable and under the influence of the person assigned? Are resources available?
>
> **Time bound.** The endpoint date when completion (success) or failure is measured (e.g. 'by 1 September 2023').

6.6 Project Planning: Deliverables, Activities and Milestones

A project will comprise a number of discrete time-bound and task-defined pieces of work or 'stages'. The activities can be completed within a set time to deliver outputs to be used in subsequent stages (or certainly in later stages) of the project. The project manager needs to monitor completion of the work and place relevant controls on its success and transfer of outputs (i.e. results and achievements) to the next stage. It is worthwhile to reiterate project objectives at the start of each stage so that team members remain clear on what needs to be done, by whom and when. Project monitoring also involves reporting to the project board on transitions between stages or any exceptions occurring within stages.

One criticism of conservation work is that evaluations of success or failure are often steered towards assessment of which activities have been carried out or which milestones have been reached (Kapos 2008). This vagueness between understanding outcomes and activity can have a significant impact on the project. For example, throughout the 1970s, 1980s and early 1990s, survey teams monitored the population of the newly discovered po'ouli in the mountain forests on Maui, Hawaii (see Box 2.2). However, continued monitoring failed to deliver knowledge on the species ecology and breeding biology in a way that would help to understand the status of the species or its potential recovery programme.

The project manager needs to establish what are the 'deliverables' of the project: which outputs will people be able to see and measure? These things are useful when deciding how to organise the project plan, matching what the project will deliver with the needs of stakeholders and the overall project goals. The project team can be involved in this exercise. Next, in order to plan how to produce the desired deliverables, the manager needs to identify the activities that will generate those desired outcomes. Activities can be organised and subdivided to identify the range of tasks necessary to complete the project. These lists of tasks and subtasks can be used to develop a project schedule that describes the sequence and timeline of project activities. Additionally, the manager might wish to set project milestones (Figure 6.3), which are useful as checkpoints in the progress of the project and support ongoing monitoring and control. Typically, milestones are fixed points in the programme of work that can be clearly observed and used as a point of celebration for the team (Clayton 2012). Milestones could be the key points between stages of the project (i.e. a point of completion of a section of work) or key outputs achieved by the team (e.g. the first hatched bird in captivity). Milestones can feature in the communication process to give people (including interested stakeholders) a sense of the structure of the project.

6.6.1 Refining and Enhancing Your Project Plan

Either during the development of a plan or more often during implementation of the work it may be necessary for you to revisit the plan and identify ways to save money or time (e.g. if faced with unexpected delays, team changes or new budget or funding constraints). Various methods can be applied during initial planning or as part of regular project reviews to produce practical improvements. The order of activity can be drawn out onto a network diagram, where each activity (drawn in a box) is

Figure 6.3 In 2009, Durrell, Wildfowl and Wetlands Trust (WWT) and partners established the very first breeding programme for the critically endangered Madagascar pochard *Aythya innotata*. In 2018, a significant milestone is to return captive-bred young to Madagascar's wetlands. (*Photo credit:* L. Woolaver.)

placed in sequence following a logical order of work. Against this, a 'critical path' (or paths) of dependent activities can be ordered, involving all activities that depend upon completion of a previous activity before they can be initiated themselves (Clayton 2012). All other activities can be planned to occur outside or parallel to this critical path. Time can be added to this critical-path analysis, denoting the amount of time for each activity. The total time for the project can be calculated from the sum of time required for all activities in the critical path from the start of the project to its completion.

Fast-tracking is a useful technique that involves optimising the sequence of activities to reduce the overall time required. Fast-tracking involves (1) identifying activities that can be run in parallel and (2) considering whether and how to revisit and shorten the critical path. Any fast-tracking has to ensure that the integrity of the critical path of activities in the project is maintained. The critical path runs through the sequence of activities that are reliant upon completion of a previous activity. All other activities outside a critical path can be flexed around the project timeline to some degree (depending on budget and resources). Identification of the options is usually performed using 'critical-path analysis'. Gantt charts are a helpful tool for visualising overall schedule and layout of the project, presenting the range of activities against a horizontal timeline for each activity (as a set of horizontal bars, one for each activity). Gantt charts can be useful to explain the interrelationships between activities, the impact of the sequence of activities in the critical path and the allowable overlaps between unrelated activities.

An alternative to fast-tracking is 'compressing' the plan. This involves adding more resources to complete a task, for example, hiring more people to carry out a task in a shorter time frame. This requires identification of (1) project cost per day, (2) number of days saved by the change, (3) cost of additional resources and (4) a cost–benefit calculation (fewer days versus additional cost). Figure 6.4 shows a simple example where costs and savings are described to justify a change in the plan.

6.6.2 Plan Protection and Regular Project Review

At various stages of planning and delivery of projects it is valuable to review the plan and to proactively anticipate potential difficulties, obstacles or changes in circumstances that might affect the success of the project. A conventional approach to strengthening a project plan is to build in 'contingencies', usually either extra time, extra money or extra resources over and above the amount required for the work. The problem with this approach is that it can be very arbitrary and resource intensive, leading to waste and potential complacency rather than sensible thinking. As an alternative, plan protection involves conducting a sensible preplanning risk analysis to finalise the overall plan before resources and time are committed to its implementation. This process is based around the concept of 'prevention better than cure'. While the approach superficially resembles a 'risk analysis', the purpose is

Site clearance for fencing
1 labourer - $50 per day
Equipment - $500

3 weeks to complete work
Cost $1250
Completion by end April

Cost of delivery of fence
in May = $2000

Project cost/day = $500
Project days = 15
Project Cost = $7500

Site clearance for fencing
3 labourers - $150 per day
Equipment - $1500

1 week to complete work
Cost $2250
Completion by mid April

Cost of delivery of fence
in April = $1250
(*discount of $750*)

Project cost/day = $500
Project days = 5
Project Cost = $2500
(*days cost **saving** versus
original* 3 *week plan
above* = **$5000**)

**Total extra cost for
compression $1000 versus** **Total benefit $ 5750**

Figure 6.4 Compression of a task in a project plan. Investing extra labour and equipment (totalling $1,000) to clear a site saves time, gains a $750 discount on delivery of the fence *and* reduces total project days required by five days (at $500 per day) for a net saving of $4,750.

more specific: the outcome for the analysis is to identify mitigation activities that should be built in as new steps within the wider project plan. In particular, the core concepts of the protecting plans process are (1) a plan can be made more robust by thoughtful risk analysis, (2) the potential impact and likelihood should be assessed before investing time and effort, (3) mitigation should be the first course of action in the face of potential risks, and (4) contingencies should be seen as a last resort: it is better to plan feasible mitigation action.

The four-step plan protection process involves employing a straightforward grid to map out the process. This is illustrated in the example of a project to build a captive breeding facility for tortoises (Figure 6.5). For each project step in the plan it is necessary to identify whether any risks are associated with that activity. In the case of the breeding centre build, two steps have been identified that carry risks: the boundary (security) walls are close to neighbouring trees, and the gate-way opens out to an adjacent road that gets heavily flooded in the rainy

Step/ Time	Activity	Risk(s)	Impact	Likelihood	Mitigation (plan protection)	Contingent Action
12	Build tortoise enclosure walls	Trees adjacent to North Wall offer access for intruders	HIGH	HIGH	Cut down all branches and/or trees adjacent to the enclosure	Procedure to shut tortoises in locked huts each night
		Intruders able to climb walls to access enclosure	HIGH	HIGH	Outer wall built to be faced in smooth stone & pointing is tight	
		Predators (mongoose) can traverse walls and access site	MEDIUM (juveniles only)	LOW		Set traps outside walls if observed
19	Lay enclosure base, access paths/vehicle entrance to courtyard	Flood damage to site in rainy season	HIGH	HIGH	Add aggregate base layer 2ft, compress & compress top layer (wacker plate both)	
		Water egress from outside site in rainy season (Ford Road entrance)	HIGH	MEDIUM	Add 10" gutter outside gate along Ford Road side of the site, plus steel gutter grate at vehicle entrance gate. Floodboard attachments fixed onto gate arch.	Deploy flood boards at gate arch on occasions of extreme rainfall
		Aggregate for base layer not available	MEDIUM	LOW		

Figure 6.5 An extract from a 'Protecting Plans' matrix showing entries for two project steps with identified risks in the construction of a captive breeding centre for endangered tortoises.

season. For each step, the process examines the potential risks associated with the activity (potential failure/breakdown), the impact if that risk occurred (high/medium/low) and the likelihood that the risk will occur. From this information it is possible to consider and prioritise (1) mitigation to devise a way to prevent this risk arising and (2) contingent action that could take place if mitigation fails or mitigation is not otherwise possible for some reason.

The final stage of the process is for identified mitigation action (i.e. plan protection) to be added as a new step (or several new steps) in the final overall project plan. In this way, the final plan will become more robust, for the sake of a few additional elements. Clearly, the cost of the mitigation action should be less than the likely cost of failure, or the project will become unmanageable. Mitigating for risks that are unlikely to occur is usually counterproductive, unless the potential impact is large. In the captive breeding centre example (Figure 6.5), the last risk, listed at the bottom, carries a likelihood that is seen as low enough that it is not necessary to prepare either mitigation or contingent action. The four mitigation actions identified in Figure 6.5 should now be built into a revised project plan for the development of the site. In this example, the contingencies will be included in future operational procedures, although sometimes contingencies may become part of the project plan itself. It is important to note that the four new mitigation steps will need themselves to be considered against the protecting plan's criteria (e.g. Is there need for permission to cut down neighbouring trees?).

6.7 Day-to-Day Project Management: Agreeing on Project Stages, Controls and Authorisation

To clarify project governance and provide the project manager with both accountability and authority to progress the work, it may be useful to agree a series of 'project stages' with the project sponsor and the steering committee (or project board). Each stage will involve a package of activities that need completion within a specific time period. Typically, a series of stages will involve the work required across the critical path of the project. Part of the agreement on the definition of each stage will be specification of the boundaries of exception for decision-making. The project manager needs to have agreed 'tolerances' for decisions based upon time, cost, risk and scope for each stage of the project (see Section 6.2).

Within a stage and within its agreed tolerances for decision-making, the project manager has authority to allocate resources, time and team members to the work that is required. Work outside these tolerances requires authorisation from the project sponsor and/or project steering group (project board). Similarly, at the boundaries between stages (i.e. at the end of one stage and before the start of the next) the project manager needs to get senior-level authorisation on the work completed. If any compromises have been required to complete the work, the sign-off by the board authorises the project to continue despite those compromises. This system protects the project manager and team while minimising subsequent delays to the work. If the project is severely compromised, then it is necessary to formally review the project plan and get senior-level authorisation of the revision before further work. The manager might wish to use key stage completion dates as milestones in the project. Typically, regular project reports to the project steering committee (or to funders or other key stakeholders) would include reference to work status against those agreed key stages within the project.

6.8 Running Project Meetings

Meetings have a purpose within a project and are an important method of communication that benefits the work being conducted by the project team. However, it is not the job of the manager to be the instigator of meetings-meetings-meetings. As project manager, you have a role based on your intellectual capability, organisation, experience and judgement – you should not waste those resources on running meetings and reporting; this is not the 'work of management', nor is micro-managing, nor is excessive 'monitoring', since these add little value, cause distraction and generally impinge on the efforts of the workforce. To make use of meetings, follow a clear meetings plan with an agreed-upon purpose and expected outcome (or outcomes), a clear start point (time available, information available or to be shared, roles to be followed, including who attends, who leads the meeting and how notes will be recorded), and an agreed-upon agenda of topics including how much time will be assigned to each topic and the process at each stage (e.g. presentation).

Ensure clear roles for participants, including a chairperson to guide the meeting through its agenda and perhaps a separate timekeeper and a note taker. Agree upon and clarify what you wish to achieve on each agenda item; is it a discussion, a decision or vote, an endorsement, a problem to solve, a plan to agree upon, or action to assign to individuals? Finally, agree upon the method you will use to record and circulate minutes, notes and information. Ensure that information is shared ahead of the meeting if needed (do not have people waste time reading during the meeting). The note taker should finalise the notes, check with the chairperson and then circulate the information (e.g. electronically, through paper copies, or a document placed on a team notice board).

6.9 Change Control

If a project has run off-plan, or a regular review identifies the need for a change of plan, the project manager needs to ensure that the change is agreed upon and documented. If the change is an exception, it should be formally reported up to the project board/sponsor. If the change is minor and within a defined project stage controlled by the project manager, then it should also be recorded for later reporting to the board during the transition to the next stage. On other occasions changes may be requested informally by the team or perhaps an external stakeholder.

In this situation, the project manager needs to be able to take a balanced approach – stick to the plan or accommodate the change. Is the suggested change trivial (or 'nice to have'), or is it potentially helpful or important? The project manager must be able to discern between the two without disengaging the person who has suggested the idea. This will mean asking for a precise statement of the change which is requested accompanied by a statement of justification (i.e. the value of the additional time, effort, cost or risk). This information enables an evaluation of costs/time/effort/risk for implementing the change. The analysis enables a further decision either by exception (passing up to the board) or by the project manager. Any change request and change decision should be documented in a project log or regular report (Clayton 2012).

6.10 Project Closure and Review

Conservation projects can be limited by funding horizons and so will have a defined end date. In reality, however, conservation outcomes need to be sustainable beyond such deadlines for the benefit of the species and ecosystems of concern. The project manager often needs to sustain the project by revisiting and reapplying for funding to add new iterations to the project cycle and extend the lifetime of the project. At these natural breaks in the project (e.g. funding cycles), it is important that the project manager encourages team members (and potentially their steering group/board) to reflect back on the last cycle and ask the following questions: Were objectives met? Were time and resources used effectively? Did the team perform well? This reflection is important information in general for the project participants but will also be useful if any follow-on work or local ownership of the work is being handed on to another team (Coppin and Barratt 2002). If elements of the project work are to be handed over to another organisation (e.g. a local team or government department), you need to plan the handover systematically. Treat this in a similar way to your team induction process. Cover issues of task, team and individual responsibilities. Part of the handover process will include full reporting of the project to all stakeholders who have held an interest in the project or who will continue an interest in any further work.

Mark the endpoint of the project (or particular project cycle) with an event for individual team members (including the project manager) to celebrate their time working together; to give each other feedback on their performance, strengths and weaknesses; and to give a chance to talk about future opportunities. The aim is to make people leave the project on a positive note with lessons learned clear in their minds and a positive sense of the people with whom they worked. It also provides the chance for people to leave the team with a positive view of the person who led them.

6.11 The Project Manager's Tool Kit

Project management requires development and delivery of the project plan. This means that the project manager needs an array of tools to aid in management of the tasks, the team and the individuals on the team. Governance, team building, project planning and protecting plans have been discussed. This section focuses on the team process skills that will enable the project manager to engage the team most effectively in day-to-day project management.

A manager needs to have a suite of skills ready to apply to managing the team and the project – its people, technology and processes. This suite of skills enables the smooth running of any project regardless of focus, specialism or outcomes, and they relate to the flow of work and activity rather than the specific content (which is based on technical know-how). Process skills include situation assessment, goal-setting, decision-making, problem-solving, project planning and plan protection. These are mental skills that the project manager may use to guide thinking but can also be applied in group situations to ensure a systematic and consistent approach to managing the work. Of course, the ability to judge which skills to use on which occasions is critical. For example, building a plan without a clear definition of the problem is rather pointless. So pointless, you would think, that it would be obvious, but it is not unknown for years of project planning and implementation to be undertaken in conservation when the root problem has not been properly defined.

6.11.1 Situation Assessment

Differentiating problems, decisions, project planning and plan protection is an important mental discipline. For a given list of issues addressing the programme, the project manager needs to be able to separate out each situation and then, for each, follow a series of questions: Do I know the cause, and do I need to know it? – since determining causes involves a problem-solving process (see Chapter 5 for approaches to understanding causes of perceived population decline). Do I have to make a decision? – if so, then identify a decision-making process. Does this issue involve a plan of action that needs protection against risks? – therefore select a protecting plans process. Does this issue involve complex deadlines, resources and many people? – if so, use project management.

6.11.2 Problem-Solving

If a problem is encountered (e.g. poor performance, errors, erratic team behaviour, a complaint) it is useful to follow a systematic process to frame the problem clearly (as a precise 'problem statement') and then to unpack potential causes. Once possible causes have been highlighted, it is important to seek data on those causes to ensure that relevant and impactful improvement is pursued. Methods such as the 'six honest men', 'five whys', 'cause and effect analysis' and 'force-field analysis' can be useful.

Six Honest Men. Based on the Kipling poem, this mental routine prompts you to consider some questions in order to test any assumptions or ambiguities in your problem statement. If you have a problem, you should consider: *what, why, who, where, when* and *how*. A combination of these questions (and variations on each) will help to clearly frame the problem (Figure 6.6).

Five Whys. This is a thinking method used to avoid focusing on symptoms of much deeper-seated problems. It ensures that you seek to deal with causes, not symptoms. If you have a problem or issue of concern, (1) clearly state what the problem/issue is, (2) ask why is this problem occurring? (this will usually identify a reason for the problem/ issue), (3) ask yourself again why is that newly identified reason/problem occurring?, and (4) repeat the process through a sequence of five 'whys'. By the fifth 'why', you should reach the root cause.

Cause and Effect (Fishbone) Diagram. As popularised in the Japanese industrial revival of the 1970s and 1980s, this approach can be applied to the complex types of problems encountered in conservation. The technique allows a team to share ideas that are structured onto a diagram. This process allows ideas to be themed and provides opportunities to identify major areas where data collection is required to support further analysis. The observed 'effect', or problem statement, is written on the right of the diagram. A fishbone of four to six major

Figure 6.6 Conservation biologists from Durrell using 'six honest men' (in French) to begin to unpick the causes behind anthropogenic burning within a protected area. (*Photo credits:* Jamieson A. Copsey.)

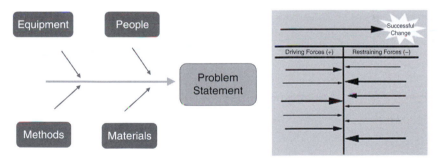

Figure 6.7 Examples of a Fishbone cause-and-effect diagram (left) and a force-field analysis chart (right).

themes is constructed; commonly used 'cause categories' include people, equipment, material, process, environment and measurement ('P–E–M–P–E–M'). Individual ideas of specific causes are suggested by team members and are posted under the relevant theme on the diagram (Figure 6.7). Sometimes ideas are identified that are root causes of an earlier suggestion, so they can be indicated as sub-branches of the ideas on the diagram. It is sometimes helpful to ask the question 'why?' after a suggested cause because this might stimulate further ideas. Once the diagram has been completed and answers exhausted, the team can discuss and agree upon preventative actions, any data collection needed prior to action and who will be responsible, as well as when and how progress will be reviewed.

Force-Field Analysis. This is a similar technique for categorising ideas using a brainstorming discussion. For a given situation (or performance issue), team members are asked to identify things that will improve the situation ('driving forces') and things that will worsen or impede the situation ('restraining forces'). Once people run out of ideas and the two lists are completed, the group rates each idea on a scale (e.g. 1–10) to show the magnitude of that force. These ratings could be informed by data (e.g. the impact of particular threats). Additionally, the ease of applying or eliminating the force can be rated (e.g. 1–10) and both impact/ease ratings multiplied to give an index rating. Once ratings have been calculated, a force-field diagram can be drawn (Figure 6.7) with larger arrows indicating the stronger-rated forces. The team can visually assess which restraining forces to address and potentially which driving forces could be addressed to aid improvement. It is generally better to concentrate on eliminating or reducing restraining forces since this will give natural momentum to the existing driving forces so that change will be more likely to occur.

6.11.3 Decision-Making

Decision-making takes many forms. A project manager might have to make a decision alone or with others, in a short time frame or after long reflection, address complexities or straightforward unimportant issues. The level of involvement of other people will depend on the authority of the project leader and the relative influence of others. Within the project, the governance structure will guide who decides and how. Involvement also relates to the people's competence, willingness, capacity, expertise and knowledge, interest and investment (in the outcomes of the decision). A significant amount of management time is spent making decisions. Some of these will be straightforward, repeating modes faced on previous occasions;

Box 6.3 *Decision Alternatives in Managing Recovery of Hawaiian Birds (VanderWerf et al. 2006)*

In 2002, the Po'ouli Working Group needed to choose the next step to conserve the highly endangered po'ouli. The population survived as a tiny population of a few individuals in the Hanawi Natural Forest Reserve on Maui, Hawaii. Alternatives from the 1999 Environmental Assessment were discussed, plus new ideas and a 'no further action' option. However, none of the alternatives were universally supported by participants, and serious risks were associated with each. The alternatives held strong advantages and disadvantages, but the chance of success was low in each case.

A systematic approach to identifying specific alternatives was undertaken. It was agreed that habitat management and control of introduced predators and alien weeds were integral to any strategy and should be continued regardless of which option was chosen. These activities were removed from the decision options and enabled a clearer decision-making boundary. To overcome the deadlock, team members were able to identify seven specific alternatives:

1. No manipulation of wild adult birds; hope population increases in response to habitat management.
2. Repeat the recent translocation but with the second female.
3. Capture two or three birds for aviary at Hanawi; then release upon pair-bond formation or some later date.
4. Catch two or three birds to breed in aviary in Hanawi; then manage the nest, first clutch kept in captivity.
5. Catch two or three birds for aviary to assess acclimation to take into captivity or release if not feasible.
6. Catch two or three birds and remove them from Hanawi to a captive breeding facility.
7. Catch two or three birds and remove them to a field aviary at a more accessible location.

A structured decision approach was used to help evaluate and compare the alternatives.

Alternative (brand of vehicle)	Must 1: four-wheel drive	Must 2: engine snorkel	Must 3: roof rack	Want 1: cost ~$20,000	Want 2: diesel engine	Want 3: CD player	Want 4: GPS system	Total
				Weight: 10	7	4	7	
Hummer	✓	✓	✓	7 = 70	6 = 42	7 = 28	5 = 35	175
Daewoo	✓	✓	X	–	–	–	–	–
Bravia	✓	✓	✓	9 = 90	6 = 42	4 = 16	4 = 28	176
Oldsmobile	✓	✓	✓	6 = 60	7 = 49	8 = 32	6 = 42	183
Saab	X	✓	✓	–	–	–	–	–

Figure 6.8 Decision matrix. A simplified example for replacing a project vehicle. The second alternative ('Daewoo') and the fifth alternative ('Saab') fail to meet the 'musts' and so are rejected. In this case, the decision makers have given alternative four, the Oldsmobile, the highest overall score, so against their criteria, that is the tentative best choice.

many will be relatively trivial. In simple terms, a mental decision process involves (1) clarifying the aim of the decision (e.g. 'to ...'), (2) identifying alternatives and likely outcomes, and (3) picking the most appropriate alternative. In some cases, picking the alternative can be simple. For example, to decide which of two volunteers should take on a particular task, with all skills and experience otherwise equal, you could simply employ the toss of a coin – it is fair, unbiased and gives an outcome – one person chosen. However, most decisions require more complex processing. An additional factor is the speed of decision; some decisions need an instant response, while others allow more considered processing and weighing of evidence.

When information is complex or alternative actions are not obvious, where the involvement of others is needed or where outcomes are important, a systematic 10-step decision–making process is useful (Figure 6.8) and provides a documented description of the rationale behind the decision

Step 1: Write down the decision statement describing the goal you wish to achieve. Avoid including more than one decision (detected by the word 'and'), avoid negative statements (e.g. 'How not to ...') and avoid including alternative courses of action. Test the statement for unconscious decisions: for example, 'which new vehicle to buy' implies 'new' and 'buy' and blocks other possible options, such as buying a used vehicle, renting a vehicle or obtaining the vehicle using a lease arrangement.

Step 2: *Establish the decision objectives*, which can be identified by considering (a) what are the desired results (what to accomplish? when? what to avoid/create/improve/maintain?), (b) what resources are available (how much money? personnel? equipment? how much time?), and (c) consider any implied restrictions (legislation? deadlines? time? money? authority? rules?). Review and tighten up the wording in the objectives, and clarify any that are vague or ambiguous.

Step 3: *Classify the objectives.* Not all are equally important; some must be accomplished, while others may be merely desirable. 'Must' criteria help to filter out decision alternatives. A 'must' is defined where (a) success depends on it, (b) it is practical and can be measured, and/or (c) it is mandatory. Identifying mandatory objectives is an important step; a mistake would raise doubts about the final decision. There should be only a few musts. If in doubt about a must, make it a 'want'; for example, 'Must cost no more than £10,000' – what if the cost is £10,120? If it isn't an obvious 'must', then relegate it to a 'want'.

Step 4: *Weight the wants.* This step enables you to consider the relative value of the rest of the objectives – the wants. You can do this by rating each using a fairly arbitrary arithmetic range, say from 1–10. Give the weight '10' to your most important want, and weight the rest in relation to the top one.

Step 5: *Generate alternatives.* Frequently the alternative courses of action are fairly obvious, e.g. the choice of which equipment to buy based on alternatives from manufacturers. This step is more difficult when alternatives are not obvious, at which point consider (a) personal experience, (b) other people's experience, (c) your boss, (d) other specialists, and (e) a structured brainstorming session with colleagues.

Step 6: *Measure the alternatives against the musts.* Screen out any alternatives that do not satisfy the mandatory requirements (see Figure 6.8). Sometimes an alternative fails a 'must', but a 'gut feeling' suggests that it might be the best alternative. This means that either the gut feeling is wrong or the specification has not been set properly and so needs a return to step 1. Sometimes none of the alternatives meet the musts: either find a new alternative or admit that the specification is too restrictive.

Step 7: *Compare alternatives.* Establish the degree to which the alternatives meet the 'want' elements in the specification. To do this, use an arithmetic scale again: 10 = best, and 1 = worst. The easiest method is to chart this information onto a decision matrix (see Figure 6.8). Rate each alternative horizontally across the page. Finally, multiply the score by the weight of the wants (step 4) to produce a 'weighted score'. Assess each alternative by adding the weighted scores together to give a total.

Step 8: *Make the tentative decision,* indicated as the alternative with the highest total. However, this choice will need to be tested (step 9). Consider where this choice picked up the marks? Did it get a high score in heavily weighted wants or lightly weighted wants or both? Is it merely the least undesirable?

Step 9: *Assess potential drawbacks.* Test whether the tentative choice is less satisfactory than seems apparent. Is there anything about the situation not yet taken into account? Have circumstances altered since the decision process was started? Is there any bias around this alternative? Consider potential draw-backs under the headings 'Probability' and 'Seriousness'. If the tentative decision proves untenable after this check, re-examine the next-highest-scoring alternative until the decision stands up.

Step 10: *Make the final choice.* This method will not automatically take the decision. It simply guides the consideration of informa-tion to enable logical judgements.

6.12 Evaluating Projects

Since the 1970s, conservation management has revolved around formal conservation management planning methods, but these approaches have been criticised for being excessively restrictive and often detrimental to the immediate recovery needs of the species concerned (Clark et al. 2002). More recent conservation management frameworks have arisen (Hockings et al. 2006; Conservation Measures Partnership 2004), but these do not consider performance or human resources and financial management. As an alternative, the 'Conservation Excellence Model'

(Black and Groombridge 2010), which is derived from established business evaluation models, is focused on the effectiveness of the overall system or organisation that embodies a conservation programme from design and implementation through to its operation and review (Black et al. 2011). Biodiversity is placed as the 'customer' of the conservation intervention or programme of work, allowing a project to be viewed using a number of novel perspectives:

1. Biological results, trends, and scientific projections relating to species, their habitats or direct threats are considered 'biodiversity results' and are the 'bread and butter' concerns of conservation professionals (i.e. interactions of animal and plant populations, geophysical variables in ecosystems, threats to species and ecosystems). It additionally includes embedded human issues such as human–wildlife conflict (e.g. predation, crop raiding, exploitation, harassment) or general human landscape use (e.g. hunting, extraction, harvesting yields). These are the things important to survival of species and ecosystems.
2. Other result measures with significant practical influence on the work of conservation are considered as 'conservation program results' (timescales, budgets, technical outcomes and deliverables, performance against objectives, financial results and project milestones). These are the things noticed by people running (or funding) the project.
3. Since volunteers and local community members are often directly engaged in conservation work alongside official employees, measures of employee and community results are included in 'people and local community results'. Levels of involvement in the programme (e.g. numbers of community volunteers, participants in meetings) are included alongside employee metrics.
4. Societal impacts are placed in the 'impact on wider society' criterion, including indirect measures such as well-being (e.g. safety, welfare, income), and outcomes from human–wildlife conflict, such as economic loss, or societal benefits from human activity in the landscape such as income from agriculture or other off-take.

Various methods of Conservation Excellence assessment can be conducted (Moore et al. 2018), but a self-assessment by the project team is usually the most feasible approach. Team members can be assigned questions under one or more criteria and can gather a combination of results, documented activities (from routine project reports and meetings minutes) and interviews with staff and stakeholders using questions derived from the conservation excellence model criteria.

182 · **Simon A. Black**

However, it is the strengths, areas for improvement and conclusions drawn from the assessment that are the most important elements of the review.

6.13 Summary

Key points from this chapter:

- Governance is critical to successful project management. The project sponsor has a key role to play in ensuring that decision-making does not slow the project or impact upon its effectiveness.
- Project planning involves a series of techniques. However, the most important aspect of planning is the ability to review and update the plan according to circumstances.
- The project manager needs to be effective in communicating the plan through clearly defined and enduring project purpose, vision and goals, defined as practical objectives (which will be continually reviewed).
- The effectiveness of day-to-day project work can be enhanced by the use of clear and consistent processes for running meetings, making decisions and solving problems. The project manager needs to balance his or her attention to the task (the project work), the team and individuals.
- When evaluating the outcomes of a completed project, consider both the outcomes ('results') and the approaches involved, linking people, process and performance elements of the work. The Conservation Excellence Model is a useful framework for assessing this range of issues.

References

Beckhard, R. (1972). Optimizing team building effort. *Journal of Contemporary Business* 1(3): 23–32

Black, S. A. and Groombridge, J. J. (2010). Use of a business excellence model to improve conservation programs. *Conservation Biology* 24: 1448–58.

Black, S. A., Meredith, H. M. R. and Groombridge, J. J. (2011). Biodiversity conservation: applying new criteria to assess excellence. *Total Quality Management* 22: 1165–78, available at http://dx.doi.org/10.1080/14783363.2011.624766.

Blue Iguana Recovery Program (2017). Our Vision, available at www.blueiguana.ky/recovery/programme/our-vision/on 24/5/2017.

Boersma, P. D., Kareiva, P., Fagan, W. F., Clark, J. A. and Hoekstra, J. M. (2001). How good are endangered species recovery plans? *BioScience* 51: 643–49.

Butchart, S. H. M., Walpole, M., Collen, B. et al. (2010). Global biodiversity: indicators of recent declines. *Science* 328: 1164–68.

Clark, J. A., Hoekstra, J. M., Boersma, P. D. and Kareiva, P. (2002). Improving U.S Endangered Species Act recovery plans: key findings and recommendations of the SCB Recovery Plan Project. *Conservation Biology* 16: 1510–19.

Clayton, M. (2012). *Brilliant Project Leader*. Pearson, Harlow.

Conservation Measures Partnership (2004). *Open Standards for the Practice of Conservation*, version 2.0. Washington, DC.

Coppin, A. and Barratt, J. (2002). *Timeless Management*. Palgrave Macmillan, New York, NY.

Covey, S. R. (1989). *The 7 Habits of Highly Effective People*. Simon & Shuster, New York, NY.

Doran, G. T. (1981). There's a S.M.A.R.T. way to write management's goals and objectives. *AMA Forum* 70(1): 35–36

Hockings, M., Stolton, S., Leverington, F., Dudley, N., and Courrau, J. (2006). *Evaluating Effectiveness: A Framework for Assessing Management Effectiveness of Protected Areas*. IUCN, Gland.

IFC (2007). *Stakeholder Engagement: A Good Practice Handbook for Companies Doing Business in Emerging Markets*. International Finance Corporation, Washington DC, available at www.ifc.org.

Kapos, V., Balmford, A., Aveling, R. et al. (2008). Calibrating conservation: new tools for measuring success. *Conservation Letters* 1(4): 155–64.

Moore, A. A., Weckauf, R., Accouche, W. F. and Black, S. A. (2018). The value of consensus in rapid organisation assessment: wildlife programmes and the Conservation Excellence Model, Total Quality Management & Business Excellence, DOI: 10.1080/14783363.2018.1444472.

Powell, A. (2008). *The Race to Save the World's Rarest Bird: The Discovery and Death of the Po'ouli*. Stackpole Books, Mechanicsburg, PA.

VanderWerf, E. A., Groombridge, J. J., Fretz, J. S. and Swinnerton, K. J. (2006). Decision analysis to guide recovery of the po'ouli, a critically endangered Hawaiian honeycreeper. *Biological Conservation* 129(3): 383–92.

Westrum R. (1994). An organisational perspective: Designing Recovery Teams from the Inside Out. In Clark T.W., Reading, R.P. and Clarke A (Eds) Endangered Species Recovery: Finding the Lessons, Improving the Process. Island Press, Washington DC.

7 · *Managing Island Threats*
Eradication and Sustained Control of Invasive Species

JOHN PARKES

7.0 Introduction

The impacts of invasive alien species are greater on islands than elsewhere. Realistically, incursions cannot be stopped altogether, but they can be managed and subsequent impacts mitigated. With invasive species management, prevention is usually better than cure. However, in many instances, the introduced species are already established and may have had a severe impact on native biodiversity. In other instances, insufficient legislation or its implementation leaves biodiversity 'hotspots' (including many islands) open to invasion.

This chapter addresses what can be done to combat the impacts of invasive species, with a particular focus on invasive vertebrates, the cause of numerous endemic species extinctions worldwide. We do not intend to provide a comprehensive review of invasive species management theory but instead to identify the fundamental steps to take in following an eradication or sustained long-term control process, learning from work conducted primarily on islands. We begin with considering the need to understand and engage key stakeholders throughout the process and go on to suggest how we can prioritise our efforts. Feasibility studies are often lacking in invasive management projects, so we reflect on the importance of building in this stage. Finally, we spend time discussing important attributes in designing early detection, rapid response (EDDR) approaches, eradication and sustained control programmes, ending with some thoughts on some concerns for the future. By the end of the chapter we intend for the reader to be clearer about key points to consider if faced with an invasive vertebrate management project.

7.1 Know Your People

Throughout this book we have emphasised the need to 'know your species' when it comes to understanding why it is in decline (see Chapter 5), the biology and ecology of an invasive species that may be threatening your target (see Chapter 4) or how to increase the population size of the species under threat (see Chapters 9 and 10). When managing an invasive species, it is also critical to understand the people who have a vested interest in the species ('stakeholders'; see Section 6.4). Once an invasive species accesses an island, country or other zone of concern, a typical pest project consists of a sequence of linked phases each involving different work and different actors and aimed at different audiences (Figure 7.1).

Management of people with their different values is often a critical component of invasive species management (Parkes 1993a), as it is for any project designed to engage them in some form of activity (see Chapter 11). It is difficult to think of a project involving invasive species management that does not involve people as proponents, antagonists, regulators, legislators, landowners, taxpayers, advocates or objectors for any number of reasons that give them a stake in the project (Boudjelas 2009). Stakeholder opposition has caused many projects to stumble: the rejected proposal to eradicate animal pests from Great Barrier Island in New Zealand (Ogden and Gilbert 2011); the delayed eradication of rodents on Lord Howe Island proposed in 2001, funding approved in 2012, but yet to begin due to local opposition (Wilkinson and Priddel 2011); or, worse still, started and then abandoned rabbit eradication on Clarion Island in Mexico (Parkes 2002). Managing stakeholders is not usually a core strength of biologists, and managers of projects with contentious issues should seek advice from people with social science skills in the process (e.g. skills for facilitating pig eradication from Santa Cruz Island in California; Morrison 2007; and Pacific Invasives Initiative at www.pacificinvasivesinitiative.org for guidance on stakeholder engagement).

It is vital to involve the most important stakeholders early on in the project design process (Yaffee et al. 1996). This may require stakeholder identification to begin months before people are brought together to stand a chance of getting the right people together in the right place at the right time; only then can you develop workshops to engage multiple stakeholders and initiate participatory planning (Westley and Miller 2003). The analysis of which stakeholders are the priority groups to involve at different points in an eradication or sustained control project can be relatively simple, involving

Figure 7.1 Project cycle diagram. (*Source:* From Pacific Invasives Initiative, http://pacificinvasivesinitiative.org.)

1. Identifying all potential stakeholders that could be involved (gathered from consultation with local partners).
2. Grouping stakeholders according to their impact on project success or the impact of the project on the particular stakeholder group. This should involve consideration and inclusion of stakeholders that may oppose the project as well as those that may be supportive.
3. Deciding how best to engage the priority groups within the decision-making process.

Sutherland (2000) suggests a five-stage process of stakeholder identification: (1) primary stakeholders (intended beneficiaries of the process), (2) secondary (involved in the implementation of the project), and (3) external (concerned with the outcome but not directly involved). The process derives the needs and interests of each stakeholder group in relation to the problem, considering whether or not these interests will conflict with or support desired project outcomes (4). The final stage (5) involves selection of the priority groups based on their position within the project and how their needs and interests could affect the project (see Section 6.4).

7.2 Project Prioritisation, Selection and Justification

Proposals to manage invasive species arise in many ways. Some are local decisions to manage a confined problem involving local people, but others are the result of a formal prioritisation process. Generally, funders do not have enough money to act against all possible invasive species, so some prioritisation has to be undertaken. This can be done by ranking the impacts of particular invasive species or groups of invasive species and dealing with those which are most urgent or where benefits can be maximised (e.g. Parkes and Murphy 2003). Alternatively, this may involve ranking assets (e.g. threatened species or representative sites) and managing their key threats (Walker et al. 2012).

The first step in a project cycle is to define the problem more precisely (see Section 6.11.2). A fundamental point to understand is which invasive species is affecting which value (e.g. other species of conservation concern). The audience of this phase is primarily the people or beneficiaries who are advocating that something needs to be done – it aims to get buy-in from these main stakeholders and to ensure that the wider community of interest is either supportive or reconciled to the actions. Justifying a project can be simple when the problem caused by a target invasive species is clear to all – the invasive arrives, and native species rapidly vanish (e.g. the arrival of ship rats *Rattus rattus* on Big South Cape Island in 1963 drove at least seven endemic species to extinction in a few years; Bell 1978). Bitter experience shows that the arrival of some invasive species can lead to significantly reduced abundance and functionality of native species or even their extinction, especially on islands (see Section 4.2).

Diagnosis of cause and effect can be subtle when the effect takes decades to emerge or complicated when more than one invasive species is involved. For example, ship rats *R. rattus* arrived on Lord Howe Island in 1918 and caused the extinction of five species, so eradication of the rats is a prerequisite for plans to recover or restore native populations (Hutton et al. 2007). Among the birds that survived the arrival of rats on Lord Howe Island is the endemic woodhen *Tricholimnas sylvestris*, whose population decline led to a project with captive breeding and release and threat control (Miller and Mullette 1985). It was thought that the ship rats had caused the decline in woodhen numbers. However, the birds survived in places with plenty of rats but not in places accessible to feral pigs *Sus scrofa* – the real culprit. Pigs were eradicated by the early 1980s, and an attempt to eradicate rats and mice is currently planned for winter 2018 (Wilkinson and Priddel 2011 and www.lhirodenteradica tionproject.org).

Sometimes the nature of the problem is assumed from well-known experiences in other places. For example, red foxes *Vulpes vulpes* are a major predator of small animals on mainland Australia (Saunders et al. 1995) and so are predicted to cause similar problems on Tasmania if the few detected there in 1998 manage to establish (Parkes and Anderson 2011). A major attempt to remove the incursion began in 2002, mostly using bait containing compound 1080, although outcomes are unclear (indeed it is debated whether foxes ever established in Tasmania; Marks et al. 2014).

An exotic species may have no catastrophic or obvious impact, so some projects may be justified without any evidence (or at least without evidence from the site) simply as a precaution (Box 7.1; Figure 7.2). Precautionary responses are usually not suitable for

---

Box 7.1 *A Subtle Problem: Impact of Common Mynas on Native Birds*

The common myna *Acridotheres tristis* (Figure 7.2), native to India, has been introduced to many islands in the Pacific, Indian and Atlantic oceans, as well as eastern Australia and northern New Zealand. It is sometimes kept in the pet trade and has the common propensity to hitch rides on ships. People do not like the bird because it is a nuisance and sometimes damages crops and fruit, but does it pose a threat to native biodiversity such that attempts to eradicate the bird are justified?

Three sources of evidence implicate mynas in the decline of native species.

Indirect Evidence from Trends. Mynas invaded Canberra in 1968, spreading across urban, suburban and rural areas around this Australian city of 370,000 people. The increase and spread of mynas coincided with a decrease in abundance of three native cavity-nesting birds and eight small birds – six natives and two introduced (Grarock et al. 2012). It is not clear whether this is cause and effect or if declines can be reversed when mynas are controlled (King 2010). At a smaller scale, Freifeld (1999) noted that collared kingfishers *Halcyon chloris* were significantly more abundant in places with the fewest mynas on Tutuila Island in American Samoa. Again, whether this relates to mynas or just different habitat preferences is unclear.

Direct Evidence from Cause and Effect. Myna activities and harassment of particular native species around nests cause a problem. For example, the fledging rate of the endangered Tahitian flycatcher *Pomarea nigra* correlated with the number of interactions between mynas and flycatchers around flycatcher nests. Flycatcher nests that failed had experienced twice the level of myna interactions than nests that succeeded (Blanvillain et al. 2003).

Evidence from Control or Eradication. Evidence exists that when mynas are controlled or eradicated, native species increase in abundance. As examples, when mynas were controlled around flycatcher nests in Tahiti, the failure rate of the nests fell to zero from 39 per cent (Ghestemme 2011). On the New Zealand island of Moturoa, control of mynas was followed by significant increases in some other birds, including the native tui *Prosthemadera novaeseelandiae* (Tindall et al. 2007). Rats were also controlled in these experiments, so again the evidence is confounded.

This uncertainty has stopped some but not all attempts to eradicate or control mynas (Copsey and Parkes 2013). A recent successful eradication of common mynas on Denis Island in the Seychelles – using a combination of live decoy traps and shooting in three phases from 2010–14 – has demonstrated that such goals are attainable, at least on small islands, with sustained effort and commitment of all stakeholders (Feare et al. 2016).

Figure 7.2 Common myna *Acridotheres tristis*, Mauritius (*Photo credit:* Nik C. Cole.)

sustained control strategies unless designed as a preliminary experiment to demonstrate the impact by reducing the invasive species population. If no impact is mitigated by trial projects, it is difficult to justify expansion into a fully sustained control project in favour of spending the money elsewhere.

7.3 Feasibility Study

Proponents of invasive species management too often launch into action before understanding whether the desired approach will achieve its goals. A failed attempt to eradicate Indian musk shrews from the islet of Ile aux Aigrettes, Mauritius (Varnham et al. 2002) provides a small-scale example of where an initial feasibility study could have changed the outcome. In other instances, socio-cultural or economic factors may complicate attempts to eradicate or manage invasive species; it is important to understand how human behaviour might influence project outcomes before action is initiated (see Chapter 11).

The options in managing invasive species that breach the border range from early detection and rapid response, eradication or sustained control through to deciding to do nothing. Each positive strategy has its own particular constraints that need to be overcome before it can be

Box 7.2 *Judging Whether Feral Cats Can Be Eradicated*

Feral cats *Felis catus* are major threat to native animals on islands (Duffy and Capece 2012) and mainlands (Dickman 1996). Proposals exist for eradicating cats from many islands, e.g. Guadalupe Island in Mexico, Kaho'olawe Island in Hawaii, Rota Island in the Northern Marianas Islands, Bruny Island in Australia, Stewart Island in New Zealand and Floreana Island in the Galapagos Islands (Parkes et al. 2014a). These are all large islands (up to 173,000 ha), so any eradication attempt will be expensive and outcomes not certain. Many of the islands are populated, have domestic cats and have exotic rodents as primary prey for the cats.

Fortunately, there are plenty of successful precedents for cat eradication. Campbell et al. (2011) recorded eighty-three successful eradication projects on islands up to 29,000 ha in size, but the particular constraints on any island need to be analysed as well as the costs, which become significant for larger islands. The presence of rodent prey and whether they should be left, targeted first or targeted simultaneously are issues (L. Luna-Mendoza, personal communication). Legal constraints on some control methods, physical constraints on some islands (e.g. unexploded bombs on Kaho'olawe Island), the management of domestic cats and the impact on non-target species (e.g. eastern quolls *Dasyurus viverrinus* on Bruny Island in Tasmania) also need careful consideration.

As part of Mexico's plans to eradicate cats on five large islands, decision-makers wanted an estimate of the effort, and thereby the cost, required for eradication. An analysis of precedents showed that one-hit methods (e.g. aerial baiting targeting the cats or targeting rodents with cats as secondary kills) almost always left survivors that had to be removed by other methods. Further, there was no constant recipe for ground-based methods (see Table 7.5). Detailed data on the effort to eradicate cats were available from six large islands (see Table 7.4). Despite the variety of methods used and their order of application, an average of at least 544 (range 140–1,449) person-days' effort per 1,000 ha was required to eradicate the cats and validate success (Parkes et al. 2014b). This places financial constraints relative to island size, but the lack of consistent approaches suggests an opportunity for improving efficiency. The inability to kill 100 per cent of the cats with one-off aerial baiting (as achieved with rodents) also suggests that finding out why some survive should be a priority for research.

considered a viable option, such as how long the project might take and how much it will cost, who will fund the project and for how long, what techniques will be most effective, and what skills are required/available to achieve a measurable success (Table 7.1). The stakeholders in this phase of a project are those who have to approve the project – and fund it. Important secondary stakeholders at this phase are others who can stop the project, a potential constraint of which the primary decision-makers will want to be aware, at least to persuade such people of the project's merits.

7.4 Early Detection, Rapid Response

Early detection, rapid response (EDRR) is the appropriate management response to an exotic species incursion before it establishes and spreads (NISC 2003). An EDRR system requires a surveillance process. This may be either passive, relying on people doing other things to find and report a new exotic species, or active, where high-risk areas (ports, airports, etc.) where new species are likely to be first seen are deliberately searched, or a mix of both (Jarrad et al. 2011). In all events, the system requires that the putative new incursion is reported and diagnosed – is it really a new species? The third part is having a process ready with a rapid response to remove the incursion before it becomes established. 'Rapid' is both how quickly managers can detect, confirm and begin to react to an incursion and how quickly they can remove the incipient population before it establishes and spreads. The time available for this varies among species since while some take time, others have a very short phase between arrival and spread.

A good template for a systematic, proactive national EDRR system is the exotic disease system (SINEXE) developed for incursions of exotic plant and animal disease in Mexico. SINEXE began in 2009 and relies on trained field staff and private veterinarians to detect possible new diseases, mostly in livestock. Clinical symptoms can be sent by smartphone or laptop computer and any physical samples delivered to one or more of 21 laboratories for diagnosis, the results of which are is then sent same-day to the appropriate government agency for rapid response. In 2012, the system investigated 31,502 cases (www.senasica .gob.mx).

A common problem in applying EDRR is the lag between detection and response. In Guam, little fire ants *Wasmannia auropunctata* were detected at their point of incursion, but delays in response

Table 7.1 *Strategic Options and Their Implications for Project Planning to Manage Invasive Species*

Strategy	Time frame	Funding requirements	Best capacity	Intervention frequency
Early detection, rapid response (EDRR)	Short: from detection to before the invasive species establishes	Contingency funds	'Fire-fighter' teams; skills depend on the invasive species	Once
Eradication	Short: deadlines for success planned	Sufficient one-off funds	Professional teams best; can be external	Once
Sustained control: to zero density	In perpetuity: to manage immigrants	Sufficient one-off funds, then ongoing funds contingent on incursion rates	Flexible options depending on case	Match frequency of incursions
Sustained control: to a target density	In perpetuity	Sufficient one-off funds to reduce the population, then ongoing fund to harvest at appropriate frequencies	Flexible options depending on case	Either fixed (for stable populations) or flexible (for populations with cyclic or erratic increases)

allowed these pests to spread across much of the island (Raymundo and Miller 2012). Sometimes a prompt response from the person detecting the incursion is all that is required. A brush-tailed possum *Trichosurus vulpecula* found on Ririwha Island in New Zealand was detected by the landowner's dog and promptly destroyed (Parkes 2010). The discovery in England of an exotic lizard *Posarcis siculus* in imported stones was diagnosed and the incursion eliminated for a few hours' effort and without regulatory fuss (Hodgkins et al. 2012).

Other rapid responses require more planning, approval and effort depending on the extent of the incursion, the nature of the invasive species and the availability of control tools and funds. An invasive marine alga *Caulerpa taxifolia* was discovered in a lagoon in California in June 2000. Containment and control began 17 days later using emergency funding set aside for oil spills, and the expenditure of US$1.2 million per year has at least contained the incursion (Anderson 2005). The eradication of 10 populations of salt marsh mosquito *Ochlerotutus camptorrhyncus* found in New Zealand in 1998 took 11 years and cost US$56 million (Kay and Russell 2013).

When an incursion becomes an established invasion, the response changes from 'rapid' to a more formal assessment of options (eradication, range limitation, sustained control or doing nothing). This point in time is debatable, determined by the point at which the invasive species starts to breed and spread and the costs of action; are costs low enough to be funded out of a contingency budget or high enough to require the formal judgement of options?

7.5 Eradication

Established invasive species can be eradicated (permanently and completely removed, including seeds and other cryptic propagules) if certain obligate rules can be met and if constraints unique to each case can be managed or overcome. Choosing eradication as a management goal when it is not intrinsically possible leads to either suboptimal management (repetition rather than sustained control) or, worse, abandonment of the project when success is not achieved. The obligate rules have been variously described but in essence are that (1) all individuals capable of breeding must be put at risk, (2) individuals must be removed faster than they can replace their losses at all densities, (3) there must be no reinvasion (Parkes 1990), and (4) the net benefits must outweigh the biological costs associated with the control methods (permanent effects on non-

Table 7.2 *Largest Islands from Which Some Types of Invasive Vertebrate Species Have Been Eradicated*

Taxon	No of Species	No successful eradications	Largest island confirmed (ha)
Marsupialia (possums and wallabies)	2	20	Rangitoto/Motutapu (3,820)
Insectivora (hedgehogs and shrews)	2	5	Rangitoto/Motutapu (3,820)
Rodentia (rats, mice and coypus)	6	405	Macquarie (12,985)
Leporidae (rabbits and hares)	2	105	Macquarie (12,785)
Canidae (dogs and foxes)	4	61	Attu (90,250)
Mustelidae (stoats and mink)	4	21	South Uist (32,026)
Viverridae (mongooses)	2	7	Fajou (120)
Felidae (cats)	1	109	Marion (29,000)
Procyonidae (racoons)	1	4	Helgesen (80)
Equiidae (horses and donkeys)	2	17	Isabela (458,812)
Suidae (pigs)	1	42	Santiago (58,465)
Cervidae (deer)	4	3	Santa Rosa (22,565)
Bovidae (goats, cattle and sheep)	3	150	Isabela (458,812)
Cercopithecidae (macaques)	1	1	Desecheo (152)
Birds	12	26	NA
Reptiles	2	2	NA
Amphibians	1	1	NA

target species) and the ecological consequences of removing the invasive alien species (Parkes and Panetta 2009). If the basic rules are met, then all that remains to resolve are the usual constraints of money, capacity, legal issues and social consents.

These rules, especially 'no reinvasion', are easiest to meet on islands, of which a growing number (Keitt et al. 2011) have had one or more invasive species removed (Table 7.2). One or more of 49 species of vertebrates have been successfully eradicated from 935 islands in 41 countries (see www.eradicationsdb.fos.auckland.ac.nz or http://diise.islandconservation.org for further information). We do not as yet seem to have reached the limit of what is feasible for certain widespread invasive species, and new projects are underway or being proposed for very large-scale projects (Table 7.3) and for the eradication of species not yet featuring in the lists of eradication successes (http://diise .islandconservation.org).

Aerial baiting of rodents is attempted by applying toxic baits usually in a single or double baiting over a week or two. Most early failures on such islands can be attributed to flaws in the application of bait, competition for bait by other species or reinvasion from adjacent islands. Recent failures have occurred on tropical islands in the absence of these classical flaws, and in such cases, the abundance of natural preferred non-bait food has been suggested as a cause (Parkes and Fisher 2011), the solution being to either find a time of year when natural food is least available and/or increase the palatability of the bait. Success rates are high on islands with distinct seasons (Parkes et al. 2011), while, conversely, lack of seasonal breeding may increase the risk of failure as juvenile rodents are not exposed to bait for some reason.

Putting aside scale-independent risks, how might the size of the island relate to risk of failure?

- If each rodent has a minute chance, for any reason, of surviving an aerial baiting, then the probability that any survive increases with population size relative to island size. This suggests a potential limit on the size of island that could be attempted since the locating and killing any such survivors become intractable.
- Larger islands tend to be more complex with more habitats and topographies and are often inhabited by people, making bait delivery to all parts of the island more difficult, but tractable.

Eradication can also be successful on larger land masses where the invasive species has patchy distributions allowing one or more populations to be removed, e.g. feral goats in New Zealand (Parkes 1993b). Knowing where the invasive species is and is not – a delimitation survey – is critical. Weeds in particular, with non-obvious seed banks and potentially discontinuous distributions, require significant effort to delimit where they are and are not present at the start of a project (Panetta and Lawes 2005). Scale becomes important as managers consider larger islands (Table 7.3).

Knowing whether or not a proposed eradication will be feasible can be determined by either looking at similar projects conducted elsewhere or via analysis of the particularities of the project itself: can the rules be met,

Table 7.3 *Some Current Large-Scale Attempts Awaiting Confirmation of Success and Proposals to Eradicate Invasive Vertebrate Species from Islands*

Species	Island	Area (ha)	Proposal/attempt	Reference
Castor canadensis	Tierra del Fuego	7 million	Proposal	Malmierca et al. (2011)
Rattus rattus, *Felis catus*, *Mus muscatus*	Floreana	17,125	Proposal	Hanson and Campbell (2013)
Felis catus	Guadalupe	24,171	Proposal	Aguirre, personal communication
Rattus norvegicus	South Georgia	104,000 of 375,000	Outcome pending	Black et al. (2012)
Mus musculus	South Georgia	4,932 of 375,000	Outcome pending	Black et al. (2012)
Felis catus	Dirk Hartog	67,000	Outcome pending	Algar et al. (2011)
Felis catus	Soccoro	13,200	Early indications of success	A. Aguirre, personal communication

are funds available and are constraints overcome (Box 7.2)? Based on precedence, we can be confident of eradication of rats where success rates exceed 90 per cent (Parkes et al. 2011) and the techniques are well established (Cromarty et al. 2002). However, we would be less confident with, for example, musk shrews *Suncus murinus* with only two successful eradications and one failure on small islands and no standard control methodology (Varnham et al. 2002).

Eradication projects can either attempt to remove 100 per cent of the target invasive species in one operation (e.g. aerial baiting with anticoagulant toxins for rodents) or through a series of control events (e.g. most shooting, trapping and plant eradication exercises; see Table 7.4). For a one-off intervention, everything must work on the day: start rules, meticulous planning and fail-safe backup systems are required before the project begins (Broome et al. 2014). No information on success or failure is gleaned from the operation itself; unless immediate monitoring can both detect and locate any survivors to allow some reactive control (Samaniego-Herrera et al. 2013), managers have to wait until failure becomes obvious (observed repopulation) and then consider options for reattempting the exercise.

Samaniego-Herrera et al. (2013) used a 200-m grid of wax tags across the 82-ha Isabel Island in Mexico to determine if rats *R. rattus* survived a standard aerial baiting. Before the baiting, the authors had estimated the probability that a wax tag in a rat's home range would be chewed by a rat to estimate the probability that the array of wax tags (or arrays at shorter spacing) would detect any single surviving pregnant female rat immediately after the baiting or any offspring over the next 30 months. In this operation, no rats survived, but the model shows that an array of 50×50 m would have over 90 per cent chance of detecting and locating a single survivor, which could then be promptly targeted by spot poisoning or trapping. The method only works on islands where such a grid of tags can be deployed.

In contrast, the second, more prolonged type of eradication (e.g. trapping for cats, hunting for ungulates or removing plants) provides all sorts of information as it proceeds. Catch-per-unit effort (Table 7.4) data and the location of animals killed or seen but not killed can be used to change tactics as the project proceeds and to estimate the probability that no more trapped, seen or shot means that none are left. Ramsey et al. (2009, 2011) used the data from successful attempts to eradicate feral pigs *S. scrofa* and feral cats *F. catus* from Santa Cruz and San Nicolas islands in California, respectively, to estimate this probability and to prescribe how

Table 7.4 *Effort (per 1,000 ha) to Eradicate Cats from Large Islands*

Island	Estimated no. of cats/1,000 ha	Total effort (person-days/1,000 ha	Effort = total person-days/1,000 ha (across years)		
			Phase 1	Phase 2	Phase 3
Marion	117	359+	241 (1986–89)	118 (1989–91)	? (1992–93)
Macquarie	60	491	165 (1996–98)	192 (1999–2000)	134 (2001–2)
Ascension	61	546	220 (2002)	113 (2002–3)	213 (2003–6)
San Nicolas	10	140+	~70 (2009)	~70 (2010)	?
Little Barrier	51+	1,449	954 (1977–79)	487 (1980)	8 (1980)
Baltra	44 – 59	277+	? (2001)	192 (2001–3)	85 (2003–4)

Note: The phases are initial reduction, removal of survivors and surveillance/validation, respectively.
Source: From Parkes et al. (2014b).

Table 7.5 *Number of Islands from Which Cats Have Been Eradicated by Various Control Methods*

Control method	No. of islands	Mean island size (ha)	Largest island
Leg-hold traps alone	4	624	Rottnest (1,705 ha)
Cage traps alone	2	332	Port Cros (640 ha)
Leg-hold + cage traps	1	1,020	Alegranza (1,020 ha)
Unspecified traps alone	3	185	Reevesby (373 ha)
Various traps + hunting, no dogs	10	1,440	Macquarie (12,784 ha)
Various traps + hunting, with dogs	14	970	San Nicolas (5,896 ha)
Hunting alone	4	357	Trinidade (1,000 ha)
1080 baiting alone	2	2,956	Faure (5,800 ha)
Brodifacoum baiting alone	1	1,277	Mayor (Tuhua) (1,277 ha)
1080 + secondary control	11	4,185	Marion (29,000 ha)
Brodifacoum + secondary control	4	1,450	Rangitoto/Motutapu (3,820 ha)
PAPP + secondary control	1	120	Tasman (120 ha)
Several toxins + secondary control	6	717	Raoul (2,943 ha)

Source: After Parkes et al. (2014a).

much more surveillance would be required to raise the probability to some level considered acceptable to the managers. This level of acceptability might depend on the monetary and political costs of having to redeploy the control effort if eradication were falsely declared.

Sequential eradication projects can be planned in phases. The first phase attempts to reduce the population to low densities as quickly as possible using techniques that maximise the proportion killed at first encounter and so teach survivors least. Often surviving individuals have avoided the initial control method and are wary of it, or they are individuals living in refugia where the method does not work. A change of tactics is often advisable. The second phase aims to remove the survivors (Table 7.4). The final phase validates whether absence of evidence of survivors is truly absence of the invasive species.

Thinking about the sequence of methods and data they provide is a key to efficiency and to reduce risks of funder fatigue in this type of project. The Santa Cruz feral pig eradication in the Galapagos Islands removed all 5,036 pigs on the 25,000-ha island in 411 days. It began with trapping, as this method does not disturb pigs outside the trap, followed by aerial shooting, which kills a very high percentage of the pigs, and finally ground hunting with dogs, which targets pigs living in areas where they can avoid the helicopter (Parkes et al. 2010). This sequence was pre-planned and resulted in the project being completed in half the time taken on nearby Santa Rosa Island (21,450 ha) and a tenth of the time taken on Santiago Island (58,465 ha) (Parkes et al. 2010).

Increasingly, eradication projects are targeting suites of sympatric invasive species either sequentially (Morrison 2011), as on Santa Cruz Island (sheep, feral bees, pigs, golden eagles and turkeys), or simultaneously, as on Rangitoto/ Motutapu islands, where removal of brush-tail possums and brush-tail rock wallabies (Mowbray 2002) was followed by mice, ship rats, Norway rats, Polynesian rats, feral cats, rabbits, hedgehogs and stoats (Griffiths 2011). Multi-species projects need thorough consideration before implementation because it is rare that the entire suite of pests and weeds can actually be eradicated or controlled in a single operation. The programme design must consider

- *Will removing one invasive species allow another to increase and make matters worse?* Eradicating goats from Guadalupe Island in Mexico had benefits for endangered native plants but allowed exotic grasses to flourish, encouraging introduced mice and therefore feral cats (Luna-Mendoza et al. 2007). The ideal would have been to eradicate the exotic plants (impossible in reality), the mice and most of the cats in an aerial baiting (beyond the limited local budget), any remaining cats (currently planned) and then goats (which were removed in 2006).
- *Can a single technique remove all invasive species?* If there are only rodent species on the island, then aerial baiting can eradicate all species. However, while aerial baiting kills directly and indirectly (e.g. predators from secondary poisoning), it rarely kills them all, and secondary methods have to be immediately planned and deployed. Secondary methods are usually species specific and so are more difficult to integrate tactically and logistically.

Eradication projects in places inhabited by people have also been successful and are being planned for some significant islands, e.g. the Juan

Fernandez Islands in Chile (Glen et al. 2013), Lord Howe Island in Australia (Wilkinson and Priddel 2011) and Great Barrier Island in New Zealand (Ogden and Gilbert 2011). Here social sciences are a critical element of the planning process if the project relies on human behavioural change (Boudjelas 2009; see also Chapter 11) .

7.6 Sustained Control

Sustained control is a more complex strategy than eradication, requiring an understanding of

1. How the asset (species, habitat or ecosystem) affected by the invasive species responds as densities of the invasive population are reduced. This may be linear (any reduction in invasive species density gives some benefit), curved (benefits increase unequally with invasive density) or with sharp thresholds (no benefits unless the invasive species is reduced below a particular density). This knowledge informs the setting of target invasive species densities and off-take levels (Choquenot and Parkes 2001; Norbury et al. 2015).
2. *Invasive species population dynamics, in particular, the rate of increase of a controlled population* (Parkes 1993a). Some invasive species have regular seasonal breeding systems and mortality rates that vary only with population densities driven by availability of resources such as food, so changes in populations levels are relatively predictable under sustained control. Red deer *Cervus elaphus*, for example, have an intrinsic rate of increase r of about 0.27, which means about a third of their numbers must be culled annually to maintain low densities (Caughley 1977). Other invasive species have a 'boom-bust' lifecycle and may only be a problem at high densities. Intervention strategies may also be intermittent either to interrupt the occasional 'boom' (although difficult when the population is in maximum breeding mode) or to focus control at times and places where the impacts on native species are most acute (Ruscoe and Pech 2010).
3. *The most efficient and acceptable way to apply these interventions.*

When reinvasion (i.e. invasive species immigration) is certain, even the technical extirpation of an entire population is, in practice, a form of sustained control since ongoing effort is still required to keep the population at zero. Pest-proof fencing to defend areas cleared of the

Figure 7.3 Fenced reserve (18 ha) at Macraes Flat, Otago, New Zealand. Introduced mammals have been removed inside the fence to protect native plants, birds and lizards (see Reardon et al. 2012). (*Photo credit:* John Parkes.)

pests is an example (Figure 7.3). Isolation of peninsulas offers the most cost-effective approach: the shortest fence to protect the largest area, assuming that the invasive species to be excluded cannot swim around the ends. Fences can exclude all mammals – although mice are proving a problem in some places (Young et al. 2013) – but are expensive at ~US$250/m (Scofield et al. 2011) and require variable ongoing costs to maintain and react to the inevitable breaches. A trial using small dead-end holes in a New Zealand fence showed that most holes were breached within a day (Connolly et al. 2009), so detection of breaches and removing immigrants through constant electronic or physical vigilance are vital (Innes et al. 2012). Critics also note the catastrophic consequences of massive breaches of fences erected in areas subject to cyclones and hurricanes.

The cost-effectiveness of fencing is an important consideration. Scofield et al. (2011) and Innes et al. (2012) compared the costs to reduce the target invasive species to zero or near-zero densities (nearly the same as the initial costs to remove them from within the fence) but spend the fence construction and maintenance costs on control in buffer zones (Barron et al. 2013). The costs and benefits of fencing versus buffer zones need to be explored, but such an analysis will emerge as both options are being conducted in many places in New Zealand and elsewhere.

If a control method can achieve extirpation with little or no extra cost, it should be pursued, even when the asset can be protected at some higher invasive species density, for example, control methods that have a cost per unit area that is independent of pest density (aerial toxic baiting) when achieving extirpation allows managers to limit immigration with buffer control or fences. However, when the control method comes with a cost per animal or plant removed, costs per unit rise exponentially as density approaches zero (Pople et al. 1998), so removing more invasive species than necessary becomes a trade-off; excess spend could be used on another project. Biological control agents also provide a form of sustained control. A successful bio-control project has the advantage of providing ongoing control of the target species for no ongoing costs, but the disadvantage is that its effects often wane over time (Box 7.3; Figure 7.4).

Box 7.3 *Risks and Benefits of Bio-control: Rabbits and Cacti*

Introducing a new species to control an invasive species has the potential to achieve control at low ongoing cost, assuming that the bio-control agent establishes, spreads and affects the invasive species. The European rabbit *Oryctolagus cuniculus* and nopales cactus *Opuntia* spp. (Figure 7.4) are two contrasting but common invasive species for which applied bio-control measures have (1) no benefit and catastrophic adverse effects, (2) major benefits with little or no adverse side effects, or (3) major benefits at some places but potential adverse risks at others.

1. **No Benefit and Bad Consequences.** Rabbits are a major invasive species in Australia and New Zealand, and the scale and cost of conventional poisoning, shooting and habitat modification are very high. The first attempt at bio-control was made in the 1880s in New Zealand with the introduction of stoats *Mustela erminea* and ferrets *Mustela furo* as rabbit predators. This was based on a misunderstanding of the relationship between predators and their primary and secondary prey (Pech et al. 1995), resulting in little effect on rabbit populations but a catastrophic effect on

---

Figure 1.1 The aye-aye *Daubentonia madagascariensis* of Madagascar. Madagascar supports 21 per cent of the world's primate genera and 36 per cent of primate families, making it the highest priority for primate conservation globally. (Mittermeier et al. 2010; *photo credit*: Georgia Dicks).

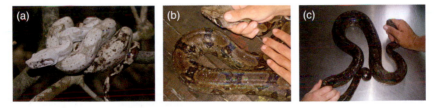

Figure 2.1 Phenotypic variation of boa constrictors between the Cayos Cochinos, Bay Islands and mainland Honduras. (a) Hog Island boa from the Cayos Cochinos Archipelago; (b) Bay Island boa from the island of Utila; and (c) mainland Honduran boa. (*Photo credit:* Stephen Green.)

Figure 2.5 Po'ouli *Melamprosops phaeosoma*, one of the most evolutionarily distinct Hawaiian honeycreepers and once one of the world's rarest birds, prior to its recent extinction. (*Photo credit:* Jim J. Groombridge.)

Figure 3.4 Field teams on Mauritius that worked with critically endangered species on the brink of extinction required a particular sense of humour. (*Image credit:* Wayne Page.)

Figure 4.2 Male Lesser Antilles iguana *Iguana delicatissima* displaying. Hybridisation with the introduced *Iguana iguana* is threatening the species across its Caribbean range. (*Photo credit:* Gerardo Garcia.)

Figure 5.4 The extinct raven parrot *Lophopsittacus mauritianus* of Mauritius, a species whose ecology and morphology have been hypothesised through examination of an early sculpture and sketches. (*Photo credit:* Julian Pender Hume.)

Figure 6.2 Cayman blue iguana: 'We envision a population of at least one thousand Grand Cayman blue iguanas, living freely within protected areas, reproducing naturally and continuing to evolve in step with their ever-changing natural environment.' By 2012, the population had risen to 750, resulting in a down-listing of the species from critically endangered to endangered. (*Photo credit:* John Binns.)

Figure 9.1 New Zealand hihi *Notiomystis cincta*, one species where explicit management decisions, based on a perceived understanding of the system, allowed for monitoring to challenge what we thought was the situation. (*Photo credit:* E. Wilson.)

Figure 9.2 Mauritius parakeet *Psittacula eques*. An experimental approach and ongoing learning and revision to understanding the most effective management contributed to its recovery. (*Photo credit:* S. Tollington.)

Figure 9.3 New Zealand short–tailed bat *Mystacina tuberculate*, one species for which structured decision-making involving primary stakeholders led to common agreement as to how best to conserve them. (*Photo credit:* S. Parsons.)

Figure 9.5 Mauritius orange-tailed skink *Gongylomorphus* sp., a great example of a species recovered from almost definite extinction through action in the absence of detailed information on the species. (*Photo credit:* N. Cole.)

Figure 10.1 Snapshots in time: before (a) and after (b) restoration efforts. (a) Round Island (1960), 22.5 km off the north coast of Mauritius, prior to the removal of European rabbits *Oryctolagus cuniculus* and goats *Capra aegagrus* and multispecies restoration efforts. Note limited vegetation and evidence of extreme soil erosion. (b) A similar spot on Round Island (2014). Note the recovery of more diverse plant life, which now provides important habitats for native seabirds and endemic reptiles, including Telfair's skink *Leiolopisma telfairii*, once widespread across Mauritius and now restricted to three offshore islands (*Photo credits:* (a) De Speville; (b) Nik Cole.)

Figure 11.1 Life in the marsh. A typical house built of reeds and located within the reed bed surrounding Madagascar's largest lake, Lac Alaotra. People rely on the lake for their livelihoods, though underlying socio-economic pressures may contribute to unsustainable land use practices (*Photo credit:* Jamieson A. Copsey.)

(a)

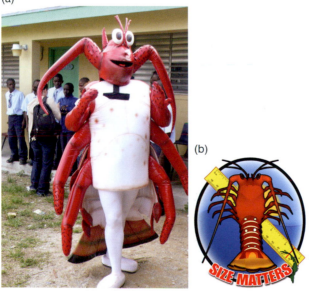

(b)

Figure 11.3 (a) Spike the lobster, the mascot of a social marketing campaign to influence harvesting of undersized lobsters in the Bahamas. (b) The campaign slogan 'Size Matters'. The campaign identified a barrier to fishers avoiding harvesting undersized lobsters: they had nothing to measure them with! The campaign distributed size gauges to fishers for this purpose. (*Photo credit:* Amy Doherty (Rare) 2010.)

PURPOSE

A statement which provides a relevant and enduring focus for all involved.

The project purposed to restore high altitude forest (Box 6.1) on Maui, Hawaii is relevant today, next year and for decades into the future.

RELATIONSHIPS

People's interactions are a product of both the way we set up the programme and the personalities of those involved.

Demanding work conditions and shared accommodation for field-based teams makes it vital to eliminate any work irritations, and to agree a common set of values or team principles to maintain good morale (Box 6.2).

PROCESSES

Conservation activities and the order of those tasks should be managed end-to-end as a process, including the interfaces between differing areas of work.

Work to protect the Caribbean spiny lobster (*Panulirus argus*) in the Bahamas, identified that even fishers aware of regulations needed a method to measure their catch. Provision of tools enabled a significant reduction of undersized catches and saw recovery of the lobster population (Box 11.3).

Ecosystem recovery on Gunner's Quoin, Mauritius (**Box 10.2**) required connected processes of alien species eradication, habitat recovery and translocation with embedded monitoring to aid learning and improvement.

GOALS

Goals align short-term effort in line with overall purpose.

Efforts to recover the St Lucia Parrot *Amazona versicolor* were enabled once goals were shifted towards changing knowledge, attitude and regard that local people had towards the species (Chapter 5, Chapter 11, section 11.4.3). The purpose of saving the species nevertheless remained unchanged.

Recent recovery of the Island Fox *Urocyon littoralis* on the Californian Channel Islands (Box 8.2) required different goals on each island; on some invasive species removal, on others vaccination, and on one the reintroduction of Bald Eagles to reinstate balance across the ecosystem.

ROLES

Role clarity ensures, even in remote teams, that people work with confidence and authority.

Specialists (e.g. veterinarians and geneticists) provide practitioners in Mauritius (Box 3.3) with data to support management of Echo parakeets *Psittacula eques* including translocation.

Figure 12.1 An illustration of the Beckhard model in relation to conservation practice, drawing on examples from preceding chapters.

secondary prey, several of New Zealand's native animals (King and Murphy 2005).

2. **Benefits and Few Costs.** Uniquely for a mammal, two viral diseases have been discovered that cause high mortality specifically in rabbits. Myxomatosis is a benign disease of New World lagomorphs that is fatal to European rabbits, whereas rabbit haemorrhagic disease is a novel virus that appeared in domestic rabbits in the 1980s. Both were introduced to Australia after appropriate risk analyses and the latter to New Zealand illegally (risk analysis had recommended, it not be imported). Both have proved effective bio-control agents with no direct downside risks to other species, although evolution – of resistance in rabbits and virulence in viruses – may be reducing the efficacy of the control (Cooke and Fenner 2002).

3. **Benefits to Some and Risks to Others.** Prickly pear cactuses (mostly *O. stricta*) were introduced to Australia in the nineteenth century to support a cochineal dye industry. By 1925, they had covered 24 million hectares. A moth *Cactoblastis cactorum* from the plants' homeland in South America was introduced in 1925 and rapidly reduced the cactus' previous invasion in eastern Australia to the status of a minor weed problem (Hosking et al. 1988). This solution has been replicated in several other countries (in the Caribbean and Africa) but conversely is an unwelcome risk to the spectacular diversity of cactuses in the southern United States and Mexico (Hoffman et al. 2000). The moth was discovered in Florida in 1989, but Mexico has so far kept it at bay. In 2006, the moth was found on the islands of Contoy and Mujeres (off the Yucatan Peninsula) and promptly eradicated using pheromone trapping – a successful example of EDRR (Koleff et al. 2010).

Sustained control is a form of harvesting, so a question often raised is whether recreational or commercial harvesting of an invasive species might act as a control system. The answers depend on the situation. For example, the lion fish *Pterois volitans*, native to the tropical Pacific Ocean, escaped into the Atlantic Ocean in 2001 and is spreading south through the Caribbean, destroying native ecosystems and the livelihoods of fishing communities. The Mexican government is encouraging fishers

Figure 7.4 Cactus habitat on Espiritu Santo Island, Sea of Cortes, Mexico. (*Photo credit:* John Parkes.)

to harvest the lion fish, but this is unlikely to have much effect on the spread of the pest (Barbour et al. 2011). Conversely, harvesting of red deer *Cervus elaphus* and Himalayan thar *Hemitragus jemlahicus* for game meat in New Zealand has seen removal of over 90 per cent of these populations from non-forested habitats with major conservation benefits to native plants (Parkes 2006), sustainable if the market for the meat remains economically viable.

7.7 Project Design, Planning and Implementation

Once a problem is identified, an appropriate strategy is selected and someone has agreed to funding, the project needs to be organised, governed (see Section 6.2) and managed to actually deliver the work on time and on budget (Box 7.4). Large projects usually have a governance group (similar to a board of directors) to represent the interests of the main stakeholders (e.g. funding agencies, key government agencies responsible for the land or the function, relevant private land owners and NGOs) involved in aspects of the project.

Box 7.4 *Project Design: The Santa Cruz Pig Eradication*

Santa Cruz is a large (25,000-ha) island off the coast of California owned by The Nature Conservancy and the Channel Islands National Park. These agencies began restoring the native ecosystems by removing cattle in 1988 and sheep in 1990, but this may have allowed feral pigs to increase, which (along with the demise of the resident bald eagles) encouraged establishment of golden eagles from mainland California. Aside from preying upon piglets, golden eagles took endangered island foxes as secondary prey, so eradicating the pigs and replacing golden eagles with bald eagles (which rarely take large evasive prey) was required to avert this trophic cascade (Morrison 2011).

The agencies fenced the island into five large zones to restrict the movements of feral pigs and make eradication easier, after which a call for tender was issued to professional pest-control contractors to eradicate the pigs. The agencies retained a governance role, but the contractor provided the project and operational management. A critical step involved setting the eradication as a fixed-price contract. The contractor was paid an instalment upon signing the contract, some halfway through, but the final substantial payment was made only when no pigs were deemed to remain. This system encouraged efficiency and effectiveness because the sooner the contractor could reliably claim success, the larger was its profit. The funding agencies gained by shortening the time frame to success (Parkes et al. 2010) and incidentally avoided potentially substantial litigation costs during the project.

The challenge was how to judge whether the contractor's claim of eradication success was true. Solving this problem had to be fair, to avoid the contractor unnecessarily continuing after all pigs had been eliminated, thereby wasting time and resources and eroding goodwill (critical since the agencies need to keep such capacity available for other tasks), yet nor was it sensible to prematurely accept the completion and then have to redeploy effort should the claim prove false. The solution was to require the contractor to keep good records of effort by different methods and success in terms of pigs removed. Contracts used GPS to assess where hunting or surveillance was done and where pigs were killed or seen and radio-telemetered pigs, dogs and hunters. Daily debriefs and flexible planning provided the data to allow an independent assessor to tell the funders (1) the probability that no further pigs would be discovered after the contractor claimed success and (2) a prescription of surveillance in time and space for no more pigs being found, which would raise this probability to an agreed level of comfort for the agencies (Ramsey et al. 2009).

With funds, an aim and some organisation structure in place, the details of who does what and when are set out in an operational plan (see Section 6.6). Plans can be highly prescriptive (as in aerial baiting for rodents) or highly adaptive (responding to information from the operation as it is gathered). The basic tools available for invasive species managers are well established – traps, snares, toxins and sprays, bullets (or arrows) and even bio-control (Box 7.3; Figure 7.4). Mascall (1590) recorded more than 30 trap types and one lure to control foxes in the fourteenth century. Novel fertility control tools such as chemical agents (Turner and Kirkpatrick 1991), adding living or dead agents to affect immunological systems and cause sterility (Tyndale-Biscoe 1994) and manipulating genomes using gene drives and CRISPR technologies to introduce adverse traits into wild populations (Esvelt and Gemmell 2017; Thresher 2008) are being cautiously researched. These provide options to manage some invertebrates but few practical solutions, as yet, for free-ranging vertebrate invasive species (Duckworth et al. 2006).

While some await the novel 'super-tool', development of the traditional toolkit has improved efficiency and effectiveness (see the papers on techniques in Veitch et al. 2011). For example, in New Zealand, aerial baiting using compound 1080 in cereal or carrot baits (Figure 7.5) has long been used to control rabbits and brush-tail possums – with ship rats and stoats as desired by-kill (Nugent et al. 2011). In 2010, 438,000 ha were treated in this way. This is costly and controversial (PCE 2011), prompting research to improve the target specificity and to reduce environmental and operational costs. Recent aerial baiting has reduced the amount of bait used from 20 to 30 kg of bait/ha to as low as 0.17 kg/ha with no loss of efficacy (Nugent and Morriss 2013).

Biological control has mitigated the impacts of many invertebrate and plant invasive species (Murphy and Evans 2009). However, attempts aimed at vertebrates have either proved a disaster

Figure 7.5 Aerial baiting in mountainous country in New Zealand. (*Photo credit:* G. Nugent.)

(e.g. mustelid introductions to control rabbits in New Zealand; King and Murphy 2005), or the effects are limited over time (e.g. targeted viral diseases of rabbits limited by evolutionary attenuation of the virus (myxomatosis) or rabbits evolving resistance (rabbit haemorrhagic disease), as described in Box 7.3 and Figure 7.4; Cooke and Fenner 2002).

7.8 Assessment and Review

Measuring success in EDRR and eradication projects is straightforward – either the invasive species has been removed or it has not. Less simple is the judgement of whether lack of evidence is evidence of absence, unless appropriate data are collected during the project. There is a growing literature on ways to make an objective judgement, much based on military surveillance and search and rescue models (Koopman 1980) using Bayesian approaches (e.g. Ramsey et al. 2009, 2011) or various models based on decision-framework theories (Regan et al. 2006; Rout et al. 2009).

Measuring the effects of a sustained control project is much more complex. Ideally, the logical link between the intensity and frequency of control (the number removed), residual densities of the invasive species and the impacts on assets at this density needs to be known or estimated, either a priori (e.g. Choquenot and Parkes 2001; see also examples in Hone 1994) or by adaptive management as the project proceeds (Parkes et al. 2006). There is a growing array of devices and methods to monitor the presence or changes in abundance of invasive species (e.g. Sinclair et al. 2006). Some new tools combine the use of cameras in drone aircraft and standard line-transect analyses, now being adapted for wildlife management (Pierce Jones et al. 2006).

7.9 Concerns for the Future

It is difficult to be optimistic about the possibility of reversing ongoing global mixing of the world's biota (see Chapter 4), and in the very long term, this trend may have little effect on global biodiversity as a new steady state with similar numbers of species will evolve (Rosenzweig 2001). The questions facing current managers include how to (1) manage the manageable to keep some of the native species that would otherwise disappear or places whose ecosystems would be transformed by invasive species and (2) recognise what is not manageable with current technologies and instead seek new technologies. Which invasive species to target is a value-based question; some invasive species are valued and their presence defended by some communities, e.g. game animals. Since sustained-control culling is merely a subset of resource harvesting, perhaps compromises exist for some species in some places where eradication is not realistic but control is desirable (Parkes 2006).

While island species are most at risk from invasive species (e.g. Genovesi 2011), their situation is most manageable because border biosecurity is simpler with no land borders such that some invasive species already present can be eradicated (Keitt et al. 2011). Eradication of insular invasive species, although barely keeping up with new incursions for some taxa such as rats (Russell et al. 2008), is a growing conservation activity, and a call to arms (Genovesi 2011; Saunders et al. 2011) alongside ambitious plans for larger islands provides hope – success breeds success!

Some vertebrate invasive species cannot currently be managed with eradication or control tools capable of effective application at a wide scale, for example, devising suitable bait for musk shrews and brown tree snakes, which prefer live prey. Additionally, the relatively few successful attempts against birds probably reflects the less obvious impacts of exotic birds relative to mammals and thus lower motivation to act rather than an absence of tools per se (although see Box 7.1 for an example of a recent island bird eradication). Current control methods for aquatic species limit management to small scales at best, and the 'do nothing' option is sensible in most cases.

The costs to eradicate widespread populations of invasive invertebrates and plants are often very high, and often conditions of success cannot be met. For example, of 18 invasive plant species in California, eradication became increasingly difficult as the scale of infestation increased, with only 25 per cent of populations covering between 100 and 1,000 ha being eradicated (Rejmánek and Pitcairn 2002). However, heroic efforts against invasive plants on islands have led to some successes or at least case studies that suggest a way forward (West 2002). Further investment in research on control tools is a prerequisite.

There are many invasive animal species for which we now have the tools to manage and even eradicate populations under certain circumstances. Given the growing body of experience that exists, we are in a stronger position now than ever to contend with the threats they pose (Buddinghagen and Tye 2015). The question is whether or not new technologies and our ability to apply them can keep pace with the rise in the tide of invasive species worldwide. Furthermore, as we move our attention from simply restoring threatened species to restoring or establishing lost ecological roles, sometimes through the use of 'ecological replacements' (see Section 10.5), we are likely to enter an era where we are seeking to control or eradicate some introduced populations and nurturing others. We are now faced with a growing number of 'novel ecosystems' (see Section 10.1), systems that have been significantly modified from their pre-anthropogenic form. In certain situations, we will find introduced species that confer ecosystem-level benefits and so should be encouraged. The distinguishing feature will be whether or not the introduced population is causing harm (invasion) or providing benefit (e.g. re-establishing a lost ecological role) to that system. Not only therefore will we need to learn fast how to respond to growth in the introduction and invasion of particular species, but we will also need to develop smarter systems for goal setting (see Section 6.5) and prioritisation of invasive species management programmes.

7.10 Summary

Key points from this chapter:

- Invasive species management on islands has informed the development of 'good practice' guidelines for planning the stages of an eradication or sustained control project.
- The identification and engagement of relevant stakeholders at different points in the invasive species management process can be critical to the success of the project.
- Justifying which species should be the priority for management can be complicated by the lag time between invasive species arrival and perceived impacts.
- Early detection, rapid response (EDRR) is the appropriate management response to an exotic species incursion before it establishes and spreads and becomes and invasive species.
- Eradication requires all individuals capable of breeding to be put at risk; individuals must be removed faster than they can be replaced; and there must be no reinvasion.
- Sustained control is a more complex strategy than eradication because it requires monitoring the condition of the species or system being affected by the invasive species to know whether or not control is having the desired positive effect.
- Needs for the future include directing research at finding new technologies to deal with currently unmanageable invasive species and for more robust systems for prioritising effort.

References

Algar, D., Johnston, M. and Hilmer, S. S. (2011). A pilot study for the proposed eradication of feral cats on Dirk Hartog Island, Western Australia, pp. 1–16 in C. R. Veitch, M. N. Clout and D. R. Towns (eds.). *Island Invasives: Eradication and Management* (Occasional Paper of the IUCN Species Survival Commission 42). IUCN, Gland.

Anderson, L. W. K. (2005). California's reaction to *Caulerpa taxifolia*: a model for invasive species rapid response. *Biological Invasions* 7: 1003–16.

Barbour, A. B., Allen, M. S., Frazer, T. K. and Sherman, K. D. (2011). Evaluating the potential efficacy of invasive lionfish (*Pterois volitans*) removals. *PLoS ONE* 6: e1966 (doi:10:1371/journal.pone.0019666).

Barron, M., Ruscoe, W., Clarke, D. et al. (2013). Pest control across boundaries. *Kararehe Kino Vertebrate Pest Research* 21: 16–17, available at www.landcareresearch.co.nz/publications/newsletters/kararehe-kino.

Bell, B. D. 1978. The Big South Cape Island rat irruption, pp. 33–40, in P. R. Dingwall, I. A. E. Atkinson and C. Hay (eds.), *The Ecology and Control of Rodents in New Zealand Nature Reserves* (Department of Lands and Survey Information Series No. 4). Department of Lands and Survey Information, Wellington.

Black, A., Poncet, S., Wolfaardt, A. et al. (2012). Rodent eradication on South Georgia: preparation and evaluation. A summary report of activities during the 2011–12 field season. Report to UK Overseas Territories Environment Programme, London.

Blanvillain, C., Salducci, J. M., Tuturai, G. and Maeura, M. (2003). Impact of introduced birds on the recovery of the Tahiti flycatcher (*Pomarea nigra*), a critically endangered forest bird of Tahiti. *Biological Conservation* 109: 197–205.

Boudjelas, S. (2009). Public participation in invasive species management, pp. 93–106 in M. N. Clout and P. Williams (eds.), *Invasive Species Management*. Oxford University Press, Oxford.

Broome, K. G., Cox, A., Golding, C. et al. (2014). *Rat Etradication Using Aerial Baiting: Current Agreed Best Practice Used in New Zealand*. Department of Conservation, Wellington.

Buddenhagen, C. E. and Tye, A. (2015). Lessons from successful plant eradications in Galapagos: commitment is crucial. *Biological Invasions* 17: 2893–912.

Campbell, K. J., Harper, G., Agar, D. et al. (2011). Review of feral cat eradications on islands, pp. 37–46 in C. R. Veitch, M. N. Clout and D. R. Towns (eds.), *Island Invasives: Eradication and Management* (Occasional Paper of the IUCN Species Survival Commission No. 42). IUNC, Gland.

Caughley, G. (1977). *Analysis of Vertebrate Populations*. Wiley, London.

Choquenot, D. and Parkes, J. (2001). Setting thresholds for pest control: how does pest density affect resource viability? *Biological Conservation* 99: 29–46.

Connolly, T. A., Day, T. D. and King, C. M. (2009). Estimating the potential for reinvasion by mammalian pests through pest-exclusion fencing. *Wildlife Research* 36: 410–21.

Cooke, B. D. and Fenner, F. (2002). Rabbit haemorrhagic disease and the biological control of wild rabbits, *Oryctolagus cuniculus*, in Australia and New Zealand. *Wildlife Research* 29: 689–706.

Copsey, J. and Parkes, J. (2013). Institutional capacity building for invasive bird management in the Pacific, in *Biodiversity Conservation Lessons Learned Technical Series 20*. Conservation International, Apia.

Cromarty, P. L., Broome, K. G., Cox, A. et al. (2002). Eradication planning for invasive alien animal species on islands: the approach developed by the New Zealand Department of Conservation, pp. 85–91 in C. R. Veitch and M. N. Clout (eds.), *Turning the Tide: The Eradication of Invasive Species* (Occasional Paper of the IUCN Species Survival Commission No. 27). IUCN, Gland.

Dickman, C. R. (1996). *Overview of the Impacts of Feral Cats on Australian Native Fauna*. Australian Nature Conservation Agency, Canberra.

Duckworth, J. A., Byrom, A. E., Fisher, P. and Horn, C. (2006). Pest control: does the answer lie in new biotechnologies?, pp. 421–434 in R. B. Allen and

W. G. Lee (eds.), *Biological Invasions in New Zealand* (Ecological Studies 186). Springer-Verlag, Berlin.

Duffy, D. C. and Capece, P. (2012). Biology and impacts of Pacific invasive species: 7. The domestic cat (*Felis catus*). *Pacific Science* 66: 173–212.

Esvelt, K. M. and Gemmell, N. J. (2017). Conservation demands safe gene drive. *PLOS Biology* (doi.org/10.1371/journal.pbio.2003850).

Feare, C. J., van der Woude, J., Greenwell, P. et al. (2016). *Eradication of Common Mynas Acridotheres tristis from Denis Island.* Pest Management Science, Seychelles (doi 10.1002/ps.4263).

Freifeld, H. B. (1999). Habitat relationships of forest birds on Tutuila Island, American Samoa. *Journal of Biogeography* 26: 1191–213.

Genovesi, P. (2011). Are we turning the tide? Eradications in times of crisis: how the global community is responding to biological invasions, pp. 5–8 in C. R. Veitch, M. N. Clout and D. R. Towns (eds.), *Island Invasives: Eradication and Management* (Occasional Paper of the IUCN Species Survival Commission No. 42). IUCN, Gland.

Ghestemme, T. (2011). French Polynesia: Impacts of Introduced Birds on the Last Population of the Tahiti Monarch. *PII News*, December 2011, pp. 3–5.

Glen, A. S., Atkinson, R., Campbell, K. J. et al. (2013). Eradicating multiple invasive species on inhabited islands: the next big step in island restoration? *Biological Invasions* 15: 2589–603.

Grarock, K., Tidemann, C. R., Wood, J. and Lindenmayer, D. B. (2012). Is it benign or is it a pariah? Empirical evidence for the impact of the common myna (*Acridotheres tristis*) on Australian birds. *PLoS One* 7: e40622.

Griffiths, R. (2011). Targeting multiple species: a more efficient approach to pest eradication, pp. 172–76 in C. R. Veitch, M. N. Clout and D. R. Towns (eds.), *Island Invasives: Eradication and Management* (Occasional Paper of the IUCN Species Survival Commission No. 42). IUCN, Gland.

Hanson, C. and Campbell, K. (2013). *Floreana Island Ecological Restoration: Rodent and Cat Eradication Feasibility Analysis*, version 6.0. Island Conservation, Santa Cruz, CA.

Hodgkins, J., Davis, C. and Foster, J. (2012). Successful rapid response to an accidental introduction of non-native lizards *Podarcis siculus* in Buckinghamshire, UK. *Conservation Evidence* 9: 63–66.

Hoffman, J. H., Moran, V. C. and Zimmerman, H. G. (2000). The renowned cactus moth *Cactoblastis cactorum*: its natural history and threat to *Opuntia* floras in Mexico and the United States of America. *Diversity and Distributions* 6: 259–69.

Hone, J. (1994). *Analysis of Vertebrate Pest Control.* Cambridge University Press, Cambridge.

Hosking, J. R., McFadyen, R. E. and Murray, N. D. (1988). Distribution and biological control of cactus species in eastern Australia. *Plant Protection Quarterly* 3: 115–23.

Hutton, I., Parkes, J.P. and Sinclair, A. R. E. (2007). Reassembling island ecosystems: the case of Lord Howe Island. *Animal Conservation* 10: 22–29.

Innes, J., Lee, W., Burns, B. et al. (2012). Role of predator-proof fences in restoring New Zealand's biodiversity: a response to Scofield et al. (2011). *New Zealand Journal of Ecology* 36: 232–38.

Jarrad, F. C., Barrett, S., Murray, J. et al. (2011). Improved design method for biosecurity surveillance and early detection of non-indigenous rats. *New Zealand Journal of Ecology* 35: 132–44.

Kay, B. and Russell, R. (2013). *Mosquito Eradication: The Story of Killing Campto.* CSIRO Publishing, Canberra.

Keitt, B., Campbell, K., Saunders, A. et al. (2011). The Global Islands Invasive Vertebrate Eradication Database: a tool to improve and facilitate restoration of island ecosystems, pp. 74–77 in C. R. Veitch, M. N. Clout and D. R. Towns (eds.), *Island Invasives: Eradication and Management* (Occasional Paper of the IUCN Species Survival Commission No. 42). IUCN, Gland.

King, C. M. and Murphy, E. C. (2005). Stoat, pp. 261–87 in C. M. King (ed.), *The Handbook of New Zealand Mammals.* Oxford University Press, Melbourne.

King, D. H. (2010). The effect of trapping pressure on trap avoidance and the role of foraging strategies in anti-predator behaviour of common mynas (*Acridotheres tristis*). *Canberra Bird Notes* 35: 85–107.

Koleff, P., González, A. I. and Born-Schmidt, G. (2010). *National Strategy on Invasive Species in Mexico*, available at www.conabio.gob.mx.

Koopman, B.O. (1980). *Search and Screening: General Principles with Historical Applications.* Pergamon Press, New York.

Luna-Mendoza, L. M., Aguirre-Muñoz, A., Keitt, B., Junak, S. and Henry, R. W. (2007). The restoration of Guadalupe Island, revisited. *Fremontia* 35: 14–17.

Malmierca, L., Menvielle, M. F, Ramadori, D. et al. (2011). Eradication of beaver (Castor canadensis), an ecosystem engineer and threat to southern Patagonia, pp. 87–90 in C. R. Veitch, M. N. Clout and D. R. Towns (eds.), *Island Invasives: Eradication and Management* (Occasional Paper of the IUCN Species Survival Commission No. 42). IUCN, Gland.

Marks, C. A., Obendorf, D., Pereira, F., Edwards, I. and Hall, G. P. (2014). *Opportunistically Acquired Evidence Is Unsuitable Data to Model Fox (Vulpes vulpes) Distribution in Tasmania.* Wildlife Society Bulletin, Canberra (doi:10.1002/wsb.448).

Mascall, L. (1590). *A Booke of Fishing with Hook and Line and Other Instruments There unto Belonging.* John Wolfs, London.

Miller, B. and Mullette, K. J. (1985). Rehabilitation of an endangered Australian bird: the Lord Howe Island woodhen *Tricholimnas sylvestris* (Sclater). *Biological Conservation* 34: 55–95.

Morrison, S. A. (2007). Reducing risk and enhancing efficiency in non-native vertebrate removal efforts on islands: a 25-year multi-taxa retrospective from Santa Cruz Island, California, pp. 398–409 in G. W. Witmer, W. C. Pitt and K. A. Fagerstone (eds.), *Managing Vertebrate Invasive Species: Proceedings of an International Symposium, Fort Collins, Colorado.* USDA National Wildlife Research, Washington, DC.

(2011). Trophic considerations in eradicating multiple pests, pp. 208–12 in C. R. Veitch, M. N. Clout and D. R. Towns (eds.), *Island Invasives: Eradication and Management* (Occasional Paper of the IUCN Species Survival Commission No. 42). IUCN, Gland.

Mowbray, S. C. (2002). Eradication of introduced Australian marsupials (brushtail possum and brushtailed rock wallaby) from Rangitoto and Motutapu Islands,

New Zealand, pp. 226–32 in C. R. Veitch and M. N. Clout (eds.), *Turning the Tide: The Eradication of Invasive Species*, IUCN Invasive Species Specialist Group.

Murphy, S. T. and Evans, H. C. (2009). Biological control of invasive species, pp. 77–92 in M. N. Clout and P. Williams (eds.), *Invasive Species Management*. Oxford University Press, Oxford.

National Invasive Species Council (2003). *General Guidelines for the Establishment and Evaluation of Invasive Species Early Detection and Rapid Response Systems*, version 1. NISC, Department of the Interior, Washington, DC.

Norbury, G. L., Pech, R. P., Innes, J. and Byrom, A. E. (2015). Density-impact functions for terrestrial vertebrate pests and indigenous biota: 'rules of thumb' for conservation managers. *Biological Conservation* 191: 409–20.

Nugent, G. and Morriss, G. A. (2013). Delivery of toxic bait in clusters: a modified technique for aerial poisoning of small mammal pests. *New Zealand Journal of Ecology* 37: 246–55.

Nugent, G., Warburton, B., Thomson, C., Sweetapple, P. and Ruscoe, W. A. (2011). Effect of prefeeding, sowing rate and sowing pattern on efficacy of aerial 1080 poisoning of small-mammal pests in New Zealand. *Wildlife Research* 38: 249–59.

Ogden, J. and Gilbert, J. (2011). Running the gauntlet: advocating rat and feral cat eradication on an inhabited island – Great Barrier Island, New Zealand, pp. 467–71 in C. R. Veitch, M. N. Clout and D. R. Towns (eds.), *Island Invasives: Eradication and Management* (Occasional Paper of the IUCN Species Survival Commission No. 42). IUCN, Gland.

PCE (2011). *Evaluating the Use of 1080: Predators, Poisons and Silent Forests*. Parliamentary Commissioner for the Environment, Wellington, available at www.pce.parliament.nz.

Panetta, F. D. and Lawes, R. (2005). Evaluation of weed eradication programs: the delimitation of extent. *Diversity and Distributions* 11: 435–42.

Parkes, J. P. (1990). Feral goat control in New Zealand. *Biological Conservation* 54: 335–48.

(1993a). The ecological dynamics of pest-resource-people systems. *New Zealand Journal of Zoology* 20: 223–30.

(1993b). Feral goats: designing solutions for a designer pest. *New Zealand Journal of Ecology* 17: 71–83.

(2002). *Potential Use of Rabbit Haemorrhaic Disease Virus (RHDV) as a Biocontrol Agent for European Rabbits (Oryctolagus cuniculus) on Clarion Island* (Landcare Research Contract Report LC0203/15). Mexico.

(2006). Does commercial harvesting of introduced wild mammals contribute to their management as conservation pests?, pp. 407–20 in R. B. Allen and W. G. Lee (eds.), *Biological Invasions in New Zealand*. Springer-Verlag, Berlin.

(2010). *Restoration of Ririwha (Stephenson or Mahinepua) Island: Eradicating the Rats* (Landcare Research Contract Report LC0910/25). Mexico.

Parkes, J. and Murphy, E. (2003). Management of introduced mammals in New Zealand. *New Zealand Journal of Zoology* 30: 335–59.

Parkes, J. P. and Panetta, F. D. (2009). Eradication of invasive species: progress and emerging issues in the 21st century, pp. 45–60 in M. N. Clout and P. Williams (eds.), *Invasive Species Management*. Oxford University Press, Oxford.

Parkes, J. P. and Anderson, D. (2011). What is required to eradicate red foxes (Vulpes vulpes) from Tasmania?, pp. 477–80 in C. R. Veitch, M. N. Clout and D. R. Towns (eds.), *Island Invasives: Eradication and Management* (Occasional Paper of the IUCN Species Survival Commission No. 42). IUCN, Gland.

Parkes, J. and Fisher, P. (2011). *Review of the Lehua Island Rat Eradication Project* (Landcare Research Contract Report LC129). Mexico.

Parkes, J., Robley, A., Forsyth, D. and Choquenot, D. (2006). Adaptive management experiments in vertebrate pest control in New Zealand and Australia. *Wildlife Society Bulletin* 34: 229–36.

Parkes, J. P., Ramsey, D. S. L., Macdonald, N. et al. (2010). Rapid eradication of feral pigs (*Sus scrofa*) from Santa Cruz Island, California. *Biological Conservation* 143: 634–41.

Parkes, J., Fisher, P. and Forrester, G. (2011). Diagnosing the cause of failure to eradicate introduced rodents on islands: brodifacoum versus diphacinone and method of bait delivery. *Conservation Evidence* 8: 100–6.

Parkes, J., Fisher, P. and Robinson, S. (2014a). *Eradication of Feral Cats on Large Mexican Islands: A Discussion of Options and Feasibility* (Landcare Research Contract Report LC1115). Mexico.

Parkes, J. P., Fisher, P., Robinson, S. and Aguirre-Muñoz, A. (2014b). Eradication of feral cats from large islands: an assessment of the effort required for success. *New Zealand Journal of Ecology* 38: 307–14.

Pech, R. P., Sinclair, A. R. E. and Newsome, A. E. (1995). Predation models for primary and secondary prey species. *Wildlife Research* 22: 55–63.

Pierce Jones, G., Pearlstine, L. G. and Percival, H. F. (2006). An assessment of small unmanned aerial vehicles for wildlife research. *Wildlife Society Bulletin* 34: 750–58.

Pople, A. R., Clancy, T. F., Thompson, J. A. and Boyd-Law, S. (1998). Aerial survey methodology and the cost of control for feral goats in Western Queensland. *Wildlife Research* 25: 393–407.

Ramsey, D. S. L., Parkes, J. and Morrison, S. A. (2009). Quantifying eradication success: the removal of feral pigs from Santa Cruz Island, California. *Conservation Biology* 23: 449–59.

Ramsey, D. S. L., Parkes, J. P., Will, D., Hanson, C. C. and Campbell, K. J. (2011). Quantifying the success of feral cat eradication, San Nicolas Island, California. *New Zealand Journal of Ecology* 35: 163–73.

Raymundo, M. L. and Miller, R. H. (2012). Little fire ant, *Wasmannia auropunctata* (Roger) (Hymenoptera: Formicidae), established at several locations on Guam. *Proceedings of the Hawaiian Entomological Society* 44: 85–87.

Reardon, J. T., Whitmore, N., Holmes, K. M. et al. (2012). Predator control allows critically endangered lizards to recover on mainland New Zealand. *New Zealand Journal of Ecology* 36: 141–50.

Regan, T. J., McCarthy, M. A., Baxter, P. W. J., Panetta, F. D. and Possingham, H. P. (2006). Optimal eradication: when to stop looking for an invasive plant. *Ecology Letters* 9: 759–66.

Rejmánek, M. and Pitcairn, M. J. (2002). When is eradication of exotic pest plants a realistic goal?, pp. 249–53 in C. R. Veitch, M. N. Clout and D. R. Towns (eds.), *Turning the Tide: The Eradication of Invasive Species* (Occasional Paper of the IUCN Species Survival Commission No. 27). IUCN, Gland.

Rosenzweig, M. L. (2001). The four questions: what does the introduction of exotic species do to diversity? *Evolutionary Ecology Research* 3: 361–67.

Rout, T. M., Salomon, Y. McCarthy, M. A. (2009). Using sighting records to declare eradication of an invasive species. *Journal of Applied Ecology* 46: 110–17.

Ruscoe, W. A. and Pech, R. P. (2010). Rodent outbreaks in New Zealand, pp. 239–51 in G. R. Singleton, S. R. Belmain, P. R. Brown and B. Hardy (eds.), *Rodent Outbreaks: Ecology and Impacts*. International Rice Research Institute, Los Baños.

Russell, J. C., Towns, D. R. and Clout, M. N. (2008). *Review of Rat Invasion Biology: Implications for Island Biosecurity* (Science for Conservation 286). Department of Conservation, Wellington.

Samaniego-Herrera, A., Anderson, D. P., Aguirre-Muñoz, A. and Parkes, J. P. (2013). Rapid assessment of rat eradication after aerial baiting. *Journal of Applied Ecology* 50: 1415–21.

Saunders, G., Coman, B., Kinnear, J. and Braysher, M. (1995). *Managing Vertebrate Pests: Foxes*. Australian Government Publishing Service, Canberra.

Saunders, A., Parkes, J. P., Aguirre-Muñoz, A. and Morrison, S. A. (2011). Increasing the return on investments in island restoration, pp. 492–95 in C. R. Veitch, M. N. Clout and D. R. Towns (eds.), *Island Invasives: Eradication and Management* (Occasional Paper of the IUCN Species Survival Commission No. 42). IUCN, Gland.

Scofield, R. P., Cullen, R. and Wang, M. (2011). Are predator-proof fences the answer to New Zealand's terrestrial faunal biodiversity crisis? *New Zealand Journal of Ecology* 35: 312–17.

Sinclair, A. R. E., Fryxell, J. M. and Caughley, G. (2006). *Wildlife Ecology, Conservation, and Management*. Blackwell, Oxford.

Sutherland, W. J. (2000). *The Conservation Handbook: Research, Management and Policy*. Blackwell Scientific, Oxford.

Thresher, R. E. (2008). Autocidal technologies for the control of invasive fish. *Fisheries* 33: 114–21.

Tindall, S. D., Ralph, C. J. and Clout, M. N. (2007). Changes in bird abundance following common myna control on a New Zealand island. *Pacific Conservation Biology* 13: 202–12.

Turner, J. W. and Kirkpatrick, J. F. (1991). New developments in feral horse contraception and their potential application to wildlife. *Wildlife Society Bulletin* 19: 350–59.

Tyndale-Biscoe, H. (1994). Virus-vectored immunocontraception of feral mammals. *Reproduction, Fertility and Development* 6: 9–16.

Varnham, K. J., Roy, S. S., Seymour, A. et al. (2002). Eradicating Indian musk shrews (Suncus murinus, Sorocidae) from Mauritian offshore islands, pp. 342–49 in C. R. Veitch, M. N. Clout and D. R. Towns (eds.), *Turning the Tide: The Eradication of Invasive Species* (Occasional Paper of the IUCN Species Survival Commission No. 27). IUCN, Gland.

Veitch, C. R., Clout, M. N. and Towns, D. R. (eds.) (2011). *Island Invasives: Eradication and Management* (Occasional Paper of the IUCN Species Survival Commission 42). IUCN, Gland.

Walker, S., Stephens, R. T. T. and Overton, J. M. C. (2012). A unified approach to conservation prioritisation, reporting and information gathering in New Zealand. *New Zealand Journal of Ecology* 36: 243–51.

West, C. J. (2002). Eradication of alien plants on Raoul Island, Kermadec islands, New Zealand, pp. 365–73 in C. R. Veitch, M. N. Clout and D. R. Towns (eds.), *Turning the Tide: The Eradication of Invasive Species* (Occasional Paper of the IUCN Species Survival Commission No. 27). IUCN, Gland.

Westley, F. W., and Miller, P. S. (eds.). (2003). *Experiments in Consilience: Integrating Social and Scientific Responses to Save Endangered Species*. Island Press, Washington, DC.

Wilkinson, I. S. and Priddel, D. (2011). Rodent eradication on Lord Howe Island: challenges posed by people, livestock, and threatened endemics, pp. 508–14 in C. R. Veitch, M. N. Clout and D. R. Towns (eds.), *Island Invasives: Eradication and Management* (Occasional Paper of the IUCN Species Survival Commission No. 42). IUCN, Gland.

Yaffee, S., Phillips, A., Frentz, I. et al. (1996). *Ecosystem Management in the United States: An Assessment of Current Experience*. Island Press, Washington, DC.

Young, L. C., VanderWerf, E. A., Lohr, M. T. et al. (2013). Multi-species predator eradication within a predator-proof fence at Ka'ena Point, Hawai'i. *Biological Invasions* 15: 2627–38.

8 · *Leading Species Recovery*
Influencing Effective Conservation

SIMON A. BLACK

8.0 Introduction

Leadership can determine whether a conservation project succeeds or fails. This implies two potential causes: (1) particular leadership approaches which may be either helpful or unhelpful to conservation, or (2) specific leaders (individual people) whose personal approach (behaviour) is either helpful or unhelpful. On islands, leaders need to build effective teams that can work in relatively self-contained contexts and can continue to learn and improve. Leaders must identify ways to lead and manage their projects to create an environment where people can carry out effective conservation work.

This chapter explores different styles of leadership, highlighting which approaches are best suited for the management of species and habitat recovery programmes. We examine the core theories and perspectives that inform individual leaders on how to behave in a way that will help their project team to succeed. The chapter stresses the importance of teams, how to create them and how to manage morale and motivation in what is inevitably a tiring and emotive process. Recognising that projects have natural high and low points, we explore how to manage staff through these stages, including aspects of managing people which are presented as a practical reference guide. We pay particular attention to the value of 'systems thinking' in influencing our perspective on helpful ways to lead conservation projects, drawing on experience from island species recovery projects to do so. Finally, the chapter considers the importance of the 'project champion' who sticks with the project and provides both leadership and encouragement throughout the process.

8.1 An Overview of 'Leadership' and 'Management'

Leadership has been quoted as the single most important factor in determining whether a project succeeds or fails (Dietz et al. 2004). For anyone with the responsibilities of leading and managing a project, at some point the questions of 'what is leadership?' and 'what is management?' are brought to mind. In the absence of previous experience or training, it is common for new leaders to establish a loose 'command and control' mentality based on hierarchies of 'boss' and 'subordinates'. A more enlightened project leader might recognise a need to be inspiring, motivating, charismatic and energetic and would also identify the need to encourage and enthuse team members to behave in similar ways. At a superficial level, it is possible to observe that (1) some leaders become successful, (2) many are about average and (3) a few have a dismal time and 'just don't have what it takes'. Are leaders born rather than made? Unsurprisingly, these questions are not solely a concern of conservation managers. Considerations of leadership, management style, behaviour and personality have been debated by many practitioners, psychologists, organisational theoreticians, social scientists and management gurus. The debate on management and leadership is an interesting diversion, but when you are leading a project with scant resources, possibly in a remote area, it is necessary to take a pragmatic view of what leadership means and how to do it effectively.

8.1.1 Leadership versus Management

Before we go into these theories in more detail, we first need to address the issue of 'leadership versus management'. Bennis (1999) suggests that 'the manager does things right; the leader does the right thing'. 'Management' is a fairly new discipline, coming to the fore in the early 1900s, while 'leadership' has a history going back for as long as we have had leaders (Coppin and Barratt 2002). Debates have raged for more than 50 years about the difference between 'management' and 'leadership', but we can now say in the first decades of the twenty-first century that an emerging consensus recognises that effective leadership and management are intertwined. Modern thinking on leading and managing increasingly recognises that a leader's role is not one that is remote and strategic but rather is based on a good understanding of what is happening on the ground (Mintzberg 2009; Hamel 2009). This offers some clues as to how to lead conservation projects – you need to do both.

At a practical level, a conservation manager should keep several aspects at the forefront of his or her thinking. From a leadership perspective, common themes include inspiring others, enabling people to use their capabilities, encouraging and reinforcing people's effort, seeking better ways of working and achieving results and setting an example. From a management perspective, planning (e.g. for invasive species eradications; see Chapter 7), delegating, and reviewing progress are important. If we add the need for a practical understanding of human psychology (of the team and oneself), then the skill mix appears to get very complicated.

Seddon (2003) suggests that leadership is all about influence. If so, then the way a project leader views his or her role (as manager and leader) and the behaviour he or she exhibits will be reflected in the influence that leader has on the team. What type of leadership will get the best out of people and the best results for a project? After all, it is all about recovering species and ecosystems rather than winning 'manager of the month' awards. However, it is people who do the work, who generate ideas, who make mistakes and who influence stakeholders, so leaders need to develop a solid understanding of the links between human perspectives, expectations, attitudes, commitments, responsibilities, behaviour and work.

8.1.2 A Short History of Well-Known Leadership Theories

Management literature still has no agreed-upon definition of 'leadership' (Kennedy 1996; Seddon 2003), although various types of leadership models have emerged over time (Table 8.1), largely driven by the ideas of American scholars and practitioners (Muczyk and Holt 2008). The traditional 'command and control' or 'scientific management' philosophy arose in the early 1900s (Holling and Meffe 1996; Grint 2010) in businesses such as the Ford Motor Company. The ideas were extended with quasi-military leadership concepts in the 1940s (Kennedy 1996). This philosophy of managing people through mechanistic control of units of work (tasks) using punishment and reward was initially superseded in the 1950s and 1960s as industrial psychology identified new, behavioural theories such as 'theory Y' (McGregor 1957) and 'situational leadership' (Hersey and Blanchard 1969). The 1960s saw a re-emergence of control-type philosophies in the form of transactional management using more sophisticated methods (including management by objectives), while the 1970s saw a trend of inspiring transformational,

Table 8.1 *Summary of Common Leadership Theories*

Theory	Summary
Command and control	*What:* mechanistic, pseudo-military, top-down, autocratic *Why important:* a common 'default' approach adopted by many managers *Assumed benefits:* 'strong leadership', or 'it is good when people need directing' *Problems:* bureaucracy, reduces thinking and learning, efficiency versus effectiveness *Further reading:* Seddon (2003); Teerlink and Ozley (2000)
Theory X and theory Y	*What:* A leader's perspective on people at work drives assumptions and style *Why important:* Theory X (authoritarian) contrasts with theory Y (participative) *Assumed benefits:* Theory Y follows a better understanding of human motivation *Problems:* people exist on a continuum, but what is the best approach and why? *Further reading:* McGregor (1957)
Situational leadership	*What:* leaders adapt behaviour according to followers' maturity and motivation *Why important:* focuses on managing an individual or team on a specific task *Assumed benefits:* enables an approach that adapts to the needs of workers *Problems:* can lose the bigger picture: why are we doing this? *Further reading:* Hersey and Blanchard (1977)
Transactional-transformational models	*What:* behaviourally based model; leader emphasised ('saviour', 'hero') *Why important:* the dominant models encountered in business schools today *Assumed benefits:* enables change and high performance, getting more out of people, leaders can learn 'transformational' behaviours *Problems:* causes ego-centred leaders, people are perceived as a problem, assumes people need motivating, reduces dissent and debate (learning) *Further reading:* Peters (1987); Kouzes and Posner (2007)
Servant leadership	*What:* power based on mutuality (listening, empathy, stewardship, persuasion)

Table 8.1 *(cont.)*

Theory	Summary
	Why important: an alternative that favours growth and community
	Assumed benefits: high identification of employees with aims of the leader
	Problems: attributes often difficult to fulfil and require a long-term approach
	Further reading: Greenleaf (2002)
Systems thinking	*What:* Enable people to work purposefully, understand and seek improvement.
	Why important: relates behaviour to people, work, results and knowledge
	Assumed benefits: philosophy fits well with needs of species conservation
	Problems: leaders must commit to the philosophy and unlearn old habits
	Further reading: Deming (1982); Senge (1990)

value-based leadership. This spawned the emergence of 'transactional-transformational' leadership (Burns 1978) involving clear vision, values, credibility, technical competence, conceptual skills, judgment, experimentation and involvement (Peters 1987; Heifetz and Laurie 1997; Bennis 1999).

As the 'negative' (or, at least, unsophisticated) aspects of transactional models such as 'punishment and reward' became less attractive in the 1980s, transformational leadership alone became the dominant philosophy (Kennedy 1996; Kouzes and Posner 2007). Major corporate leaders were presented as heroes and saviours of their companies. Nevertheless, elements of this ideology have since been shown to be context specific, for example, individualism, status-consciousness and risk-taking are contingent upon the national or regional culture of followers (Muczyk and Holt 2008). Few alternatives have emerged in Western management thinking since, although 'servant leadership' is one that has been useful in some organisations. In recent years, the 'distributed leadership' approach has been applied in organisations with multiple business units (Gronn 2002), in which the focus is placed upon the capability of dispersed teams to undertake the work. With team locations remote from the central leadership team, the leadership functions are carried out by different people at different times (Bolden 2011), so the leadership actions of any individual leader are much less important than the collective leadership provided by members of the organisation (Yukl 1999).

8.2 Adapting the Approach to Followers' Needs

Hersey and Blanchard's (1977) model of 'situational leadership' characterised different leadership styles in terms of the amount of task behaviour and relationship behaviour the leader provides to followers. The key principle that they identified was that no one style is considered optimal for all leaders to use all the time. They indicated that the correct style will depend on the person or group being led (the follower) and the particular task they are being set. This is an important notion for conservationists in leadership roles; they need to adapt their style to the people on the team and the work that those people need to do. Firstly, the leader has to recognise that workers have various levels of competence and commitment within their roles. Good leaders (1) identify each person's competence in terms of professional development and personal motivations and (2) use a flexible leadership style, applying directive behaviours (i.e. clearly telling people what to do, how, where and when and closely supervising the work) or supportive behaviours (i.e. listening, supporting, encouraging, coaching, facilitating) to maximise the potential of their staff.

Against these behaviours, Hersey and Blanchard (1977) categorised all leadership styles into four behaviour types: directing, coaching, supporting and delegating, each relevant to different situations. The situation is defined in terms of the 'task' and the 'maturity' of the worker. The specifics of the task are important; a person might be generally skilled, confident and motivated in his or her job, but when asked to perform a task requiring new skills, that person should be treated more as a beginner. A leader should be looking to make the team as self-sufficient as possible – able to take on tasks and be responsible for their delivery. A good leader may start by directing tasks but will be able to coach, support and then fully delegate the task to team members as they mature in their skills and experience.

8.3 The Importance of People

The challenge for the conservation leader is to identify and apply the leadership skills that make sense when managing the team and the project

Figure 8.1 Ulysses S. Seal, chairman of the IUCN Conservation Breeding Specialist Group (CBSG), 1979–2003. According to this highly respected professional, who had facilitated more than 200 species recovery workshops in more than 60 countries, 'the one common feature that many successful conservation projects have is a charismatic and inspirational leader that has a clear vision, can motivate the staff and can manage morale'. (*Photo credit:* IUCN SSC Conservation Planning Specialist Group (CPSG).)

as a whole (Figure 8.1). Inevitably this requires significant interpersonal skills, since leadership involves people. Nevertheless, these skills should complement the management activities within the project, such as goal-setting, decision-making and problem-solving.

Leadership depends on followers, so, by definition, a leader must be able to influence followers. The most enduring models of leadership of the last 30 years emphasise less the charisma of the leader and instead focus more on the leader's requirement to engage followers. For example, Kouzes and Posner (2007) identify the need for leaders to set an example based on clear values, inspire followers with a clear vision, be ready to encourage others to experiment and take opportunities, enable people to get on with work and recognise and celebrate the achievements of the team. Coppin and Barratt (2002) discuss timeless qualities of management and include the characteristic of 'mutuality', defined in terms of trust, win–win mentality and the ability to coach, give recognition, review performance and promote fun. In essence, these are aspects of working with people, ensuring that they are engaged, contributing and feeling part of the team. Deming (1982) encourages people to develop a basic understanding of human psychology to inform how they manage their teams. Better leaders tend to believe in self-motivation that comes from within their people.

Nevertheless, work is more than just belonging; it is about getting things done. Adair's (1979) 'action centred leadership', describes three elements that leaders should take into account: the task, the team and the individual team members. To manage successfully, a leader should not overemphasise one aspect over others, although the focus might shift on occasion (e.g. if a problem arises in the task or an individual needs particular attention). This can be useful to keep in mind as a starting point when thinking about your team (for example, see Box 6.2).

8.4 Empowerment, Motivation and the Fear Factor

Conservation is often a tiring and emotive process in which projects will have natural high and low points from the team's point of view. Managing morale and motivation in this environment is an important role for the conservation leader. A key issue in management is how people are motivated: extrinsically (through rewards) or intrinsically (through self-motivation) or a combination of both. To understand these issues more clearly, a quick overview of the key motivational theories is useful.

8.4.1 Maslow's 'Hierarchy of Needs'

One of the earliest breakthroughs in describing human motivation was Abraham Maslow's (1970) 'hierarchy of needs'. This suggested that as humans' basic physiological needs are met, they are motivated to pursue higher-level needs such as safety (law and order, protection but also job security), belonging (relationships, including within a work group), esteem (achievement, responsibility, reputation) and self-actualisation (higher sense of purpose and fulfilment). This suggests that as a manager running a team, if basic and safety needs are met, the leader needs to ensure that team members have a sense of belonging and then, through their work, a sense of achievement and ultimately self-fulfilment. This resonates with the situational leadership model because once workers are comfortable in their tasks, the leader should look to seek higher levels of performance by providing an opportunity to learn more, achieve more and take on more responsibility.

8.4.2 Hertzberg's 'Motivators' and 'Hygiene Factors'

Frederick Herzberg's (2003) most famous article in *Harvard Business Review* emphasised that 'you cannot motivate people'. Instead, he argues, you can only provide conditions in which employees are more or less likely to be self-motivated or de-motivated. Herzberg identified two sets of conditions: one involved factors that influence people's motivation at work ('satisfiers'), whereas the other set involved factors that de-motivate people ('dissatisfiers'). These two groups were not mutual; it is easy for leaders to think that they are doing the right things to motivate while erroneously ignoring the things that de-motivate, and this may unwittingly undermine the leader's best efforts. For example, for a field team working in relatively tough environmental conditions, being provided with equipment that makes their time more comfortable and enjoyable is likely to create an environment in which people could feel motivated. Conversely, ignoring their requests for mosquito nets, electricity or sleeping mats would frustrate them and dissipate their inherent motivation for the job. A second important point is that motivation is different from movement – in Herzberg's analogy, you can kick a dog and it will move, but it is not motivated.

8.4.3 The Fundamentals of Motivation

Ultimately, motivation theory and observed practices encountered in thousands of organisations repeatedly tell us one thing: you cannot motivate people; they can only motivate themselves. Furthermore, recent research has indicated that higher worker performance in cognitive tasks (i.e. anything more than the most menial activity) relates to increases in the worker's degrees of autonomy, mastery and purpose (Ryan and Deci 2000). With motivation, we are interested in behaviour and the intentions behind a worker's behaviour, or the ABC of motivation: antecedents, behaviour and consequences. Sensible influence of the outputs (achievement of purpose, establishment of their levels of mastery of skills and autonomy in enacting the work) will influence the effectiveness of work performance. A basic tenet of behavioural analysis is to view behaviours as a function of a person and his or her environment: something occurs that precedes behaviour (the antecedent) and influences the behaviour, resulting in a consequence (an outcome). We can't change a person, but we can influence the way he or she behaves by shaping the environment within which he or she works. Although effort is placed into antecedents such as training, persuading and briefing to ensure that people are correctly focused, in practice, it is the consequences of actions that are the greatest determinant of behaviours. In Box 6.1 we saw how the Maui Forest Bird Recovery Project (MFRBP) leader requires new staff to have discussions with community members about the purpose of MFBRP at a public event. This approach demands that new staff make efforts during induction to understand the purpose of MFBRP – if they do not, they will appear unconvincing and unprofessional and will be uncomfortable at the public event. This perceived 'consequence' means that staff members must prepare themselves thoroughly and consult colleagues before the event (the antecedent). The outcome is that new people better understand their team and its purpose and can carry that knowledge into their role (behaviour) more effectively.

It is important that consequences are carefully designed. The 'theory of planned behaviour' (Ajzen 1991) tells us that people tend to weigh decisions on the favourability of outcome, social pressure and level of control over the action, often on an irrational basis. Motivations and subsequent behaviours are influenced by myriad internal and external factors. Do not expect to set consequences to make people 'jump' without experiencing unintended consequences elsewhere (the work, the team or the individual's reactions). 'Command and control' erroneously assumes a cause-and-effect link with reward and punishment. However, psychological studies repeatedly demonstrate that while setting task-specific standards for routine tasks has a positive impact on performance, the effect on more complex tasks (more commonly encountered in conservation) is negative or at best maintains motivation (Bryan and Locke 1967; Elliot and Harackiewicz 1994). As a straightforward first step to effective management, instead of applying standards, targets and rewards, a leader should make expectations clear so that people consciously consider what is important and focus on the purpose of the work. In other words, people take it upon themselves to be purposeful and autonomous and therefore seek to develop mastery of the work.

8.5 Managing Individuals: Win–Win and the Basics of Working Relationships

Conservation programmes can often engage teams in working together in relatively extreme conditions, shared living accommodation and close proximity over days, weeks or even months. In island conservation, this is particularly common, and the boundaries between work and social lives may blur to some degree. As a leader, it is advantageous to know your team members not only in terms of their skills abilities and motivations but also in terms of their interests, constraints and aspirations, even at a social level. The value of friendships at work is relatively understudied, misunderstood or ignored in management literature. At the very least, a leader must show integrity – a consistency of personal values and expectations applied in work and social settings. This sense of completeness or wholeness of approach is a big demand on the conservation leader; no one is perfect. Nevertheless, a leader needs to have a clear understanding of values and principles before applying actions and methods.

Additionally, there are other fundamentals of managing relationships within the team that are useful to encourage a climate of trust, understanding, sharing and learning (Covey 1989) based around the concept of 'win-win'. The notion of valuing oneself and valuing other persons and maintaining that position even when others do not behave in a similar fashion offers the opportunity of an acceptable outcome or workable compromise being reached without unnecessary conflict or emotional 'game playing'. This modelling of an 'assertive' approach grew out of pioneering work on behavioural psychology (Smith 1975) in the 1960s that arose from emerging theory and practice in psychology, neuroscience and psychotherapy. The concept is built on the reality of how human beings process and recall experiences, but also the impact of verbal, non-verbal behaviour and emotions on a person's state (Peters 2012). At a practical level it is useful to encourage behaviours that build trust, empathy, listening and responsiveness. A leader needs staff to know when they are performing or behaving inappropriately (and to respond to the leader's requirements) as much as a leader might want them to feel positive when things go right; a climate of trust and respect will allow both. The 'win-win' behaviours that arise from a sense of value for oneself and other people are likely to identify mutually positive outcomes. Win-lose or lose-win behaviour is subversive and eventually leads to everybody losing. In the absence of trust, things may repeatedly go wrong, and morale will decline. A leader who aggressively challenges or demands from staff may win in the short term (while others put up with the behaviour or demands), but in the long term the leader will lose out once people stop responding, hide bad news, refrain from giving ideas or leave.

8.6 The Importance of Team Development

There are several good reasons for engaging workers to collaborate together as a cohesive team (Figure 8.2): better understanding of higher-

Figure 8.2 Team development training, Madagascar. Participants from local conservation organisations work together to determine how to move a ball around the team as quickly as possible. (*Photo credit:* Jamieson A. Copsey.)

level decisions, more support for plans, stronger participation in implementation of action, increased contribution to problem-solving and more involvement and ownership of shared decisions. In order for teams to fulfil their intended role of improving organisational effectiveness, it is critical that teams develop into working units that are focused on their goal, mission or reason for existing (see Section 6.3). An effective project leader not only will expect the team to mature and develop over time but also will proactively develop the team to high performance quickly. All teams go through a number of stages of maturity. Without conscious effort, a team's development might be erratic or even dysfunctional. Tuckman (1965) describes how teams mature through four stages: forming (meeting and establishing team purpose and familiarity), storming (vying for power, setting boundaries, questioning and establishing trust), norming (establishing stable behavioural expectations, team processes and work procedures and roles) and performing (member's delegates work, team decision-making, problem-solving and improvement), essentially a continuum of development. The stages are observed in the behaviours, activities and experiences of team members. Importantly, the speed at which a team moves from 'forming' to 'performing' can be managed and enhanced by careful consideration of team processes, including selection, induction, staff development, information sharing, decision-making, problem-solving, project management and feedback. Secondly, a team can stall at one stage for weeks, months or years if relevant group processes are not enacted. Thirdly, if members join or leave, the overall dynamics of a team revert back to the 'forming' stage. The speed at which a team progresses through the stages is a measure of the effectiveness of both the team and the leader. In 1975, Tuckman added a fifth stage 'adjourning', which relates to the breakup of the team on completion of the task and how leaders need an awareness of, and ability to manage, the sensitivities and emotional aspects that project closure entails.

8.7 The Case for Using Systems Thinking When Leading Conservation Projects

A conservation leader needs to combine a series of skills and rarely carries the sole role of 'professional manager'. Normally, technical, scientific or social-scientific competence will form a significant proportion of the role. A leadership approach (in terms of thinking and behaviour) that complements the technical demands of the role is vital. A leadership approach that contradicts the technical demands of conservation work has time and again proven to be counterproductive as it separates the manager's focus from the needs of the project and the pressures on the team. The experiences described by various authors make this apparent, as best summarised by Black, Groombridge and Jones (2011) as:

1. *Goals that are unachievable* (scope, time scale, or incorrect or unrealistic assumptions).
2. Organisational structures that are *excessively hierarchical or bureaucratic* or have functional divisions.
3. A *lack of timely information sharing* due to bureaucracy or apathy or simple errors in practice.
4. *Poor decision-making* due to hierarchy, risk aversion or uninformed viewpoints and lack of data.
5. Ideologically-driven *team members who do not commit to or agree with a programme's culture*.
6. *Methodological dissonance across the programme*, including different technical preferences.

7. *Time wasted on essentially unsolvable issues* outside or not yet under the project's influence.
8. *An adherence to procedure and protocol* that stifles innovations in practice or experimentation.
9. *Failure to learn* from mistakes or to seek advice or wrongly delegating key decisions to outsiders.
10. Rigid people management and a *failure to identify and work to people's strengths* within the team.

Box 8.1 *Can a Change in Leadership Approach Have an Impact on Conservation Results?*

The recovery of the California condor illustrates changes in leadership approaches over time alongside the measurable changes in population status (Black, Groombridge and Jones 2011; Box 8.1, Figure 8.3).

Trends in the California condor population were compared with observable stages in programme management and patterns of leadership since the 1940s, knowing the changes in personnel and jurisdiction overseeing the programme. The population curve is shown by a thick black line indicating total individuals (estimates where indicated), and the

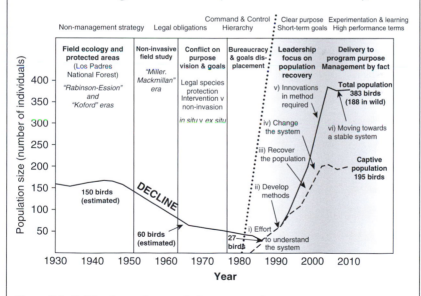

Figure 8.3 California condor population status and programme management trends. Note correlation between shift in leadership approach and species recovery.

captive population is shown by a dashed black line. Various management team phases are indicated by vertical lines (Koford 1953; Miller et al. 1965; Phillips and Nash 1981; Snyder and Snyder 2000; USFWS 2010; Wilbur 1978). A change in leadership approach is indicated by the vertical dotted line. It is clear that there is significant purposefully managed progress using a different philosophy since the 1980s. However, would a similar approach work where resources are more limited and set within the confines of island conservation?

The spectacularly successful recovery of the Mauritius kestrel is a case in point. The recovery pattern is strikingly similar to that of the California condor (Figure 8.4). By the early 1980s, the programme was set the task of managed withdrawal due to the pitifully few surviving individuals. Nevertheless, the local programme leader, Carl Jones, took it upon himself to attempt a long-term recovery but focusing on achievable short-term goals. After years of experimentation, trial, error, increasing knowledge of the species and effective methods, the recovery began to take shape. The result is a significant free-living wild population requiring virtually no human intervention. The leadership focus, use of people, learning culture, experimentation and decision-making based on knowledge are all characteristics of systems thinking, a natural outcome, perhaps, from employing an open-minded, practical biologist endeavouring to work a solution for a species within a complex, open island ecosystem.

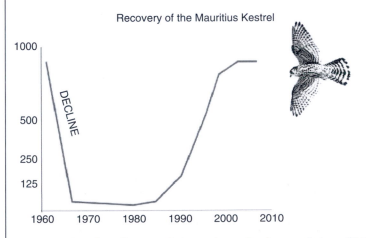

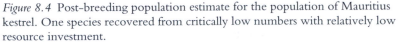

Figure 8.4 Post-breeding population estimate for the population of Mauritius kestrel. One species recovered from critically low numbers with relatively low resource investment.

The challenge for the conservation leader is to use approaches that avoid these problems yet are able to maintain structure and progress in the project which they are managing. Conservation programmes are 'open systems', which provide an additional layer of complication. From both a philosophical and a practical point of view, a conservation leader needs a perspective that incorporates open systems, leadership, management of people, innovation of methods and an overall focus on purpose and results. Black, Groombridge and Jones (2011) identify this as 'systems thinking', an approach best suited for leaders in conservation and that also allows a distributed approach to leadership if teams are expected to work remotely and to adapt to local conditions and challenges. However, systems thinking requires perspectives quite different to the common default leadership style ingrained in people from childhood and often throughout the education system (Deming 1993; Scholtes 1998). To illustrate this contrast between systems thinking and command and control (Seddon 2003), a useful summary is provided in Table 8.2.

Table 8.2 *Comparison of Command and Control versus Systems Thinking*

	A systems thinking leader will be informed by these perspectives	These traditional approaches show an absence of systems thinking
Organisation design	Outside-in, derived from core work processes, self-managing teams	Top-down hierarchy, functional procedures, depend on individuals
Attitude to customers/users [a]	What matters to customers/users? [a] Cooperative: value, speed, reliability	Contractual: adversarial, price-based, 'fit with what we offer'
Attitude to suppliers	Cooperative/ partnerships: value, speed and reliability, long term, eliminate cost	Contractual: adversarial, price-based, 'see how we squeeze you'
Ethos	Learning, team-based, sharing, integrity, vision	Control, individualism, 'politics' and rivalry
Attitude to employees	Trust and responsibility; people are the solution, with huge potential for growth	People are the problem, lack potential, need 'carrot & stick'

Table 8.2 *(cont.)*

	A systems thinking leader will be informed by these perspectives	These traditional approaches show an absence of systems thinking
Decision-making	Integrated with workers	Separated from workers
Leadership	Inclusive, situational, based on expertise	Exclusive, fixed, based on position/hierarchy/ seniority
Communication	Based on knowledge and understanding, for people placed to make decisions	Based on passing information, limited to managers, top down
Learning and development	An investment for all, critical for success and improvement	A cost, privilege of the few
Measurement	'What & why' focus: relate to purpose, capability, variation, lead and lag metrics	'What' focus: output, targets, standards, related to budget
Pay and reward	Reward capability and achievement	Reward attendance

[a] In conservation, customers/users will be species, habitats and human communities in the ecosystem.
Source: From Black et al. (2011).

Recently, mainstream management thinkers have moved away from considering the leader solely as 'strategic' and transformational towards engaging in a leadership role that is closer to operational activity (Hamel 2009; Mintzberg 2009). Theories in organisation development and human psychology appear to confirm this need, identifying how leadership processes contribute to the achievement of organisational purpose, and that leadership is linked to system characteristics and dynamics (Zaccaro and Klimoski 2001). The application of systems thinking in organisations originated in the 1930s and 1940s (Shewhart 1931; von Bertalanffy 1969; Deming 1982) and encourages leaders to optimise links between manager behaviour, work rules, structure, decision-making, skills, methods and results (Senge 1990; Scholtes 1998; Seddon 2003). Systems thinking emphasises not the leader as such but the effectiveness of the organisation. A systems thinking leader's role is one of 'working on the system'; a fundamental change from 'working on people', as advocated by the various command-and-control, behavioural and transformational models (Seddon 2003).

A project manager needs to develop four areas of competence: personal capabilities (including decision-making, analytical skills, planning, self-awareness, time management and communication skills), leadership capabilities (managing teams and participating as a team member) and organisational skills (knowledge of stakeholders, awareness of policies, budgets, procedures and internal politics) alongside the technical and scientific knowledge required for the job (Black and Copsey 2014a).

As a leader with many pressures on time and energy, it is worth focusing on the most relevant areas in which to develop knowledge. We suggest that the specific areas of knowledge are defined by the way that human activity, motivations and organisations operate within the wider environment of human society and its place within natural landscapes and ecosystems. Ed Deming was the first to frame these core areas of theory, for which he used the term 'profound knowledge' (Deming 1993), but many influential authors have followed his lead. Since Deming first presented these ideas to Japanese industrialists in the 1950s, the disciplines of psychology, neuroscience, statistics and organisational behaviour have advanced, yet these core theories remain relevant (Black and Copsey 2014b).

Due to the durability of Deming's framework, we suggest that conservation leaders should invest effort in developing a practical understanding of the following four areas of competence:

- Psychology of motivation, behaviour and interpersonal skills (respect, mutuality, responsiveness)
- Understanding systems, management conditions, goals, rules and expectations on behaviour
- Applying theories of knowledge to decisions, research and managing uncertainty
- Understanding the difference between chance outcomes and meaningful patterns in data

At a practical level, this suggests that a leader's thinking and approach influence the focus, operation, structure, policy, goal-setting and decision-making in his or her organisation (Scholtes 1998; Seddon 2003). All these aspects are less well explained by other management theories yet are relevant to current demands placed on leaders within the conservation sector. In its truest sense, systems thinking incorporates an understanding of human behaviour (essentially a natural system), organisations and rules (human-made systems), technology (manufactured hardware and materials) and the processes in place to manage the work that we do. In conservation we would add the need to understand other natural systems (i.e. climate, geology, ecology, ecosystems, species biology, physiology and behaviour, including invasive species and disease).

8.8 What Does Systems Thinking Involve?

A quick check through textbooks and web articles will expose the reader to a range of other 'systems theories' that include information technology/computing, management information systems and the like. Our perspective relates to the best-known proponents of systems thinking, including Deming (who promoted it from the 1920s through the 1990s) and Senge (who has done the same since the 1990s) with a focus on human organisations and the interaction of people, work, information, rules, decisions, materials, equipment and outputs of work.

8.8.1 Projects within Natural and Social Systems

If we lead a project that deals with an open system involving the natural world and the human stakeholders who interact with it (see Chapter 11), then the purpose of our programme should reflect that understanding. If we are to work effectively, we need to see our interventions as influencing the elements of the system that make a difference to the species and ecosystems which are of concern to us. Purpose defines the system that you are going to manage. Clarity of purpose is vital if a project is to have the correct reference point for goals, actions and decisions (Black 2015). A 'goal' is a discrete milestone that is agreed upon to guide a distinct set of actions. Most projects or teams will have several goals (see Section 6.5 and Section 9.1.1). The important discipline required from a leader is to ensure that goals are assigned to the overall project purpose and that specific goals are mutually supportive, not counterproductive. A good test for a goal is 'how does this help us to achieve our overall purpose?'

Decision-making around goals requires a good or growing understanding of the needs of the target subject, which for the purposes of this book are threatened species and the ecosystems in which they live. A systems thinking conservation leader should therefore continually seek to better understand the needs of the species (e.g. its genetic status; see Chapter 3) and ecosystems of concern (e.g. wider impacts of invasive species; see Chapter 4), as this information forms the basis of decision-making (notwithstanding other factors of economics, land ownership, jurisdiction, value or societal needs, which may also need to be taken into account).

8.8.2 Integrating All Aspects of the Work

There is no separation between 'soft' aspects such as people's behaviour, thinking, emotions, decisions and communication and 'hard' aspects such as equipment, machinery, money, products and resources – all these factors interact. If you change one factor, it will affect, to some degree, everything else. For example, if one team member is disaffected by work or a personal situation, it easily rubs off on other people on the team and might affect the work or influence bad decisions. A systems thinking leader needs to consider a number of core processes that are undertaken by the team during a project or an ongoing conservation programme. Aside from occasional work on various 'support processes' (such as administration, recruitment, health and safety), the main focus will be on three core processes: the task process, the team process and the individual process(es):

- **Task Core Process.** This is the work being undertaken to deliver the conservation outcome. The output measures for the project/programme should relate to these core work processes.
- **Team Core Process.** How the team operates, its development, how it runs meetings, how it solves problems, how it makes decisions, how it sets goals, how it inducts new people, how it trains people.
- **Individual Core Process(es).** How each individual develops, personal skill acquisition, personal goal-setting, how each person gives and receives feedback, personal career development.

Clearly, the work, the team and the individual processes cross over in many ways. For example, if we set goals for the team, we need to consider the purpose of the project in relation to the work, the way the team defines those goals and how each individual might contribute to those goals.

8.8.3 Managing Knowledge, People and Resources

One might think management is based on rational information (costs, data, facts), yet often this is not the case; objectives can be defined on somewhat arbitrary terms, and decisions can be based on partial, often misinterpreted facts, such as differences ('variance') between one month's results and the next or this year's results versus last year's. Systems thinking requires a better understanding of variation in data both temporally and spatially (Black and Copsey 2014b). Also, although we may wish to make decisions based on known data, we do not know everything, and some things are frankly not worth measuring or too difficult to measure. In such cases, a leader and his or her team need to make the best guess, but based on a sound rationale (or 'theory', as Deming would describe it). A good leader will know when to make judgments in the light of limited data by using a reasonable rationale (observations, experience or best available knowledge). In conservation, notions such as the 'precautionary principle' serve well (e.g. as with the case of invasive species; see Section 4.4.3). A good leader also adapts approaches as new knowledge arises.

An effective leader also recognises the risks of having a de-motivated workforce. Conservation requires motivated people who will observe things in their work, make suggestions, imagine solutions and work together as a team to improve the situation for species and ecosystems. The systems thinking leader must use a basic understanding of human psychology to manage his or her team (see Section 8.4). In principle the leader must be respectful and treat colleagues and other stakeholders as rational people who, nevertheless, may still respond in 'irrational' or emotive ways to poor management. Efforts to conserve the Hawaiian crow *Corvus hawaiiensis* were hampered for years by a breakdown in the relationship between the scientific team and local landowners to the point where, aside from vocal support of the conservation of the bird, landowners prevented scientists from entering the protected habitats in which the remaining few individual crows persisted (Walters 2006). The two parties refused to cooperate on a point of principle, not on the basis of the logical, recognised need of the species. It is in situations such as this that understanding helpful and unhelpful management behaviour becomes critical.

A systems thinking leader will recognise that people doing the job need to understand all relevant information to carry out that work, including how their work affects other activities and results. By inference, workers are best placed to make decisions that influence that work, assuming that they have the relevant skills and expertise. This is pertinent to conservation projects, where often highly skilled scientists and technicians are engaged in the work. It is unsurprising that conservation projects have suffered where technical experts have been prevented from making decisions and implementing actions that they see are necessary and useful. Too often there have been delays further up the organisational chain of command that have proven fatal to species recovery.

The po'ouli *Melamprosops phaeosoma* is a well-known case of recent likely extinction (Powell 2008). In the final stages of its decline, field-based teams of biologists were used to monitor the status, breeding biology and feeding ecology of the remaining population (a handful of individual birds). However, on the few occasions when observations were made – such as when nests were discovered – those local experts had little opportunity to make conservation decisions. For example, the only nest ever observed by scientists was poorly positioned and exposed to inclement weather, and its recently hatched chicks soon died as a result of climatic effects. Observers had no authority to intervene or use the initial discovery of the nest to take hatched birds into captive breeding (a well-established method at that time). As a result, knowledge was not gained, hatched chicks were lost and an entire generation of po'ouli never fledged or reached adulthood. Subsequent attempts by the team to recover the remaining adult birds were consistently hampered by slow authorisation of the team to enact decisions in the field. The failure of the po'ouli recovery was sadly as much a failure to delegate authority to knowledgeable experts who could carry out work on the ground as it was the impact of invasive species, disease or habitat loss. A systems thinking leader will look to avoid this problem by engaging people for their ideas, insights and knowledge at the level nearest to the work on the ground.

8.8.4 Differentiating Fundamental Changes from One-Off Events

It is a fundamental observation that systems (particularly natural systems) are dynamic and ever changing. However, there are essentially two types of systems: systems that are stable and systems that are unstable. Conservation systems that show species in uncontrollable decline would be considered unstable, as would systems in which a species is in uncontrollable ascendancy (such as an alien invasive species population explosion). A stable system is one in which the variation in system status (measured by some suitable indicator) is in a 'steady state' and predictable within well-understood limits. Although this type of measurement and monitoring can be difficult in natural systems (population status is one of the few aspects that can be reliably and cost-effectively measured), the conservation leader should be aware of the principle and seek patterns in data rather than comparing one-off data measures or pairs of points in an attempt to identify 'trends'. Second, the leader needs to recognise and differentiate those changes in data that are one-off anomalies (driven by 'special' causes) and changes that are driven by 'common' causes, which indicate a fundamental shift in the system (Black 2015; Pungaliya and Black 2017). This concept matches the idea of statistical 'outliers' – scientists would not make predictions or recommend changes based on a data point that is clearly an outlier. From a practical conservation science perspective, however, a separate investigation into why the outlier occurred might be important, noting that the findings should be considered separate from the general issues experienced in the current system.

8.8.5 Developing a Learning Culture Focused on Improvement

One of the most important aspects of systems thinking is for the leader to encourage a culture of continuous learning within the team (Figure 8.5). This means that people are unafraid to raise problems or ask awkward questions, are prepared to challenge the assumptions of others and there is a culture of openness to discussion, debate and informed dissent. This can be a challenge for many leaders but can be encouraged as a positive aspect

Figure 8.5 Improvement and learning. The best leaders know when to bring in experts to support key aspects of their project and develop staff competencies. Here a veterinarian is supporting a team in Mauritius in taking blood extractions from wild birds out in the field. (*Photo credit:* Mauritian Wildlife Foundation.)

of team interactions by applying the correct balance between celebrating successes and recognising and openly discussing failures among the team. A 'Shewhart cycle' of continuous learning helps to inform this process of test, evaluation and decision-making.

Deming (1982) popularised Shewhart's cycle for accelerated learning as a mental model for applying scientific principles to management. The basic elements are (1) *check* to seek information that indicates what is happening now, (2) *act* on outcomes of the analysis – what are the conclusions or hypotheses that need testing? – (3) *plan* to devise and prepare the intervention or test, and (4) *do* by implementing the plan of action. The cycle repeats with a return to check (i.e. monitor the outcomes of the 'do' phase), which may use scientific data but can also use 'softer' information such as people's opinions (e.g. surveys that are formalised collections of opinions). The cycle is repeated (*check-act-plan-do-check-act-plan-do-check* ...) to ensure verification and knowledge to inform future plans and activity through continuous learning. This fits closely with Caughley's (1994) five-step model for conservation:

1. Use the scientific method to deduce why the population declined and which agent caused the decline. Do not assume that the answer is already provided by folk wisdom, lay or scientific convention (*check, act*).
2. Remove or neutralise the agent of decline (*plan, do*).
3. Release a probe group to confirm that the causes of decline have been deduced correctly (*do, check*).
4. If so, restock unoccupied areas by translocation or, if the remnant population is too low to risk further reduction, breed up a protected stock as fast as possible, as near to the problem site as possible, and release it as soon as possible (*act, plan, do*).
5. Monitor the subsequent re-establishment (*check, act* and repeat the cycle).

8.9 Putting It All Together When Leading Your Team

Those five major concepts that describe systems thinking fit well with conservation biology (Caughley 1994). The conservation leader can apply the disciplines of conservation science while integrating complementary methods for managing the project team and other stakeholders (see Chapter 6). The advantage of the systems thinking approach is that it enables action-based research at the point where learning is applied to the activities of conservation. Practitioners can apply science to management and management to science rather than waiting for professional researchers to define hypotheses, collect data, analyse and report outcomes against hypotheses.

Understanding how to manage a project as a 'system' requires a perspective on the whole system and an ability to use relevant knowledge to inform action. A clear focus for the purpose of your programme will be the ecosystems (and perhaps human social systems) that you are trying to improve. At a fundamental level, this means a focus on the needs of the species and ecosystems of concern. This perspective informs measures of success, goals, plans, strategies and decision-making. It enables experimentation, frames acceptable risk taking (following the precautionary principle) and prevents the potential for goal displacement caused by alternative agendas. Against these requirements, the pragmatic boundaries set by budgets, capacity, location and geography can be offset and priorities can be identified. The best way to illustrate this concept is to consider the need for different approaches to recovering various island species in the same location. If we take the recovery of native birds on the island of Guam (Box 8.2), all have been exposed to an identical threat, the invasive brown tree snake (Wiles et al. 2003). However, despite a common impact on each species, the solution for each differed.

Box 8.2 *The Importance of Understanding Species' Needs*

A species' needs will relate to its biology and ecology and the impact of threats. There are many cases in conservation biology where a fundamental understanding (or misunderstanding) of any of these factors has either enabled or hindered effective conservation of species. A species' needs are both biological and contextual, based on a best understanding of both the species itself and its threats.

Case 1: Impact of Invasive Brown Tree Snakes *Boiga irregularis* on Native Birds on Guam

A dozen native bird species, some endemic, have been exposed to the threat posed by the invasive brown tree snake (Wiles et al. 2003). Despite the common impact on each population (Figure 8.6), the solution for each species has differed greatly. For the Pacific swiftlet, no conservation action was required because the species has adapted

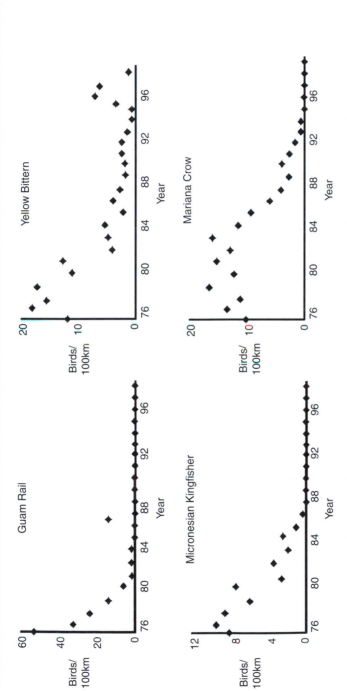

Figure 8.6 Population trends for several different Guam birds 1976–98. Note the decline in all four species coinciding with the invasive spread of the brown tree snake. (*Source:* After Wiles et al. 2003.)

to use human habitation as a nesting site (areas that tree snakes generally avoid). For other species, straightforward relocation to unaffected or predator-free offshore islets with suitable habitat was sufficient to enable recovery. Some species required intensive captive breeding, while others needed longer-term habitat development and renewal. Unfortunately, in some instances the wrong strategy was taken for the wrong species; for example, the Guam rail was successfully raised in captivity (in which the species thrived), yet the effort progressed without the development of suitable wild habitat. As a result, the wild population, despite reintroduction, continues to suffer.

Case 2: Recovery of the Channel Island Fox

The recent recovery of the endemic island fox *Urocyon littoralis* to the Channel Islands off the coast of California is an example where close understanding of differing threats in different ecosystems has been the key to effective action (Coonan et al. 2010). Six distinct subspecies of this small fox occur on six Channel Islands, but the causes of decline on each island have differed. On Santa Cruz Island, the fox population rapidly declined due to predation by recently established golden eagles (previously discouraged from colonising by the local population of bald eagles, which previously disappeared due to DDT contamination). While the remaining few foxes were taken into captivity for captive breeding, any possible success with release demanded complete removal of the golden eagles; high levels of mortality in reintroduced foxes continued even when most eagles had been removed. Part of this included removal of abundant golden eagle prey (feral pigs, goats and deer), which enabled hyperinflation of the eagle population. After final removal of golden eagles and reintroduction of bald eagles (which do not predate foxes), a stable ecosystem has seen recovery of the fox population.

In contrast, Santa Catalina Island, which is free of golden eagles, saw a 90 per cent decline in the fox population within a few years due to canine distemper carried by accidentally introduced racoons from the mainland. Captive breeding, vaccination and release enabled fox population recovery.

The lessons from Guam are twofold. Firstly, identify action based on species needs, and adapt the system to enable recovery. Secondly, if you take the wrong perspective, what previously seems like good practice becomes poor and ineffective practice.

The starting point for a project is to establish a purpose that is relevant to the needs of the species and ecosystems of concern. For highly endangered species suffering cataclysmic decline, needs relate to threats (invasive predation, human behaviour, exploitation, etc.) and recovery. For endangered species threatened as a result of small population size, needs may be defined in terms of population management. In some cases, the same species can be affected by threats in different ways in different contexts, as demonstrated by different populations of Channel Island foxes on the California Channel Islands (Box 8.2). This is not an intellectual exercise requiring years of preparatory research; instead, it is about prioritisation of effort. Once a programme of effective work is established, it is possible to examine key scientific questions to better understand and optimise the systems of concern. In blunt terms, there is a place for a hunch or educated guess if many factors are unknown, but a conservation leader must quickly build that hunch into scientific understanding that will soundly inform and optimise the work of the programme in question. This progression of understanding is an application of the 'theory of knowledge' (Deming 1993).

8.10 The Role of the 'Project Champion'

The conservation sector tends to lean towards the 'heroic leader' because we work in a resource stretched sector where the leaders have to keep close to the work and the teams and communities who support that work. However, there are dangers associated with a heroic leader focus: ego–driven behaviour, lack of willingness by others to raise alternative views and a reliance on the leader for decisions. None of these reflects good leadership. The conservation leader must be conscious of a need to (1) serve the purpose of the project and not one's own purpose or ambition, (2) be prepared to question one's own approach, values and priorities, (3) enable opportunities of team members to question or give alternative views, and (4) enable people close to the work to make decisions.

To get the right mental balance between being the energy and driver of the project and not being the sole source of momentum, it is helpful for leaders to see themselves as 'project champions'. In this role, the leader sticks with the project and provides both leadership and encouragement throughout the process. The important thing to keep in mind is to ensure that your personal aims are subservient to the aims of the programme (or project) as a whole. However, part of championing a species does come from within the leader – his or her personal enthusiasm or passion for the species or ecosystem in question. You need to be an advocate for species (and sometimes human communities) that do not have a voice of their own or for whom needs are not easily otherwise expressed. To lead a successful conservation programme, a leader should seek a better way of working, focused on the needs of the species and ecosystems of concern. Black, Groombridge and Jones (2011) suggest a range of aspects (Box 8.3) that provides a useful framework of points to consider in becoming an effective conservation leader.

Box 8.3 *The Qualities and Abilities of an Effective Conservation Leader (after Black et al. 2011)*

Vision and Goals

Establish a stable, shared long-term vision and a common sense of purpose.

Identify what is happening to, or affecting, biodiversity (populations, productivity, threats).

Set clear short-term goals, ensure flexible planning and measure performance against project aims.

Consider the views of stakeholders and partners.

Ensure that planning starts with an understanding current performance relative to programme purpose.

Ensure that staff members embrace project aims and culture (vision, understanding the system, goals).

Advocate good governance, particularly in large, complex projects.

Ensure congruency between plans, action on the ground and results.

Hands-on Leadership

Be orientated towards 'hands-on' management, working with staff.

Possess highly developed biological and/or operational skills appropriate to the programme.

Prioritise the work by asking key questions, checking results and empowering staff to get the job done.

Know people's strengths, and channel their energy and passion to maximum effect.

Understand cultural differences, and manage people's expectations and viewpoints sensitively.

Involve the people doing the work in data analysis, decisions and implementing changes.

Place responsibility and control of information in the hands of people who do the work.

Ensure that an understanding of what matters to biodiversity steers the work people do.

Have two-way communication meetings, with an emphasis on clarifying, testing and listening.

Ensure that managers lead, spend time with staff, listen to concerns and enable contributions.

Improvement and Learning

Expect the project (and its needs) to evolve through time.

Give people the opportunity to ask for training, and provide it on a just-in-time basis.

Be receptive to and seek out alternative solutions.

Understand risk, and make suitable contingencies.

Enable staff to challenge, share and learn from mistakes without fear, but expect high standards.

Appraise the system rather than people; manage morale, celebrate success, learn from failures.

Make improvements based on biodiversity needs and process performance, not arbitrary targets.

Recognise the difference between neglect and lack of capability (training, experience or resources).

Allow people doing the work the freedom to experiment with methods to improve.

Consider Both Project Details and the Big Picture

Know the project's sphere of influence and solvable problems.

Focus both internally and externally, understanding intra- and inter-organisational dynamics.

Establish budgets and a fund-raising strategy, and determine relevant financial and non-financial measures.

Base information, technology and resource needs on how they help people's core work.

Create an attitude of cooperation with project partners, sharing information to improve work.

Anticipate unexpected outcomes; integrate management flexibility alongside professional rigour.

Be prepared to seek specialist advice from external sources.

Determine whether data on staff, communities or society would be useful for the programme.

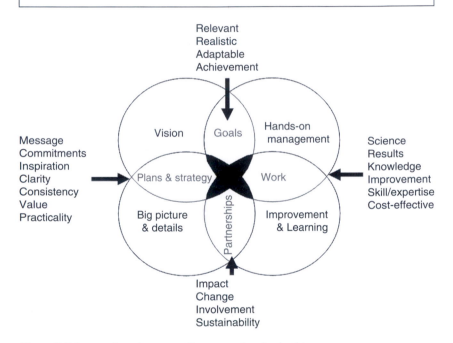

Figure 8.7 Interacting elements of conservation leadership.

8.11 The Next Steps: Leading Improvement in Your Programme

Leadership is a dynamic process. Figure 8.7 illustrates the interactions between elements of leadership behaviour (Black, Groombridge and Jones 2011). At the interface between these various behaviours are the deliverable elements of work that people do well or not. The behaviours of 'vision' and 'hands–on management' combine to generate an ability to set, revise and monitor meaningful goals for the project team. Bridging the aptitude for 'hands-on management' and 'improvement and learning' is the ability to manage the work through meaningful use of science, development of knowledge and skills and application of cost-effective interventions. 'Improvement and learning' combined with a sense of 'both the big picture and details' provide a basis for managing partnerships with other project stakeholders to deliver improvements. Finally, a combined sense of 'vision' and 'big picture and details' offers a basis for planning and strategic decision-making that provide clarity and generate energy, imagination and commitment in the team.

8.12 Summary

Key points from this chapter:

- Leadership is about influence, driven by credibility. Motivation of the team is linked to these aspects; do not confuse movement with motivation (a kicked dog moves but is not motivated to move).
- A leader must focus the team on the needs of species and ecosystems and build a better understanding of the system in which they work, including biological, social and economic aspects.
- A systems thinking approach complements conservation biology and takes into account the needs of other stakeholders. Leadership is about substance not style; style should be adapted to context. The substance of leadership remains constant, focused on the purpose of the project.
- Managing people throughout a project lifecycle needs to be conducted in a consistent manner.
- An effective leader will share a clear long-term vision, provide 'hands-on' management, be able to switch between attention to detail and the 'big picture' and encourage learning, improvement and innovation.

References

Adair, J. (1979). *Action-Centred Leadership*. Gower, Aldershot.
Ajzen, I. (1991). The theory of planned behavior. *Organizational Behavior and Human Decision Processes* 50: 179–211.
Bennis, W. (1999). The leadership advantage. *Leader to Leader* 12: 18–23.
Bertalanffy, L. V. (1969). *General Theory of Systems*. Braziller, New York, NY.
Black, S. A. (2015). A clear purpose is the start point for conservation leadership. *Conservation Letters* 8(5): 383–84.

Black, S. A. and Copsey, J. A. (2014a). Purpose, process, knowledge, and dignity in interdisciplinary projects. *Conservation Biology* 28(5): 1139–41.

(2014b). Does Deming's 'system of profound knowledge' apply to leaders of biodiversity conservation? *Open Journal of Leadership* 3: 53–65.

Black, S. A., Groombridge, J. J. and Jones, C. G. (2011). Leadership and conservation effectiveness: finding a better way to lead, *Conservation Letters* 4: 329–39.

Bolden, R. (2011). Distributed leadership in organizations: a review of theory and research. *International Journal of Management Reviews* 13: 251–69.

Bryan, J. F. and Locke, E. A. (1967). Parkinson's law as a goal-setting phenomenon. *Organizational Behavior and Human Performance* 2(3): 258–75.

Burns, J. M. (1978). *Leadership*. Harper & Row, New York, NY.

Caughley, G. (1994). Directions in conservation biology. *Journal of Animal Ecology* 63: 215–44.

Coonan, T. J., Schwemm, C. A. and Garceon, D. K. (2010). *Decline and Recovery of the Island Fox*. Cambridge University Press, Cambridge.

Coppin, A. and Barratt, J. (2002). *Timeless Management*. Palgrave Macmillan, New York, NY.

Covey, S. R. (1989). *The 7 Habits of Highly Effective People*. Simon & Shuster, New York, NY.

Deming, W. (1982). *Out of the Crisis*. MIT Press, Cambridge MA.

(1993). *The New Economics*. Massachusetts Institute of Technology, Center for Advanced Engineering Study, Cambridge, MA.

Dietz, J. M., Aviram, R., Bickford, S. et al. (2004). Defining leadership in conservation: a view from the top. *Conservation Biology* 18(1): 274–78.

Elliot, A. J. and Harackiewicz, J. M. (1994). Goal setting, achievement orientation, and intrinsic motivation: a mediational analysis. *Journal of Personality and Social Psychology* 66(5): 968.

Greenleaf, R. K. (2002). *Servant Leadership* (25th anniv. edn). Paulist Press, New York, NY.

Grint, K. (2010) leadership: A very short introduction. Oxford University Press, UK.

Gronn, P. (2002). Distributed leadership as a unit of analysis. *Leadership Quarterly* 13: 423–51.

Hamel, G. (2009). Moonshots for management. *Harvard Business Review* 87: 91–98.

Hersey, P. and Blanchard, K. H. (1969). Life cycle theory of leadership. *Training Development* 23: 26–34.

Hersey, P. and Blanchard, K. H. (1977). *Management of Organizational Behavior: Utilizing Human Resources*, 3rd edn. Prentice-Hall, Englewood Cliffs, NJ.

Herzberg, F. (2003). One more time: how do you motivate employees?. *Harvard Business Review* 81: 1.

Heifetz, R. A. and Laurie, D. L. (1997). The work of leadership. *Harvard Business Review* 75: 124–34.

Holling, C. S. and Meffe, G. K. (1996). Command and control and the pathology of natural resource management. *Conservation Biology* 10: 328–37.

Kennedy, C. (1996). *Managing with the Gurus: Top Level Guidance on 20 Management Techniques*. Vintage Press, New York, NY.

Koford, C. B. (1953). The California condor. National Audubon Society Research Report No. 4, pp. 1–154.

Kouzes, J. M. and Posner, B. Z. (2007). *The Leadership Challenge*, 4th edn. Jossey-Bass, San Francisco, CA.

Maslow, A. (1970). *Motivation and Personality*, 2nd edn. Harper & Row, New York, NY.

McGregor, D. (1957). The human side of enterprise. *Management Review* 46: 22–28.

Miller, A. H., McMillan, I. and McMillan, E. (1965). The current status and welfare of the California condor. National Audubon Research Report No. 6, pp. 1–61.

Mintzberg, H. (2009). *Managing*. Berrett-Koehler, San Francisco, CA.

Muczyk, J. P. and Holt, D. T. (2008). Towards a cultural contingency model of leadership. *Journal of Leadership and Organizational Studies* 14(4): 277–86.

Peters, S. (2012). *The Chimp Paradox*. Vermillion, London.

Peters, T. (1987). *Thriving on Chaos*. Alfred A. Knopf, New York, NY.

Phillips, D. and Nash, H. (1981). *The Condor Question: Captive or Forever Free?* Friends of the Earth, San Francisco, CA.

Powell, A. (2008). *The Race to Save the World's Rarest Bird: The Discovery and Death of the Po'ouli*. Stackpole Books, Mechanicsburg, PA.

Pungaliya, A. V. and Black, S. A. (2017). Insights into the recovery of the palila (*Loxioides bailleui*) on Hawaii through use of systems behaviour charts. *International Journal of Avian and Wildlife Biology* 2(1):7.

Ryan, R. M. and Deci, E. L. (2000). Self-determination theory and the facilitation of intrinsic motivation, social development, and well-being. *American Psychologist* 55(1): 68.

Scholtes, P. (1998). *The Leader's Handbook*. McGraw-Hill, New York, NY.

Seddon, J. (2003). *Freedom from Command and Control*. Vanguard Press, Buckingham.

Senge, P. (1990). *The Fifth Discipline: The Art and Practice of the Learning Organisation*. Doubleday, New York, NY.

Shewhart, W. A. (1931). *Economic Control of Quality of Manufactured Product*. Van Nostrand, New York, NY.

Smith, M. J. (1975). *When I Say No I feel guilty*, Bantam Books, New York, NY.

Snyder, N. and Snyder, H. (2000). *The California Condor: A Saga of Natural History and Conservation*. Academic Press, London.

Teerlink, R. and Ozley, L. (2000). *More than a Motorcycle: The Leadership Journey at Harley Davidson*, HBS Press, Boston, MA.

Tuckman, B. (1965). Developmental sequence in small groups. *Psychological Bulletin* 63(6): 384–99.

USFWS (US Fish and Wildlife Service) (2010). California condor recovery program population size and distribution. Available at www.fws.gov/hoppermountain/CACORecoveryProgram/ CurrentStatus.html (last accessed October 2010).

Walters, M. J. (2006). *Seeking the Sacred Raven: Politics and Extinction on a Hawaiian Island*, Island Press, Washington, DC.

Wilbur, S. R. (1978). The California condor, 1966–76: a look at its past and future. *US Fish & Wildlife Service North American Fauna* 72: 1–136.

Wiles, G. J., Bart, J., Beck, R. E., Jr. and Aguon, C. F. (2003). Impacts of the brown tree snake: patterns of decline and species persistence in Guam's avifauna. *Conservation Biology* 17(5): 1350–60.

Yukl, G. (1999). An evaluation of conceptual weaknesses in transformational and charismatic leadership theories. *Leadership Quarterly* 10(2): 285–305.

Zaccaro, S. J. and Klimoski, R. J. (2001). *The Nature of Organizational Leadership: Understanding the Performance Imperatives Confronting Today's Leaders*. Jossey-Bass, San Francisco, CA.

9 · Conserving Island Species
Journey to Recovery

CARL G. JONES, NIK C. COLE, STEFANO
CANESSA, ALIÉNOR L. M. CHAUVENET,
DEBORAH J. FOGELL AND JOHN G. EWEN

9.0 Introduction

Many of the greatest conservation successes have been on islands, with
species restorations providing us with hope that these are widely achievable. It is clear that if some of the more endangered species are to survive,
they are going to require long-term care, which for animals may include
translocation, supplemental feeding, predator and competitor control,
disease management and the provision of safe breeding sites. Embracing
interventionist approaches to species recovery means that many extinctions are avoidable.

This chapter summarises experiences from New Zealand and
Mauritius to illustrate the necessary steps of species recovery. We
highlight the need for clearly defined recovery objectives followed by
careful identification and comparison of alternative strategies to achieve
these objectives. In addition, we explicitly acknowledge uncertainty and
how this influences our risk attitude and how best to address it in
recovery planning and implementation.

9.1 The Journey of Species Recovery

A project to recover a species typically goes through broad overlapping
stages as it progresses from its inception, reaches maturation and achieves
its *fundamental objectives* (Jones 2004; see below). A project starts with
getting to know the species and understand its problems. This grows
into developing approaches to mitigate the limiting factors and then
monitoring how the population responds to management – and then
adjusting as required. Once recovery has been achieved, there is a need to
continue with the best options for maintaining or increasing species

numbers, including monitoring to detect any future problems (Jones 2004; see Section 5.2).

Recovering threatened species requires diagnosis (see Chapter 4) and then correction of problems. Solving problems requires making choices, and these decisions can be difficult to make for reasons such as (1) a failure to correctly identify what the problem is, (2) a mix of fundamental objectives that may be in conflict, (3) not knowing all the recovery options available, (4) a lack of information about the species to be able to predict how it will respond to management, and (5) how to select the best options to achieve the fundamental objectives. Breaking down recovery strategies can remove perceived barriers and guide the selection of approaches that have the best chance of success.

It is our experience that planning and decision-making (see Section 6.8) frequently lack clarity about what the fundamental objectives are and an understanding of the stages through which the project will likely progress. Conservationists are often poor at developing and stating their fundamental objectives (McCarthy 2014; Ewen, Soorae and Canessa 2014a). Equally, pointing out poorly defined fundamental objectives is often met with surprise because groups frequently believe that these objectives and the stages through which a project will go (see Section 6.6) are obvious, even though members of the group will have a range of different interpretations of what these fundamental objectives are!

A second barrier is a tendency to be risk averse; this is usually to avoid possibly doing more harm. Risk arises due to uncertainty. Learning to work with uncertainty is necessary because this is a feature of all threatened species recovery programmes (see Section 8.7). Uncertainty can be minimised by the compilation, evaluation and use of relevant information. Data can be from studies on the species, from surrogate species or from expert judgement. Recognising which uncertainties are hindering decisions helps focus research and monitoring.

Our approach proposes a set of steps: (1) knowing what you want to achieve (objectives), (2) exploring what management approaches could be used (alternative options), (3) developing a priori hypotheses about predicted outcomes of management, and (4) testing hypotheses and developing intervention techniques. In the remainder of this chapter we develop these four thematic steps and end with four case studies that illustrate how these steps can be applied to inform the development of our species recovery efforts.

9.1.1 Setting Objectives

Objectives express our values, and choices based on these are the cornerstone of any recovery programme. In this chapter we focus on two core types of objective:

1. **Fundamental Objectives (Synonymous with Project Goals).** These are the ultimate things that we care about and that should define our management choices. In all cases of threatened species recovery these will include a wish to prevent species extinction (or some other articulation of improving a species' current status). However, there are often additional fundamental objectives behind our choices, for example, recovering an ecosystem function (see Chapter 10). All need to be clearly stated.

2. **Means Objectives.** These are how we go about achieving our fundamental objectives and reflect our knowledge of what is wrong and how to manage a species. These approaches are dynamic and may be modified as we get to know the problems more thoroughly (see Section 8.8.4) or as their impact changes as populations grow. For example, we may want to improve productivity in one of our bird species. This may be achievable by providing artificial nest sites to promote breeding, but we then find that nest parasites have a strong negative influence on productivity in these boxes. This scenario would then open up a range of possible management options aimed at increasing productivity, including perhaps removing the boxes, modifying the boxes so that they are less attractive to parasites or directly controlling the parasites. Understanding and combining relevant approaches require careful attention to ensure that our choices will have the best chances of success. Keeping in mind that productivity is a means to population recovery, if something else achieves population recovery better, we should focus management there.

Care needs to be taken that the right problem is being solved. Refining management around a *means objective* (e.g. productivity) is valid as long as it supports the *fundamental objective* of species recovery. For example, our work with hihi *Notiomystis cincta* (an endemic passerine from New Zealand; Figure 9.1) often focuses on showing the benefits to productivity from supplemental feeding. However, in one population, the improved productivity had a highly uncertain impact on reversing negative population growth, the fundamental objective we really care about,

Figure 9.1 New Zealand hihi *Notiomystis cincta*, one species where explicit management decisions, based on a perceived understanding of the system, allowed for monitoring to challenge what we thought was the situation. (*Photo credit:* E. Wilson.) (A black-and-white version of this figure will appear in some formats. For the colour version, please refer to the plate section.)

largely because adult survival remained low (Armstrong et al. 2007). Focusing on means objectives is common and blinkers recovery actions (Ewen, Soorae and Canessa 2014a), at worst leading to failed recovery actions because the wrong threats were being addressed. The debate between whether we prioritise genetic management or exotic predator management of island species is another scenario that captures this issue well (Jamieson 2007). Both are important, their effects variable and on different temporal scales – only assessing these and projecting outcomes against the fundamental objective (e.g. species increase or population persistence) can allow rational management decisions.

Objectives should be clear, concise, jargon-free statements with measurable indicators. Valid measures can be assigned, e.g. the probability of extinction in 20 years, and be natural values, proxy values or constructed scales. We give objectives in our case studies and recommend that readers learn more about this step in any species management (e.g. Gregory et al. 2012).

9.1.2 Developing Options

Many species will already be well known, but all the practitioners should be familiar with the life history and ecology of the animals with which they are working; they should 'know their species'. Gathering information about the species is essential for developing valid recovery options. The greater the familiarity with the species, the more confidence one can have in decisions made. The practitioner should develop 'deep knowledge' about their species or be able to transfer skills from a similar species to the focal one. The most successful practitioners we work with are so skilled that they are able to make intuitive decisions about how to manage a species recovery that are often correct. However, as an approach, it remains essential that decision-making is done in a structured and transparent way (see Section 6.8). Intuitive decisions can be great but are very difficult for others to engage with and learn from. Initial steps entail a compilation of all the available published and unpublished information. Additional information can come from interviews with local naturalists and others with knowledge of the species (e.g. hunters) (see Section 5.1.3).

Species recovery work should include evaluation of taxonomic status not only because more taxonomically distinct populations may be of greater conservation importance if a fundamental objective is maximising genetic diversity (see Chapter 3) but also because mixing populations of distinct genetic provenance may reduce population viability. Hybridisation can be an unintentional result of mixing populations during conservation translocations. This has occurred, for example, with some kiwi (Apterygidae) and rail (Rallidae) translocations in New Zealand (Miskelly and Powlesland 2013). The resulting populations of hybrids may perform well at an ecological or population level, but their role in either parent species' management is questionable if the goal is to preserve genetic uniqueness. In a hypothetical case, maximising genetic diversity may conflict with maximising persistence. This thorny issue has led to some interesting debate (Weeks et al. 2015).

The status of many species is poorly known, with uncertain or misleading data on numbers, distributions and population trends. Population numbers and distribution need regular appraisal to determine whether our interventions are working. In addition, it is important to compile knowledge of life history so that population data on productivity and survival can be more accurately interpreted. For animals, the important data include the number of age classes (juvenile, non-breeding adult age classes, and breeding adult age classes) with their survival estimates and measures of reproduction (clutch or litter size, breeding frequency and success by breeder age class). Having an idea of reproduction and survival can allow projections under different management options.

Further, knowledge on feeding ecology, dispersal behaviour and causes of mortality can provide key insight into habitat quality and causes of decline.

Understanding the causes of decline (see Chapter 5) is central to any attempts at recovering a failing population. The factors that limit animal populations have been the focus of much research, beginning with the development of a coherent theoretical framework in the 1940s and 1950s (Lack 1954, 1966; Newton 1998). Most animal populations are naturally regulated by relatively few variables, of which food, availability of safe breeding sites, predation, competition and disease are the most important (Newton 1998). It can be assumed that one or more of these factors will be limiting the populations of most critically endangered species. Island ecosystems have been profoundly affected by human-induced change, including habitat destruction, direct hunting and the negative impacts of introductions of non-native and invasive species. The negative impact of rats on island ecosystems is one major example (Dingwall et al. 1978; Atkinson 1985; Jones et al. 2016). However, non-native species of many taxa, including disease-causing parasites and viruses, have also caused widespread population declines and extinctions. In Hawaii, non-native avian malaria *Plasmodium relictum* and avian poxvirus *Poxvirus avium* are implicated in the collapse of entire avian communities (Atkinson and La Pointe 2009; Paxton et al. 2016). Climate change is predicted to accelerate the collapse of the remaining Hawaiian bird communities, as warming temperatures allow expansion of the range of mosquitoes, which act as vectors for both parasites, into high-altitude forest refuges.

The combined effects of ecosystem changes have compromised the natural ecological functions of many islands. At worst, conservationists have to work with systems that are disrupted by the loss of interactions caused by species extirpations and extinctions. Novel solutions to missing ecological interactions, for example, through ecological replacements, are discussed in Section 10.5.

9.1.3 Uncertain Outcomes and Developing A Priori Hypotheses

Decision-making and the planning of our recovery projects require that we make predictions of what the effects of alternative options will be. We need to choose whether and how to intervene. There is a choice to do nothing because of a lack of information or a choice to collect more baseline data before intervening, and these should be treated as active choices. In all cases, however, practitioners should be encouraged to capture their ideas about the causes of species rarity and use them to derive management options. Knowledge and action do not have to be independent options, since doing something provides information, supporting or refuting, your hypothesis, which then can be acted upon.

Generating a priori hypotheses can help to clarify difficult decisions in at least two ways. Firstly, we may be confident that we understand the cause of rarity but are uncertain on how best to manage it. Here uncertainty hinders our choice of the best management option. To solve this, we could use expert judgement (New Zealand short-tailed bat *Mystacina tuberculata*, Section 9.3.1) or data from a closely related species (Mauritius orange-tailed skink *Gongylomorphus* sp., Section 9.3.2) to make predictions about alternative solutions in the focal population and/or compare alternative options using experiments (Mauritius parakeet *Psittacula eques*, Section 9.3.3, and Hihi *Notiomystis cincta*, Section 9.3.4). Monitoring then provides the information required to judge and, if necessary, improve management. Secondly, we may have competing hypotheses about what is causing rarity. Careful consideration of these hypotheses allows one to choose the best option. For example, predator control may be most important if poor reproductive success is driven by predation, whereas supplementary feeding may be best if poor reproductive success is driven by food availability. Where only one option can be used, it is still possible to express expectations, compare the results to those predictions and then consider alternatives in a 'passive adaptive management' framework (Canessa et al. 2016).

9.1.4 Testing Hypotheses and Developing Techniques

We recognise that management interventions and learning from these interventions are frequently done on highly endangered species limited by small sample sizes. However, this reinforces, rather than diminishes, the need for a strong theoretical basis for planning and why trial and error is risky (Armstrong et al. 2015). Our work in Mauritius has shown that interventions sometimes require modification before they become functional. For example, with both the pink pigeon and the Mauritius parakeet (Figure 9.2), we suspected that seasonal food shortages were affecting the populations. When feeding trials were conducted with

Figure 9.2 Mauritius parakeet *Psittacula eques*. An experimental approach and ongoing learning and revision to understanding the most effective management contributed to its recovery. (*Photo credit:* S. Tollington.) (A black-and-white version of this figure will appear in some formats. For the colour version, please refer to the plate section.)

the pink pigeon, they took the food immediately, and productivity increased (Swinnerton 2001). This provided good support for the hypothesis, although by attracting them to a feeding station cats were also attracted that killed some pigeons, so predator control had to be implemented (Swinnerton 2001). Supplemental feeding Mauritius parakeets was more problematic, and there was difficulty in getting them to recognise the food provided (Jones and Duffy 1993). The wild Mauritius parakeets only started to take supplemental food after copying supplemental feeding of released captive-reared birds (Jones et al. 1998, 2013c). Similarly, it was hypothesised that Mauritius parakeets, a cavity nesting species, were limited by nest-site availability. Initial nest box trials were unsuccessful because the parakeets apparently did not recognise the boxes as potential breeding sites, but they learned to use these again by copying released captive-bred birds (Jones et al. 1998, 2013c). However, after two decades of effort, over half the Mauritius parakeet population now take supplemental food (increasing productivity), and over three-quarters of breeding pairs are using nest boxes (reducing nest predation) (Jones et al. 2013c).

Captive individuals or closely related species can provide useful subjects for testing various manipulations for use on wild birds. Many of the skills required by, and clutch and brood manipulations used on, Mauritius kestrels, pink pigeons, Mauritius parakeets, olive white-eyes and Mauritius fodies were developed and perfected using captives.

9.2 Intensive Species Management in the Absence of Knowledge about Limiting Factors

In some cases, with the most endangered species, the most appropriate strategy may be a broad management strategy that addresses the most likely limiting factors to improve productivity and survival, an approach that has been used successfully in bird species in both Mauritius and New Zealand (Jones 2004; Jones and Merton 2012). For example, the Chatham Island black robin and Mauritius parakeet restoration programmes initially both addressed the species' extreme rarity by providing supplemental feeding, enhancing and protecting nest sites, controlling/excluding predators and competitors around nest sites and the control of parasites at nest sites (Butler and Merton 1992; Jones and Duffy 1993; Jones 2004). These management actions were implemented even though it was not definitively known at the time what was causing declines in either species. Equally, it may not be known which of the management interventions was most responsible for recovery, although monitoring during these initial recovery steps may provide solid clues. In both the black robin and parakeet examples, the managers were being guided by previous knowledge and experience with passerine and parrot biology and conservation management. Learning, however, can be applied at a time when the species has started to recover and can be used to promote long-term sustainable management by refining care and the removal of unnecessary procedures. This has recently been the focus of research on Mauritius olive white-eyes (Ferrière et al., submitted) and Mauritius parakeets (Section 9.3.3).

Ultimately, to ensure the persistence of a declining population, one must try to improve survival and/or productivity. Knowing that there are few factors that control populations, we have deployed various interventions to address one or more of these limiting factors across the species on which we have worked (Table 9.1).

9.3 Case Studies of Steps to Species Recovery

9.3.1 Translocation of New Zealand Short-Tailed Bats

In this example, recovery planning was hampered by uncertainty about the outcomes of management, which, in turn, led to potential

Table 9.1 *Causes of Population Decline and Examples of Management Options Used in Recovery of Mascarene and New Zealand Species*

Causes of decline	Management options	Our published examples
Food shortage	Supplementary feeding	• Mauritius kestrel (Cade and Jones 1994; Jones et al. 1991, 2013a) • Pink pigeon (Jones et al. 2013b; Jones 2008; Jones and Swinnerton 1997) • Mauritius parakeet (Tollington et al. 2015; Jones et al. 2013c; Jones and Duffy 1993; Jones and Swinnerton 1997) • Hihi (Armstrong et al. 2007; Chauvenet et al. 2012; Walker et al. 2013) • Olive white-eye (Ferrière et al., submitted) • Mauritius fody (Cristinacce et al. 2008, 2009).
Competition for food	Feeder design	• Pink pigeon (Jones 2008) • Mauritius parakeet (Jones 2008)
Nest-site competition	Nest-site design	• Mauritius kestrel (Jones et al. 1991, 1994, 2013a) • Mauritius parakeet (Jones et al. 2013c).
Predation on adults	Predator control, eradication or exclusion	• Mauritius kestrel (Jones et al. 1991) • Pink pigeon (Jones et al. 1992, 2013b)
Predation at nests	• Predator control/ exclusion • Egg and brood manipulations	• Mauritius kestrel (Jones et al. 1991, 1994, 2013a) • Mauritius parakeet (Jones 2008; Jones et al. 2013c) • Olive white-eye (Maggs et al. 2015) • Mauritius kestrel (Jones 1987; Jones et al. 1991, 1994, 2013a; Jones and Owadally 1988; Nicoll et al. 2006; Butler et al. 2009) • Mauritius parakeet (Jones et al. 1998)
Nest-site limitation	• Nest boxes • Enhancing nest sites	• Mauritius kestrel (Cade and Jones 1994; Jones et al. 1991, 1994, 2013a)

Table 9.1 *(cont.)*

Causes of decline	Management options	Our published examples
		• Mauritius parakeet (Jones et al. 1998, 2013c)
		• Hihi (Ewen et al., in press)
		• Mauritius kestrel (Jones et al. 1991, 1994)
		• Mauritius parakeet (Jones et al. 1998, 2013c)
		• Round Island petrels (Tatayah 2010)
Nest-site parasites	Treatment of nests with insecticides	• Hihi (Ewen et al. 2009)
		• Mauritius parakeet (Jones et al. 1998)
		• Mauritius fody (unpublished)
Disease transmission at feeders	Hygiene and feeding protocols	• Hihi (Ewen et al., in press)
		• Pink pigeon (Bunbury et al. 2008)
		• Mauritius parakeet (Tollington et al. 2015)
Disease transmission between populations	• Disease risk assessments • Screening and quarantine	• Hihi (Dalziel et al. 2016)
		• Short-tailed bat (see Section 9.3.1)
		• Pink pigeon (Jones and Swinnerton 1997)
		• Mauritius parakeet (Jones et al. 1998)
		• Mauritius fody (Cristinacce et al. 2008, 2009)
		• Hihi (Ewen et al. 2012)

risks. Furthermore, uncertainty was difficult to reduce; little information existed, and collecting it through further studies would entail the same risks that would be encountered implementing management. Rather than ignore that uncertainty or let it stall the process, it was openly expressed. This was in terms of its quantitative extent and the stakeholders' attitude towards what was acceptable and what was not.

Lesser short-tailed bats (Figure 9.3) are one of only two extant native land mammal species in New Zealand and are comprised of three subspecies (northern, central and southern). The current threats faced by the

Figure 9.3 New Zealand short-tailed bat *Mystacina tuberculate*, one species for which structured decision-making involving primary stakeholders led to common agreement as to how best to conserve them. (*Photo credit:* S. Parsons.) (A black-and-white version of this figure will appear in some formats. For the colour version, please refer to the plate section.)

bats are relatively well known, being common to most endangered New Zealand species: predation and competition by exotic mammals, along with habitat loss (Lloyd 2001; O'Donnell et al. 2010). Translocation to predator-free islands or reserves has been proposed as a valuable management tool to secure each subspecies (Molloy 1995). Although this tool has been applied successfully to island insect, bird and reptile species in New Zealand, there is considerable uncertainty about the possible outcome of a bat translocation; little information exists and few past attempts have been made, with no success. Bat ecology and past experiences point to two key issues: strong homing behaviour and disease. Although homing, where translocated bats leave the release site to return home, has never been studied in short-tailed bats, some evidence exists for long-tailed bats *Chalinolobus tuberculatus* in New Zealand (Guilbert et al. 2007) and other microbat species on other continents (reviews by Davis 1966; Griflin 2017). Homing was suggested as a cause of several failed bat translocation attempts in the past (Tomich 1986; Lloyd 1994). To make matters worse, one attempt to translocate short-tailed bats to Kapiti Island (in 2006) initially appeared successful in reducing homing but ultimately

Table 9.2 *Fundamental Objectives of Short-Tailed Bat Translocation Planning*

Objective	Measurable indicator
Improve persistence of translocated subspecies	Extinction probability in 50 years
Maximise safety of the source population	Extinction probability in 50 years
Maximise Maori values	Constructed scale of Maori (vital essence of life or well-being) based on *whakapapa* (connections and location), *kaitiakitanga* (sustainable resource management) and *tapu-noa* (rules of good behaviour that can represent advice for health and safety; normally answers are binary: *tapu* is prohibited; *noa* is the opposite).

failed when the translocated bats developed an unidentified and highly infectious disease (Gartrell 2007). The agent that caused the failure of the 2006 attempt remains unknown because it could not be identified despite extensive testing (Gartrell 2007).

Overall Management Hypothesis. Bats will return to their source population after translocation and release at a destination site, with the risk of carrying a highly infectious pathogen with them from the new location.

Objectives. Although the first fundamental objective of a short-tailed bat translocation is the persistence of the subspecies, consultation with stakeholders highlighted a strong desire to avoid risks to the extant populations. This referred not only to the overall species persistence, of which extant populations are the key component, but also to a more general desire to avoid negative impacts as a result of management. This attitude was especially important to the values of local Maori communities (Table 9.2).

Alternative Options. Since the perceived key drivers of translocation success are homing and disease and these are related to the age of translocated individuals and the distances between source and destination sites, we explored several combinations of translocation methods and sets of sites (summarised in Table 9.3).

Table 9.3 *Summary of Potential Translocation Strategies*

Article I.	Age class captured at source	Captive phase and location	Release strategy
1	Pregnant females	Pregnant females held at destination to give birth	Release adult females at destination
			After delay period, release juveniles destination
2	Pregnant females	Pregnant females held at source to give birth	Release adult females at source
			After delay period, release juveniles at destination
3	Pre-flight juveniles	Juveniles held at destination	Delayed and staggered release of juveniles at destination
4	Post-flight juveniles	Juveniles held at destination	Delayed and staggered release of juveniles at destination
5	Adult males and pregnant females	Males and pregnant females held at destination to give birth	Release adults at destination
			After a delay period, release juveniles at destination
6	Pregnant females	Pregnant females held at destination to give birth	Release juveniles at destination
			After a delay period, release adult females at destination

Consequences and Decisions. To evaluate the pros and cons of different management strategies, it was necessary to measure their expected outcomes, particularly as regards homing probabilities and disease. Given that no short-tailed bat-specific empirical data are available, we formalised expert opinion (using best-practice approaches; McBride et al. 2012) and summarised the literature on similar species. For homing, we considered that the likelihood of attempting to home, and of successfully doing so, will be mostly influenced by the age of the released

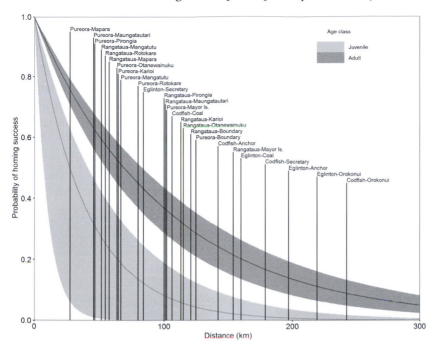

Figure 9.4 Probability of successful homing, if attempted, for each of the candidate source-destination combination of sites. Sites were determined by an expert bat panel and do not represent views of all site-based stakeholders (the required next step in this species recovery process). The distance between each site pair is superimposed on the general homing-distance relationship, estimated via expert evaluation of available information.

individuals (adults being more strongly imprinted on their birth site and more likely to navigate and survive a long flight back). Using an inverse exponential dispersal function, with observations about the home range of bats and information from other species, we estimated the potential homing distance to fall within a range of 80–120 km for adults and 10–60 km for juveniles. We used this estimate, with its explicit range of uncertainty, to assess the probability of homing for all possible combinations of source and release sites (Figure 9.4).

For disease, we enlisted a panel of third-party expert veterinarians to obtain an additional opinion about the possible cause of the disease encountered in the failed translocation to Kapiti Island. We provided them with all available information about that experience. Through a guided discussion for differential diagnosis, we asked them to state and quantify their belief that the causative agent belonged to one of the categories identified by Sainsbury and Vaughan-Higgins (2012): destination, carrier or transport hazard. Although experts noted the speculative nature of the expressed beliefs given the scarce information about the aetiology of the disease, they found themselves mostly in agreement that the agent was a carrier hazard. Although this procedure could not eliminate uncertainty, it helped focus and guide follow-up discussions about potential actions.

Expressing beliefs about homing and disease quantitatively was not aimed at providing a false sense of certainty, nor were the estimates taken as absolute truth; rather, they served as a guide to discussions which, as long as the corresponding uncertainty was properly recognised, helped to put all stakeholders and experts on the same knowledge level. Adults would be the most likely vector of disease, given their higher chance of surviving the homing trip, so they would be a poor choice for scenarios in which homing would occur. When releasing juveniles, even if disease occurred and juveniles did home on their own, their lower expected survival during the homing flight, possibly further reduced by the disease itself, reduced the risk of carrying the disease back to the source site.

As a result, the recovery group perceived an advantage in releasing juveniles, without involving adults, mostly reflecting the desire to avoid disease risks. From the group's position, the priority was minimising potential damage. Avoiding disease risk offset the potential failure of the translocation when moving juveniles, presumed to have lower survival than adults. For the same reason, the northern subspecies of short-tailed bat, with only one extant population, was considered too precarious to risk experimenting with, although it would certainly be a future candidate once a successful method was established. Finally, the southern subspecies was perceived to be a possible candidate, but the distances and complexity in managing a translocation over remote terrain and large distances meant that feasibility might be limited.

In summary, the threats driving the decline of the short-tailed bat in New Zealand are relatively clear, but insufficient information and the inherent complexity of the system hindered the choice of a reliable strategy, in particular, since uncertainty about homing and disease leads to risks perceived as unacceptable by most stakeholders, particularly indigenous communities. By (1) clarifying the objectives and attitudes towards risk of those stakeholders and (2) clearly stating the opinions of experts about expected outcomes while openly recognising uncertainty, we found the common ground to focus discussions and break the decision deadlock. The next step in short-tailed bat conservation will be to engage support from key stakeholders at the proposed source and destination sites, secure resources to implement the current best action, monitor its outcomes and compare it with the current predictions to assess success or make adjustments as needed.

9.3.2 Rescue of Mauritius Orange-Tailed Skink from Asian Musk Shrew Invasion

For the case of the orange-tailed skink (Figure 9.5), we predicted a risk of imminent, unavoidable and irreversible invasion by a non-native mammalian predator, for example, the Asian musk shrew *Suncus murinus*, which had a high probability of causing the extinction of the single island population of this threatened species. However, there was limited prior knowledge of the abundance, biology, ecology and past distribution of the skink. After stakeholder consultation, it was agreed that the potential risk of invasion warranted rapid intervention to translocate the skink to a second secure island. There were stakeholder

Figure 9.5 Mauritius orange-tailed skink *Gongylomorphus* sp., a great example of a species recovered from almost definite extinction through action in the absence of detailed information on the species. (*Photo credit:* N. Cole.) (A black-and-white version of this figure will appear in some formats. For the colour version, please refer to the plate section.)

concerns that the action of removing skinks could be detrimental to the source population and uncertainty as to whether an invasion would occur. Based upon what was known, using data from surrogate species and sparse historical information on the skink's ecosystem, we implemented management to minimise the impact to the source population while maximising the probability of establishment of a second population through translocation.

The orange-tailed skink was discovered on Flat Island (253 ha; 11.5 km NNE of Mauritius) in 1995 (Bhuiyan and Bell 1995) representing the only known population of this sub-fossorial slit-eared skink. Although the skink's taxonomic position has yet to be formally described, it is considered a distinctive subspecific lowland form of the Macchabé skink *Gongylomorphus fontenayi*, which exists in the upland forests of the south-west mountains of Mauritius (Freeman 2003). The eradication of introduced mammalian predators (*Felis catus, Mus musculus* and *Rattus rattus*) from Flat Island in 1998 (Bell 2002) led to an increase in abundance of the surviving reptile species, including the orange-tailed skink. Between 2001 and 2002, the effective population size of orange-tailed skinks was estimated at between 810 and 6,000 individuals (Freeman 2003; Nichols and Freeman 2004). However, the absolute abundance of skinks on the island remained unknown, with fewer than 200 individuals being seen since their discovery. An ecological study in 2004 suggested that the skinks were mostly restricted to small, isolated areas of deep leaf litter in mature, non-native *Sapindus trifoliatus* forest (Ross et al. 2008). In August 2007, it was learnt that Flat Island had been leased for the enhancement of tourism, but little was known regarding what development was planned for the island. By November, we understood that facilities were to be constructed on the island and predicted that without bio-security protocols being strictly enforced (which was unlikely for numerous reasons), infrastructural development and related activities would lead to the introduction of invasive predators, such as the Asian musk shrew (Cole 2007). Ecosystems that have evolved in the absence of terrestrial mammals are particularly prone to the impacts of musk shrew invasions, as observed in Mauritius and Guam (Jones 1993; Fritts and Rodda 1998; Cheke and Hume 2008). There are no known methods for eradicating shrews from islands of more than a few hectares (Morris and Morris 1991; Varnham et al. 2002, Seymour et al. 2005). To safeguard against the potential invasion of Flat Island by shrews, it was proposed that a second orange-tailed skink population should be established on the closed island nature reserve, Gunner's Quoin (70 ha; 4 km N of Mauritius) (Cole 2007). In addition to a translocation, it was recommended that the Flat Island population should be researched to obtain a better understanding of the abundance, biology and ecology of the skink (Cole 2007) and to monitor any outcomes of a possible predator incursion. Gunner's Quoin was selected because it was the only location with areas of perceived suitable habitat and free from non-native predators. However, Gunner's Quoin was already a focal reintroduction site for the threatened Telfair's skink *Leiolopisma telfairii*, a known predator of slit-eared skinks (Jones 1993). In February 2007, 250 adult Telfair's skinks had been released on the island (Cole et al. 2009). There was concern that released orange-tailed skinks would be predated before they could establish.

Overall Management Hypotheses. The translocation of orange-tailed skinks will lead to the establishment of a secure population without this translocation affecting the source population. Secondly, if Asian musk shrews invaded the source island, this would cause a population crash and likely extinction of that orange-tailed skink population.

Objectives. There was a clear objective hierarchy in this management scenario (Table 9.4). Of fundamental importance was to ensure the persistence of orange-tailed skinks. However, there was uncertainty as to whether a non-native predator invasion would occur to the skink's island home and how a proposed translocation would affect the source population. There was clear risk aversion to negative outcomes stemming from any intervention. In this case, maximising the persistence of both the source and the destination sites was articulated as two sub-objectives.

Table 9.4 *Objectives Hierarchy for Orange-Tailed Skink Rescue Operation*

Objective	Measureable indicator
Minimise extinction of orange-tailed skink	Probability of extinction 20 years
Minimise extinction of Flat Island population	Probability of extinction 20 years
Minimise extinction of Gunner's Quoin population	Probability of extinction 20 years

Alternative Options. In this case, there were two main options. Either establish a second population to safeguard against a non-native mammalian predator invasion to Flat Island or not. If a translocation was to be attempted, then there was need to also consider the number of individuals to move and when best to move them given the changing ecosystem at the destination site (due to the establishing Telfair's skink population).

Consequences and Decisions. We used a mix of predictive modelling and post-intervention monitoring to inform and learn from our decisions. Firstly, we predicted that island-wide extinction would occur rapidly if shrews invaded. Given this, we focused our modelling to determine the number of orange-tailed skinks that we could translocate and when best to do so given the establishing Telfair's skink population. In both cases we used programme *Vortex* (Lacy 1993) to visualise predicted outcomes using a mix of information sources to parameterise our models, often with very limited data.

Firstly, to model our harvest of the source population, we worked with the most conservative source population estimate of at least 810 individual orange-tailed skinks (Freeman 2003). Using apparent survival estimates, reproductive rates and environmental impact data we had obtained from the closely related Bojer's skink *Gongylomorphus bojerii*, we estimated the number that could be removed without causing a source population extinction risk above 20 per cent within a 20-year period from any one of seven isolated populations on the island (Figure 9.6a). We then estimated probabilities of destination population extinction within a similar 20-year period with different release group sizes at intervals of 20 up to 140 individuals (more than we expected to catch), with and without possible predation pressure from Telfair's skink predation (Figure 9.6b). Exposing Bojer's skinks to Telfair's skink predation causes a 5 per cent reduction in survival (unpublished data 2007).

Secondly, timing of a translocation was important both because of local seasonal conditions and because of the risk of Telfair's skink predation pressure. The onset of the rainy season, from mid-January to February, was prioritised as an ideal time to translocate reptiles due to the increase in relative abundance of food resources, reptile body condition and survival (Cole et al. 2009). To understand more about the changing predation pressure from an establishing Telfair's skink

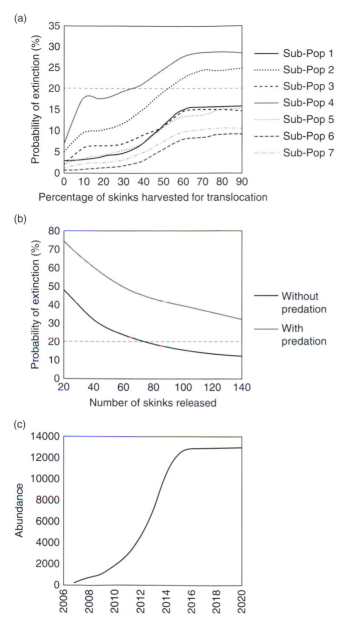

Figure 9.6 (a) The probability of extinction 20 years after harvesting up to 90 per cent of each of the seven known subpopulations of orange-tailed skinks on Flat Island. (b) The probability of extinction 20 years after release of up to 140 orange-tailed skinks with and without Telfair's skink predation on Gunner's Quoin. (c) The predicted growth of the translocated Telfair's skink population on Gunner's Quoin.

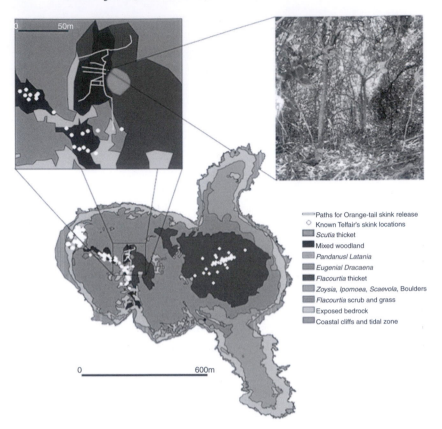

Paths for Orange-tail skink release
○ Known Telfair's skink locations
Scutia thicket
Mixed woodland
Pandanus/ Latania
Eugenia/ Dracaena
Flacourtia thicket
Zoysia, Ipomoea, Scaevola, Boulders
Flacourtia scrub and grass
Exposed bedrock
Coastal cliffs and tidal zone

Figure 9.7 Planned predator-free release site for orange-tailed skinks on Gunner's Quoin in November 2007.

population, we also modelled their establishment, our belief being that to enhance post-release orange-tailed skink survival, we needed to translocate before the reintroduced Telfair's skink population had grown and dispersed across the island. By November 2007, our monitoring showed that the establishing Telfair's skinks population had started to reproduce and had a mean (95 per cent confidence intervals) adult abundance of 128 (94–193) individuals. Our model projections based on Telfair's skink demographic data predicted that there would be 704 individuals by November 2008 (Figure 9.6c). Furthermore, Telfair's skinks had not yet colonised all suitable habitat for orange-tailed skinks such that they could still be released into a predator-free site (Figure 9.7).

Using the preceding projections to support our case, we decided to move ahead with a translocation of approximately 80 orange-tailed skinks. This represented ~10 per cent of the abundance estimate of skinks on Flat Island, where up to 30 per cent of skinks could be removed from the smallest subpopulation without exceeding our extinction-risk threshold. A quick release was needed before major infrastructural works were expected to begin and before Telfair's skinks further expanded on Gunner's Quoin. Despite having only two months to plan, we conducted the translocation in February 2008.

Post-release monitoring has supported our emergency choices (Cole 2011; Cole and Goetz 2013). Firstly, shrews were detected in 2010 following infrastructural development on Flat Island. A further 300 orange-tailed skinks were translocated to Gunner's Quoin in response, but within Telfair's skink occupied areas (no unoccupied areas remained by this time). Post–shrew invasion monitoring on Flat Island showed rapid population growth and spread of shrews, leading to the extirpation of orange-tailed skinks in 2011. Second, the Gunner's Quoin translocations of orange-tailed skinks appear to have been successful, although obtaining abundance estimates has been difficult without adversely disrupting the habitats they occupy. Indications are that orange-tailed skinks are now well established on Gunner's Quoin; their area of occupancy has increased from less than 1 ha to more than 18 ha.

In summary, the importance of action despite very limited information was justified, and the extinction of the orange-tailed skink was prevented. In this case there was a heavy reliance on information from surrogate species and similar systems, from the basic risk of accidental predator invasion through to parameterising projection models. Projection models were regarded as important to better visualise our expert judgements of alternative outcomes, thereby helping inform management choices and justification of these to government permitting agencies and other stakeholders.

9.3.3 Nest-Box Placement and Hygiene for Managing the Mauritius Parakeet

Emerging infectious diseases are key contributors to the current biodiversity crisis (Brooks and Ferrao 2005; Yap et al. 2015) and are increasingly the focus of direct management intervention. On Mauritius, one major threat has been the emergence and spread of a circo virus, beak and feather disease virus (BFDV), that causes psittacine beak and feather disease. BFDV first became a major concern in Mauritius parakeet management during a 2005 outbreak (Kundu et al. 2012). This disease causes feather discolouration. In mild infections, the birds may get a few yellow instead of green feathers, and they may recover. Chronic cases of the disease are terminal; the birds develop symmetrical feather dystrophy, and the feathers are deformed, brittle and usually break, with the birds loosing wing and tail feathers. The birds have a suppressed immune system.

The Mauritius parakeet is the last surviving endemic parrot in the Mascarene Islands (Figure 9.2). They were once the world's rarest parrot, numbering fewer than 20 individuals in the early 1980s (Jones et al. 2013c). Intensive management has successfully recovered the species to 142 known breeding pairs in the wild in late 2016 and a population of between 600 and 700 birds in 2017. This was achieved by boosting productivity via the provision of nest sites, supplemental feeding, clutch and brood manipulations and the reintroduction of captive reared birds (Jones et al. 2013c).

A down side to this management was the expression and spread of psittacine beak and feather disease. In an attempt to reduce BFDV spread, management including cross-fostering and captive rearing with subsequent release was halted in 2005. Supplementary feeding and visiting nests have continued but with new bio-security measures. As is the case elsewhere (e.g. Department of the Environment and Heritage 2005), the standard mitigation for BFDV transmission is the application of more stringent hygiene and bio-security protocols. For example, nest-site bio-security for Mauritius parakeets now includes wearing medical barrier suits while accessing nests and disinfecting nest sites with an industrial antiviral solution (Virex, Kilco International, Ltd.) at the end of each season. It was uncertain, however, whether these labour-intensive and expensive measures reduce BFDV transmission.

Overall Management Hypothesis. Bio-security protocols at nests will reduce the transmission of BFDV to nestlings.

Objectives. In this case, our management decision was framed as a single objective, to reduce BFDV in Mauritius parakeet nestlings. This objective had two measurable indicators: prevalence of virus in broods and viral load in individual nestlings. We recognise this as a means objective, and critical evaluation of how managing BFDV will improve Mauritius parakeet recovery is ongoing.

Alternative Options. Here we kept the management choice fairly simple: either implement recommended hygiene and bio-security protocols (see earlier) or not.

Consequences and Decisions. In this case, we chose to use a controlled experiment to test our hypothesis (Fogell et al., unpublished data). Two experimental groups were allocated based on natural geographic separation of the population into two subgroups. We implemented a reciprocal experimental design over two breeding seasons whereby in breeding season one we undertook standard BFDV mitigation, involving wearing medical barrier suits while accessing the nests and disinfecting the nest boxes with Virex prior to the breeding season in subgroup one, whereas no mitigation measures were applied in subgroup two. In breeding season two, these treatments were swapped. Over a third breeding season, standard mitigation measures were applied to 14 of 34 nest sites in subgroup one and 17 of 63 nest sites in subgroup two, distributed at a gradient away from supplementary feeding stations, to account for any in-group variation. In this experiment, our treatment refers to where BFDV mitigation is used compared to our control, where BFDV mitigation is not. In all cases nestling parakeets were blood sampled at 45 days of age, and both prevalence (proportion of brood infected) and infection intensity (viral load derived via quantitative PCR) were determined (Fogell et al., unpublished data).

Our experiment showed that while bio-security protocols implemented at nest sites were effective at reducing the incidence of BFDV infection in nestlings, they were not effective at reducing viral load. Instead, the results indicated that both viral incidence in a brood and the intensity of individual BFDV infection were more strongly linked to the distance at which a nestling was produced away from a supplementary feeding station (Figures 9.7 and 9.8). Work on Mauritius parakeets has suggested a link between the impact of psittacine beak and feather disease on nestlings and whether their parents are supplementary food users (Tollington et al. 2015). Additionally, individual viral load has been strongly correlated to the severity of psittacine beak and feather disease in Cape parrots (Regnard et al. 2015). Therefore, it appears that targeted bio-security at feeding stations to mitigate transmission may be more beneficial to the Mauritius parakeet population than the time-consuming and costly bio-security at nest sites, and this has become the subject of our continuing applied research.

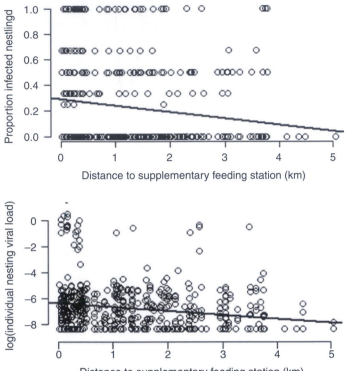

Figure 9.8 (Above) The proportion of nestlings in a brood that tested positive for BFDV on PCR testing of 45-day-old nestlings. (Below) Viral load of nestlings sampled at 45 days of age tested using quantitative PCR. Both panels show the relationship to distance from the nearest supplementary feeding station.

In summary, this example shows how carefully designed experiments can be used to test the effectiveness of management. Embedding experiments into management in this way can help continually evaluate and refine what we do in an evidence-based manner.

9.3.4 Supplementary Feeding and Demographics of the New Zealand Hihi

Supplementary feeding has proven to be a successful management option for many species. However, its use is not always accompanied by critical evaluation of its need nor consideration of what happens as populations successfully respond and grow, thereby increasing the costs incurred by managers in providing an ever-increasing food supply (Ewen et al. 2014). In this example we show how detailed monitoring can help us learn how populations respond to management and, importantly, how monitoring informs whether the response is as we expected. We introduce studies about supplementary feeding a reintroduced population of hihi on Kapiti Island, a large offshore island with regenerating forest. This hihi population was established successfully in the early 1990s. Managers on Kapiti are attempting to find the optimal balance between adequate provisioning and management cost.

Hihi are a threatened endemic passerine of New Zealand (Figure 9.1). Once widespread across northern New Zealand, hihi had become restricted to a single offshore island by about 1890 due to human-driven ecological change. Reintroduction and intensive post-release support, in addition to protection of the remnant population, has resulted in an increase to six populations and about 400 additional individuals spread across these sites. Hihi feed on a mix of nectar, fruit and invertebrates. Reintroduced populations are supported with food supplementation, the provision of nesting boxes (some sites) and control of parasites (some sites). To date, we have been unsuccessful in establishing a population with minimal management (predator control only), and we regard successful establishment of hihi without intensive management support as an acid test for ecological restoration in northern New Zealand.

Overall Management Hypothesis. Regenerating forest at reintroduction sites provides insufficient nectar and fruit for hihi.

Objectives. There are three fundamental objectives behind using supplementary food for hihi recovery across New Zealand: one directly related to the conservation benefit, of increased productivity and improved survival derived from feeding, the second related to management costs and the third on a desire for hihi populations to exist in as natural a setting as possible (supplementary feeding being viewed as artificial) (Table 9.5).

Alternative Options. The population on Kapiti has experienced two long periods of management, one without supplementary feeding, during which the population size remained low (up to 2001), and one where supplementary feeding was provided ad libitum, during which the population experienced rapid growth (after 2001). However, in 2009, the logistic difficulty of providing food to

Table 9.5 *Fundamental Objectives of Supplementary Feeding of Hihi*

Objective	Measurable indicator
Increase number of hihi	Number of adults in population
Reduce cost of management	Constructed scale of hours of effort between 0 (no feeding) and 100 (ad libitum)
Increase natural setting of hihi	Binary – presence or absence of supplementary feeding

a growing population (biological objective) then forced managers to evaluate how they could respond to increasing demands for food (cost objective) (Chauvenet et al. 2012). Chauvenet et al. (2012) had already showed that hihi were unlikely to persist without supplementary feeding such that the third objective was weighted low and not considered further for management planning in this population. This led island managers to trial a feeding regime that focused on reducing cost to manageable levels (through a 25 per cent reduction of the amount of food provided at peak ad libitum; 'first cap' in Figure 9.9). While this reduced cost, it also caused the population to decline (Figure 9.9a). The hihi recovery group then worked together through a structured decision-making process to select a new supplementary feeding strategy (Ewen et al. 2014). This decision process used monitored outcomes of the three trialled alternatives: (1) no feeding, (2) ad libitum feeding, and (3) a 25 per cent reduction on maximal feeding reached under ad libitum, alongside three additional options which varied where and how much food was made available (predictions based on expert judgement) (Ewen et al. 2014). A decision was made to redistribute where feeding stations were placed (closer together to reduce management cost) and an increase in the food provided (capped at levels provided at the previous peak under ad libitum; 'second cap' in Figure 9.9a). This management action was predicted to result in a population increase back close to the previous abundance seen under ad libitum feeding at a predicted cost slightly lower than achieved with the 25 per cent reduction trial (see Ewen et al. 2014: table 1). This decision was implemented in late 2013, and the population response continues to be monitored (Chauvenet et al., unpublished data; Figure 9.9b).

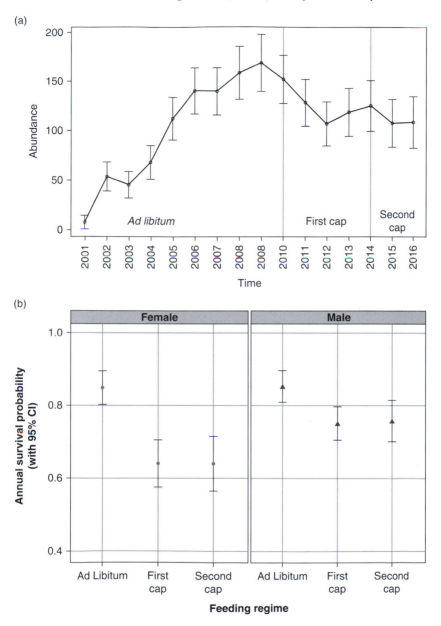

Figure 9.9 (a) Change in population size of hihi on Kapiti Island through three alternative supplementary feeding regimes. (b) Adult female and male annual survival estimates under the three alternative supplementary feeding regimes. Estimates of abundance (POPAN Jolly-Seber parameterisation) and survival (Cormack-Jolly-Seber models) were investigated using the software MARK. (*Source:* Cooch and White 2009.)

Consequences and Decisions. The majority of birds produced on Kapiti Island are caught in their first year and provided with unique colour ring identifiers. Constant-effort annual population surveys are done to generate an encounter (re-sighting) history, which is used to model the population's size and demography (Chauvenet et al. 2012). Monitoring results clearly show the response of the population to varying forms of feeding management (Chauvenet et al. 2012; Chauvenet et al., unpublished data; Figure 9.9a).

Initial monitoring of the management response, following the structured decision-making exercise, shows that the population has stabilised but not recovered to ad libitum levels (Figure 9.9a). Moreover, survival rates for males and females remain lower following implementation of the two feeding caps (Chauvenet et al., unpublished data; Figure 9.9b). Continued iterations of this decision are possible at any time as priorities change (e.g. an optimal decision depends partly on how much weight is given to the cost objective relative to the biological objective of population size). Importantly, as monitoring results are obtained, they can be compared to prior predictions and used to update our knowledge of the system and consider alternatives if our original predictions are not supported. In this case, our biological predictions are not currently well supported by monitoring data.

It is possible that external factors that were not considered when deciding on management have played a role in this pattern. For example, hihi are susceptible to climate such as increased temperature and high variation in rainfall patterns (Chauvenet et al. 2013). In addition, there is an indication that management costs were overestimated (i.e. the cost saving by moving feeding stations closer together was greater than predicted). A future iteration of this decision process can include updated information on both cost and how the population is responding, and we may choose to adjust current management.

9.4 Summary

Key points from the chapter:

• Clearly defining what we want to achieve allows us to compare how alternative options may help us get there, and predicting the outcome of alternative management options requires us to know, or judge, something about the species and its environment.

- We need to know, or suspect, what the key threatening processes are and remain open to the fact that our knowledge will be uncertain. By stating this uncertainty and making key elements of it the focus of monitoring and research, we can develop greater clarity.
- Choosing the best management strategy for conservation of endangered species is made difficult by uncertainty. Our attitude towards uncertainty is expressed as risk, and this shapes the way conservation management decisions are made. Risk attitudes are best expressed on the basis of clear objectives and explicit predictions of outcomes with uncertainty.
- Problems facing species are frequently too complicated for intuition or for the informal use of commonsense decisions alone, so we need to appreciate the value of a more formalised problem-solving and decision-making process.
- Managing and recovering threatened species are not quick processes and will likely involve large multi-stakeholder groups working together. There are, however, pitfalls with diverse representation that can drive division if sometimes conflicting views are not embraced and resolved carefully. Multi-objective problem-solving methods offer a helpful set of tools to assist in these scenarios

References

Armstrong, D. P., Castro, I. and Griffiths, R. (2007). Using adaptive management to determine requirements of re-introduced populations: the case of the New Zealand hihi. *Journal of Applied Ecology* 44: 953–62.

Armstrong, D. P., Moro, D., Hayward, M.W. and Seddon, P. J. (2015). Introduction: the development of reintroduction biology in New Zealand and Australia, in D. P. Armstrong, D. Moro, M. W. Hayward and P. J. Seddon (eds.), *Advances in Reintroduction Biology of Australian and New Zealand Fauna*. CSIRO, Clayton South.

Atkinson, C. T. and LaPointe, D. A. (2009). Introduced avian diseases, climate change, and the future of Hawaiian honeycreepers. *Journal of Avian Medicine and Surgery* 23: 53–63.

Atkinson, I. A. E. (1985). The spread of commensal species of *Rattus* to oceanic islands and their effects on island avifaunas, pp. 35–81 in P. J. Moors (ed.), *Conservation of Island Birds* (ICBP Technical Publication 3). Cambridge University Press, Cambridge.

Bell, B. D. (2002). The eradication of alien mammals from five offshore islands, Mauritius, Indian Ocean, pp. 40–45 in C. R. Veitch and M. N. Clout (eds.), *Turning the Tide: The Eradication of Invasive Species*. Invasive Species Specialist Group, Species Survival Commission, World Conservation Union, Gland.

Bhuiyan, J. and Bell, M. (1995). A Report of Ile Plate, Ilot Gabriel and the Adjoining Lagoon. Unpublished report, National Parks and Conservation Service, Reduit.

Brooks, D. R. and Ferrao, A. L. (2005). The historical biogeography of co-evolution: emerging infectious diseases are evolutionary accidents waiting to happen. *Journal of Biogeography* 32: 1291–99.

Bunbury, N., Jones, C. G., Greenwood, A. G. and Bell, D. J. (2008). Epidemiology and conservation implications of *Trichomonas gallinae* infection in the endangered Mauritian pink pigeon. *Biological Conservation* 141: 153–61.

Butler, D. and Merton, D. (1992). *The Black Robin: Saving the World's Most Endangered Bird*. Oxford University Press, Oxford.

Butler, S. J., Benton, T. G., Nicoll, M. A. C. Jones, C. G. and Norris, K. (2009). Indirect population dynamic benefits of altered life-history trade-offs in response to egg harvesting. *American Naturalist* 174(1): 111–21.

Cade, T. J. and Jones, C. G. (1994). Progress in restoration of the Mauritius kestrel. *Conservation Biology* 7: 169–75.

Canessa, S., Guillera-Arroita, G., Lahoz-Monfort, J. J. et al. (2016). Adaptive management for improving species conservation across the captive-wild spectrum. *Biological Conservation* 199: 123–31.

Chauvenet, A. L. M., Ewen, J. G., Armstrong, D. P. et al. (2012). Does supplemental feeding affect the viability of translocated populations? The example of the hihi. *Animal Conservation* 15: 337–50.

Chauvenet, A. L. M., Ewen, J. G., Armstrong, D. P. and Pettorelli, N. (2013). Saving the hihi under climate change: a case for assisted colonization. *Journal of Applied Ecology* 50: 1330–40.

Cheke, A. S. and Hume, J. P. (2008). *Lost Land of the Dodo: An Ecological History of Mauritius, Réunion and Rodrigues*. A&C Black, London.

Cole, N. (2007). Proposed Translocation of the Orange-Tail Skink. Unpublished report, Mauritian Wildlife Foundation, Vacoas.

  (2011). Driven to Extinction: The Invasion of the Musk Shrew Suncus murinus on Flat Island. Unpublished report, Durrell Wildlife Conservation Trust, Jersey.

Cole, N. and Goetz, M. (2013). Mauritius Reptile Recovery Programme: Conservation status of the orange-tailed skink, in *A Report Submitted to the National Parks and Conservation Service, Ministry of Agro-Industry*. Government of Mauritius, Vacoas.

Cole, N., Jones, C. G., Buckland, S. et al. (2009). The Reintroduction of Endangered Mauritian Reptiles, Technical Report, Mauritian Wildlife Foundation, Vacoas.

Cooch, E. and White, G. (2009). Analysis of Data from Marked Individuals: A Gentle Introduction. Program MARK, available at www.phidot.org/software/mark/docs/book/.

Cristinacce, A., Ladkoo, A., Switzer, R. A. et al. (2008). Captive breeding and rearing of critically endangered Mauritius fodies *Foudia rubra* for reintroduction. *Zoo Biology* 27: 255–68.

Cristinacce A., Switzer, R. A., Cole, R. E. et al. (2009). The release and establishment of Mauritius fodies *Foudia rubra* on Ile aux Aigrettes, Mauritius. *Conservation Evidence* 6: 1–5.

Dalziel, A., Sainsbury, A. W., McInnes, K., Jakob-Hoff, R. and Ewen, J. G. (2016). A comparison of disease risk analysis tools for conservation translocations. *Ecohealth* (doi: 10.1007/s10393-016-1161-5).

Davis, R. (1966). Homing performance and homing ability in bats. *Ecological Monographs* 36: 201–37.

Department of the Environment and Heritage (2005). Threat Abatement Plan for Psittacine Beak and Feather Disease Affecting Endangered Psittacine Species. Available at www.environment.gov.au (last accessed 10 December 2015).

Dingwall, P. R., Atkinson, I. A. E. and Hay, C. (1978). *The Ecology and Control of Rodents in New Zealand Nature Reserves*, (Information Series 4). New Zealand Department of Lands and Survey, Wellington.

Ewen, J. G., Armstrong, D. P., Empson, R. et al. (2012). Parasite management in translocations: lessons from an endangered New Zealand bird. *Oryx* 46: 446–56.

Ewen, J. G., Soorae, P. S. and Canessa, S. (2014a). Reintroduction objectives, decisions and outcomes: global perspectives from the herpetofauna. *Animal Conservation* 17(S1): 74–81.

Ewen, J. G., Walker, L., Canessa, S. and Groombridge, J. J. (2014b). Improving supplementary feeding in species conservation. *Conservation Biology* 29: 341–49.

Ewen, J. G., Thorogood, R., Brekke, P. et al. (2009). Maternally invested carotenoids compensate costly ectoparasitism in the hihi. *Proceedings of the National Academy of Sciences USA* 106: 12798–802.

Freeman, L. M. (2003). The Ecology and Conservation Genetics of the Gongylomorphus Skinks of Mauritius. PhD Thesis, Queen Mary, University of London.

Fritts, T. H. and Rodda, G. H. (1998). The role of introduced species in the degradation of island ecosystems: A case history of Guam. *Annual Review of Ecology and Systematics*, 29: 113–40.

Gartrell, B. D. (2007). Dermatitis of the pinnae in lessor short-tailed bats *Mystacina tuberculata* translocated to Kapiti Island. *Kokako* 14: 25–31.

Gregory, R., Failling, L., Harstone, M. et al. (2012). *Structured Decision Making: A Practical Guide to Environmental Management Choices*. Wiley, Chichester.

Griflin, J., Walker, M., Greif, S. and Parsons, S. (2007). Evidence of homing following translocation of the long-tailed bat (*Chalinolobus tuberculatus*) at Grand Canyon Cave, New Zealand. *New Zealand Journal of Zoology* 34: 239–46.

Guilbert, J., Walker, M., Greif, S. and Parsons, S. (2007). Evidence of homing following translocation of long-tailed bats (*Chalinolobus tuberculatus*) at Grand Canyon Cave, New Zealand. *New Zealand Journal of Zoology* 34: 239–46.

Jamieson, I. G. (2007). Has the debate over genetics and extinction of island endemics truly been resolved? *Animal Conservation* 10: 139–44.

Jones, C. G. (1987) The larger land birds of Mauritius, pp. 208–300 in A. W. Diamond, (ed.), *Studies of Mascarene Island Birds*. Cambridge University Press, Cambridge.

(1993). The ecology and conservation of Mauritian skinks. *Proceedings of the Royal Society of Arts and Sciences of Mauritius* 5: 71–95.

(2004). Conservation and management of endangered birds, pp. 269–301 in W. J. Sutherland, I. Newton and R. E. Green (eds.), *Bird Ecology and Conservation: A Handbook of Techniques*. Oxford University Press, Oxford.

(2008). Practical conservation on Mauritius and Rodrigues: steps towards the restoration of devastated ecosystems, chap. 10, pp. 226–59 in A. S. Cheke and J. P. Hume (eds.), *Lost Land of the Dodo*. T&AD Poyser, London.

Jones, C. G. and Owadally, A. W. (1988). The life histories and conservation of the Mauritius kestrel *Falco punctatus*, pink pigeon *Columba mayeri*, and echo parakeet *Psittacula eques*. *Proceedings of the Royal Society of Arts and Sciences Mauritius* 5(1): 79–130.

Jones, C. G. and Duffy, K. (1993). Conservation management of the echo parakeet *Psittacula eques echo*. *Dodo* 29: 126–48.

Jones, C. G. and Merton, D. V. (2012). A tale of two islands: the rescue and recovery of endemic birds in New Zealand and Mauritius, in J. G. Ewen, D. P. Armstrong, K. A. Parker and P. J. Seddon (eds.), *Reintroduction Biology: Integrating Science and Management*. Wiley Blackwell, Chichester.

Jones, C. G. and Swinnerton, K. J. (1997). Conservation status and research for the Mauritius kestrel, pink pigeon and echo parakeet. *Dodo* 33: 72–75.

Jones, C. G., Heck, W., Lewis, R. E., Mungroo, Y. and Cade, T. J. (1991). A summary of the conservation management of the Mauritius kestrel *Falco punctatus* 1973–1991. *Dodo* 27: 81–99.

Jones, C. G., Swinnerton, K. J., Taylor, C. J. and Mungroo, Y. (1992). The release of captive bred pink pigeons *Columba mayeri* in native forest on Mauritius: a progress report July 1987–June 1992. *Dodo* 28: 92–125.

Jones, C. G., Heck, W., Lewis, R. E. et al. (1994). The restoration of the Mauritius kestrel *Falco punctatus* population. *Ibis* 137: S173–80.

Jones, C. G., Swinnerton, K. J., Thorsen, M. and Greenwood, A. (1998). The biology and conservation of the echo parakeet *Psittacula eques* of Mauritius, pp. 110–123 in *Proceedings of IV International Parrot Convention*. Tenerife, Spain.

Jones, C. G., Burgess, M. D., Groombridge, J. J. et al. (2013a). Mauritius kestrel *Falco punctatus*, pp. 300–6 in R. J. Safford and A. F. A. Hawkins (eds.), *The Birds of Africa*, vol. VIII: *The Malagasy Region*. Christopher Helm, London.

Jones, C. G., Bunbury, N., Zuel, N., Tatayah, V. and Swinnerton, K. J. (2013b). Pink pigeon *Nesoenas mayeri*, pp. 484–89 in R. J. Safford and A. F. A. Hawkins (eds.), *The Birds of Africa*, vol. VIII: *The Malagasy Region*. Christopher Helm, London.

Jones, C. G., Malham, J., Reuleaux, A. et al. (2013c). Echo parakeet *Psittacula eques*, pp. 517–22 in R. J. Safford and A. F. A. Hawkins (eds.), *The Birds of Africa,* vol. VIII: *The Malagasy Region*. Christopher Helm, London.

Jones, H. P., Holmes, N. D., Butchart, S. H. et al. (2016). Invasive mammal eradication on islands results in substantial conservation gains. *Proceedings of the National Academy of Sciences USA* 113(15): 4033–38.

Kundu, S., Faulkes, C. G., Greenwood, A. G. et al. (2012). Tracking viral evolution during a disease outbreak: the rapid and complete selective sweep of a circovirus in the endangered echo parakeet. *Journal of Virology* 86: 5221–29.

Lack, D. (1954). *The Natural Regulation of Animal Numbers*. Oxford University Press, Oxford.

(1966). *Population Studies in Birds*. Oxford University Press, Oxford.

Lacy, R. C. (1993). Vortex, a computer simulation model for population viability analysis. *Wildlife Research* 20: 45–65.

Lloyd, B. (1994). Preliminary Report on the Transfer of Short-Tailed Bats *Mystacina tuberculata* from Codfish Island to Ulva Island. Unpublished report, New Zealand Department of Conservation, Wellington.

(2001). Advances in New Zealand mammalogy 1990–2000: short-tailed bats. *Journal of the Royal Society of New Zealand* 31: 59–81.

Maggs, G., Nicoll, M., Zuël, N. et al. (2015). *Rattus* management is essential for population persistence in a critically endangered passerine: combining small-scale field experiments and population modelling. *Biological Conservation* 191: 274–81.

McBride, M. F., Garnett, S. T., Szabo, J. K. et al. (2012). Structured elicitation of expert judgments for threatened species assessment: a case study on a continental scale using email. *Methods in Ecology and Evolution* 3: 906–20.

McCarthy, M. A. (2014). Contending with uncertainty in conservation management decisions. *Annals of the New York Academy of Sciences* 1322: 77–91.

Miskelly, C. M. and Powlesland, R. G. (2013). Conservation translocations of New Zealand birds, 1863–2012. *Notornis* 60: 3–28.

Molloy, J. (1995). *Bat (Peka Peka) Recovery Plan (Mystacina, Chalinolobus)*. Threatened Species Unit, New Zealand Department of Conservation, Wellington.

Morris, P. A. and Morris, M. J. (1991). Removal of Shrews from the Ile aux Aigrettes. Unpublished report, Mauritian Wildlife Appeal Fund, Port Louis.

Newton, I. (1998). *Population Limitation in Birds*. Academic Press, London.

Nichols, R. A. and Freeman, K. L. M. (2004). Using molecular markers with high mutation rates to obtain estimates of relative population size and to distinguish the effects of gene flow and mutation: a demonstration using data from endemic Mauritian skinks. *Molecular Ecology* 13: 775–87.

Nicoll, M. A. C., Jones, C. G. and Norris, K. (2006). The impact of harvesting on a formerly endangered tropical bird: insights from life history theory. *Journal of Applied Ecology* 43: 567–75.

O'Donnell, C., Christie, J., Hitchmough, R., Lloyd, B. and Parsons, S. (2010). The conservation status of New Zealand bats, 2009. *New Zealand Journal of Zoology* 37: 297–311.

Paxton, E. H., Camp, R. J., Gorresen, P. M. et al. (2016). Collapsing avian community on a Hawaiian island. *Science Advances* 2: e1600029.

Regnard, G. L., Boyes, R. S., Martin, R. O., Hitzeroth, I. I. and Rybicki, E. P. (2015). Beak and feather disease virus: correlation between viral load and clinical signs in wild cape parrots (*Poicepahlus robustus*) in South Africa. *Archives of Virology* 160: 339–44.

Ross, T. N., Pernetta, A. P., Jones, C. G. and Bell, D. J. (2008). Sexual size dimorphism and microhabitat use of the orange-tail skink (*Gongylomorphus* spp.) on Flat Island, Mauritius: conservation implications. *Amphibia-Reptilia* 29: 349–59.

Sainsbury, A. W. and Vaughan-Higgins, R. J. (2012). Analyzing disease risks associated with translocations. *Conservation Biology* 26: 442–52.

Seymour, A., Varnham, K., Roy, S. et al. (2005). Mechanisms underlying the failure of an attempt to eradicate the invasive Asian musk shrew *Suncus murinus* from an island nature reserve. *Biological Conservation* 125: 23–35.

Swinnerton, K. J. (2001). The Ecology and Conservation of the Pink Pigeon *Columba mayeri* in Mauritius. PhD thesis, University of Kent, Canterbury.

Tatayah, R. V. V. (2010). The Breeding Biology of the Round Island Petrel Pterodroma arminjoniana and Factors Determining Breeding Success. PhD thesis, University of Mauritius, Mauritius.

Tollington, S., Greenwood, A., Jones, C. G. et al. (2015). Detailed monitoring of a small but recovering population reveals sublethal effects of disease and unexpected interactions with supplemental feeding. *Journal of Animal Ecology* 84: 969–77.

Tomich, P. (1986). *Mammals in Hawaii*. Bishop Museum Press, Honolulu.

Varnham, K. J., Roy, S. S., Seymour, A. et al. (2002). Eradicating Indian musk shrews (*Suncusmurinus*, Soricidae) from Mauritian offshore islands, pp. 342–49 in C. R. Veitch and M. N. Clout (eds.), *Turning the Tide: The Eradication of Invasive Species*. Invasive Species Specialist Group, Species Survival Commission, World Conservation Union, Gland.

Walker, L. K., Armstrong, D. P., Brekke, P. et al. (2013). Giving hihi a helping hand: assessment of alternative rearing diets in food supplemented populations of an endangered bird. *Animal Conservation* 16: 538–45.

Weeks, A. R., Moro, D., Thavornkanlapachai, R. et al. (2015). Conserving and enhancing genetic diversity in translocation programs, in D. P. Armstrong, M. W. Hayward, D. Moro and P. J. Seddon (eds.), *Advances in Reintroduction Biology of Australian and New Zealand Fauna*. CSIRO, Clayton South.

Yap, T. A., Koo, M. S., Ambrose, R. F. et al. (2015). Averting a North American biodiversity crisis: a newly described pathogen poses a major threat to salamanders via trade. *Science* 349.

10 · *Restoring Island Ecosystems*
Managing the Recovery Process

CARL G. JONES AND JAMIESON A. COPSEY

10.0 Introduction

There are now relatively few, if any, 'pristine' ecosystems remaining. Islands exemplify the impacts that anthropogenic change can bring about; change that has often been so severe that it is hard to imagine or to recreate perfectly a pre-human state, with original species assemblages and relationships. We are increasingly conscious of how habitat degradation can lead to reduced resilience of these systems to external shocks, such as extreme weather events. This situation presents us with a number of challenges, at the crux of which is the question of how we manage these 'novel' ecosystems to maintain maximum biodiversity and ecological function. Beginning with the recovery of threatened species, we can start to understand how current ecosystems are functioning and where there might be ecological gaps that need to be filled. Through species we can begin to understand the ecological roles that would have existed and, where possible, restore lost links and species assemblages and, where not, create new relationships that help build resilience, species diversity and ecological roles.

In this chapter we reflect on the extent to which we can restore historical systems and enhance ecological function, with reference particularly to work on islands and drawing heavily on our experience in Mauritius. We revisit the concept of habitat management to mitigate the factors limiting population growth of threatened species, a process that has been common practice in game bird management for hundreds of years. We consider the main stages that are involved in habitat restoration, drawing heavily on lessons from islands where invasive plant and animal management is often a requirement. We look at the point at which we restore threatened vertebrates to the system and in which order, ending with an analysis of the role of ecological replacements to fulfil the function of extinct species.

10.1 Motivations for the Management of Novel Ecosystems

There is little question that we are losing biodiversity at an unprecedented rate. Within the last 40 years, global populations of the major vertebrate groups have halved (WWF 2014). The degradation of ecosystems worldwide is reducing their resilience to extreme events, such as flooding or storm surges (Costanza et al. 2014), with knock-on effects for humans along with other species; these events are only likely to become more severe and frequent as climates change (WWF 2014). In Chapters 2 and 3 we explored our growing understanding of the impact of genetic loss on species and their ability to evolve and change and avert extinction. In Chapter 4 we discussed the growing homogenisation of the world's islands as the biota they support consist of an increasingly similar suite of introduced species, invading degraded habitats and threatening remaining endemic wildlife. The challenge we face is to restore threatened species within functioning ecosystems that are resilient enough to respond more effectively to a changing world and conserve maximum biodiversity.

Where ecosystems are degraded but endemic or native species still exist, we should be striving to restore them and re-establish as best we can the original species assemblages and inter relationships. In this way we can succeed in maintaining maximum diversity. Where species are missing but are required to perform particular ecological roles (e.g. seed dispersal), then we should seek out alternative species that could fill the gap without causing negative impacts elsewhere – not an intervention to be carried out lightly given what we know of the unintentional impacts of introduced species (see Chapters 4 and 7). Species play roles within ecosystems, so in addition to being influenced by the state of the system, they can in return influence its health and functionality (Mascaro et al. 2013).

Species recovery projects can drive ecosystem management and restoration. This may be through the species providing a focus for public concern and investment in interventions to conserve the wider system and community assemblages: a 'flagship' species approach (Frankel and Soulé 1981). Successful efforts to restore the St Lucia parrot *Amazona versicolor* in St Lucia, Caribbean, is one such example (Birdlife International 2013; Box 11.5). In other situations, in order to meet the needs of the focal species, it may be necessary to manage particular qualities or scales of land or particular trophic levels, thereby satisfying the needs of other species within the system: the 'umbrella' species approach (Frankel and Soulé 1981). For example, habitat management recommendations to conserve the Californian Channel Island fox *Urocyon littoralis* (Cypher et al. 2014; Box 8.2) are likely to benefit the native species on which it depends. An interesting twist with this example concerns removal of previously transient, non-breeding golden eagles *Aquila chrysaetos*, which had become established on the islands, creating an additional trophic level *above* the foxes and a threat to their long-term viability. In particular cases, species may be 'keystone' species within the system – species that perform a particular function that is necessary to maintain certain biotic and/or abiotic processes (Power 1996; Cortés-Avizanda 2015). Loss of fruit bats from island systems could have serious ecological and economic repercussions as at least 448 products come from 289 species of plants that rely on fruit bats for pollination or seed dispersal (Fujita and Tuttle 1991). In each of these situations, the conservation of one species can result in positive gains for other components of the system.

An understanding of the system and how to intervene to conserve individual species can build confidence to take on larger challenges, including restoration of whole ecosystems (Figure 10.1, Box 10.1). Ecosystems are complex, and our understanding of how biotic and abiotic factors interact either historically or in the present is limited. However, by adopting threatened species and their needs as our 'entry point' into understanding this complexity, we can begin to see where changes have occurred that have led to the system's failure to maintain the species within.

For vertebrates at least, ecosystems provide

- Foraging sites that provide sufficient food and water year around
- Safe breeding sites, and
- Adequate cover providing secure
  - Resting sites,
  - Protection from the extremes of weather, and
  - Protection from predators.

These factors will determine productivity and mortality and the balance between the two for any given species. The relative importance of each of these factors can vary within species and within individuals, an extreme example being the contrasting ecological

Figure 10.1 Snapshots in time: before (a) and after (b) restoration efforts.
(a) Round Island (1960), 22.5 km off the north coast of Mauritius, prior to the

requirements of the tadpole and adult forms of many amphibians. The critically endangered Puerto Rican crested toad *Peltophryne lemur* is the only endemic toad of Puerto Rico and was thought to be extinct for over 40 years until 1965, when individuals were rediscovered in the north of the island (USFW 1992). Threats to the species have included habitat loss, the impact of invasive species and pesticide contamination (USFW 1992). The species breeds in temporary ponds following heavy rains, and the availability of such sites in its remaining habitat has limited its recovery. Efforts to restore the population through captive breeding and release have included the development of artificial breeding ponds, similar in function to the cattle troughs used when farming was a more common land use practice. While the species is still critically endangered, there are signs of released toads returning to these artificial sites to breed (Zippel 2005).

Loss of habitat within ecosystems has been shown to have multiple impacts on species and species assemblages. It can reduce trophic chain length (Komonen et al. 2000) and change interactions between species (Taylor and Merriam 1995). It has been shown to reduce the number of specialist, large-bodied species (Gibbs and Stanton 2001) and reduce breeding success (Kurki et al. 2000), dispersal success (Bélisle et al. 2001), predation rate (Bergin et al. 2000) and foraging success rate. As our understanding of the relationship between habitat change and species productivity and mortality has grown, it has become possible to manipulate habitats to increase holding capacity. Game bird managers have been doing this for more than a century and have taken habitat management to more extreme lengths than have hitherto been applied to endangered species.

Caption for Figure 10.1 (cont.)

removal of European rabbits *Oryctolagus cuniculus* and goats *Capra aegagrus* and multispecies restoration efforts. Note limited vegetation and evidence of extreme soil erosion. (b) A similar spot on Round Island (2014). Note the recovery of more diverse plant life, which now provides important habitats for native seabirds and endemic reptiles, including Telfair's skink *Leiolopisma telfairii*, once widespread across Mauritius and now restricted to three offshore islands (*Photo credits:* (a) De Speville; (b) Nik Cole.) (A black-and-white version of this figure will appear in some formats. For the colour version, please refer to the plate section.)

10.2 Historical Lessons from Game Bird Management

Habitat management for the benefit of certain game bird species demonstrates how human intervention to artificially maintain particular habitat types can promote biodiversity conservation. The aim here is not to simply leave 'nature' to its own devices or even to recreate landscapes to their pre-anthropogenic state but to manage the system for the benefit of key species and species assemblages.

The endemic race of the willow grouse in the British Isles, the red grouse *Lagopus lagopus scoticus* population, is kept at high densities by habitat management and predator control and is perhaps the best example of the long-term management of an endemic bird taxon. Red grouse depend upon heather moorland that is managed to sustain high densities of grouse for shooting. Heather moorland is a distinctive habitat dominated by ling heather *Calluna vulgaris*. Three-quarters of the world's heather moors are restricted to the United Kingdom, and about half of this is managed for grouse (Moors for the Future Partnership 2007). Many moors are pure stands of heather; others may have varying amounts of grassland or blanket *Sphagnum* bog. The heather is managed by burning the older rank heather in narrow strips on a rotation to produce a mosaic of different-aged growth. The grouse nest on the ground typically among the older heather that provides more cover. Burning encourages young growth, the main food of adult grouse (Hudson 1992). Management of the moorlands in this way has had some positive knock-on effects for other otherwise declining species within the United Kingdom. For example, there is evidence that populations of black grouse *Tetrao tetrix*, lapwing *Vanellus vanellus* and curlew *Numenius arquata* are benefitting from these management regimes (Grant et al. 2012).

The motivation behind this habitat management may not have been for biodiversity conservation purposes, and in fact, there is counterevidence to demonstrate that for other species the management regime has detrimental effects (Grant et al. 2012). However, this example is instructive for conservation managers. Firstly, it shows how, through understanding a particular species' habitat requirements, it is possible to elevate population densities of target species beyond that which could have been sustained within the system in the absence of management. Secondly, it demonstrates how, through management, it is possible to have positive consequences for wider species assemblages that would otherwise be compromised within a human-dominated landscape. Such interventions are now being applied to island systems across the world as a means to conserve threatened species and restore ecological function.

10.3 Ecological Restoration of Islands: Identifying What to Restore

Habitat loss and subsequent loss of species and ecological function have been particularly pronounced on islands as a consequence of their relatively small physical size, biogeography (impoverished biota, evolution in isolation, broad ecological niches) and overwhelming human colonisation (Ewel et al. 2013). Conservation interventions on islands are therefore often designed to restore threatened species. Both usually involve manipulation at the species level to increase the abundance of some (see Chapter 9) and the reduction of others (see Chapter 7). When the aim goes further to restore ecological function, it can be difficult to determine the most appropriate reference point. Should we look to restore ecosystems with their associated species assemblages back to what was there 50 years ago, 100 years ago, 500 years ago or the last ice age? The development of 'ecological histories' (see Section 5.1) can be informative in helping to construct a view of what certain ecosystems looked like prior to human contact. It would, though, be naive to assume that we can turn back the clock in all situations, and in many others it is more prudent to consider them as managed human-made, novel ecosystems (see Hobbs, Higgs and Hall (2013) for a full review of this paradigm). However, even the most degraded systems (Box 10.1) can begin to be rebuilt in particular on islands where their bounded nature makes restoration of some pre-anthropocene species assemblages and ecological functions a realistic goal.

Box 10.1 *Use of Technology to Understand Food Webs and (Re)Build Functioning Systems*

Ecosystem processes that must be re-established, or initiated, in order to restore or create function include the flux of nutrients and energy through a system. A thorough understanding of the food web of a dysfunctional ecosystem can help to pinpoint the missing links that must be reinstated to restore the system and is particularly important when the system is likely to consist of novel elements due to either species extinction or our patchy understanding of the pre-anthropogenic state.

The first step towards understanding food web dynamics is to analyse the diets of the species present in the ecosystem to establish trophic links. Traditional methods of non-invasive dietary analysis include the micro-histological examination of remains in faeces or regurgitates and direct observation of feeding. However, such methods are time consuming and require considerable expertise (Holechek et al. 1982), and taxa can rarely be identified to the species level. An alternative is to use molecular methods, which have been shown to be superior in terms of taxonomic resolution (Ando et al. 2013; Soininen et al. 2009) and less intensive in terms of labour and expertise. One molecular method involves coupling DNA bar-coding with next-generation sequencing (NGS) (Pompanon et al. 2012). A DNA barcode is a short fragment of DNA that is conserved within species but exhibits consistent interspecific differences. It is possible to amplify DNA barcodes from many species in tandem by using universal primers. NGS allows the amplified DNA in a pooled sample, extracted from faeces or other samples containing a mix of dietary items, to be sequenced. Providing that the DNA barcodes for all taxa in the sample are present in a DNA barcode reference library, the taxa can be identified.

We have begun to piece together the food webs of Round Island and Ile aux Aigrettes (Mauritius) by using DNA bar-coding and NGS. The central aim of this work is to determine how grazing by an analogue species, the Aldabra giant tortoise *Aldabrachelys gigantea*, is altering plant community composition and structure and how this, in turn, affects two endemic species, the pink pigeon *Nesoenas mayeri* (Ile aux Aigrettes only) and Telfair's skink *Leiolopisma telfairii*. This project focuses solely on herbivory and has involved comprehensive DNA bar-coding of the entire flora of the two islands to compile a DNA barcode reference library. This is a novel way to assess the impacts of taxon replacements, and our findings will be valuable for deciding future directions of restoration work in Mauritius and elsewhere.

The history of restoring islands began with the removal of invasive mammals and was done largely to provide habitat for endangered bird species and to remove exotic predators. New Zealand was at the forefront of this development in the 1960s due to a combination of government leadership and planning and public recognition of the need to take radical steps to prevent further biodiversity loss (Rauzon 2007). In 1961, goats were eradicated on Cuvier Island (181 ha), Hauraki Gulf (New Zealand). By this point, the North Island saddlebacks *Philesturnus carunculatus rufusater* and red-crowned parakeets *Cyanoramphus n. Novaezelandiae* had become extinct on the island (Atkinson 1988). The last feral cats were removed in 1964, and in 1968, the first reintroduction of 29 saddlebacks began, followed later by red-crowned parakeets. Following the success of this project, multiple other restoration efforts have been undertaken across the offshore islands of New Zealand (see Atkinson (1988) for a summary of the early work). Efforts that paralleled the work on Cuvier Island were begun to restore Nonsuch Island (6 ha), Bermuda, in 1962 (Murphy and Mowbray 1951). Again, this work was driven by concern for the decline of a native bird, the Bermuda petrel *Pterodroma cahow*, believed to be extinct until its rediscovery in 1959. In this case multiple species of invasive vertebrate and invasive plant species were removed from the island. Salt marsh vegetation and mangrove trees were restored along with freshwater swamp habitats, and then the process of re-establishing locally extinct or threatened fauna began. The endangered white-eyed vireo *Vireo griseus bermudianus*, the yellow-crowned night heron *Nycticorax violacea* – known only from fossil bones (see Section 5.1.1) – the green turtle *Chelonia mydas* and a top shell sea snail *Cittarium pica* were all reintroduced. The top shell was established to provide shells for an endangered species of giant land-based hermit crab *Coenobita diogenes* (Atkinson 1988). Finally, a recovery programme for the recently rediscovered Bermuda petrel was launched. From the initial rediscovered 18 pairs, the global population of the species now stands at approximately 250 individuals (Madeiros 2011).

Our ability to begin to restore degraded ecosystems has increased exponentially in recent years, with new techniques available for us to eradicate problematic invasive species (see Chapter 7). On 23 March 2015, the last of a three-stage process to eradicate rats from the 580-km^2 island of South Georgia, Antarctica, was completed

(South Georgia Habitat Restoration Project 2015). By 2007, introduced Arctic foxes *Alopex lagopus* had been removed from 99 per cent (445) of the Aleutian Islands (>202,000 ha), native seabird populations subsequently recovering by up to a factor of 5 within 10 years of fox clearance (Rauzon 2007). The Aleutian Canada goose *Branta canadensis leucopareia* increased from fewer than 1,000 birds in 1975 to over 100,000 and was subsequently removed from the US endangered species list (Ebbert and Byrd 2002).

10.4 Lessons from Islands: Stages in the Recovery Process

Examples from islands illustrate how ecosystem restoration takes on an iterative nature, with small changes made to the system being followed by checks to see what the impacts have been, either at the species or the ecosystem level. As discussed in Chapters 6, 7 and 8, projects need to begin with clear goals in mind and be broken down into achievable and relevant steps, which build the confidence of those involved to take on larger challenges. Initial concern for individual species shifts to management to maintain or restore ecological function to the wider ecosystem as our skills, ecological understanding and degree of public and political support required for successful intervention expands. In this section we hope to provide some clarity concerning the restoration process, drawing heavily on evidence from islands. Our aim is not to provide a prescriptive 'recipe for success' (as no single approach is right for all situations all the time) but to inform our thinking about how to plan future restoration projects and the re-establishment of ecological functions. From at least an island perspective it is possible to conceive of five logical and incremental stages, with monitoring and evaluation running alongside each but considered right from the start.

10.4.1 Establish a Baseline (Stage 1)

The rate of global environmental change can make it difficult to determine what the 'original' composition was for a given ecosystem. Ecological histories can provide invaluable – if patchy – reference points from which to determine the extent of change that has occurred, drawing from a range of data sources including travellers' logbooks, museum artefacts and hand-drawn early maps (see Figure 5.3). While each of these data sources has its own limitations (see Section 5.1.2), they can help us to develop a 'broad brush' view of what the pre-human habitat may have looked like and therefore point to what would be appropriate to be re-established. Furthermore, the identification of 'reference sites', or comparable islands that lack the existence of known threats (e.g. introduced invasive species), can help greatly in developing a sense of what islands identified for restoration might have once looked like (Towns et al. 2016). For example, attempts to establish the restoration goals for the Mercury Islands, New Zealand – which were degraded through the introduction of invasive vertebrates – were helped through comparisons made with six non-invaded islands. The non-invaded islands provided good evidence of a much more vibrant and diverse reptile, seabird and invertebrate community that may once have existed on the Mercury Islands prior to the arrival of introduced vertebrates. These comparisons helped to establish restoration goals (Towns et al. 2016).

Once the baseline has been approximated, it is then possible to begin to clarify restoration goals, which can be based on returning the system to approximately what it may have looked like at a certain time in the past or around identification and (re-)development of ecological function (Towns et al. 2016). The former requires greater clarity around historical ecosystem structure, while the latter focuses more on understanding how existing components of the system interact. Clearly, it is possible to adopt a middle way that seeks to restore historical species assemblages but recognises that as species are returned to the system and their behaviour and impacts are monitored, missing ecological roles will become apparent. In the case of Tiritiri Island, Hauraki Gulf (New Zealand), the goal was to restore the island to the state it was in at the point of European settlement in the mid-1830s but not to go back further before the point at which Polynesians settled on the island (Atkinson 1988). This example highlights that setting restoration goals is as much a social process as a biological one (Cairns 2000).

10.4.2 Remove Invasive Alien Vertebrates (Stage 2)

There have to date been more than 1,200 successful eradications globally, mostly focusing on vertebrates and largely on single species (Glen et al. 2013). Scaling up these efforts could generate significant benefits to biodiversity globally. A recent study of 968 threatened seabird islands globally revealed that 74 per cent of these were not inhabited by humans, and 96 per cent of them were located within high- to middle-income countries, providing a real opportunity for restoration interventions given the relative lack of socio-economic barriers to such work (Spatz et al. 2014). As detailed in Chapter 7, our abilities to remove particularly problematic invasive species have increased exponentially in the last few decades, though we are not as yet able to deal with them all (e.g. brown tree snakes in Guam; see Box 8.2), and many more are only just starting to reveal themselves as problems on islands (e.g. Indian musk shrew in Mauritius; Varnham et al. 2002). Our aim here is not to explain how to remove invasive vertebrates (see Chapter 7 for such details) but to highlight some of the results you can expect, both positively and negatively, and so be prepared for them. We also recognise that vertebrates are not the only problematic fauna facing island systems. However, given the global reach and impact of some core invasive mammalian vertebrate species and our ability to remove them and begin ecosystem restoration, it is appropriate to single them out for consideration.

Three species of rat (Norway rat *Rattus norvegicus*, black rat *R. rattus* and the Polynesian rat *R. exulans*) are between them now present on at least 90 per cent of islands worldwide (Towns et al. 2006). The ecosystem-level impacts they have following establishment (see Section 4.2) result in significant habitat degradation and endemic species loss. Conversely, their eradication alone can result in widespread ecosystem recovery, including the reappearance of once thought extinct plants and the recovery of native fauna (e.g. invertebrate, reptiles, land birds and seabird populations). This pattern of recovery can be seen following the eradication of a range of vertebrate species. For example, three years after the removal of rabbits *O. cuniculus* from Round Island (Mauritius) in 1986, three native tree species had regenerated, and there was a marked increase (up to 20-fold) in the abundance of five threatened endemic reptiles (North et al. 1994).

Given the degraded state of many ecosystems, in particular, on islands, not all introduced species should be considered ripe for removal, where the goal is restoring ecological function. In Mauritius, for example, introduced honey bees were the major flower visitors of 58 per cent (43) of plant species within a weeded conservation management area (Kaiser 2006), indicating their potential value in plant reproduction despite their novel status. Furthermore, the removal of certain species can result in undesired consequences. The removal of particular invasive species (e.g. introduced herbivores) may result in other invasive species switching their prey focus more towards native or endemic wildlife. In other situations, the removal of one predatory invasive may allow another to increase in abundance and have an impact on endemic wildlife, a concept known as 'meso-predator release' (Prugh et al. 2009). The severe decline in the native sea eagle *Haliaeetus albicilla* in Finnish island archipelagos coincided with the invasion of the American mink *Mustela vison*. Recovery of the eagle population since the 1960s is reducing mink activity and could well reduce the population of this predatory invasive (Salo et al. 2008). These examples underscore three fundamental lessons about the restoration process:

1. Understand not only what is missing within the system (where possible) but also what is present and how they might interact.
2. Ensure that your monitoring of the system is effective so that you can detect the unforeseen as well as the predicted.
3. Accept that despite the preceding, things will happen that you did not expect, but be willing to accept this and act with this 'imperfect' knowledge (Black and Copsey 2014; see also Section 8.8.2), observe and respond accordingly.

As our ability to eradicate invasive alien species increases, so does the stretch of the goals we can begin to aim for. In the Galapagos Islands, initial work to eradicate feral goats from the 12-ha island Plaza Sur in 1971 has now been expanded to aim for their removal across the whole archipelago, including their removal from Santiago Island, an island more than 58,000 ha in size; work is now in process to remove goats from the more than 500,000 ha of Isabela Island (Carrion et al. 2011). The removal of goats from these islands has resulted in the recovery of the endangered Galapagos rail *Laterallus spilonotus* on multiple islands following vegetation recovery, increases in the populations of eight threatened plant species (including one feared extinct) and the recovery of native plant communities on multiple islands (Carrion et al. 2011). As illustrated here, the removal of individual invasive fauna (and in particular invasive mammalian vertebrates) can be sufficient to stimulate the recovery of threatened species and whole ecosystems. In other situations, however, additional work is required to attain species- or system-level recovery goals, beginning with the active removal of invasive plants.

10.4.3 Remove Invasive Alien Plants (Stage 3)

In some cases, the removal of invasive alien vertebrates can also withdraw a control on the growth of invasive plants. The eradication of goats from Santiago Island, Galapagos, resulted in the introduced invasive blackberry *Rubus niveus* becoming an increasing problem in the highland areas, compounded by the spread of its seeds by native birds (Carrion et al. 2011). Control measures are now in place to try to contain the species, and bio-control agents are being explored for application by Galapagos National Parks. Removal of rabbits on Round Island (Mauritius) resulted in growth of hitherto unreported exotic plants (e.g. *Desmanthus* and *Desmaodium*) and the proliferation of exotic grasses (Box 10.1).

Removal of invasive alien plants can be achieved through physical (e.g. burning, uprooting, ring-barking, grazing, mulching, tilling and removal of leaf litter), chemical (e.g. use of herbicides including inject-able forms) and/or biological means. Alternatives include rebalancing soil chemistries left by invasive plant growth through direct applications (e.g. the application of sawdust to reduce high nitrogen levels left by the build-up of biomass from dead yellow bush lupin *Lupinus arboreus* in grassland areas; Alpert and Maron 2000). At small scales – such as when an invasive plant is in the early stages of establishment or on offshore islets – physical removal may be sufficient. For example, between 1986 and 2005, more than 90 per cent of the 25-ha island of Ile aux Aigrettes, Mauritius, had been weeded manually at least once and more than 60 per cent multiple times. Weeding became progressively easier as plant biomass was reduced. Of the 53 native plant species now established on the island, four are endangered, nine vulnerable and four are rare species (Cheke and Hume 2008). Similar efforts on the Mauritius main-land have resulted in weeded plots beginning to show signs of regenera-tion, with gaps closing within native vegetation over three to five years (Figure 10.2).

Herbicide use has proved more effective at reducing invasive plant cover, biomass and density over physical methods, although when used alone it may not confer any significant gains for native plant species recovery (Kettenring and Adams 2011). As with the eradication of invasive alien vertebrates (see Section 7.5), the application of a suite of removal methods can be the most effective way to achieve success (Kettenring and Adams 2011). Preventing reinvasion or the spread of more problematic species into vacant spaces is an important

(a)

(b)

Figure 10.2 Comparisons of weeded (a) and non–weeded plots (b) within and outside of conservation management areas (CMAs), Black River Gorges National Park, Mauritius. (*Photo credit:* Jamieson A. Copsey.)

consideration, as it is with invasive vertebrate control or eradication. We should increasingly view the removal of invasive alien plants and animals as simply the start of the restoration process – the creation of a 'clean slate' on which to start re-creating (or creating) species assemblages and functional ecosystems.

10.4.4 Re-establish Plant Communities (Stage 4)

Invasive plant removal does not necessarily lead to native plant regeneration. Removal of one species may provide resources for other invasive species to take hold, potentially more damaging to the ecosystem than the first. A lack of sufficient source stock ('propagule pressure'; see Section 4.4.3) may limit the ability of endemic or native species to re-colonise even with the successful control of invasive species (Kettenring and Adams 2011). Going further, active re-vegetation should be considered an important component of invasive plant control projects, creating barriers to re-invasion. However, before launching into a full-scale re-vegetation effort, there is a need for trial (re-)introductions of cultivated plants, with adequate monitoring (Atkinson 1988), to test the feasibility of the techniques and the suitability of the site and the species for reintroduction.

Alongside monitoring should come support for plants during the establishment phase, in particular, for those that are threatened or whose populations are likely to be badly affected by restoration activities. The failure to restore the threatened shrub *Scalesia affinis* on Santa Cruz in the Galapagos Archipelago through artificial propagation and planting out into the wild was linked to a lack of understanding of what the particular microhabitat requirements were for the species that needed to be recreated (Atkinson et al. 2009). Post-reintroduction care of plants is often neglected and is to be recommended until they have become well established and may include watering, mulching, removing weeds, controlling pests and disease and hand pollination and collection of seeds. Of the thousands of seeds and plants propagated and planted out on Round Island, Mauritius, in the 1980s and 1990s, less than 0.1 per cent of them survived due primarily to water stress and competition (Tatayah et al. 2007). Since this time watering systems have been installed and plants are weeded, shaded from the sun and protected through individual, circular fences from burrowing seabirds. The result is an increase in survivorship to 95 per cent (for up to three months) and stabilisation at 85 per cent after one year (Tatayah et al. 2007).

The fencing of individual plants has to be done with great care because building a cage around a plant may attract attention to it. In Rodrigues, after the fencing of the last *Ramosmania rodriguesii* – and at the time the last known wild *Hybiscus liliflorus* – interest in the species grew, and both plants had branches and leaves pulled off to make herbal remedies. It was alleged that since they were fenced, they must have magical or medicinal properties. The *Hybiscus* subsequently died in part due to the excessive attention it was getting. Fencing may also alter microclimates or allow weeds to grow unchecked by herbivores and smother the focal plant. Caging usually has to be done with supportive management and is probably essential in many cases to provide protection for critically endangered plants. See Marren (2005) for a discussion on caged flowers.

Once vegetation communities are well established and cared for, they can become important refugia for the rarer species. In Hawaii, recovery of the critically endangered Maui parrotbill, or 'kiwikiu', *Pseudonestor xanthophrys* is believed to be restricted by the availability of suitable habitat. While the species currently persists in moist forest, breeding success is low, and this is thought to be in part an artefact of the destruction of its historical drier forest habitat (Mounce et al. 2013). Efforts to restore the species include the fencing of existing mesic forest followed by the removal of invasive species and active restoration of the parrotbill's food plants (Figure 10.3). Once established, the plan is to

Figure 10.3 Maui Forest Bird Recovery Project team carrying seedlings out to experimental restoration plots in Nakula Natural Area Reserve, Maui, Hawaii. (*Photo credit:* Maui Forest Bird Recovery Project, www.mauiforestbirds.org.)

translocate captive-bred birds into the restored habitat to form a new, protected population (Mounce and Leonard 2012).

10.4.5 Replace Missing Vertebrates (Stage 5)

In some instances, restored habitats will naturally be re-colonised by native vertebrates. Natural seabird population recovery in the Mercury Islands, New Zealand, has been greatly facilitated by the eradication of invasive vertebrates. A prediction is that the functional role of seabirds within this island group (e.g. through the importation of additional nutrients) could be restored within as little time as the next 50 years (Towns et al. 2016). In Mauritius, creation of fenced, weeded upland areas resulted in an increase in the number of other native passerines. Point counts in the weeded plots and in unmanaged forest showed that the numbers of native birds were related to forest quality, with the highest numbers of native birds being found in areas of full-canopy forest. These managed plots are also chosen preferentially by pink pigeons over surrounding degraded areas of forest.

The reintroduction of threatened species for conservation purposes can contribute to wider ecosystem recovery and the reduction of threats to other native species. On the coralline islet of Ile aux Aigrettes, Mauritius, reintroduction of Telfair's skink *Leiolopisma telfairii* correlated with a significant reduction in the population of introduced giant African land snails *Achatina fulica*, possibly assisted through selective predation (Copsey et al. 2011). Going further, as our understanding of ecosystems and what was once there grows (e.g. through the development of ecological histories), we can begin to develop goals around the restoration of lost ecological roles. We can make informed guesses about where there may be vacant niches that can be filled through the replacement of missing species.

On island systems, such goals may be of particular importance due to the often limited range of species filling specific roles within the system. The interaction between island flora and fauna provides a useful illustration of this point (Kaiser-Bunberry et al. 2009). Reptiles can play a disproportionate role as seed dispersers and pollinators on islands compared to on continental systems, broadening their niches beyond that found in many continental species to capitalise on readily available fruit and nectar resources. On Ile aux Aigrettes, Mauritius, the endemic gecko *Phelsuma ornata* is seen as a 'super generalist', acting as primary pollinator for a range of endemic plant species (Olesen et al. 2002). Loss of such species from the system has therefore potentially serious ramifications for island plant communities.

The replacement of missing vertebrates should be undertaken with a clear idea not only of the goal in mind but also the sequence in which that goal is to be achieved. By establishing species at lower trophic levels to begin with, it is possible not only to track their progress in performing particular ecological functions (e.g. as seed dispersers or grazers) but also to ensure that they are sufficiently secure to withstand either competition or predation from later reintroductions (Box 10.2).

Box 10.2. *Re-establishing Reptile Communities to Gunners Quoin, Mauritius*

Gunner's Quoin, located approximately 8 km from the north shore of Mauritius and measuring 76 ha in area, is one of over a dozen islets under protection and ongoing ecological restoration. Following baseline studies (referencing historic texts, museum specimens and paleontological records) to determine the pre-human state of the island, invasive plants and vertebrates were systematically removed. Species eradicated included the brown rat *R. norvegicus*, introduced to the island in the mid–1800s, which had subsequently caused the extirpation of Telfair's skink *L. telfairii* and the keel-scaled boa *Casarea dussumieri*. Black-naped hares *Lepus nigricollis* and rabbits *Oryctolagus cuniculus* were also eliminated by 1998. Removal of the rat (predator) and lagomorphs (herbivores) from Gunner's Quoin allowed the smaller surviving reptile species (e.g. lesser night gecko *Nactus coindemirensis*, ornate day gecko *P. ornata*) and native plants to demonstrate signs of recovery, as revealed by before and after population monitoring.

Native plant re-establishment was followed by return of the missing vertebrates, beginning in 2007 with 250 Telfair's skinks translocated to Gunner's Quoin from nearby Round Island. Skinks were carefully selected from all areas of the source population, tagged with passive integrated transponders (PITs), health screened and quarantined in holding units for two to three days. The quarantine period allowed skinks to pass the contents of their gastrointestinal tract so as not to accidently introduce exotic plants with the reptile translocations. Annual surveys (e.g. transect lines/distance sampling, mark-recapture sampling) on Gunner's Quoin provided data on population, body condition, overall health status, etc. that could be compared with what is known from the source population. Annual dietary (faecal) analysis of the Telfair's skink has been conducted to examine food selection and to determine what impact the skinks may be having, if any, on invertebrates, fruit and plant material and other vertebrates (other native lizards). Translocated Telfair's skinks consumed the fruit and seeds of multiple imperilled plants, promoting seed dispersal and assisting efforts to re-colonise the island with native vegetation.

By 2010, mark–recapture studies indicated that there was population recruitment, with individuals having hatched and matured on Gunner's Quoin, in addition to surviving adults from the 2007 translocation. Tissue sampling was used across years to test for genetic robustness, assessing whether there was a need to supplement individuals into the growing Gunner's Quoin population. In 2012, an additional 100 Telfair's skinks were translocated to Gunner's Quoin, following the above-mentioned procedures, to enhance genetic variability. Dedicated study informed a predictive population growth model, which estimated that Gunner's Quoin Telfair's skinks would soon start to experience density-dependent effects (i.e. competition for food and space).

Orange-tailed skinks *Gongylomorphus* cf. *fontenayi* were translocated to Gunner's Quoin (82 individuals in 2008, 300 individuals in 2010) to establish an assurance population as the source population on nearby Flat Island was experiencing recreational tourist development. By 2013, orange-tailed skinks had begun colonising areas outside of release sites, and the introduced population was composed of individuals of all age classes, including young of the year, indicating reproduction and recruitment. Morphometric and genetic data collection is ongoing for comparison with the pre-disturbance source.

With a robust prey base established and the removal of exotic predators, the reintroduction of a Mauritian apex predator, the keel-scaled boa, could proceed. In April 2012, researchers collected additional population baseline data, as well as health and disease screening, from the sole boa population on Round Island. Boa translocation from Round Island to Gunner's Quoin took place in October 2012. Release boxes were set up across an array of release sites on Gunner's Quoin. In total, 60 adult boas were collected from across Round Island to maximise genetic variability, screened for disease, PIT tagged, and maintained short term in holding facilities to time release under optimal conditions. Following strict bio-security protocols, groups of boas were transported to Gunner's Quoin via helicopter over several days. On Gunner's Quoin, boas were placed individually into release boxes. Following sunset, the boxes were opened. Boas were released in adjacent male-female pairs at a stocking density calculated based on home range size of individuals from the source population and prey (skink) density. The release boxes were left in place as potential refuge sites. Life-history data from captive and wild boas were used to develop a predictive population growth model for Gunner's Quoin. Additionally, genetic sampling demonstrated that boas reintroduced to Gunner's Quoin represent the genetic diversity of the Round Island source population at large. In late 2013, a juvenile boa was found during surveys, representing the first confirmed hatching of a wild keel-scaled boa outside of Round Island since the mid-1800s. This observation also confirmed that Gunner's Quoin has microclimate conditions suited for successful egg incubation, as well as habitat appropriate for juvenile survival.

Where possible, we should naturally try to restore species to their former range or support existing populations to increase in size to the point at which they are once again performing their original ecological roles. However, increasingly, the endemic or native species no longer exist. Under these circumstances, we must consider how far we are willing to go to restore ecological function and conserve maximum biodiversity, if this is our goal.

10.5 Ecological Replacements

The introduction of species outside of their natural range has contributed significantly to the current biodiversity crisis. However, under certain conditions, such a strategy can be justified on conservation grounds. These conservation introductions have been widely practiced in New Zealand, where all populations of kakapo *Strigops habroptilus* and little spotted kiwi *Apteryx owenii* are on islands where these species have never previously occurred (Bell and Merton 2002). In these instances, the goal has been the conservation of threatened species, removing them from threats that cannot be controlled. As we begin to think more about restoring ecological function as our goal, we can consider taking this approach a step further, introducing sometimes non-threatened species outside their historic range in order to replace extinct species, thereby establishing them as 'ecological replacements'.

10.5.1 Development of the Concept

On European nature reserves, cattle, horses and sheep are now used commonly to maintain grazing climax communities. These herbivores are often different to the native species that once existed but have become extinct, extirpated or greatly reduced in number. Selective (back-)breeding of various domestic and semi-domestic breeds has resulted in the development of Konik horses and Heck cattle that are morphologically, behaviourally and ecologically close to their extinct wild ancestors, the wild horse or tarpan *Equus ferus* and wild cattle or auroch *Bos primigenius* (Bunzel-Druke 2001). Both 'wild types' are now free roaming within Europe, fulfilling a lost ecological role.

There have been several introductions of different subspecies to replace an extinct race, such as the introduction of a mix of seven different races of peregrine falcons to North America to replace the Eastern form of the *anatum* race of peregrine falcon *Falco peregrinus* spp. (Cade and Burnham 2003) or the introduction of the North African red-necked ostrich *Struthio camelus camelus* to replace the Arabian subspecies *Struthio camelus syriacus* to Saudi Arabia (Islam et al. 2008). The primary use of these replacements has been to reactivate lost ecological interactions due to the loss of particular native or endemic species. Given the overwhelming threats to many species and systems, it is likely that the movement of particular animals and plants outside of their historical range, either for conservation or ecological purposes, is going to increase in coming decades. It is important therefore that we consider some guiding principles to inform our responsible application of the process.

10.5.2 Guiding Principles

A landmark paper on species replacement and the protocols that should be adhered to is provided by Atkinson (1990). He suggested the possibility of introducing the alpine living rock wren *Xenicus gilviventris* to an island to replace the now-extinct lowland *X. longipes*. The paper provides a list of critical questions, highlighting three main criteria that need to be considered when choosing an ecological replacement species:

1. **Ecological Equivalence to the Extinct Species.** The closer the replacement is to the extinct species in ecological needs, the better.
2. **Taxonomic Closeness to the Extinct Species.** Choosing replacement species that are in the same genus is desirable, although probably not essential.
3. **Conservation Importance.** Some replacements may themselves be in need of conservation action, and clearly, these should have priority over non-endangered taxa.

If the replacement is taxonomically very close to the extinct form (i.e. a subspecies, sister species or in the same super-species) and ecologically similar, then there is every possibility that the introduction will be successful. Donlan et al. (2006) argue the importance of genetic relatedness when selecting analogue species, and Hutton et al. (2007) postulate that the closer the relatedness, the better and that one should substitute subspecies, before species, before genus. Hutton et al. (2007) caution that any substitutions based on ecological function above the level of genus should be avoided. This seems unduly restrictive since taxonomic closeness alone may not be enough in the choice of a replacement; in many radiations, a closely related species may have a very different ecology (see the example of finches in Galapagos or honey creepers in Hawaii, Box 2.2). Ecological closeness may override the need for taxonomic affinity, assuming that the purpose is to restore an ecological function that has been lost by extinction. As a result of convergence, there are many distantly related groups that serve similar functions.

In the Mascarene Islands in the Indian Ocean, the idea to replace extinct species dates back over three decades (Cheke 1975; Temple 1981) and is now being developed for reptiles and birds (Cheke and Hume 2008). The first suggestions were to introduce from Mauritius to the neighbouring island of Reunion the Mauritius kestrel *Falco punctatus*, pink pigeon *Nesoenas mayeri*, echo parakeet *Psittacula eques* and Mauritius fody *Foudia rubra*, replacing the closely related species/races that had become extinct (Dubois kestrel *F. douboisi*, Reunion pink pigeon *N. duboisi*, double-collared parakeet

P. eques, Reunion fody *F. delloni*). A possible first step along this route has been taken with the introduction of exotic tortoises onto the Mauritian islands of Ile aux Aigrettes and Round Island. These tortoises are being used to replace the extinct *Cylindrapsis* tortoises and to try and re-create the grazing climax community that has been largely lost (Griffiths et al. 2013; Pearce and Jones 2016). There are additional candidate parrot species that may help to re-fill ecological roles linked to seed dispersal for a range of fruiting trees in Mauritius and potentially in the wider Indian Ocean region (Box 10.3).

Box 10.3 *Replacing Lost Seed Dispersers to the Western Indian Ocean Islands*

The islands of the Seychelles and Mascarenes had at least 10 different species that were endemic; these have now been largely extirpated (Cheke and Hume 2008), and only two species survive. The parrots were important components of the bird communities and would have been effective seed predators as well as seed dispersers. The native forests of many of the Indian Ocean islands are highly degraded, with many of the plants reproducing poorly due, in some cases, to the loss of pollinators and seed dispersers. This is particularly true of many of the endemic canopy trees of Mauritius that are not regenerating adequately and show poor dispersal. Some of these trees produce fruit with fleshy epicarps and hard seeds, and these species have evolved to be distributed by vertebrates. The search for the most likely dispersal agents for some of these trees has been the subject of much debate.

Most of this discussion has centred on the tambalacoque *Sideroxylon grandiflorum*, a canopy tree that produces spherical fruits (~50 mm in diameter) with a fleshy epicarp and a very hard seed. It has been suggested that these seeds were originally spread by dodos that ingested the fruit and passed the seeds in their droppings (Temple 1977). This hypothesis has now been debunked (Witmer and Cheke 1991), although other dispersal agents for the tambalacoque have been suggested, including giant tortoises.

What this argument fails to emphasise is that there are a whole host of Mauritian canopy trees spread over several families that have hard seeds that are protected by a fleshy and edible epicarp. These fruits come in a range of sizes, suggesting that several different species were involved in dispersal. The tambalacoque has two closely related species on Mauritius that produce very hard seeds that are similar in form but are of different sizes. *Sideroxylon sessiliflorum* produces medium-sized fruits (~20–25 mm in diameter), and *Sideroxylon boutonianum* produces small fruits (~12 mm in diameter).

There were a limited number of frugivorous vertebrates on Mauritius that could be likely candidates for dispersing fruit. The fruit bat *Pteropus niger* is known to feed extensively on the fruits of some trees and to spread their seeds. However, the seeds of some native trees are very much harder than would be required to withstand the assaults of a feeding fruit bat; these would probably have been parrot dispersed. The fleshy epicarp would have been eaten by the parrots, but they would have had difficulty in opening the seeds, which they would have dropped, often well away from the host plant. The still-surviving echo parakeet feeds on the hard-seeded fruits of colophane *Canarium paniculatum* and tambalacoque. They eat the fleshy epicarp and reject the seeds. A species favoured by the echo parakeet that produces very hard seeds is the colophane batard *Protium obtusiflorum*. When the fruit ripens, the epicarp splits open, revealing three very hard seeds covered with an edible pink–red pulp. The parakeets feed on the red pulp and reject the seeds, thus dispersing them. It is likely that the now-extinct and distinctive medium-sized Thirioux's grey parrot *Psittacula (Coracopsis?) bensoni* and the large raven parrot *Lophopsittacus mauritianus* (see Figure 5.4) would have been important seed dispersers. It is possible that the tambalacoque has such a hard seed because it had to withstand the onslaught from the beak of the extinct raven parrot.

It would be desirable to replace these parrots to try and reactivate some of the lost seed dispersal systems. The raven parrot was strongly dimorphic in size, and it would be difficult to find a suitable replacement. Hume (2007) suggests that based on beak and body morphology, the hyacinth macaw *Anodorhynchus hyacinthinus* and palm cockatoo *Probosciger atterimus* are reasonable analogues, or possibly one of the *Calyptorhynchus* cockatoos. No introductions can be entertained until extensive feeding studies had been conducted and perhaps until we learn a bit more about the raven parrot from osteological and DNA studies and further studies of sub-fossil remains. Concern over the 'invasibility' of these species would also need to be addressed before permitting any such introduction (see Chapters 4 and 7).

There were six or more taxa of *Psittacula* parakeets on Indian Ocean islands. Only the echo parakeet *Psittacula eques* from Mauritius survives and would be the most appropriate taxon that could be used to replace the nominate form from Reunion. It could also be introduced to Rodrigues as a possible analogue for the Newton's parakeet *P. exsul*. The extinct Seychelles parakeet was closely related to the Alexandrine parakeet *P. eupatria*, with which it shares a similar morphology, and this species would be the obvious candidate for a replacement, or if we are looking for a taxon of conservation value, then an introduction of the echo parakeet may be more appropriate.

10.5.3 Cautions with Ecological Replacement

The use of analogues for some extinct species that were highly distinctive and where little is known about their biology is unrealistic, since accurate ecological replacements could not at present be chosen with any confidence. Hence, lost species such as the dodo and the Rodrigues solitaire must be regarded as irreplaceable with any currently extant taxon (see Box 1.2). The use of ecological replacements needs to proceed with care to ensure that there are no major negative impacts upon native species, with the introduced one potentially becoming invasive (see Chapters 4 and 7). Initial studies on the use of replacement species and those on which the techniques and protocols are developed should therefore be based on species that can be carefully controlled or contained on small islands.

The choice of flightless birds as analogues allows, in most cases, the luxury of being able to closely monitor the released animals and, if necessary, to be able to remove them with relative ease. In many cases it will be appropriate that replacement species are maintained in managed populations for the first few generations, while their impact is being evaluated. The guidelines for the introduction of replacement species need to be more rigorous than those currently employed with reintroductions and translocations. Greater emphasis will need to be expended on post-introduction monitoring (see Chapter 9) and to study the ecology of the species, evaluating whether it is fulfilling its proposed role.

10.6 Ecosystem Management: Look to the Future

Ecosystems are dynamic, responding to abiotic as well as biotic change brought about in part by human activity. Where possible, we should seek out historical reference points to inform our species or wider ecosystem recovery goals. There is still much to be done to develop ecological histories for islands as well as continental areas based on a mix of qualitative and quantitative and historical and current data (see Chapter 5). However, it would be naive to assume that we can return modern-day ecosystems to their 'pre-human' state, particularly in the face of current global climate change (Harris et al. 2006); rather, we should be moving towards the management of resilient systems able to cope with future change and able to support maximum biodiversity over the long term.

Species are likely to remain the catalyst for such developments as concern for these tangible units of life drives many restoration efforts. They are at the heart of an ambitious (and contentious) proposal to 're-wild' continental areas or large islands with whole communities of substitute animals. The concept of 're-wilding' can be broadly defined as the (re-)introduction of species to restore ecosystem function, although variations occur in large part based on the degree of human intervention accepted in its management (Nogués-Bravo et al. 2016). 'Pleistocene re-wilding' seeks to restore the large animal community of North America as it existed 13,000 years ago. There are suggestions to introduce cheetah, lion, horses, African and Indian elephants and Bactrian camels to replace extinct but similar species (Donlan et al. 2006). Re-wilding has also been proposed for New Zealand (Atkinson 1988), Madagascar (Burney 2003), South America (Galetti 2004) and Siberia (Zimov 2005; Donlan et al. 2006). However, the use of replacements is a controversial issue, with several scientists arguing caution (Caro 2007) or being in direct opposition (Cajal and Tonni 2006; Rubenstein et al. 2006).

'De-extinction' is now being discussed as a distinct possibility, bringing with it a raft of ethical, political and other issues to address. Could the woolly mammoth *Mammuthus primigenius* be 'resurrected' through genetic engineering to begin to restore the Arctic Steppe in place of the less ecologically rich tundra? Or could the Tasmanian tiger *Thylacinus cynocephalis*, lost within the last 100 years, be reinstated to the Tasmanian landscape? Seddon et al. (2014) present a list of 20 possible de-extinction candidates, including the New Zealand moa *Dinornis* spp., the Madagascan elephant bird *Aepyornis* sp./*Mulleromis* sp. and the saber-toothed cat *Smilodon*. They go on to apply the current 2013 IUCN

Reintroduction Guidelines (IUCN/SSC 2013) to help inform the selection of species for which benefits of their 'reintroduction' would outweigh the costs.

The merging of technological advances with our current understanding, confidence and ability to begin to manage ecosystems and the species within for enhanced function presents many more opportunities for successful conservation intervention. We should begin with the 'low-hanging fruit': locations where, among other characteristics, the removal of key threats (e.g. invasive alien species) is feasible, native wildlife was well known prior the arrival of these threats and lost species or ecological replacements are present elsewhere (Hutton et al. 2007). Islands continue to represent some of the best opportunities for such ecosystem-wide interventions given their bounded nature. However, there are examples where our management at the ecosystem level has extended to the continents, including one of the largest restoration efforts in the world to restore 700 km^2 of dry forest in Costa Rica (Janzen 1988).

As our ability to restore ecological function increases to include those areas inhabited or used by humans, so too will the need to confer anthropological benefits through a range of ecosystem services (Cairns 2000). Value judgements will need to be made over which species and roles are priorities for removal or replacement, taking into account the needs of a range of stakeholders and what their 'fundamental objectives' might be (see Section 9.2.1). The concept of re-wilding raises many issues of human concern and requires careful thought before being put into practice. Islands may again provide us with an opportunity to trial these ideas within relatively controlled systems. However much traction this concept gains, it should be remembered – for the sake of islands and their place in our conservation thinking – that the origin of these ideas has its recent genesis among the biologists of New Zealand and the Mascarenes.

10.7 Summary

Key points from this chapter:

• While species-specific management interventions may be required over the long term for their continued persistence, we should develop larger visions around the recovery of functioning ecosystems able to support maximum biodiversity.

- We need to understand how habitat loss is affecting particular species if we are to intervene appropriately to conserve them and restore functional elements.
- Our understanding of habitat management within the conservation sector has been greatly influenced by early work to remove invasive alien species from islands.
- Where restoration is our goal, we need to establish ecological baselines. Where the focus is on maintaining or restoring ecological function, we can work more with our understanding of existing systems.
- While removal of alien invasive species will remain an integral step in the restoration of many systems, in particular, on islands, it should also include planning for the re-establishment of native species (with post-release care and monitoring).
- Ecological replacements represent an alternative where key species have gone extinct. However, care must be taken with their use (with close monitoring and readiness to intervene) to ensure that they do not exacerbate threats to native biodiversity.

References

Alpert, P. and Maron, J. L. (2000). Carbon addition as a countermeasure against biological invasion by plants. *Biological Invasions* 2(1): 33–40.

Ando, H., Setsuko, S., Horikoshi, K. et al. (2013). Diet analysis by next-generation sequencing indicates the frequent consumption of introduced plants by the critically endangered red-headed wood pigeon (*Columba janthina nitens*) in oceanic island habitats. *Ecology and Evolution* 3(12): 4057–69.

Atkinson, I. A. E. (1988). *Presidential Address: Opportunities for Ecological Restoration.* New Zealand Journal of Ecology 11: 1–12.

(1990). Ecological restoration on islands: prerequisites for success: ecological restoration of New Zealand Islands. *Conservation Sciences Publication* 2: 73–90.

Atkinson, R., Jaramillo, P. and Tapia, W. (2009). Establishing a new population of *Scalesia affinis*, a threatened endemic shrub, on Santa Cruz Island, Galapagos, Ecuador *Conservation Evidence* 6: 42–47.

Bélisle, M. and St Clair, C. C. (2001). Cumulative effects of barriers on the movements of forest birds. *Conservation Ecology* 5(2): 9.

Bell, B. D. and Merton, D. V. (2002). *Critically Endangered Bird Populations and Their Management* (Conservation Biology Series). Cambridge University Press, Cambridge.

Bergin, T. M., Best, L. B., Freemark, K. E. and Koehler, K. J. (2000). Effects of landscape structure on nest predation in roadsides of a Midwestern agroeco-system: a multiscale analysis. *Landscape Ecology* 15(2): 131–43.

BirdLife International (2013). *Amazona versicolor. The IUCN Red List of Threatened Species 2013*, e.T22686387A48052131, available at http://dx .doi.org/10.2305/IUCN.UK.2013–2.RLTS.T22686387A48052131.en (last accessed 5 March 2016).

Black, S. A. and Copsey, J. A. (2014). Purpose, processes, knowledge and dignity are missing links in interdisciplinary projects. *Conservation Biology* 28 (5): 1139–41.

Bunzel-Drüke, M. (2001). Ecological substitutes for wild horse (*Equus ferus Boddaert*, 1785 = *E. przewalskii Poljakov*, 1881) and aurochs (*Bos primigenius Bojanus*, 1827). *Natur-und Kulturlandschaft* 4(9).

Burney, D. A. (2003). Madagascar's prehistoric ecosystems, pp. 47–51 in S. Goodman and J. Benstead (eds.), *The Natural History of Madagascar*. University of Chicago Press, Chicago, IL.

Cade, T. J. and Burnham, W. (eds.) (2003). *Return of the Peregrine: A North America Saga of Tenacity and Teamwork*. Peregrine Fund, Boise.

Cairns, J. (2000). Setting ecological restoration goals for technical feasibility and scientific validity. *Ecological Engineering* 15(3): 171–80.

Cajal, J. L. and Tonni, E. P. (2006). Re-wilding in South America: is it possible?. *Mastozoología Neotropical* 13(2): 281–82.

Caro, T. (2007). The Pleistocene re-wilding gambit. *Trends in Ecology and Evolution* 22(6): 281–83.

Carrion, V., Donlan, C. J., Campbell, K. J., Lavoie, C. and Cruz, F. (2011). Archipelago-wide island restoration in the Galapagos Islands: reducing costs of invasive mammal eradication programs and reinvasion risk. *PLoS ONE* 6(5): e18835.

Cheke, A. S. (1975). An undescribed gecko from Agalega: *Phelsuma agalegae* sp. nov. *Bulletin of the Mauritius Institute* 8: 33–48.

Cheke, A. and Hume, J (2008). *Lost Land of the Dodo: An Ecological History of Mauritius, Reunion and Rodrigues*. Yale University Press, New Haven, CT.

Copsey, J. A., Shelbourne, G., Grice, R. and Goder, M. (2011). Possible control of introduced giant African land snails (*Achatina* spp.) by the reintroduced endemic skink *Leiolopisma telfairii*, Ile aux Aigrettes, Mauritius. *Management of Biological Invasions* 2: 39–45.

Cortés-Avizanda, A., Colomer, M. A., Margalida, A. et al. (2015). Modeling the consequences of the demise and potential recovery of a keystone-species: wild rabbits and avian scavengers in Mediterranean landscapes. *Science Reports* 5: 17033

Costanza, R., de Grootb, R., Sutton, P. et al. (2014). Changes in the global value of ecosystem services. *Global Environmental Change* 26: 152–58.

Cypher, B. L., Madrid, A. Y., Job, C. V. H. et al. (2014). Multi-population comparison of resource exploitation by island foxes: implications for conservation. *Global Ecology and Conservation* 2: 255–66.

Donlan, C., Berger, J., Bock, C. E. et al. (2006). Pleistocene rewilding: an optimistic agenda for twenty-first century conservation. *American Naturalist* 168(5): 660–81.

Ebbert, S. E. and Byrd, G. V. (2002). Eradications of invasive species to restore natural biological diversity on Alaska Maritime National Wildlife

Refuge, pp. 102–9 in C. R. Veitch and M. N. Clout (eds.), *Turning the Tide: The Eradication of Invasive Species*. IUCN Invasive Species Specialist Group, Gland.

Ewel, J. J., Mascaro, J., Kueffer, C. et al. (2013). Islands: Where novelty is the norm, pp. 29–44 in R. J. Hobbs, E. S. Higgs, and C. M. Hall (eds.), *Novel Ecosystems: Intervening in the New Ecological World Order*. Wiley, Chilchester.

Frankel, O. H. and Soule, M. E. (1981). *Conservation and Evolution*. Cambridge University Press, Cambridge.

Fujita, M. S. and Tuttle, M. D. (1991). Flying foxes (Chiroptera: Pteropodidae): threatened animals of key ecological and economic importance. *Conservation Biology* 5(4): 455–63.

Galetti, M. (2004). Parks of the Pleistocene: recreating the Cerrado and the Pantanal with megafauna. *Natureza and Conservacao* 2: 93–100.

Gibbs, J. P. and Stanton, E. J. (2001). Habitat fragmentation and arthropod community change: carrion beetles, phoretic mites, and flies. *Ecological Applications* 11(1): 79–85.

Glen, A. S., Atkinson, R., Campbell, K. J. et al. (2013). Eradicating multiple invasive species on inhabited islands: the next big step in island restoration?. *Biological Invasions* 15(12): 2589–603.

Grant, M. C., Mallard, J., Leigh, S. and Thompson, P. S. (2012). *The Costs and Benefits of Grouse Moor Management to Biodiversity and Aspects of the Wider Environment: A Review*. RSPB, Sandy.

Griffiths, C. J., Zuel, N., Jones, C. G., Ahamud, Z. and Harris, S. (2013). Assessing the potential to restore historic grazing ecosystems with tortoise ecological replacements. *Conservation Biology* 27(4): 690–700.

Harris, J. A., Hobbs, R. J., Higgs, E. and Aronson, J. (2006). Ecological restoration and global climate change. *Restoration Ecology* 14(2): 170–76.

Hobbs, R. J., Higgs, E. S. and Hall, C. (2013). *Novel Ecosystems: Intervening in the New Ecological World Order*. Wiley, New York, NY.

Holechek, J. L., Vavra, M. and Pieper, R. D. (1982). Botanical composition determination of range herbivore diets: a review. *Journal of Range Management* 35(3): 309–15.

Hudson, P. J. (1992). *Grouse in Space and Time: The Population Biology of a Managed Gamebird: The Report of the Game Conservancy's Scottish Grouse Research Project and North of England Grouse Research Project*.Game Conservancy Limited, London.

Hume, J. P. (2007). *Reappraisal of the Parrots (Aves: Psittacidae) from the Mascarene Islands, with Comments on Their Ecology, Morphology, and Affinities*. Magnolia Press, Orlando, FL.

Hutton, I., Parkes, J. P. and Sinclair, A. R. E. (2007). Reassembling island ecosystems: the case of Lord Howe Island. *Animal Conservation* 10(1): 22–29.

Islam, Z. U. M., Ismail, K. and Boug, A. (2008). Re-introduction of the red-necked ostrich, *Struthio camelus camelus*, in Mahazat as-Sayd Protected Area in central Saudi Arabia. *Zoology in the Middle East* 44(1): 31–40.

IUCN/SSC (2013). *Guidelines for Reintroductions and Other Conservation Translocations*, version 1.0. IUCN Species Survival Commission, Gland.

Janzen, D. H. (1988). Management of habitat fragments in a tropical dry forest: growth. *Annals of the Missouri Botanical Garden* 75(1): 105–16.

Kaiser, C. N. (2006). Functional Integrity of Plant–Pollinator Communities in Restored Habitats in Mauritius. PhD dissertation, Universität Zürich.

Kaiser-Bunbury, C. N., Memmott, J. and Müller, C. B. (2009). Community structure of pollination webs of Mauritian heathland habitats. *Perspectives in Plant Ecology, Evolution and Systematics* 11(4): 241–54.

Kettenring, K. M. and Adams, C. R. (2011). Lessons learned from invasive plant control experiments: a systematic review and meta-analysis. *Journal of Applied Ecology* 48(4): 970–79.

Komonen, A., Penttilä, R., Lindgren, M. and Hanski, I. (2000). Forest fragmentation truncates a food chain based on an old-growth forest bracket fungus. *Oikos* 90(1): 119–26.

Kurki, S., Nikula, A., Helle, P. and Linden, H. (2000). Landscape fragmentation and forest composition effects on grouse breeding success in boreal forests. *Ecology* 81(7): 1985–97.

Madeiros, J. (2011). Cahow report. *Bermuda Audubon Society Newsletter* 22(1): 5–6.

Marren, P. (2005). Caged flowers. *British Wildlife* 17(1): 33.

Mascaro, J., Harris, J. A., Lach, L. et al. (2013). Origins of the novel ecosystems concept, pp. 45–57 in *Novel Ecosystems: Intervening in the New Ecological World Order*. Wiley, Chilchester.

Moors for the Future Partnership (2007). Looking after Moorland Habitats, Sustainable Uplands and Moors for the Future Research Note No. 14, available at www.moorsforthefuture.org.uk/sites/default/files/documents/MFF%20RN14%202007%20Looking%20after%20grouse%20moor%20habitats.pdf (last accessed 26 April 2017).

Mounce, H. and Leonard, D. (2012). Habitat Restoration Aiding the Recovery of the Maui Parrotbill, Biodiversity Science Developments in Biodiversity and Conservation Management No. 6, available at www.biodiversityscience.com/2012/04/26/habitat-restoration-maui-parrotbill/ (last accessed 16 April 2016).

Mounce, H. L., Leonard, D. L., Swinnerton, K. J. et al. (2013). Determining productivity of Maui parrotbills, an endangered Hawaiian honeycreeper. *Journal of Field Ornithology* 84(1): 32–39.

Murphy, R. C. and Mowbray, L. S. (1951). New light on the cahow, *Pterodroma cahow*. *The Auk* 68(3): 266–80.

Nogués-Bravo, D., Simberloff, D., Rahbek, C. and Sanders, N. J. (2016). Rewilding is the new Pandora's box in conservation. *Current Biology* 26(3): R87–91.

North, S. G., Bullock, D. J. and Dulloo, M. E. (1994). Changes in the vegetation and reptile populations on Round Island, Mauritius, following eradication of rabbits. *Biological Conservation* 67(1): 21–28.

Olesen, J. M., Eskildsen, L. I. and Venkatasamy, S. (2002). Invasion of pollination networks on oceanic islands: importance of invader complexes and endemic super generalists. *Diversity and Distributions* 8(3): 181–92.

Pearce, F. and Jones, C. (2016). Kestrel manoeuvres in the dark. *New Scientist* 231 (3089): 40–41.

Pompanon, F., Deagle, B. E., Symondson, W. O. et al. (2012). Who is eating what: diet assessment using next generation sequencing. *Molecular Ecology* 21(8): 1931–50.

Power M. E., Tilman, D., Estes, J. A. et al. (1996). Challenges in the quest for keystones. *BioScience* 46: 609–20.

Prugh, L. R., Stoner, C. J., Epps, C. W. et al. (2009). The rise of the mesopredator. *BioScience* 59(9): 779–91.

Rauzon, M. J. (2007). Island restoration: exploring the past, anticipating the future. *Marine Ornithology* 35: 97–107.

Rubenstein, D. R., Rubenstein, D. I., Sherman, P. W. and Gavin, T. A. (2006). Pleistocene Park: does re-wilding North America represent sound conservation for the 21st century? *Biological Conservation* 132(2): 232–38.

Salo P., Nordstrom M., Thomson R. L. and Korpimaki E. (2008). Risk induced by a native top predator reduces alien mink movements. *Journal of Animal Ecology* 77: 1092–98.

Seddon, P. J., Moehrenschlager, A. and Ewen, J. (2014). Reintroducing resurrected species: selecting de-extinction candidates. *Trends in Ecology and Evolution* 29(3): 140–47.

Soininen, E. M., Valentini, A., Coissac, E. et al. (2009). Analysing diet of small herbivores: the efficiency of DNA barcoding coupled with high-throughput pyrosequencing for deciphering the composition of complex plant mixtures. *Frontiers in Zoology* 6(1): 16.

South Georgia Habitat Restoration Project (2015). Project News Issue 27, available at www.sght.org/sites/default/files/SGHT%20Newsletter%20Aug%202015_0.pdf (last accessed 26 April 2017).

Spatz, D. R., Newton, K. M., Heinz, R. et al. (2014). The biogeography of globally threatened seabirds and island conservation opportunities. *Conservation Biology* 28(5): 1282–90.

Tatayah R. V.V ., Kett G., Zuel N. and Khadun A. (2007). Designing a plant cage to mitigate damage to seedlings by burrowing wedge-tailed shearwaters *Puffinus pacificus*, Round Island, Mauritius. *Conservation Evidence* 4: 9–12.

Taylor, P. D. and Merriam, G. (1995). Wing morphology of a forest damselfly is related to landscape structure. *Oikos* 1995: 43–48.

Temple, S. A. (1977). Plant-animal mutualism: coevolution with dodo leads to near extinction of plant. *Science* 197(4306): 885–86.
  (1981). Applied island biogeography and the conservation of endangered island birds in the Indian Ocean. *Biological Conservation* 20(2): 147–61.

Towns, D. R., Atkinson, I. A. and Daugherty, C. H. (2006). Have the harmful effects of introduced rats on islands been exaggerated? *Biological Invasions* 8(4): 863–91.

Towns, D. R., Borrelle, S. B., Thoresen, J., Buxton, R. T. and Evans, A. (2016). Mercury Islands and their role in understanding seabird island restoration New Zealand. *Journal of Ecology* 40(2): 235–49.

USFWS (US Fish and Wildlife Service) (1992). *Recovery Plan for the Puerto Rican Crested Toad (Peltophryne lemur)*. US Department of the Interior, Atlanta.

Varnham, K. J., Roy, S. S., Seymour, A. et al. (2002). Eradicating Indian musk shrews (*Suncus murinus*, Soricidae) from Mauritian offshore islands, pp. 342–49 in *Turning the Tide: The Eradication of Invasive Species*. IUCN SSC Invasive Species Specialist Group, Gland.

Witmer, M. C. and Cheke, A. S. (1991). The dodo and the tambalacoque tree: an obligate mutualism reconsidered. *Oikos* 1991: 133–37.

WWF (2014). *Living Planet Report 2014: Species and Spaces, People and Places*. World Wildlife Fund, Gland.

Zimov, S. A. (2005). Pleistocene Park: return of the mammoth's ecosystem. *Science* 308: 796–98.

Zippel, K. (2005). Zoos Play a Vital Role in Amphibian Conservation, available at http://elib.cs.berkeley.edu/aw/declines/zoo/index.html (last accessed 26 July 2005).

11 · *Engaging Island Communities*
Social Marketing and Behaviour Change

PAUL BUTLER, JAMIESON A. COPSEY
AND CHARLIE GARDNER

11.0 Introduction

Human communities around the world exploit natural resources obtained
from the land and sea to support their lives and livelihoods. On islands, the
results of this exploitation have been exacerbated due in part to the relatively
high human densities reached and their history of colonisation and rapid
natural resource exploitation. Conservation interventions to reverse these
anthropogenic effects increasingly need to engage with human communities as a complement to more ecologically oriented work. Environmental
education programmes are often developed to engage communities with
the sustainability message but have to date had varying degrees of success at
promoting more conservation-oriented behaviours.

In this chapter we first explore a more nuanced understanding of the
'community' that needs to be engaged and provide some insights into
how human behaviour change can be achieved. We then devote the rest
of the chapter to considering some of the steps involved in delivering
a social marketing campaign which – while by no means consisting of
a silver bullet – we believe are helpful in informing any conservation
project where societal change is required to reduce threats to species and
systems. We conclude with reference to the need for more effective
evaluation of environmental education programmes in general in order
to both measure impact and refine our model and methods over time.

11.1 Know Your Audience

It is becoming an increasingly common feature to include 'local communities' within conservation projects. This term is of limited utility to

conservation practitioners, however, who need to identify the target group, or groups, within the community with which to engage. A commonly held definition of a 'community' is 'groupings of people who physically live in the same space ... derive a unity from common history and cultural heritage ... [and] share interests and control over particular resources' (IIED 1994). This definition suggests that we can draw an imaginary line around a group of people and distinguish them as a 'community', separate from other communities. It also suggests that they share a common reliance on the natural resource base (including species) and that all would be equally affected by any change in access to it.

In reality, communities are much more complex than this. Rather than considering them to be largely homogeneous structures that can be communicated with as a single unit, we need to move to a more nuanced understanding of these loose social groupings. A useful way of looking at communities is as being composed of 'multiple actors with multiple interests' (Agrawal and Gibson 1999), their individual behaviour being moderated by cultural and social norms (accepted ways of behaving) and institutions that set the boundaries of 'acceptable' behaviour. This definition recognises that communities are composed of subgroups of *individuals*.

This situation is well illustrated through the case study of fishers and rice cultivators living within the same 'community' adjacent to Lac Alaotra, the largest lake in Madagascar (Box 11.1). For conservation practitioners, this example highlights that while we may wish to influence the understanding, attitudes or behaviour of a community, different groups within it are likely to require different approaches if we are to

---

Box 11.1 *Diversity within the 'Community': Lives and Livelihoods Around Lac Alaotra, Madagascar*

Lac Alaotra is the largest lake on Madagascar, covering an area of 20,000 hectares in the central highlands of the island (Andrianandrasana et al. 2005). The 23,000-hectare wetland bordering the lake supports the critically endangered Alaotran gentle lemur *Hapalemur alaotrensis* (Groves 2005). Lac Alaotra is also home to over 550,000 people who live along its shores (Plan Régional de Développement 2003; Figure 11.1).

Figure 11.1 Life in the marsh. A typical house built of reeds and located within the reed bed surrounding Madagascar's largest lake, Lac Alaotra. People rely on the lake for their livelihoods, though underlying socio-economic pressures may contribute to unsustainable land use practices. (*Photo credit:* Jamieson A. Copsey.) (A black and white version of this figure will appear in some formats. For the colour version, please refer to the plate section.)

One of the biggest threats to the wetland habitat surrounding the lake is annual burning during the dry season. In 2004 alone, the wetland was reduced to almost 47 per cent (10,816 hectares) of its previous size in this way (Durrell 2006). An anthropological study was conducted in 2007 (Copsey et al. 2009a, 2009b) to better understand the socio-economic realities of life for people living around the lake and to understand the ultimate drivers of the burning. The target stakeholder groups for the study were fishers and rice cultivators, as the dominant livelihood groups within the study village. While interview respondents expressed concern for the deterioration in the wetland habitat, there was a more pressing concern.

Small-scale fishers described how large-scale fish buyers would secure their loyalty by providing them with financing during times of difficulty, the result being that these fishers were required to sell their catches at below-market rates. Other groups of fishers described how fishing provided a useful additional income, with rice cultivation being practiced for subsistence. Fishers conveyed a desire to move into rice cultivation, perceiving that as a more reliable livelihood. However, when asked, rice cultivators described their own livelihood security issues, such as flooding of rice fields resulting in complete loss of harvests, although such impacts were less of a concern for more wealthy rice growers. Fishers and rice cultivators recognised the need to maintain the wetland habitat and limit its conversion. However, more pressing short-term concerns were what they were trying to contend with, affecting different subgroups within each livelihood sector to different degrees and in different ways. Fishers expressed support for a closed fishing season to allow stocks to recover, but they also saw this as a barrier to behavioural change due to the lack of alternative jobs during the closed season.

This case study illustrates some of the obstacles to behaviour change as well as the diversity that is often found within the 'community'. By understanding these differences, we can develop a much more realistic picture of whom we are trying to engage and what their specific concerns might be. It also raises the question, when we decide to engage with a community, to which group should we be pitching our engagement efforts?

engage them in issues that are relevant to their lives at any particular point in time. Identifying the particular group on which to target our efforts will depend on what the conservation project is trying to achieve, i.e. its goals, mission or vision (see Section 6.5). Are we simply aiming to raise levels of awareness about an environmental issue? Do we want to challenge existing attitudes? Or are we trying to facilitate a shift in what people do? In other words, do we want to change human behaviour?

11.2 From Knowledge Provision to Behavioural Change

Conservation is as much about people as it is about wildlife and wild places. People are the root cause of most of the threats that our environment faces, but they are, or can be, the solution too. Conservation without community engagement is a recipe for disaster, as is the belief that simply providing people with information will automatically result in changed behaviour – a view aligned with the 'knowledge-deficit model' (Durant et al. 1989). Increased knowledge *alone* does not typically change behaviour (Zain 2012). Many of us are aware of the damage done to the environment by driving cars or to our own health by smoking, yet many of us drive and still smoke.

Too many traditional environmental education programmes, on islands and elsewhere, focus narrowly on the transference of knowledge and information in their desire to change behaviours without under-standing and removing the barriers that prohibit change from taking place. Neither do they always make the best use of the rational and emotive arguments (Box 11.2) that help to facilitate change. Unless you make public transportation easy, cheap and ubiquitous while

---

Box 11.2 *The Elephant and Rider*

We are frequently of split mind when it comes to change, and this is no surprise, because it reflects the way we're wired. Psychologists say there are two independent systems in our brains. First, there's the rational, analytical, problem-solving side of our brain, which may think, 'I need to eat less'. But there's an emotional side of our brain that's addicted to impulse or comfortable routines. The rational side of us may understand the need to reduce carbon emissions. But the emotional side reacts with disgust if reducing emissions means we can't vacation in Hawaii.

The emotional side is much more powerful. Psychologist Jonathan Haidt (2006) says, if you want to understand your brain, picture a human rider atop an elephant. The rider represents our analytical, planning side. The rider decides, 'I need to go somewhere, and here's the direction I want to go', and sets off. But it's the elephant, the emotional side, that's providing the power. The rider can try to lead the elephant, but in any direct contest of wills, the elephant is going to win – it has a six-ton weight advantage. That power imbalance is what makes a diet hard and, by extension, any kind of change – it's not easy to think our way into change. So, if you want to lead change, in your organization or in society, you've got to speak to both sides of the brain, pointing out the direction for the rider but also motivating the elephant to undertake the journey.

To Read More: See Heath, C., & Heath, D. (2011). *Switch: How to Change Things When Change Is Hard*. Waterville, ME: Thorndike Press.

simultaneously making driving less attractive (e.g. restricted parking places and increased cost), people will continue to drive. The design of a campaign must begin with a thorough understanding of the audience and the societal norms, values, customs and behaviours that guide their lives. The messages that these campaigns deliver must be easily understood, compelling and have a clear call to action. What do we want the recipients of our message to do, and why might adopting the new behaviour be beneficial to them! It is not about us and what we need; it is about them.

Effective messaging begins with understanding the societal and conservation context in which destructive behaviours are rooted – the who, what and why that lie behind the environmental threat. The conservation context requires us to understand and articulate the desired conservation outcomes, the direct and indirect threats that affect these outcomes and the behaviours that drive them (e.g. Ervin et al. 2010). The societal context includes understanding the values, beliefs, habits and social norms of those engaged in the behaviour we are striving to change (e.g. destructive fishing, bush meat trade, etc.), as well as understanding the positive, negative and perverse incentives that may influence the prevailing and desired behaviours (Ervin et al. 2010; St John et al. 2013).

Understanding the conservation outcomes we desire, the threats that need to be reduced or mitigated and the underlying behaviours that cause the threats, as well as the context in which these are embedded, enables us to design a campaign strategy and develop a 'theory of change' (e.g. Harries et al. 2014; Rare 2014).

There is no unifying theory of behavioural change. Various models have been developed supported by varying degrees of evidence to explain what steps are involved (Table 11.1). What most agree on is that environmental behaviours are influenced by an interaction between our emotions, attitudes, beliefs, identities, knowledge, worldviews and values (Braus 2013). In addition, many also point to the need to understand the social and cultural contexts in which people operate if we are to understand how behaviours are influenced and sustained or abandoned. Some useful pointers for busy conservation managers who need to manage not only the biological aspect of species conservation projects but also the human dimension are that:

Table 11.1 *A Sample of Behavioural Change Theories That Exist*

Theory	Description	Relevance to environmental educators
Environmental citizenship behaviour model	Variables such as ecological knowledge, empathy towards the environment and knowledge of the consequences of particular behaviours combine to encourage the individual adoption of environmentally responsible behaviours.	This theory highlights the need to build the connection between people and their environment. If we can encourage personal investment in the environment and provide the skills and understanding to do things differently, we increase the likelihood of change occurring.
Value–belief–norm model	Behaviours arise as a consequence of personal belief and values. The theory highlights three value groups to be considered: biospheric (those linking people with the planet), altruistic (those which benefit the community), and egoistic (a belief in actions that benefit oneself).	Environmental education programmes that acknowledge and build on an individual's beliefs and values have a greater chance of achieving behaviour change, whether these values are largely self-centred or directed towards the wider world.
Reasonable person model	The underlying principle is that people want to understand the world around them and are motivated to help find solutions to recognised problems.	Environmental educators should involve target groups in determining their solutions to shared problems. An assumption is that people feel that they have the skills and power to effect change.
Systems thinking	This model assumes that for people to make informed decisions about actions to be	This theory encourages us to raise understanding about the interconnectedness of

Table 11.1 (cont.)

Theory	Description	Relevance to environmental educators
	taken, they must first understand how systems work and both the direct and indirect linkages between their own actions and environmental consequences.	life on Earth. Unless we can appreciate how species, habitats and ecosystems are connected (and linked back to humans), we cannot fully appreciate the social and biological ramifications of our actions.
Diffusion of innovation	This theory was developed to explain why some ideas succeed in spreading through a community, with people varying in their willingness to take up new behaviours.	This theory highlights the importance of identifying 'opinion leaders' within a community who might be more willing to take up the new actions and can influence others to do the same.
Stages of change	This theory posits that people go through stages in their adoption of new behaviours, from 'pre-contemplation' through to 'preparation', action and maintenance.	This theory identifies the value of knowing what stage a group of people are at within the behavioural change process and modifying the engagement approach accordingly.

Sources: Adapted from Jacobson et al. (2006) and Braus (2013).

1. We need to spend more time understanding what our target audience already knows, feels, believes and practices to determine how most effectively to engage them; and that, in general,
2. Knowledge does not equal behavioural change, nor does a lack of it prevent shifts in how people behave. Our cultural or spiritual beliefs

and how our behaviour is viewed by the wider social group with which we associate all exert powerful influences over how we behave; and that

3. Empowerment is the key to behavioural change. If our target audience believes that the costs (financial, social, etc.) of adopting a behaviour outweigh the benefits of changing that behaviour, there will be a reluctance to make the shift, even if the understanding and positive attitudes towards change exist. In Box 11.1, fishers around Lac Alaotra in Madagascar were in agreement with the seasonal fishing ban on the lake, but the lack of alternatives to support them and their families during this period resulted in some of them reporting that they continued to fish during this time. If we want to effect change, then we must recognise these barriers and consider how we can reduce costs and increase benefits of the change desired.

11.3 Stages in Behaviour Change

Human behavioural change is a complex and convoluted process that may not follow exactly the same steps or be categorised as linear in all situations. However, an understanding of some of the processes that people go through to change their behaviour can greatly inform current environmental education practice, where behavioural change is a desired outcome. The first points to make are that when it comes to deeply rooted practices and beliefs, individuals do not typically change their behaviour for the same reasons or at the same time, and economics is not the only driver of change.

Think about it. What are some of the reasons you might take up jogging? Perhaps you are concerned about your health or your doctor recommended it; perhaps you have joined a new group of friends that all jog in the morning. How about riding a bike to work? Maybe it is for health reasons, maybe to save money or perhaps for the sheer enjoyment of having the wind in your hair? Or what about buying that electric car? Perhaps it is to align with your environmental ethos or to be seen to be a leader. Understanding what might motivate someone will help in the design of messages that resonate with the targeted audience. People are not a single, homogeneous group all having the same beliefs and approaches to life. Neither do we all have the same propensity for change.

One way to view patterns and trends of behavioural change within a society is as the 'diffusion of an innovation' (Rogers 1995).

The concept of diffusion of innovation recognises that individuals within any group will adopt new behaviours at different rates and should be targeted in different ways. 'Innovators' are considered to be the first group to purchase a new product or adopt a new behaviour. This is a relatively small group of individuals who enjoy taking risks, like to be seen as being the first to buy or do something. Think of your friends who line up early in the morning to buy the latest phone and then cannot resist showing you just how wonderful it is and all the new applications it has and yours does not. Your message to this group is that what you are promoting is new and exciting. According to Rogers, 'early adopters' are the next group of people to buy into a new idea or product. They are often swayed by the innovators and are followed by the 'early majority' (who may need more convincing over how the benefits outweigh the costs of the new adoption). The 'late majority' and then, ultimately, the 'laggards' (again, a comparatively small group) are typically the most resistant to change and indeed may never change. Think of your friends who steadfastly refuse to use the latest iPhone.

There is often a critical point when the purchase of a new product or the adoption of a new behaviour becomes a societal trend and a new 'social norm'. Two decades ago, hybrid automobiles were a novelty and remained so for many years, but now they are widespread, and while they are not yet a new norm with the majority of drivers, they don't seem quite so scary or weird.

Societal changes begin small, but if the conditions are right and barriers to adoption are removed, they can spread quickly (Gladwell 2000). Creating societal change requires people who are connectors and the power of persuasive conversations, which is why interpersonal communication is a key component in Rare's theory of change (Rare 2014). People talking with people they trust and perceive as knowledgeable helps to facilitate and expedite change or, conversely, can grind it to a halt. You are thinking about jogging and your doctor encourages you, so what do you do? What if he or she were to strongly advise you against jogging, fearing that it might result in a heart attack? What would you do?

11.4 Social Marketing As a Behavioural Change Tool

Many behaviours are deeply rooted in cultural or social beliefs, habits and practices. To change such behaviours, you need to first understand and be able to influence the underlying social context. Such a journey takes us beyond traditional forms of environmental education into the realms of social marketing. Social marketing draws on a range of techniques to target and change specific behaviours in order to achieve a 'social good'. Such initiatives illustrate that the message being conveyed must appeal to the heart as well as the head if it is to be an impetus for attitude and behavioural change (Box 11.2).

The conservation world is only just beginning to draw on this evolving field, going beyond awareness-raising towards changing natural resource-use behaviours in order to conserve and restore endangered species and habitats. Social marketing principles encourage us to recognise that to change a behaviour, we must first identify and understand the motivations of the specific group of people whose behaviour we most want to change (Ervin et al. 2010). The approach appreciates that while the content of the message is important, so too is the medium used to convey it. One of the most potent and direct ways to change attitudes and social norms is through interpersonal communications, as individuals turn to trusted individuals to validate new information or to seek advice. Such interpersonal communication can serve multiple functions, such as clarifying how trusted opinion leaders feel about a new behaviour, verifying the risk/rewards inherent in adopting the behaviour or helping to gauge the social acceptability of the behaviour. Social marketing programs have been shown to stimulate interpersonal communication, which can then serve as a trigger to behaviour change (Rogers et al. 1999). These interpersonal communications can take place in informal one-on-one conversations or in more structured environments such as workshops and meetings.

Social marketing has been shown to be effective at changing attitudes and ultimately leading to more sustainable natural resource management practices. In Madagascar, for example, Andriamalala et al. (2013) demonstrated how such an approach led to more positive community support for locally enforced fishing regulations and a 63 per cent reduction in specific destructive fishing practices. Despite this, relatively few conservation organisations to date have adopted a social marketing approach to their public engagement and behavioural change work (Wright et al. 2015). One organisation that has pioneered the process is the conservation organisation Rare (www.rare.org; Jenks et al. 2010). In the remainder of this chapter we take a close look at the Rare model as a case study for achieving behavioural change. While we do not claim that this model provides a panacea for all situations, it does highlight a number of important steps we should consider if we see behavioural change as contributing to achieving our conservation goals (Rare 2009). It is important to note that the model itself is evolving as Rare strives to scale its impact and reduce costs.

11.5 The Rare Theory of Change Model

The Rare theory of change (ToC) is an elaboration of a behaviour change model developed by Vaughan and Rogers (2000) to understand the impact of mass media radio soap operas on reproductive health behaviours (Figure 11.2). The Rare model posits that most people adopt new behaviours in response to a changes in knowledge and attitudes, interaction and communication with peers and removing barriers and creating the enabling conditions that make behaviour adoption easier (Prochaska et al. 1992; Ervin et al. 2010; Table 11.2). Individuals are motivated by new information and the influence of peers and opinion leaders garnered through interpersonal communication (Rogers 1995). The model also assumes that many individuals carefully observe the results achieved by early adopters of the behaviour before they adopt themselves (Bandura 1994). Rare's two main additions to the Vaughan and Rogers model are (1) the importance of identifying barriers to behaviour change and including mechanisms to reduce or eliminate the barrier(s) in order to create the enabling conditions in which change can occur and (2) the inclusion of additional stages so that the model extends beyond behaviour change to include threat reduction and the desired conservation result.

It is important to note that while appearing linear, in many instances progression along the theory of change may require inputs of additional knowledge or a fostering of further interpersonal communication for progress to continue. An individual may not have formed attitudes about the behaviour in question until after he or she has communicated with peer groups and has internalized the attitudes of the groups to which he or she belongs. Further, individuals are likely to lapse after having adopted a behaviour and will need to be re-motivated. The model helps to inform the development of a public engagement programme designed to achieve specific behavioural changes, beginning with an understanding of what the societal and conservation context is for a given species or system.

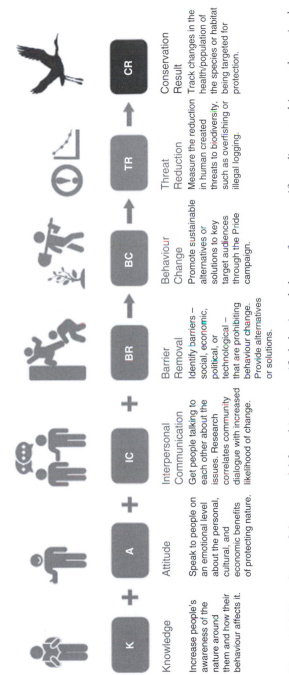

K	A	IC	BR	BC	TR	CR
Knowledge	Attitude	Interpersonal Communication	Barrier Removal	Behaviour Change	Threat Reduction	Conservation Result
Increase people's awareness of the nature around them and how their behaviour affects it.	Speak to people on an emotional level about the personal, cultural, and economic benefits of protecting nature.	Get people talking to each other about the issues. Research correlates community dialogue with increased likelihood of change.	Identify barriers – social, economic, political, or technological – that are prohibiting behaviour change. Provide alternatives or solutions.	Promote sustainable alternatives or solutions to key target audiences through the Pride campaign.	Measure the reduction in human created threats to biodiversity, such as overfishing or illegal logging.	Track changes in the health/population of the species or habitat being targeted for protection.

Figure 11.2 Rare theory of change model for achieving specific behavioural change from a specific audience to drive predetermined conservation outcomes.

Table 11.2 *A Simplified Example of How This Model Can Be Used to Develop Campaign Goals*

Theory of change stages	Goals set for each stage within the campaign
Knowledge	Local leaders and fishing communities will gain knowledge about the local law in place (*dina*) to control fishing methods used and its relevance to sustaining local fish stocks.
Attitudes	Workshops and village events will enable village leaders and the fishing community to feel more responsible for enforcing the local *dina*.
Interpersonal communication	Local leaders and the fishing community will talk among themselves about illegal fishing methods (beach seining and poison fishing) and how to halt their use locally as well as about local fishing regulations (dina).
Barrier removal	The conservation organisation running the campaign will run leadership training for local leaders and assist in the enforcement of the *dina*.
Behavioural change	Local leaders will enforce the *dina* in all situations where it is infringed. The fishing community will also report any *dina* infringements.
Threat reduction	All forms of illegal, destructive fishing techniques will be reduced, in particular, beach seining.
Conservation result	There will be an increase in the near-shore juvenile fish and reef fish abundance and diversity by 5 per cent by 2015, compared to the control site.

Source: Adapted from Andriamalala et al. (2013).

11.6 Understanding the Societal and Conservation Context

Understanding the broader context in which threats to conservation occur is the starting point for any effective social marketing program. This process (adapted from CMP Open Standards for the Practice of Conservation Version 3.0 2013) begins with understanding the conservation context. It requires clearly identifying the key biodiversity targets – the species, natural communities and ecological systems – that are important within a given area. Good conservation targets should represent the biodiversity and/or ecosystems at the site, reflect the goals of your conservation work (and that of others at the site) so that they will be affected by the campaign, be viable or restorable so that conservation efforts can be effective and be threatened so that they provide a worthwhile goal to aim for (Box 11.3; see also Section 9.1.1 and fundamental objectives). Ground-nesting terrestrial or sea birds are good examples of the sorts of species groups that might fall into these categories on islands, given their importance within island ecosystems, level of threat and vulnerability through overharvesting or predation by invasive vertebrates and their ability to be restored.

Box 11.3 *Promoting Protection Through Pride*

In the Abaco Islands of the Bahamas, size matters, at least when it comes to delivering a Rare Pride Campaign to reduce overfishing of the Caribbean spiny lobster *Panulirus argus*. Abaco is one of the Bahamas' largest exporters of the popular seafood (also known as crawfish), whose wild population has steadily declined in recent years due to overharvesting and illegal fishing techniques. Although a law was already in place to prevent harvesting lobsters with tails smaller than five and a half inches, many locals did not know about the regulation, much less abide by it. So, in 2009, Friends of the Environment launched a Pride Campaign using social marketing tools to raise awareness and reduce the harvesting and sale of juvenile lobsters.

Along the way it was discovered that even the fishers who already knew about the size restrictions had no means to actually measure their catch. So over three hundred size gauges were distributed to local fishers and more than four hundred fishers attended meetings on a proposed sustainable-catch certification training program.

Major buyers have reported that since the launch of the campaign, undersized tails being sold to them have been drastically reduced; much to their surprise, in some cases they have not received any undersized tails. With the help of the campaign mascot, 'Spike the Lobster' (Figure 11.3A), and catchy slogan, 'Size Matters' (Figure 11.3B), the campaign quickly took Abaco by storm and has since begun to spread throughout the Bahamas. A follow-up grant from Rare was provided to help launch a restaurant certification program for establishments that agree to only serve mature lobsters.

(a)

(b)

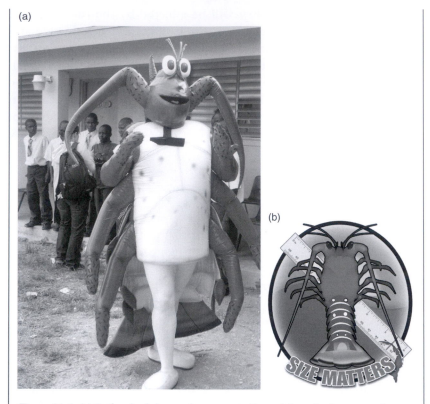

Figure 11.3 (a) Spike the lobster, the mascot of a social marketing campaign to influence harvesting of undersized lobsters in the Bahamas. (b) The campaign slogan 'Size Matters'. The campaign identified a barrier to fishers avoiding harvesting undersized lobsters: they had nothing to measure them with! The campaign distributed size gauges to fishers for this purpose. (*Photo credit:* Amy Doherty (Rare) 2010.) (A black and white version of this figure will appear in some formats. For the colour version, please refer to the plate section.)

This Pride Campaign was so successful in spreading the awareness on the importance of harvesting only mature lobster that the 'Size Matters' campaign and slogan are still talked about today, nearly ten years later, especially when August 1 nears, the date that the annual season opens for spiny lobster fishing.

Inspiring locals to adopt sustainable fishing practices is helping the Bahamas to maintain thriving fisheries and healthy marine ecosystem.

Source: Friends of the Environment (www.friendsoftheenvironment .org/.)

The second step is to identify the specific threats to the key biodiversity targets. Some of the sources of information we can turn to to help us build a picture of what is driving a species population down are given in Chapter 5. Stakeholder workshops are a useful vehicle for accessing much of this information, whereby people with a vested interest in the biodiversity target are brought together to discuss and develop a concept model of the main threats and how they are connected (Figure 11.4).

Once threats to the key biodiversity targets have been identified, there then needs to be an assessment of how threatened these biodiversity targets are. This is often summarised as a composite measure of the scope, severity and irreversibility of threats to biodiversity in order to prioritise the focus and actions of the social marketing campaign to follow. Software tools (e.g. *Miradi*; www.miradi.org) can help to conceptualise and rank threats identified by stakeholders to detail the prevailing situation at a project site. For example, Rare's campaign for sustainable fisheries management in Abaco (the Bahamas; Box 11.3), the Rare campaign manager worked with stakeholders to rank threats to the local population of the spiny lobster *Panulirus argus*. While threats such as pollution, habitat degradation, larval predation and natural disasters were all identified as important, overfishing of undersized individuals was ranked as the highest threat to this conservation target and became the focus of the campaign.

The third step is to understand *why* those threats are occurring. A good concept model includes not only the scope of the project, its key biodiversity targets and the direct threats that affect them but also the indirect threats and contributing factors that serve as root causes. Identifying and articulating these will help conservation practitioners to understand what behaviours lie behind a specific threat and who needs to be targeted. For example, deforestation may be a direct threat to a given species. Knowing this is important, but understanding why it is taking place is even more critical. Is it industrial logging that is clearing the forest or smallholders? If the latter, are they clearing the forest to open up new areas for cultivation, for construction timber or for fuel wood? Is the situation being exacerbated by a lack of area demarcation, policies that incentivise clearing, poor enforcement or corruption? If the clearing is for fuel wood, is this because there is a lack of alternate energy sources or because the smallholders cannot afford them? Unless the root causes are recognised and target audiences identified, a campaign may focus on the wrong threat, the wrong behaviour, the wrong audience or convey the wrong message.

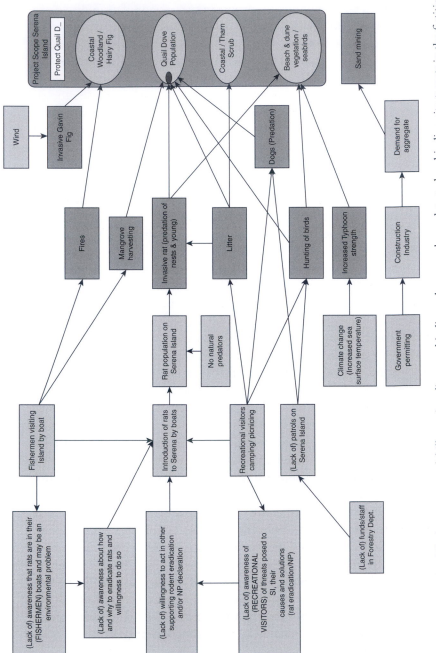

Figure 11.4 A simplified concept model illustrating direct and indirect threats as they relate to key biodiversity targets in the fictitious island of Andrea.

The fourth step is to understand the social, cultural, economic and political context in which threats take place (Ervin et al. 2010). This includes the values, norms, belief systems, practices, customs, traditions and policies (including the positive, negative and perverse incentives) that influence how individuals within society behave (Liu et al. 2015). For example, the belief that monkeys are the human form of the Hindu god Hanuman is likely to influence public views surrounding the control or eradication of invasive rhesus macaques *Macaca mulatta* in Mauritius.

Qualitative (in-depth interviews or focus group discussions with members of target audiences) and quantitative (formal knowledge, attitude and practice (KAP) surveys) research can be used to both ascertain the societal context and identify key audiences. An easy-to-use tool for creating and analysing questionnaire surveys is *SurveyPro* (Apian 2015), although others exist, including *Survey Monkey* (www.surveymonkey .com), which may also prove to be more cost-effective.

11.7 Identifying Key Audiences

Environmental education programmes often target school children or some other relatively easy to access group within society. While there may be a clear rationale behind this focus (e.g. see Box 11.4), it is all too common for such projects to fail to address sufficiently the group within society that is engaging in the behaviour we seek to influence. Social marketing approaches encourage deeper thought around the group of people (or 'stakeholders'; Section 7.1) to concentrate on if we want to achieve specific conservation goals. The target audience(s) will largely depend on the types of threats that are occurring and the types of behaviours that contribute to threats to biodiversity, assuming that it is human behaviour that is driving the problem rather than some other factor, such as disease.

Once identified, resources can be directed towards understanding how best to influence the behaviour of this group. For example, in addressing threats caused by the illegal use of dynamite to fish, conservation managers might identify fishers and their families, local fish market vendors and law enforcement agencies. In this step, it is important to understand the different ways that people learn and to identify how the target audiences are mostly likely to assimilate and understand new information and who they are likely to turn to for advice, so-called 'opinion leaders'. Key to success is the inclusion of the local stakeholders

Box 11.4 *A Focus on Empowering Children: International Eco-Schools Programme*

As Small Island Developing States (SIDS), island governments are being expected to prioritise and scale up effective education for sustainable development (ESD) to help communities build resilience and reduce the potentially tragic impacts of climate change (UNESCO 2014). One example is the European Union–funded Eco-Schools Indian Ocean programme (www.eco-schools.io) being introduced to the countries of Comoros, Madagascar, Mauritius and Zanzibar by the Indian Ocean Commission. Eco-Schools Indian Ocean is part of the International Eco-Schools programme of the Foundation for Environmental Education (FEE), an action-orientated 'whole institution approach' to ESD currently running in 62 countries worldwide (www.fee.global). Eco-Schools is a student-led approach that emphasises processes of critical reflection and action on the key issues that affect them. This contrasts with traditional 'instructive' approaches, whereby projects and objectives are driven by external experts (Wals 2010).

Students in Eco-Schools work collaboratively with multiple stakeholders from the schools and local communities to review their main environmental challenges (e.g. waste, water, energy, biodiversity, health, climate change, etc.), expanding formal curriculum learning, addressing critical issues within learning environments and developing skills and competencies through the creation of practical projects. For example, in Zanzibar, some students are addressing litter problems, energy needs and deforestation simultaneously by recycling paper waste into charcoal for their homes, while others are growing food to improve nutrition and planting trees to reduce soil erosion using wastewater recycled from local mosques.

Solutions such as these develop on crucial twenty-first century skills (www.p21.org) of collaboration, creativity and communication. They combine expert knowledge with advice from community elders, local tradespeople and craftsmen so that the resulting ESD is contextualised to meet specific needs of communities adapting to their most complex and important challenges.

in the development and design of the programme. Without this early local buy-in, campaigns are likely to fail in achieving their goals in part because they are perceived to be driven by the interests of external groups rather than coming from and aligning with the interests of the community.

11.8 Removing Barriers and Creating Enabling Conditions for Change

As noted earlier, simply changing knowledge and attitudes is often not enough to change behaviours. Social marketing campaigns not only must provide information but also must promote exchanges where the benefit of adopting a new behaviour outweighs the continuation of a current one. This is often referred to as the 'benefit exchange', whereby benefits are promoted and barriers to behaviour changes are removed. It is essential that before you begin to promote a new behaviour you are certain that the new behaviour is a viable option to the target audience and that there are few barriers to behaviour change that cannot be offset by the benefits of the change. Where the costs of changing the behaviour are unlikely to be offset, it may be better to pursue behaviour change through other means, such as lobbying the government to create and enforce legislation, rather than to try to persuade people directly. It is also critical to ensure that the campaign is fully integrated into the wider conservation goals of the programme so that the interventions identified are supportive of these goals rather than undermining them. For example, condoms distributed as part of a family planning campaign associated with a marine protected area in Madagascar were widely used by fishers to waterproof flashlights for night diving, thus reducing fisheries' sustainability and compromising the programme's goals. Insights from social marketing not only should fit in with broader institutional missions and objectives but also should even help drive them. In commercial marketing, for example, the work of the marketing team informs product development and company-wide decisions, but in conservation, it tends to remain peripheral. Social marketing for conservation should be thought of as a long-term approach rather than a one-off project aiming to change one behaviour.

Even when people are motivated to change and believe that they should, there may still be barriers that prevent them from doing so. These may be real or perceived. They may be political or financial, where economic incentives, existing policies or market conditions prevent change. Moving from conventional to organic agriculture improves the soil and can reap financial rewards once organic certification has taken place, but the process of certification is complicated and costly (especially for small, rural, often semiliterate smallholders), and the three-year transition time is risky (crop yields often dip, pests rise and new markets require sourcing). Without in-transition price premiums, guaranteed markets, pre-purchase agreements, risk insurance and technical assistance, change is hard.

Barriers might also be socio-cultural, such as when a society's values, norms, belief systems, practices, customs and traditions prevent an individual from behaving in ways that protect biodiversity and secure long-term benefits from nature. For example, curbing the practice of exotic 'prayer animal' releases by Buddhist and Taoist followers in Taiwan (Agoramoorthy and Hsu 2007; see Section 4.5.2) is likely to require more than information about the potential damage caused by introduced species. In such cases, an individual may believe that a change in behaviour will cause conflicts with friends and family members.

Some common approaches to removing barriers include the provision of tools, technologies or expertise required to support new practices. The provision of viable alternative livelihoods can encourage the shift from one practice to a more environmentally sustainable one. For example, in the Comoros Islands (Indian Ocean), conversion of forest to agricultural land poses a major threat to the islands' biodiversity; the islands experienced an estimated 24 per cent loss of forest cover between 1990 and 2015 (FAO 2015). In response, the conservation-with-development organisation *Dahari* (meaning 'sustainable' in Comorian) recognised through its interactions with local farmers that 'educating' them about the importance of maintaining the remaining forest blocks – as had happened in the 1990s – had not reduced this practice.

Instead, *Dahari* listened to community members who were fully aware of forest loss being a serious concern and who highlighted the impact of this loss on soil and water conservation. The organisation used this knowledge, combined with its biological understanding of the system, to build a theory of change detailing the links between more intensive and sustainable farming practices and forest conservation (Doulton et al. 2015). Subsequently, *Dahari* developed and trained farmers in a suite of agricultural techniques that improve yields and intensify production in lowland areas away from remaining forest while conserving water and soil (Doulton et al. 2015). While this project is still in its infancy, evidence is being gathered to show improved crop yields, soil and water conservation and farmer income, all of which is hoped to lead to a reduction in the incentive to convert remaining forest blocks. In 2015, farmers began to commit to reforesting water catchments and to protecting the remaining roost sites for the critically endangered Livingstone's fruit bat *Pteropus livingstonii.*

Sometimes, for change to happen, new policies or legislation is required. This may be to remove perverse incentives or to facilitate the legal establishment of positive ones. Municipal laws enabling the establishment of territorial use rights for fisheries coupled with reserves (TURF-reserves) – where local communities have the legal right to fish in a given area if they agree to set aside, protect and manage adjacent no-take-zones – are one example. Campaigns can also be used to garner public support for such policy changes and to encourage their political representatives to act.

In other cases, the primary obstacle to change may be cultural assumptions or preferences. A campaign needs to be cautious about trying to change these. However, there are ways to work respectfully within social norms. One way to change social norms may be to show how current values deviate from traditional values, such as references to religious mandates regarding environmental stewardship. Furthermore, religious instruction also changes in response to societal change, potentially providing positive gains for conservation. In the Cocos Islands (Indian Ocean), post-1980 shifts in Islamic teachings disapproving of and discouraging the practice of hunting sea turtles are likely to be one of the main factors leading to significant recovery of resident populations of green turtle *Chelonia mydas* and hawksbill turtle *Eretmochelys imbricata* (Macrae and Whiting 2014).

An alternate or complementary approach to removing perverse or negative incentives is to create positive new ones to compensate for the inherent inconvenience of switching behaviours. Positive incentives (e.g. tax reductions or the payment for ecosystem services, improved market access, social recognition, etc.) provide rewards for behaving in a certain way and help to promote environmentally sustainable behaviours, whereas disincentives (e.g. increased taxes, user fees, fines, penalties and social scorn) provide a punishment for continuing unsustainable resource behaviours (Ervin et al. 2010).

However, Kotler and Roberto (1989) argue that one of the key components of social marketing is that it needs to be a consensual exchange. Therefore, programmes that rely on excessive use of

Box 11.5 *Knowledge (K), Attitudes (A) and Behavioural Change: Case of the Saint Lucia Parrot*

Over the course of the past four decades, the Caribbean island of Saint Lucia has made impressive strides in changing local attitudes towards its national bird, from apathy to appreciation and pride. In the 1970s, Saint Lucians tended to view the endemic and endangered Saint Lucia parrot *Amazona versicolor* with ambivalence. It was hunted and traded, and its forest home was cleared for subsistence agriculture, fuel wood and timber. A social marketing campaign (that included songs, sermons, posters, billboards, costumes, puppets, pamphlets and community meetings) conducted by Saint Lucia's Forestry Department resulted in changed fortunes for the species. In a post-campaign survey undertaken in 1991, 97 per cent of those surveyed ($n = 496$) knew the parrot to be their national bird, 77 per cent knew it to be endemic and 55 per cent believed it to be very important to protect it (Rare, unpublished data, 1991).

A parrot sanctuary was established, the bird declared a national symbol and penalties (for hunting/trapping the bird) increased from EC\$5 to EC\$5,000 and/or a year's imprisonment. People are now aware of the species and its plight and take pride in their national bird, with the consequence that hunting and trade have been eliminated and forest destruction has slowed. Once numbering as few as 100 to 200 individuals (Butler et al., unpublished data, 1977), the population of this spectacular bird has recently been estimated to be between 1,750 and 2,250 individuals (Morton et al. 2011).

disincentives, especially administered by governments that may lack full participation and transparency, should be avoided. Nevertheless, in combination, disincentives and a targeted social marketing campaign can achieve desired conservation outcomes, as illustrated through work to recover the Saint Lucia parrot *Amazona versicolor* (Box 11.5).

11.9 Delivering the Campaign

Within the Rare model of social marketing there are a multitude of multimedia activities that can be drawn upon to engage particular target groups with a specific conservation message, including the use of billboards, songs, videos, religious sermons, radio spots and civic engagement activities (Jenks et al. 2010; Adriamalala et al. 2013; see Box 11.6). Here our concern is not to detail the use of each of these methods but to highlight a few generic points that we believe can help in the delivery of effective behavioural change programmes, in particular, where social marketing approaches are employed.

Box 11.6 *Rare Radio: Using Soap Operas to Inform and Change Behaviours*

The key to any successful social marketing project starts with tapping into the community's pre-existing culture. In the case of Saint Lucia, this meant leveraging the strong local devotion to soap operas such as *The Young and the Restless* and *The Bold and the Beautiful*. Beginning in February 1996, Rare and partners began airing a radio soap opera called *Apwe Plezi* to promote family planning, HIV prevention and related social issues. Running for three seasons until September 1998, the program took its name from the locally popular saying, 'Apwe plezi c'est la pain' (After the pleasure comes the pain).

The show featured positive role models with whom community members could come to identify but also negative ones demonstrating behaviours that those same people would collectively agree were socially unacceptable. Tony, for example, portrayed the particularly deplorable characteristics of alcoholism, physical abuse and promiscuity, whereas other transitional characters, such as Georgie, displayed similar characteristics early on but ultimately made the favourable transition to personal and sexual responsibility. These characters in particular were designed to serve as role models for the listening audience.

The impacts of the program were thoroughly assessed through a series of pre- and post-test surveys in addition to other complementary social research methods. Vaughan et al. (2000) found that among the more than 1,200 respondents to post-test surveys, 18 per cent of regular listeners reported having talked about the family planning content of the show, and 14 per cent reported having actually adopted a family planning method as a result. In pre-test surveys, 27 per cent of respondents considered it acceptable for husbands to have extramarital relations. That number dropped to 14 per cent by the time of the post-test surveys. Interestingly, condom importation to Saint Lucia increased from 45 per cent in 1998 to 143 per cent in 1999, supporting the hypothesis that *Apwe Plezi* bolstered demand for contraception among Saint Lucians. As in other developing countries, including many islands (e.g. Madagascar, Comoros), high population growth rates can have negative environmental consequences. Successful efforts to change attitudes towards contraception and family planning can help to reverse such trends (Vaughan et al. 2000).

It cannot be repeated enough that in order to be effective in our conservation work, we need to be clear about what exactly we are trying to achieve. Goal-setting with social marketing campaigns, as within other forms of public engagement activity, is of particular importance given the complexity of trying to influence what people do. As detailed in Figure 11.2, there may be a sequence of objectives that should be developed in order to act on different aspects of the problem. With a clear goal in mind, it is then possible to track back and determine what interventions are most likely to be most effective. Within goal-setting, it is important to understand – and be able to ensure that your target audience understands and can 'buy into' – the specific element(s) of biodiversity that you are seeking to conserve. For example, while there may be general concern over bush-meat hunting and its impact on mammal populations within a given habitat, social marketing approaches encourage deeper thinking over the 'product' (e.g. a named species) that we want people to 'buy' (i.e. conserve).

Rare social marketing campaigns often focus on a 'flagship' species (see Section 10.1) used to engender local pride and a desire to conserve the species and hopefully with it the wider natural community and ecosystem. This approach has proved effective with previously endangered species such as the Saint Lucia parrot (see Box 11.5). In this instance, the flagship species was threatened, and its conservation in the wild (in part through the protection of forest habitats) was likely to have positive spill-over effects for other species. Verissimo et al. (2011) provide a helpful analysis of the flagship species concept and suggest a framework for their selection, basing it partly on the attributes that appeal to the target audience and partly on the relationship between the species and the conservation issue of concern. In this way, flagship species can be chosen not from some predetermined list but tailored to the needs of the audience and the conservation issue at hand.

With your product in place, your target audience identified and theory of change developed, it is tempting to then launch the campaign. However, without a 'test run' or pilot program first, you run the risk of wasting resources and failing to achieve your goal. Piloting involves selecting a minimum of two subsets of your target audience, one of which you will test run your campaign on to see if it delivers the hypothesised change, the other being left as a control group (McKenzie-Mohr 2011). Your campaign is unlikely to be the only influence that your target audience is subject to, so by maintaining one subset as a control or comparison group (which is not exposed to the campaign), it is possible to determine whether or not your campaign has the desired effect (in terms of behavioural change) relative to other influences in society.

11.10 Sustaining Behaviour Change over Time

Marketing of all kinds is most successful when continuously reinforced. Even the biggest commercial brands continue to invest heavily in marketing, even when they have been established market leaders for decades. The long-term approach, coupled with continuity of personnel, is even more important for social marketing with local communities, much of which depends on building trust and fostering understanding through strong relationships. However, social marketing campaigns carried out by conservation non-governmental organisations (NGOs) are often tied to specific funding periods and thus time limited from their conception. For example, although the social marketing campaign to reduce destructive fishing practices in southwest Madagascar was effective in changing the attitudes and behaviour of traditional fishers (Adriamalala et al. 2013), it was only designed and funded to last for two years. This short-term, one-off approach can weaken the potential of social marketing for achieving long-term behaviour change, as any message can start to fade and weaken as the campaign comes to an end. With this proviso in place, social marketing campaigns can be effective in helping to sustain and build wider support for a new behaviour if maintained. Such a campaign can also include highly visible and local activities, such as having a flagship species' mascot march in a parade, viral text messaging and workshops that train 'para-educators'/spokespeople.

Individuals within target groups will vary in their willingness to adopt a new behaviour. Some individuals change their behaviour because they are motivated by rational and economic arguments. Others are motivated by intangible issues, such as pride of place, future generations, etc. (see Box 11.2). Campaigns should use a range of different arguments, including rational, economic, personal and emotional, in their media campaigns. They should also consider who is going to be the most effective communicator of the message. If a message comes from an influential spokesperson, such as a popular actor/musician, a community leader or a religious figure, it may be more effective in changing behaviour than if the message comes from a protected area manager. Additionally, influential people may not be famous, such as the wise neighbour, respected teacher or parish priest.

One of the best ways to reinforce a message is to hear it from different sources. For example, a parent whose child is entering an art contest on lobsters, who reads an article about lobsters in the newspaper, who sees a lobster mascot at a community meeting and who hears radio stories about the decline of lobsters is likely to begin to believe that lobsters are an important issue. This multipronged approach may be facilitated by coordinating between campaigns run by the same or different organisations. This also helps to ensure the consistency of the message heard.

A key factor driving the success of a campaign is that it be an integrated set of activities. No single marketing stimulus is likely to result in behaviour change, but the interaction of various stimuli is apt to have a reinforcing effect (Phillips et al. 2001). Conservation managers should not try to test the impact of one activity but rather the results of a series of activities around a common approach. For example, the use of an influential spokesperson is better if the message is repeated and coordinated with other campaign activities such as a radio program or school visits that discuss the message of the influential spokesperson.

11.11 Assessing and Monitoring the Impacts of Social Marketing Campaigns

Monitoring data then should be used to evaluate the effectiveness of campaign actions and, if necessary, to adapt the campaign as part of an adaptive management cycle (Gunderson 2015). Too few projects consider reliable and measurable indicators to measure progress towards achieving defined objectives and goals. Such indicators should be readily/reliably measurable using available technologies and staff, be reliable across time, be easily communicated to partners and other interested parties and measure the objective upon which the communication, education and awareness campaign is developed. Indicators should be developed for each objective, if possible. For example, if the conservation goal of a social marketing campaign is to reduce pressure on forests from illegal logging, a variety of indicators developed for objectives at each stage in the behavioural change process. Knowledge and attitude surveys could be conducted of people living adjacent to the campaign site to measure pre-/post-project change. To assess changes in social norms, values and perceptions researchers could interview people to ask how they perceived that others viewed illegal logging and whether or not they themselves had talked about the illegal logging and the benefits of forest protection with others in the community. The extent of illegal harvesting within the protected area could be measured and compared to levels prior to the campaign to engage the community to inform understanding of how the threat status had changed. Finally, to determine the change in conservation outcomes, measures such as forest integrity and fragmentation or population change within a threatened species could be employed. Many conservation projects measure change in attitudes, but this is insufficient because changed attitudes do not necessarily equate to changes in behaviour; it is therefore important to measure actual changes in behaviour or other outcomes explicitly (Verissimo 2013).

11.12 Summary

Key points from the chapter:

- Communities are composed of 'multiple actors with multiple interests', so efforts to engage at this level should identify which specific groups or individuals within the community have the greatest impact on the conservation issue of concern.
- Knowledge development does not automatically lead to behavioural change; different people will be at different stages in their knowledge, attitudes and willingness to change their behaviour at any point in time and so will require different stimuli to change.
- One approach to understanding the process of behavioural change is to view it as being stages that an individual goes through. This approach encourages conservation practitioners to spend more time understanding which stage the target audience is at in the process.

- The Rare theory of change approach begins with the conservation issue of concern and an identification of the cause–and–effect relationships between the concern and specific human behaviour.
- Changing human behaviour involves an understanding of the barriers to this change and how to influence and remove them.
- Behavioural change is a complex process that we still do not fully understand in all contexts. If we are to improve our practice, then we must build in monitoring and evaluation from the outset of our public engagement, social marketing or broad environmental education campaigns

References

Adriamalala, G., Peabody, S. T., Gardner, C. J., and Westerman K. (2013). Using social marketing to foster sustainable behaviour in traditional fishing communities of southwest Madagascar. *Conservation Evidence* 10: 37–41.

Agoramoorthy, G. and Hsu, M. J. (2007). Ritual releasing of wild animals threatens island ecology. *Human Ecology* 35(2): 251–54.

Agrawal, A. and Gibson, C. C. (1999). Enchantment and disenchantment: the role of community in natural resource conservation. *World Development* 27(4): 629–49.

Andrianandrasana, H. T., Randriamahefasoa, J., Durbin, J., Lewis, R. E. and Ratsimbazafy, J. H. (2005). Participatory ecological monitoring of the Alaotra wetlands in Madagascar. *Biodiversity & Conservation* 14(11): 2757–774.

Apian (2015). *Survey Pro 5*, available at www.apian.com/ (last accessed 16 January 2015).

Bandura, A. (1994). Social cognitive theory of mass communication, in J. Bryant and D. Zillman (eds.), *Media Effects: Advances in Theory and Research*. Erlbaum Associates, Mahway, NJ.

Braus, J. (2013). *Influencing Conservation Action: What Research Says About Environmental Literacy, Behavior, and Conservation Results*. National Audubon Society, New York, NY.

Conservation Measures Partnership (CMP) (2013). Open Standards for the Practice of Conservation Version 3.0, April 2013, available at http://cmpopenstandards .org/wp-content/uploads/2014/03/CMP-OS-V3-0-Final.pdf (last accessed 15 January 2015).

Copsey, J. A., Jones, J. P., Andrianandrasana, H., Rajaonarison, L. H. and Fa, J. E. (2009a). Burning to fish: local explanations for wetland burning in Lac Alaotra, Madagascar. *Oryx* 43(3): 403–6.

Copsey, J. A., Rajaonarison, L. H., Randriamihamina, R. and Rakotoniaina, L. J. (2009b). Voices from the marsh: livelihood concerns of fishers and rice cultivators in the Alaotra wetland. *Madagascar Conservation & Development* 4(1): 25–30.

Doulton, H., Mohamed, M., Shepherd, G. et al. (2015). Competing land-use in a small island developing state: using landscape approaches to manage sustainable outcomes in the Comoro Islands. Presented at the XIVth World Forestry Congress, Durban, South Africa, 7–11 September 2015.

Durant, J. Evans, G. and Thomas, G. (1989). The public understanding of science. *Nature* 340: 11–14.

Durrell, J. (2006). Annual Report 2006. Unpublished report, Durrell Wildlife Conservation Trust Programme, Antananarivo, Madagascar.

Ervin, J., Butler, P., Wilkinson, L. et al. (2010). *Inspiring Support and Commitment for Protected Areas through Communication, Education and Public Awareness Programs: A Quick Guide for Protected Area Practitioners* (Quick Guide Series). Rare, Arlington, VA.

Food and Agriculture Organisation (FAO) (2015). Country Report, Comoros, available at www.fao.org/3/a-az188f.pdf (last accessed 12 February 2016).

Gladwell, M. (2000). *The Tipping Point: How Little Things Can Make a Big Difference.* Little, Brown, Boston, MA.

Groves, C. (2005). Order primates, pp. 111–84 in D. E. Wilson and D. M. Reader (eds.), *Mammal Species of the World: A Taxonomic and Geographic Reference*, 3rd edn. Johns Hopkins University Press, Baltimore, MD.

Gunderson, L. (2015). Lessons from adaptive management: obstacles and outcomes, pp. 27–38 in C. R. Allen and A. Garmestani (eds.), *Adaptive Management of Social-Ecological Systems.* Springer, Netherlands.

Haidt, J. (2006). *The Happiness Hypothesis: Finding Modern Truth in Ancient Wisdom.* Basic Books, New York, NY.

Harries, E., Hodgson, L. and Noblem, J. (2014). *Creating Your Theory of Change: NPC's Practical Guide.* New Philanthropy Capital, London. Available at www .thinknpc.org/publications/creating-your-theory-of-change/ (last accessed on 20 January 2017).

Heath, C. and Heath, D. (2007). *Made to Stick: Why Some Ideas Survive and Others Die.* Random House, New York, NY.

Heath, C. and Heath, D. (2010). *Switch: How to Change Things When Change Is Hard.* Broadway Books, New York, NY.

IIED (1994). *Whose Eden? An Overview of Community Approaches to Wildlife Management.* International Institute for Environment and Development, London.

Jacobson, S. K., McDuff, M. D. and Monroe, M. C. (2006). *Conservation Education and Outreach Techniques.* Oxford University Press, Oxford.

Jenks, B. J., Vaughan, P. W. and Butler, P. J. (2010). The evolution of Rare Pride: using evaluation to drive adaptive management in a biodiversity conservation organization. *Evaluation and Program Planning* 33: 186–90.

Kotler, P. and Roberto, E. L. (1989). *Social Marketing: Strategies for Changing Public Behavior.* Free Press, New York, NY.

Liu, Z., Jiang, Z., Fang, H., Li, C. and Meng, Z. (2015). 'Consumer behaviour' change we believe in: demanding reduction strategy for endangered wildlife. *Journal of Biodiversity and Endangered Species* 3: 141.

Macrae, I., and Whiting, S. (2014). Positive conservation outcome from religious teachings: changes to subsistence turtle harvest practices at Cocos (Keeling) Islands, Indian Ocean. *Raffles Bulletin of Zoology* 30: 162–67.

McKenzie-Mohr, D. (2011). *Fostering Sustainable Behavior: An Introduction to Community-Based Social Marketing*, 3rd edn. New Society, Gabriola Island, BC.

Morton, M., Whitehead, H., Young, R., Dornelly, A. and Jean Baptiste, T. (2011). Status of the Saint Lucia Parrot *Amazona versicolor*. Report to the government of Saint Lucia.

Phillips, P., Davies, F. and Moutinho, L. (2001). The interactive effects of strategic marketing planning and performance: a neural network analysis. *Journal of Marketing Management* 17(1–2): 159–82.

Plan Régional de Développement (2003). Zone de Développement Rural Intégral de l'Alaotra (ZDRI), unpublished Report, CORDAL, Ambatondrazaka, Madagascar.

Prochaska, J. O., DiClemente, C. C. and Norcross, J. C. (1992). In search of how people change: applications to addictive behaviors. *American Psychologist* 47(9): 1102–14.

Rare (2009). *Rare Pride Leadership Development Program*. Rare, Arlington, VA.

Rare (2014). *Theory of Change for Community-based Conservation*. Rare, Arlington, VA. Available at www.rare.org/sites/default/files/ToC_Booklet_Final_Rare .pdf (last accessed on 20 January 2017).

Rogers, E. (1995). *Diffusion of Innovations*, 4th edn. Free Press, New York, NY.

Rogers, E. M., Vaughan, P. W., Swalehe, R. M. A. et al. (1999). Effects of an entertainment-education radio drama on family planning behaviour in Tanzania. *Studies in Family Planning* 30(3): 193–211.

St John, F. A. V., Keane, A. and Milner-Gulland, E. J. (2013). Effective conservation depends upon understanding human behaviour, pp. 344–61, in D. W. Macdonald and K. J. Willis (Eds.), *Key Topics in Conservation Biology 2*. Wiley-Blackwell, Chichester.

UNESCO (2014). *Roadmap Education for Sustainable Development*. Paris. Available at http://unesdoc.unesco.org/images/0023/002305/230514e.pdf.

Vaughan, P. W. and Rogers, E. M. (2000). A staged model of communication effects: evidence from an entertainment-education radio soap opera in Tanzania. *Journal of Health Communication* 5: 203–27.

Vaughan, P. W., Alleyne, R. and St Catherine, E. (2000). Effects of an entertainment-education radio soap opera on family planning and HIV prevention in St Lucia. *International Family Planning Perspectives* 26(4): 148–57.

Verissimo, D. (2013). Influencing human behavior: an underutilized tool in biodiversity management. *Conservation Evidence* 10: 29–31

Verissimo, D., MacMillan, D. C. and Smith, R. J. (2011). Toward a systematic approach for identifying conservation flagships. *Conservation Letters* 4: 1–8.

Wals, A. (2010). *Message in a Bottle: Learning Our Way Out of Unsustainability*. Wageningen University Press, Wageningen.

Wright, A. J., Veríssimo, D., Pilfold, K. et al. (2015). Making marine science matter: issues and solutions from the 3rd International Marine Conservation Congress. Competitive outreach in the 21st century: why we need conservation marketing. *Ocean & Coastal Management* 115: 41–48.

Zain, S. (2012). *Behavior Change We Can Believe In: Towards A Global Demand Reduction Strategy for Tiger*. TRAFFIC International, Cambridge.

12 · *Island Species Conservation*
What Are We Trying to Achieve and How Do We Get There?

SIMON A. BLACK AND JAMIESON A. COPSEY

12.0 Introduction

Throughout this book we have sought to identify elements of threatened species recovery projects that can contribute to success. We have drawn lessons from our understanding of both biological systems and distinctly human systems to inform our work. Threads that run through the chapters include the need for clarity of purpose and goals and to use diverse knowledge to inform our actions and learn from our mistakes.

In this chapter we apply the Beckhard organisational design model, introduced in Chapter 6, to provide a framework on which to hang an overview of the book, highlighting the need for improvements in our species conservation efforts not just around clarity of purpose and goals but also around the roles we assign to people within projects, the processes we expect them to manage and, finally, the relationships on which our work is built.

12.1 Species Conservation: Components of the Project

In Chapter 6 we introduced Beckhard's organisational design model, which provides a succinct picture of the elements that make up any species conservation project (Figure 12.1). The key for a manager is the extent to which these elements are regularly reflected upon, developed and refined to improve overall work performance and ultimately the recovery of threatened species. The model also provides us with a helpful structure upon which to 'join the dots' and present an image of species conservation and some lessons we have learnt from islands.

PURPOSE

A statement which provides a relevant and enduring focus for all involved.

The project purposed to restore high altitude forest (Box 6.1) on Maui, Hawaii is relevant today, next year and for decades into the future.

GOALS

Goals align short-term effort in line with overall purpose.

Efforts to recover the St Lucia Parrot *Amazona versicolor* were enabled once goals were shifted towards changing knowledge, attitude and regard that local people had towards the species (Chapter 5, Chapter 11, section 11.4.3). The purpose of saving the species nevertheless remained unchanged.

Recent recovery of the Island Fox *Urocyon littoralis* on the Californian Channel Islands (Box 8.2) required different goals on each island; on some invasive species removal, on others vaccination, and on one the reintroduction of Bald Eagles to reinstate balance across the ecosystem.

RELATIONSHIPS

People's interactions are a product of both the way we set up the programme and the personalities of those involved.

Demanding work conditions and shared accommodation for field-based teams makes it vital to eliminate any work irritations, and to agree a common set of values or team principles to maintain good morale (Box 6.2).

ROLES

Role clarity ensures, even in remote teams, that people work with confidence and authority.

Specialists (e.g. veterinarians and geneticists) provide practitioners in Mauritius (Box 3.3) with data to support management of Echo parakeets *Psittacula eques* including translocation.

PROCESSES

Conservation activities and the order of those tasks should be managed end-to-end as a process, including the interfaces between differing areas of work.

Ecosystem recovery on Gunner's Quoin, Mauritius (**Box 10.2**) required connected processes of alien species eradication, habitat recovery and translocation with embedded monitoring to aid learning and improvement.

Work to protect the Caribbean spiny lobster (*Panulirus argus*) in the Bahamas, identified that even fishers aware of regulations needed a method to measure their catch. Provision of tools enabled a significant reduction of undersized catches and saw recovery of the lobster population (Box 11.3).

Figure 12.1 An illustration of the Beckhard model in relation to conservation practice, drawing on examples from preceding chapters. (A black-and-white version of this figure will appear in some formats. For the colour version, please refer to the plate section.)

12.2 Defining Your Purpose

Clarity of purpose is one of the most important building blocks on which to construct species conservation projects or, in fact, any project that may be complex, long term and challenging. It defines why we are here and what we are aiming to achieve, often stretching over decades and possibly beyond the professional lifespan of the original people involved (see Section 6.5). Looking into the past (see Chapter 5), we can build an impressionistic picture of what populations and systems once looked like and help shape our sense of what we are trying to create or recreate (see Chapter 10). Our knowledge of small-population biology and genetics (see Chapters 2 and 3) now enables us to dig further back in time and sharpen the lines of evidence in the historical distribution or abundance of species that might now be in marginal habitats or critically low numbers.

Programme purpose must be informed by a proper understanding of current versus historical ecology of a species (see Chapters 2 and 5). For example, the Mediterranean monk seal *Monachus monachus* raises its pups in subterranean caves on islands in Turkey, yet this behaviour is a recent adaptation to human encroachment and disturbance of previous haul-out beaches. Breeding productivity is poor, with the species only making the best of a bad situation. A programme that simply perpetuates the current circumstances is unlikely to sustain or recover the seal population. Similarly, birds of the high-altitude forests of Maui may have opted for suboptimal habitat to find areas free of disease and alien mammalian competitors but may be less productive in those locations. These limitations need to be considered in the birds' recovery strategy.

This historical knowledge can be drawn upon by conservation managers – who clearly work in the 'now' – to inform the purpose of recovery plans and the future they are attempting to build (Figure 12.2). This knowledge provides clues to the types of interventions that will succeed and those which will not. The challenge is to know which avenues of knowledge to pursue within the limited resources we have available. The filter for this decision-making is a clear understanding of the purpose of the project.

The purpose of a project, if defined clearly and relevant to the context of the species and landscape of concern, has practical implications for the work of everyone involved, whether scientists, professionals, volunteers or members of a local community. Purpose must have a meaning that relates to the motivations of all people involved and so will, or should,

Figure 12.2 The place of conservation in time and space. A project's purpose must be relevant today, tomorrow, next year and for as long as the project has to exist.

reflect their values (see Sections 7.1 and 9.1.1). This point is well illustrated within the Rare theory-of-change model that underpins the organisation's social marketing campaigns (see Section 11.5). Step four in the Rare process is to understand the values, norms, belief systems, practices, customs and traditions that influence how individuals within society behave and so inform the development of the campaign and its 'purpose'.

Although often conservation efforts made today only bear fruit in future generations, maybe decades or even centuries ahead, the choice of a programme's purpose today will heavily influence that future. Breeding programmes for long-lived species such as the tortoises of Galapagos may only be realised after the lifetime of the professionals who currently curate those activities. Community programmes need to continue long after the scientists and field teams have left. Long-term motivations are also important in specialist replanting, such as in the high-altitude forests on Maui, the recovery of coral reefs, community tree planting in Madagascar and whole-island restoration in Mauritius (see Chapter 10). This legacy may itself be a motivation for the dedication of local people in those projects, drawing upon a reservoir of goodwill that today may still be a relatively untapped resource.

12.3 Establishing Goals and Alignment of Effort

In Chapter 9 we considered the difference between *fundamental* and *means* objectives, the former being synonymous with goals and important to distinguish as they frame what you actually want to achieve, as opposed to the 'means' by which you get there. For example, a fundamental objective might be to restore an island community of endemic species. In order to get there, one *means* objective might be to eradicate an introduced vertebrate from the island (see Chapter 7). Clarity between the two is important as they involve different resources being allocated in different ways and different perspectives on what 'success' looks like.

Skill in setting relevant goals often sets apart successful programmes from the unsuccessful. Goal-setting requires the practitioner to confront a paradox: to focus on short-term, feasible actions (often relevant to means objectives) but avoiding limitations caused by short-term thinking. Goals should be focused to deliver outputs that will help the programme to learn for the future. Acting fast is now an established concept in successful species recovery (see Chapter 8 and Section 9.3.2), with cases such as the po'ouli and Christmas Island pipistrelle bat illustrating the failures associated with not taking this approach.

A potential trap occurs when short-term goals become associated with the desire to demonstrate progress, a mode of thinking that sabotages long-term success. This is evident in programmes that set numerical 'targets'. A target is a quantified level of performance used with the intent of providing a focus for work activity. Targets are problematic in their failure to focus people on the species and ecosystems of concern or the required work (i.e. their true purpose), driven by three factors. The first problem is that 'activities' usually associated with targets are not in themselves the processes that deliver the purpose of a programme (Section 12.5). Secondly, targets are unlikely to be based upon knowledge (e.g. if a target is 'to breed 20 offspring', why not breed 21 or 50? Would breeding 19 or 17 be bad? If we raise offspring, from which parents or bloodlines should they be bred?). Thirdly, a target becomes a *de facto* purpose, distracting people's attention away from the programme's real purpose of conserving species and ecosystems, thereby risking redirection of people to work towards conflicting agendas, literally at 'cross-purposes'. Instead, the conservation manager should encourage the team to consider goals, both shared and individual, to provide a short-term focus that is entirely in line with the programme's core purpose.

At the same time, it is important, even in the light of a challenging purpose or an ambitious vision, not to waste time on unsolvable problems (see Section 8.7). In the face of threats, a programme may either focus on reduction of the threat, elimination of the threat or mitigation in the face of the continued threat. Each of these contexts will produce a completely different set of short-term goals. The programme should not simply do whatever is possible; it must do what is possible that will enable achievement of purpose and the long-term vision. Breeding lots of animals of a rare species may be possible now, but if they are unfit to survive in the wild, then the effort is futile and a waste of resources. By contrast, not making the effort to breed the species may mean loss of genetic diversity as well as loss of learning opportunities that may be vital in future years. A balance of appropriate effort is required.

Traditional detailed planning is built upon the flawed assumption that everything likely to occur is known in advance. In reality, knowledge ranges from unknowns, hunches and informed guesses, through to assumptions and inferences, towards associations and causation, up to the most concrete scientific facts (see Sections 8.8.3 and 9.2). The most effective conservation draws on the best available knowledge at the time when it is needed, and short-term goals should aim to continually inform this knowledge. Sometimes the 'near enough is good enough' analogy for knowledge still applies, and good science can explore hypotheses on the status of populations when time and resources permit, including comparisons with the historical genetic status of the population, as shown in Mauritius with population recovery of birds (see Boxes 3.2 and 3.3) and reptiles (see Box 10.2). Early intervention and recovery are essential not only to prevent extinction but also in the long-term sense of retaining genetic diversity across as mixed a group of individuals as possible (see Chapters 2 and 3). In practice, in the absence of definitive genetic knowledge of all representatives in a population, this means recovering as many individuals as quickly as possible and recruiting them into the breeding population. As practitioners, we sometimes need to set short-term goals on the basis of best available knowledge, not total or complete knowledge. Goals must be aligned and, where possible, mutually reinforcing. This can only be achieved through a solid understanding of the species and its context (see Section 9.1.2), shared discussion, awareness of current goals, agreement on new goals and an alignment by everyone involved behind the core purpose of the programme.

12.4 Roles and Apportioning Responsibility

Role clarity is important in defining not only core responsibilities and levels of authority but equally importantly the boundaries of people's work. Boundaries are important because they define the types of collaborative partnerships necessary to make the programme work. The best programmes encourage learning and improvement (see Section 8.8.5), and this relies on the willingness of staff to ask questions, identify mistakes and share experiences. Governance structures are important in defining roles such as project sponsor, project manager and other key decision makers (see Sections 6.2 and 7.7). All other roles should refer to that structure allowing people the responsibility and accountability so that they can get on with the work on the ground. Governance should enable, not stifle. Decisions need to be made by people who know the work and the needs of the species and ecosystems of concern.

Connections between areas of conservation work are also important to understand and to define within roles so that responsibilities at the interfaces do not fall between the gaps. Does the output or result of one area of work (e.g. alien species eradication) fit with another (e.g. habitat recovery and replanting)? Are captive bred animals fit for release? Is community support for a protected area strong enough to ensure future policing and monitoring by that community? Are new sources of income established so that previous destructive off-take in a recovered forest is averted? How is responsibility for completion and handover defined within people's roles, or is there a shared responsibility that is defined and agreed by the team as a whole?

Aside from the demands of working with community partners, the public or other stakeholder groups, conservation leaders also need to maximise the effectiveness of their own operational teams (see Sections 6.3, 8.6 and 8.9). This requires a sound understanding of human motivation (see Section 8.4.3) and how team members identify with the programme and their work. In order to tap into people's genuine motivation, it is necessary to enable team members to deeply identify with the purpose of the work. People working on a team should have a close affinity with the purpose of the project. This affinity allows people to commit effort, and it also enables people to commit to the 'norms' of the team – how it works, working conditions, tasks, working hours, necessary chores and routines, social interactions, support, advice, decisions and engagement in outward communications or external interactions in which the team is involved. When interactions with external stakeholders become the norm, then trust between the work of the team and the interests of affected people in local communities will grow.

In designing the structure of the programme's roles (whether at trustee, manager, practitioner, volunteer or community partner level), it is worth considering three principles of motivation from psychological theory: (1) the work needs to be relevant, simply defined and clear to understand, (2) people's efforts need to be focused on achievable goals and (3) people need to have an element of control over the action that is taken. Decision-making authority needs to be placed with the experts who have knowledge of what is happening on the ground. This requires a governance structure that ensures responsible oversight yet avoids a stifling bureaucracy.

12.5 Processes and Doing the Right Things at the Right Time

A variety of methods, techniques, activities, resources, data and information contribute to conservation work that managers need to oversee and coordinate as coherent 'processes'. The most important processes in a conservation programme must be defined from the purpose of the programme so that the work is aligned with overall direction, intentions and priorities. Over time, as the programme evolves and the content changes, processes will need to be reviewed, adapted and replaced to fit the context of the programme (see Section 9.3.3). For example, initial eradication processes for invasive plants and animals may be replaced in time by translocation processes to re-establish endemic wildlife to restored islands (see Chapter 10).

The concept of organisational processes can, however, be a stumbling block for professionals in many sectors, and wildlife conservation is no exception. A process is essentially a slice of a wider system. At its most basic, a process is a defined by (1) activities and (2) the flow between those activities. The appropriate activities and flow between them are defined by the purpose of the process. A task, or set of tasks, is not a process until defined with a specific purpose. 'Captive breeding' in itself is not a process until operational boundaries are defined by a purpose, which informs the process design. So 'captive breeding to produce individuals that survive and breed in the wild' differs from 'captive breeding of wild-sourced animals to accelerate population growth through released progeny'. Species behaviour, ecology and threats influence purpose. Similarly, invasive species management processes will be informed by understanding paths to invasion and purposes of eradication or mitigation (see Chapters 4 and 7).

Hypothesis-driven management interventions should be designed to either halt or reverse population declines and also to build understanding of the causes of decline (see Sections 9.1.2 to 9.1.4). Monitoring does not deliver conservation but should be embedded into process management to provide the knowledge required to inform decisions and actions. Emerging methods of measuring systems behaviour and assessing impacts of conservation work can be considered (see Section 8.8.4). Current gaps at the 'knowledge-action' or 'science-practitioner' boundary between scientifically focused research and practitioner needs can be overcome by identifying scientific questions that fit the need to understand the effectiveness of real work processes.

The best conservation processes are ones informed by small-scale experimentation that is up-scaled over time using knowledge derived from data and insight generated by the process itself. Techniques of island species and habitat recovery discussed in these chapters are well proven and have also been transferred and up-scaled effectively to mainland initiatives, for example, in Australia and India. As new information becomes available, conservation interventions can be modified through active, dynamic management for maximum impact (see Sections 5.5 and 5.6).

Scientific monitoring is a common component in conservation programmes (see Section 5.2) and is needed to accurately measure three things: (1) to identify changes through time (e.g. population size, range), (2) to compare differences (e.g. success of a species in different habitats), and (3) to quantify the impacts of a threat or conservation action (e.g. changes following the eradication of an invasive species). Various techniques have been discussed in preceding chapters for measuring these effects. Concepts of stochastic (random) and deterministic causes of change, particularly in assigning reasons for declines (such as human-induced decline) or recoveries (i.e. impact of conservation action) should be considered in the operational management of conservation. This is an area of significant learning for conservation science and relates to how we can close the knowledge-practice gap to enable improved conservation performance. Monitoring needs to be undertaken at various stages in the process to inform the flow (i.e. order) of activity.

12.6 Relationships

The first point that should be reiterated with regard to Beckhard's organisational design model, is that often within projects while it may seem that there are 'relationship issues', the underlying cause is often related to a lack of clarity or agreement around the purpose or goals of the project, blurring of roles or the establishment of ineffective or over-complex processes; i.e. ask yourself first whether one of these other components is in question before assuming that there are relationship issues at play! However, few conservation programmes, even on the remotest uninhabited islands, can escape the dynamic of human relationships. Most people will have to deal with colleagues on their project team. On inhabited islands, conservation efforts are embedded in a social, cultural, political and economic context. Local people may have knowledge that can inform scientific understanding of the species and ecology of the environment (see Section 5.1.3). Human interaction is largely an inevitable feature of work, be it with local communities, partner organisations, researchers, politicians and business people, yet for many scientifically trained conservation professionals it can be an unfamiliar challenge.

Work with local communities cannot be an afterthought to more conventional conservation strategies, nor should it be seen as a 'nice to have' element in a conservation plan (see Sections 7.1 and 9.3.1). Conservation interventions that aim to reverse anthropogenic effects need to engage with human communities and encourage behavioural change, and this requires an understanding of psychology (see Section 8.8 and Chapter 11). The theory of planned behaviour tells us that people's intentions differ from their ultimate actions because other controls will affect behaviour over and above an individual person's intention. We need to understand how people's behaviour may be moderated by their level of social identity and established cultural norms (i.e. accepted ways of behaving) and the expectations of institutions that set the boundaries of 'acceptable' behaviour. To do this, the needs and expectations of communities and societies should be considered in a respectful manner, even if they do not fit with the norms of the conservation project team. A win-win approach to these situations has far greater opportunity to succeed (see Section 8.5). At a fundamental level, all people we encounter should be treated with dignity.

The Rare theory-of-change model (see Section 11.5) is one approach that unpicks behavioural elements. The fundamental message from island community conservation efforts in Saint Lucia, Madagascar, Samoa and the Comores is that knowledge and attitudes can be changed. Sustainable reinforcement of these changes is achieved by developing partnerships with key community actors such as schools and businesses to maintain education and awareness implicitly within the learning and dialogue of the community. The way that conservation professionals communicate and work alongside partners should also be informed by an understanding of effective interpersonal interactions. Human relationships are often the most difficult area of professional conservation work. The priority is to keep relationships as transparent as possible. Clarity on programme purpose, goals, roles and processes will enable maintenance of working relationships and allow stakeholder engagement to be more straightforward.

12.7 Monitoring and Evaluation

Implicit in the purpose-goals-roles-processes-relationships model is the need for evaluation of each element to ensure effectiveness of the overall organisation. This book has emphasised the importance of monitoring and evaluation in covering both *fundamentals* of purpose (outcomes – the symptoms of success or failure) and *means* (causes – achievements from interventions or actions to reduce threats, usually against short-term goals). Our aim has been to present monitoring as a process by which we can check on the quality or progress of some process or action and therefore tweak it as required to achieve our goals and outcomes, or at least to inform future action if we do not succeed. A correct programme purpose is defined by a correct evaluation of context: threats, ecological history, historical status of populations, communities of species and ecosystems. Goals are defined, and their achievement is ascertained, by monitoring data (current population status, immediate threat impacts) including knowledge of current capabilities and availability of resources.

Roles should include responsibilities to measure performance to support improvement, usually connected to the processes of the programme. Processes should be evaluated in terms of the effectiveness of the work (largely operational measures) and sustained outcomes of the programme that covers the interests of the species and ecosystems of concern (population recovery, habitat recovery, landscape renewal).

Evaluation of relationships is more complex yet, with programmes linked with local human communities, no less important. Human interest and identification with particular species can influence people's motivations to enable tangible progress and continued effort (see Chapter 11). Identification of which things to evaluate (awareness, attitude, engagement, behaviour, motivations, constraints, influences) and how that relates to understanding a relevant theory of change will have significant implications in managing the practicalities of interventions. A better understanding of human psychology and behavioural change will enable conservation programmes to design interventions that tap into the interests and enthusiasm of local people for their natural heritage and the advantages of restoring species and systems for the greater good.

Monitoring data must provide enough information to close the knowledge-action boundary to enable practice to be improved without absorbing excessive resources. The best-designed monitoring and eva-luation approaches deliver the right information at the right time to enable the right decisions. If data are being collected but not used, the practitioner and scientist should ask how can these data provide insight to the programme or whether such monitoring is still relevant or if the work effort and resources must be redirected elsewhere.

12.8 Postscript

Islands represent both the present need and a future opportunity for wildlife conservation informed by the past (see Chapters 1–3 and Chapter 5). The experiences across the globe illustrate how well-purposed and well-focused species recovery programmes have enabled much wider recovery of habitats and entire ecosystems (see Chapters 7 and 9–11). As conservation practitioners, we want to organise (see Chapter 6) and lead (see Chapter 8) projects to best apply knowledge to relevant areas of need while recognising the need to act fast to avoid extinction and irreversible degradation of ecosystems.

The future challenges for island conservation are significant in the face of uncertainties relating to climate change and the socio-economic and political consequences of a rapidly expanding human population. These elements are, of course, out of the control of the conservation practitioner. This should not, however, discourage us from learning how to improve and become more effective. Programmes that can quickly understand and adapt to changing pressures and opportunities will be those which will be best able to succeed in achieving their long-term ambitions.

Conservation work, as all work, operates within a wider, intercon-nected system, going well beyond the biological focus of many conser-vation professionals' training. By accepting this and reaching out to more diverse sources of information and knowledge to inform and evaluate our conservation actions, we can achieve greater success. This book has drawn on an eclectic mix of experiences and understanding from people who have worked for decades on islands, in particular, tropical islands, to save species from extinction. The challenges described in locations such as Saint Lucia, Mauritius, New Zealand, Galapagos, Madagascar and the Hawaiian Islands are diverse yet hold common threads of insight. We hope that the lessons presented here offer strategies and practices that will enable conservation impact and success in many other locations across the globe.

Index